THE LANIER OAK, FACING THE MARSHES OF GLYNN, NEAR BRUNSWICK, GEORGIA

# SOUTHERN LIFE IN SOUTHERN LITERATURE

## SELECTIONS OF REPRESENTATIVE PROSE AND POETRY

SELECTED AND EDITED BY

MAURICE GARLAND FULTON

PROFESSOR OF ENGLISH, DAVIDSON COLLEGE

GINN AND COMPANY

BOSTON · NEW YORK · CHICAGO · LONDON
ATLANTA · DALLAS · COLUMBUS · SAN FRANCISCO

**The Athenæum Press**

GINN AND COMPANY · PRO-
PRIETORS · BOSTON · U.S.A.

# PREFACE

In this book I have endeavored to represent as adequately as might be possible within the limits of a volume of moderate size the work of the more important Southern writers. My attempt has been not merely to show the value of literary effort in the South as absolute achievement but also to emphasize its importance as a record of Southern life and character.

Taking literature in the stricter sense of fiction, essay, and poetry, I have omitted the historians, the biographers, and the political writers so frequently used to swell the bulk of Southern literature. In poetry I have endeavored to select poems which have attained some measure of general critical approval. But in some instances, especially in the Civil War poetry, I have included poems obviously without much literary merit because they were household poems of an older generation and embodied in a characteristic way the traditions and spirit of the people who loved them. For much the same reason I have included a few specimens of the vanishing survivals of old English ballads to the presence of which in the South attention has lately been turned.

In the case of the older prose writers, I have drawn upon a very limited number of the most significant works. As most of these were out of print or difficult to secure, I have tried to give a general idea of each by means of liberal excerpts and suitable summaries. Coming to the recent novelists and story-writers, whose number is almost legion, I was compelled to confine myself rigidly to the five pioneers in the new development of fiction in the eighties. The single departure from this principle in the case of William Sidney Porter (" O. Henry ") will require no explanation. I have devoted much attention to the humorous writers of the South because of my belief that, although much of this work was rough and crude, it was nevertheless very influential not only in the development of American humor but also in that of realistic fiction.

Better to fit the book to the needs of students, I have tried to organize the material effectively. The table of contents will show that the arrangement is roughly chronological, with such subdivisions as would bring together writers of the same type of literature. Further aids to students have been given in biographical notes, summaries of literary developments, explanations of unfamiliar matters in the selections, and bibliographies — all being held to the briefest compass.

I have given at appropriate places in the book acknowledgments for permission to reprint such of the selections as were under copyright, but I wish here to record in a general way grateful appreciation of the courtesy extended to me in this matter by authors and by publishers.

M. G. F.

Davidson College,
    Davidson, N. C.

# CONTENTS

## PART I. THE OLD SOUTH IN LITERATURE

### *ESSAYISTS AND DESCRIPTIVE WRITERS*

### *ROMANCERS AND STORY WRITERS*

## PART II. POETRY OF THE CIVIL WAR

## PART III. THE NEW SOUTH IN LITERATURE

### HUMORISTS

### NOVELISTS AND STORY WRITERS

## ESSAYISTS AND DESCRIPTIVE WRITERS

## POETS

# CONTENTS

# ILLUSTRATIONS

# SOUTHERN LIFE IN SOUTHERN LITERATURE

## PART I. THE OLD SOUTH IN LITERATURE

### ESSAYISTS AND DESCRIPTIVE WRITERS

#### WILLIAM WIRT

[William Wirt was born at Bladensburg, Maryland, in 1772. He was admitted to the bar in 1792 and began practice at Culpeper Court-House, Virginia. After 1799 he resided chiefly at Richmond until his appointment as Attorney-General of the United States in 1817. This position he held for twelve years, and upon his retirement from office he resided in Baltimore. He died at Washington in 1834. During Wirt's practice of law in Virginia his best-known legal argument was his celebrated speech in 1807 against Aaron Burr at the latter's trial for treason. In addition to success at the bar Wirt had the distinction of being regarded for many years as the chief man of letters in the South.]

#### THE BRITISH SPY'S OPINION OF *THE SPECTATOR*

In one of my late rides into the surrounding country, I stopped at a little inn to refresh myself and my horse; and, as the landlord was neither a Boniface nor "mine host of the garter," I called for a book, by way of killing time while the preparations for my repast were going forward. He brought me a shattered fragment of the second volume of *The Spectator*, which he told me was the only book in the house, for " he never troubled his head about reading"; and by way of con- clusive proof, he further informed me that this fragment, the only book in the house, had been sleeping unmolested on the dust of his mantelpiece for ten or fifteen years. I could not meet my venerable countryman, in a foreign land, and in this humiliating plight, nor hear of the inhuman and gothic con- tempt with which he had been treated, without the liveliest emotion. So I read my host a lecture on the subject, to which he appeared to pay as little attention as he had before done to *The Spectator*; and, with the *sang froid* of a Dutchman, answered me in the cant of the country, that he " had other fish to fry," and left me.

It had been so long since I had had an opportunity of open- ing an agreeable collection, that the few numbers which were now before me appeared almost entirely new; and I cannot describe to you the avidity and delight with which I devoured those beautiful and interesting speculations.

Is it not strange, my dear S——, that such a work should have ever lost an inch of ground? A style so sweet and simple, and yet so ornamented! a temper so benevolent, so cheerful, so exhilarating! a body of knowledge, and of original thought, so immense and various, so strikingly just, so universally useful! What person, of any age, sex, temper, calling, or pursuit, can possibly converse with *The Spectator* without being conscious of immediate improvement?

To the spleen he is as perpetual and never-failing an anti- dote as he is to ignorance and immorality. No matter for the disposition of mind in which you take him up; you catch, as you go along, the happy tone of spirits which prevails through- out the work; you smile at the wit, laugh at the drollery, feel your mind enlightened, your heart opened, softened, and refined; and when you lay him down, you are sure to be in a better humor, both with yourself and everybody else. I have never mentioned the subject to a reader of *The Spectator* who did not admit this to be the invariable process; and in such a world of misfortune, of cares and sorrows and guilt, as this is, what a prize would this collection be if it were rightly estimated!

Were I the sovereign of a nation which spoke the English language, and wished my subjects cheerful, virtuous, and enlightened, I would furnish every poor family in my dominions (and see that the rich furnished themselves) with a copy of *The Spectator*, and ordain that the parents or children should read four or five numbers aloud every night in the year. For one of the peculiar perfections of the work is, that while it contains such a mass of ancient and modern learning, so much of profound wisdom and of beautiful composition, yet there is scarcely a number throughout the eight volumes which is not level to the meanest capacity. Another perfection is, that *The Spectator* will never become tiresome to anyone whose taste and whose heart remain uncorrupted.

I do not mean that this author should be read to the exclusion of others; much less that he should stand in the way of the generous pursuit of science, or interrupt the discharge of social or private duties. All the counsels of the work have a directly reverse tendency. It furnishes a store of the clearest argument and of the most amiable and captivating exhortations, "to raise the genius, and to mend the heart." I regret only that such a book should be thrown by, and almost entirely forgotten, while the gilded blasphemies of infidels, and the "noontide trances" of pernicious theorists, are hailed with rapture and echoed around the world. For such, I should be pleased to see *The Spectator* universally substituted; and, throwing out the question of its morality, its literary information, its sweetly contagious serenity, and pure and chaste beauties of its style, and considering it merely as a curiosity,

as concentering the brilliant sports of the finest cluster of
geniuses that ever graced the earth, it surely deserves perpetual attention, respect, and consecration.

There is, methinks, my S——, a great fault in the world,
as it respects this subject: a giddy instability, a light and
fluttering vanity, a prurient longing after novelty, an impa-
tience, a disgust, a fastidious contempt of everything that is
old. You will not understand me as censuring the progress
of sound science. I am not so infatuated an antiquarian, not
so poor a philanthropist, as to seek to retard the expansion of
the human mind. But I lament the eternal oblivion into which
our old authors, those giants of literature, are permitted to sink,
while the world stands open-eyed and open-mouthed to catch
every modern, tinseled abortion as it falls from the press. In
the polite circles of America, for instance, perhaps there is no
want of taste, and even zeal, for letters. I have seen several
gentlemen who appear to have an accurate, a minute, acquaintance with the whole range of literature, in its present state of
improvement; yet you will be surprised to hear that I have not
met with more than one or two persons in this country who
have ever read the works of Bacon or of Boyle. They delight
to saunter in the upper story, sustained and adorned, as it is,
with the delicate proportions, the foliage and flourishes, of the
Corinthian order; but they disdain to make any acquaintance,
or hold communion at all, with the Tuscan and Doric plainness
and strength which base and support the whole edifice. . . .

## AN OLD VIRGINIA PREACHER

It was one Sunday, as I traveled through the county of
Orange, that my eye was caught by a cluster of horses tied
near a ruinous old wooden house in the forest, not far from
the roadside. Having frequently seen such objects before, in

traveling through those states, I had no difficulty in understanding that this was a place of religious worship.

Devotion alone should have stopped me, to join in the duties of the congregation; but I must confess that curiosity to hear the preacher of such a wilderness was not the least of my motives. On entering, I was struck with his preternatural appearance. He was a tall and very spare old man; his head, which was covered with a white linen cap, his shriveled hands, and his voice were all shaking under the influence of a palsy; and a few moments ascertained to me that he was perfectly blind.

The first emotions that touched my breast were those of mingled pity and veneration. But how soon were all my feelings changed! The lips of Plato were never more worthy of a prognostic swarm of bees than were the lips of this holy man! It was a day of the administration of the sacrament; and his subject was, of course, the passion of our Saviour. I have heard the subject handled a thousand times; I had thought it exhausted long ago. Little did I suppose that in the wild woods of America I was to meet with a man whose eloquence would give to this topic a new and more sublime pathos than I had ever before witnessed.

As he descended from the pulpit to distribute the mystic symbols, there was a peculiar, a more than human, solemnity in his air and manner which made my blood run cold and my whole frame shiver.

He then drew a picture of the sufferings of our Saviour: his trial before Pilate, his ascent up Calvary, his crucifixion, and his death. I knew the whole history; but never until then had I heard the circumstances so selected, so arranged, so colored! It was all new; and I seemed to have heard it for the first time in my life. His enunciation was so deliberate that his voice trembled on every syllable; and every heart in the assembly trembled in unison. His peculiar phrases had the force of description, that the original scene appeared to be at that moment acting before our eyes. We saw the very faces of the Jews: the staring, frightful distortions of malice and rage. We saw the buffet; my soul kindled with a flame of indignation, and my hands were involuntarily and convulsively clinched.

But when he came to touch on the patience, the forgiving meekness of our Saviour; when he drew, to the life, his blessed eyes streaming in tears to heaven, his voice breathing to God a soft and gentle prayer of pardon on his enemies, "Father, forgive them, for they know not what they do," — the voice of the preacher, which had all along faltered, grew fainter and fainter, until, his utterance being entirely obstructed by the force of his feelings, he raised his handkerchief to his eyes and burst into a loud and irrepressible flood of grief. The effect is inconceivable. The whole house resounded with the mingled groans, and sobs, and shrieks of the congregation.

It was some time before the tumult had subsided, so far as to permit him to proceed. Indeed, judging by the usual, but fallacious standard of my own weakness, I began to be very uneasy for the situation of the preacher. For I could not conceive how he would be able to let his audience down from the height to which he had wound them, without impairing the solemnity and dignity of his subject, or perhaps shocking them by the abruptness of the fall. But — no; the descent was as beautiful and sublime as the elevation had been rapid and enthusiastic.

The first sentence with which he broke the awful silence was a quotation from Rousseau: "Socrates died like a philosopher, but Jesus Christ, like a God!"

I despair of giving you any idea of the effect produced by this short sentence, unless you could perfectly conceive the whole manner of the man as well as the peculiar crisis in the discourse. Never before did I completely understand what Demosthenes meant by laying such stress on delivery. You are to bring before you the venerable figure of the preacher; his blindness, constantly recalling to your recollection old Homer, Ossian, and Milton, and associating with his performance the melancholy grandeur of their geniuses; you are to imagine that you hear his slow, solemn, well-accented enunciation, and his voice of affecting, trembling melody; you are to remember the pitch of passion and enthusiasm to which the congregation were raised; and then the few moments of portentous, death-like silence which reigned throughout the house; the preacher, removing his white handkerchief from his aged face (even yet wet from the recent torrent of his tears) and slowly stretching forth the palsied hand which holds it, begins the sentence, "Socrates died like a philosopher," — then, pausing, raising his other hand, pressing them both, clasped together, with warmth and energy to his breast, lifting his "sightless balls" to heaven, and pouring his whole soul into his tremulous voice, — "but Jesus Christ — like a God!" If it had indeed and in truth been an angel of light, the effect could scarcely have been more divine.


## DAVID CROCKETT

[David Crockett, the noted American pioneer and politician, was born in Tennessee in 1786. He was a typical backwoodsman, un-lettered but shrewd, skillful as a hunter, and fond of an out-of-doors life. He served under Jackson in the war against the Creek Indians, and in 1826 was elected to Congress. At the close of his third term in Congress he enlisted with the Texan forces then at war with Mexico, and in 1836 was one of the defenders of the Alamo, where, on March 6th, with the rest of the garrison, he was killed by Santa Anna's troops.]

## THE BEAR HUNT

In the morning I left my son at the camp, and we started on towards the harricane, and when we had went about a mile, we started a very large bear, but we got along mighty slow on account of the cracks in the earth occasioned by the earthquakes. We, however, made out to keep in hearing of the dogs for about three miles, and then we come to the harricane. Here we had to quit our horses, as old Nick himself could n't have got through it without sneaking it along in the form that he put on to make a fool of our old grandmother Eve. By this time several of my dogs had got tired and come back; but we went ahead on foot for some little time in the harricane, when we met a bear coming straight to us, and not more than twenty or thirty yards off. I started my tired dogs after him, and McDaniel pursued them, and I went on to where my other dogs were. I had seen the track of the bear they were after, and I knowed he was a screamer. I followed on to about the middle of the harricane, but my dogs pursued him so close that they made him climb an old stump about twenty feet high. I got in shooting distance of him and fired, but I was all over in such a flutter from fatigue and running that I could n't hold steady; but, however, I broke his shoulder, and he fell. I run up and loaded my gun as quick as possible, and shot him again and killed him. When I went to take out my knife to butcher him, I found that I had lost it in coming through the harricane. The vines and briars was so thick that I would sometimes have to get down and crawl like a varment to get through it all; and a vine had, as I supposed, caught in the handle and pulled it out. While I was standing and studying what to do, my friend came to me. He had followed my trail through the harricane, and had found my knife, which was mighty good news to me, as a hunter hates the worst in the world to lose a good dog or any part of his hunting tools. I now left McDaniel to butcher the bear, and I went after our horses and brought them as near as the nature of the case would allow. I then took our bags and went back to where he was; and when we skinned the bear, we fleeced off the fat and carried it to our horses at several loads. We then packed it up on our horses, and had a heavy pack of it on each one. We now started and went on till about sunset, when I concluded we must be near our camp; so I hollered, and my son answered me, and we moved on in the direction to the camp. We had gone but a little way when I heard my dogs make a warm start again; and I jumped down from my horse and gave him up to my friend, and told him I would follow them. He went on to the camp, and I went ahead after my dogs with all my might for a considerable distance, till at last night came on. The woods were very rough and hilly and all covered over with cane.

I now was compelled to move more slowly, and was frequently falling over logs and into the cracks made by the earthquakes, so I was very much afraid I would break my gun. However, I went on about three miles, when I came to a good big creek, which I waded. It was very cold, and the creek was about knee-deep; but I felt no great inconvenience from it just then, as I was overwet with sweat from running and I felt hot enough. After I got over this creek and out of the cane, which was very thick on all our creeks, I listened for my dogs. I found they had either treed or brought the bear to a stop, as they continued barking in the same place. I pushed on as near in the direction of the noise as I could, till I found the hill was too steep for me to climb, and so I backed and went down the creek some distance, till I came to a hollow, and then took up that, till I came to a place where I could climb up the hill. It was mighty dark, and was difficult to see my way, or anything else. When I got up the hill I found I had passed the dogs; and so I turned and went to them. I found, when I got there, they had treed the bear in a large forked poplar, and it was setting in the fork.

I could see the lump, but not plain enough to shoot with any certainty, as there was no moonlight; and so set in to hunting for some dry brush to make me a light; but I could find none, though I could find that the ground was torn mightily to pieces by the cracks.

At last I thought I could shoot by guess and kill him; so I pointed as near the lump as I could and fired away. But the bear did n't come; he only clumb up higher and got out on a limb, which helped me to see him better. I now loaded up again and fired, but this time he did n't move at all. I commenced loading for a third fire, but the first thing I knowed, the bear was down among my dogs, and they were fighting all around me. I had my big butcher in my belt, and I had a pair of dressed breeches on. So I took out my knife, and stood, determined, if he should get hold of me, to defend myself in the best way I could. I stood there for some time, and could now and then see a white dog I had, but the rest of them, and the bear, which were dark-colored, I could n't see at all, it was so miserable dark. They still fought around me, and sometimes within three feet of me; but at last the bear got down into one of the cracks that the earthquakes had made in the ground, about four feet deep, and I could tell the biting end of him by the hollering of my dogs. So I took my gun and pushed the muzzle of it about, till I thought I had it against the main part of his body, and fired; but it happened to be only the fleshy part of his foreleg. With this he jumped out of the crack, and he and the dogs had another hard fight around me, as before. At last, however, they forced him back into the crack again, as he was when I had shot.

I had laid down my gun in the dark, and I now began to hunt for it; and, while hunting, I got hold of a pole, and I concluded I would punch him awhile with that. I did so, and when I would punch him the dogs would jump in on him, when he would bite them badly, and they would jump out again. I concluded, as he would take punching so patiently, it might be that he would lie still enough for me to get down in the crack and feel slowly along till I could find the right place to give him a dig with my butcher. So I got down, and my dogs got in before him and kept his head towards them, till I got along easily up to him; and placing my hand on his rump, felt for his shoulder, just behind where I intended to stick him. I made a lunge with my long knife, and fortunately struck him right through the heart, at which he just sank down, and I crawled out in a hurry. In a little time my dogs all come out too, and seemed satisfied, which was the way they always had of telling me that they had finished him.

I suffered very much that night with cold, as my leather breeches and everything else I had on was wet and frozen. But I managed to get my bear out of this crack after several hard trials, and so I butchered him and laid down to try to sleep. But my fire was very bad, and I could n't find anything that would burn well to make it any better; and so I concluded I should freeze if I did n't warm myself in some way by exercise. So I got up and hollered awhile, and then I would just jump up and down with all my might and throw myself into all sorts of motions. But all this would n't do; for my blood was now getting cold, and the chills coming all over me. I was so tired too that I could hardly walk; but I thought I would do the best I could to save my life, and then if I died, nobody would be to blame. So I went up to a tree about two feet through, and not a limb on it for thirty feet, and I would climb up to the limbs and then lock my arms together around it and slide down to the bottom again. This would make the inside of my legs and arms feel mighty warm and good. I continued this till daylight in the morning, and how often I climbed up my tree and slid down I don't know, but I reckon at least a hundred times.

In the morning I got my bear hung up so as to be safe, and then set out to hunt for my camp. I found it after a while, and McDaniel and my son were very much rejoiced to see me get back, for they were about to give me up for lost. We got our breakfasts, and then secured our meat by building a high scaffold and covering it over. We had no fear of its spoiling, for the weather was so cold that it couldn't.

We now started after my other bear, which had caused me so much trouble and suffering; and before we got him we got a start after another, and took him also. We went on to the creek I had crossed the night before, and camped, and then went to where my bear was that I had killed in the crack. When we examined the place, McDaniel said he wouldn't have gone into it, as I did, for all the bears in the woods.

We then took the meat down to our camp and salted it, and also the last one we had killed; intending in the morning to make a hunt in the harricane again.

We prepared for resting that night, and I can assure the reader I was in need of it. We had laid down by our fire, and about ten o'clock there came a most terrible earthquake, which shook the earth so that we rocked about like we had been in a cradle. We were very much alarmed; for though we were accustomed to feel earthquakes, we were now right in the region which had been torn to pieces by them in 1812, and we thought it might take a notion and swallow us up, like the big fish did Jonah.

In the morning we packed up and moved to the harricane, where we made another camp, and turned out that evening and killed a very large bear, which made eight we had now killed in this hunt.

The next morning we entered the harricane again, and in a little or no time my dogs were in full cry. We pursued them, and soon came to a thick canebrake, in which they had stopped their bear. We got up close to him, as the cane was so thick that we couldn't see more than a few feet. Here I made my friend hold the cane a little open with his gun till I shot the bear, which was a mighty large one. I killed him dead in his tracks. We got him out and butchered him, and in a little time started another and killed him, which now made ten we had killed; and we knowed we couldn't pack any more home, as we had only five horses along; therefore we returned to the camp and salted up all our meat, to be ready for a start homeward next morning.

The morning came, and we packed our horses with meat, and had as much as they could possibly carry, and sure enough cut out for home. It was about thirty miles, and we reached home the second day. I had now accommodated my neighbor with meat enough to do him, and had killed in all, up to that time, fifty-eight bears during the fall and winter.

As soon as the time come for them to quit their houses and come out again in the spring, I took a notion to hunt a little more, and in about one month I killed forty-seven more, which made one hundred and five bears which I had killed in less than one year from that time.


## JOHN JAMES AUDUBON

[John James Audubon was born near New Orleans in 1780 of French and Spanish extraction. He was educated in Paris, where he had lessons in painting from the celebrated painter J. L. David. Returning to America in 1798, he settled on an estate of his father's near Philadelphia, and gave himself up to the study of natural history, and especially to the drawing of birds. Afterwards he was for a time a merchant in various Southern cities. Finally he gave up all regular business pursuits and spent his time roaming hither and thither in the forests making observations of animal and of bird life. His greatest production, "The Birds of America," published from 1831 to 1839, consisted of five volumes of biographies of birds and four volumes of portraits of birds, the latter volumes containing over four hundred drawings, colored and life-size.]

## EARLY SETTLERS ALONG THE MISSISSIPPI

Although every European traveler who has glided down the Mississippi at the rate of ten miles an hour has told his tale of the squatters, yet none has given any other account of them than that they are "a sallow, sickly-looking sort of miserable being," living in swamps and subsisting on pignuts, Indian corn, and bear's flesh. It is obvious, however, that none but a person acquainted with their history, manners, and condition can give any real information respecting them.

The individuals who become squatters choose that sort of life of their own free will. They mostly remove from other parts of the United States after finding that land has become too high in price, and they are persons who, having a family of strong and hardy children, are anxious to enable them to provide for themselves. They have heard from good authorities that the country extending along the great streams of the West is of all parts of the Union the richest in its soil, the growth of its timber, and the abundance of its game; that, besides, the Mississippi is the great road to and from all the markets in the world; and that every vessel borne by its waters affords to settlers some chance of selling their commodities, or of exchanging them for others. To these recommendations is added another, of even greater weight with persons of the above denomination, namely, the prospect of being able to settle on land, and perhaps to hold it for a number of years, without purchase, rent, or tax of any kind. How many thousands of individuals in all parts of the globe would gladly try their fortune with such prospects I leave to you, reader, to determine.

As I am not disposed too highly to color the picture which I am about to submit to your inspection, instead of pitching on individuals who have removed from our eastern boundaries, and of whom certainly there are a good number, I shall introduce to you the members of a family from Virginia, first giving you an idea of their condition in that country previous to their migration to the West. The land which they and their ancestors have possessed for a hundred years, having been constantly forced to produce crops of one kind or another, is completely worn out. It exhibits only a superficial layer of red clay, cut up by deep ravines, through which much of the soil has been conveyed to some more fortunate neighbor residing in a yet rich and beautiful valley. Their strenuous efforts to render it productive have failed. They dispose of everything too cumbrous or expensive for them to remove, retaining only a few horses, a servant or two, and such implements of husbandry and other articles as may be necessary on their journey or useful when they arrive at the spot of their choice.

I think I see them harnessing their horses and attaching them to their wagons, which are already filled with bedding, provisions, and the younger children; while on their outside are fastened spinning wheels and looms, and a bucket filled with tar and tallow swings betwixt the hind wheels. Several axes are secured to the bolster, and the feeding-trough of the horses contains pots, kettles, and pans. The servant now becomes a driver, riding the near saddled horse; the wife is mounted on another; the worthy husband shoulders his gun; and his sons, clad in plain, substantial homespun, drive the cattle ahead and lead the procession, followed by the hounds and other dogs.

Their day's journey is short and not agreeable. The cattle, stubborn or wild, frequently leave the road for the woods, giving the travelers much trouble; the harness of the horses here and there gives way, and immediate repair is needed. A basket which has accidentally dropped must be gone after, for nothing that they have can be spared. The roads are bad, and now and then all hands are called to push on the wagon or prevent it from upsetting. Yet by sunset they have proceeded perhaps twenty miles. Fatigued, all assemble around the fire which has been lighted; supper is prepared, and a camp being run up, there they pass the night.

Days and weeks, nay months, of unremitting toil pass before they gain the end of the journey. They have crossed both the Carolinas, Georgia, and Alabama. They have been traveling from the beginning of May to that of September, and with heavy hearts they traverse the neighborhood of the Mississippi. But now, arrived on the banks of the broad stream, they gaze in amazement on the dark, deep woods around them. Boats of various kinds they see gliding downward with the current, while others slowly ascend against it. A few inquiries are made at the nearest dwelling, and assisted by the inhabitants with their boats and canoes, they at once cross the river and select their place of habitation.

The exhalations rising from the swamps and morasses around them have a powerful effect on these new settlers, but all are intent on preparing for the winter. A small patch of ground is cleared by the ax and fire, a temporary cabin is erected; to each of the cattle is attached a bell before it is let loose into the neighboring canebrake, and the horses remain about the house, where they find sufficient food at that season. The first trading boat that stops at their landing enables them to provide themselves with some flour, fishhooks, and ammunition, as well as other commodities. The looms are mounted, the spinning wheels soon furnish yarn, and in a few weeks the family throw off their ragged clothes and array themselves in suits adapted to the climate. The father and sons meanwhile have sown turnips and other vegetables, and from some Kentucky flatboat a supply of live poultry has been purchased.

October tinges the leaves of the forest; the morning dews are heavy, the days hot and the nights chill; and the unacclimatized family in a few days are attacked with ague. The lingering disease almost prostrates their whole faculties. Fortunately the unhealthy season soon passes over, and the hoarfrosts make their appearance. Gradually each individual recovers strength. The largest ash trees are felled, their trunks are cut, split, and corded in front of the building; a large fire is lighted at night on the edge of the water; and soon a steamer calls to purchase the wood and thus add to their comforts during the winter. This first fruit of their industry imparts new courage to them; their exertions multiply; and when spring returns the place has a cheerful look. Venison, bear's flesh, and turkeys, ducks, and geese, with now and then some fish, have served to keep up their strength, and now their enlarged field is planted with corn, potatoes, and pumpkins. Their stock of cattle too has augmented; the steamer which now stops there, as if by preference, buys a calf or pig together with their wood. Their store of provisions is renewed, and brighter rays of hope enliven their spirits.

Who is he of the settlers on the Mississippi that cannot realize some profit? Truly none who is industrious. When the autumnal months return, all are better prepared to encounter the ague which then prevails. Substantial food, suitable clothing, and abundant firing repel its attacks; and before another twelvemonth has elapsed the family is naturalized. The sons have by this time discovered a swamp covered with excellent timber, and as they have seen many great rafts of saw logs, bound for the mills of New Orleans, floating past their dwelling, they resolve to try the success of a little enterprise. Their industry and prudence have already enhanced their credit. A few cross-saws are purchased, and some broad-wheeled "carry-logs" are made by themselves. Log after log is hauled to the bank of the river, and in a short time their first raft is made on the shore and loaded with cordwood. When the next freshet sets it afloat, it is secured by long grapevines or cables until, the proper time being arrived, the husband and sons embark on it and float down the mighty stream.

After encountering many difficulties they arrive in safety at New Orleans, where they dispose of their stock, the money obtained for which may be said to be all profit, supply themselves with such articles as may add to their convenience or comfort, and with light hearts procure a passage on the upper deck of a steamer, at a very cheap rate on account of the benefit of their labor in taking in wood or otherwise.

And now the vessel approaches their home. See the joyous mother and daughters as they stand on the bank! A store of vegetables lies around them, a large tub of fresh milk is at their feet, and in their hands are plates filled with rolls of butter. As the steamer stops, three broad straw hats are waved from the upper deck, and soon husband and wife, brothers and sisters, are in each other's embrace. The boat carries off the provisions for which value has been left, and as the captain issues his orders for putting on the steam, the happy family enter their humble dwelling. The husband gives his bag of dollars to the wife, while the sons present some token of affection to the sisters. Surely, at such a moment, the squatters are richly repaid for all their labors.

Every successive year has increased their savings. They now possess a large stock of horses, cows, and hogs, with abundance of provisions and domestic comfort of every kind. The daughters have been married to the sons of neighboring squatters, and have gained sisters to themselves by the marriage of their brothers. The government secures to the family the lands on which, twenty years before, they settled in poverty and sickness. Larger buildings are erected on piles, secure from inundations; where a single cabin once stood, a neat village is now to be seen; warehouses, stores, and workshops increase the importance of the place. The squatters live respected, and in due time die regretted by all who knew them.

Thus are the vast frontiers of our country peopled, and thus does cultivation, year after year, extend over the western wilds. Time will no doubt be, when the great valley of the Mississippi, still covered with primeval forests interspersed with swamps, will smile with cornfields and orchards, while crowded cities will rise at intervals along its banks, and enlightened nations will rejoice in the bounties of Providence.


## WILLIAM ELLIOTT

[William Elliott was born in Beaufort, South Carolina, in 1788. After graduating from Harvard, he returned to South Carolina. Except for some early incursions into politics, he chiefly devoted himself to the management of his estates, and, as a writer and lecturer on agricultural and other subjects, became widely known. He contributed to one of the newspapers of Charleston the series of sporting sketches which were collected and published in 1846 under the title of "Carolina Sports by Land and Water." He died in Charleston, South Carolina, in 1863.]


### A DEER HUNT

It was a glorious winter's day — sharp, but bracing. The sun looked forth with dazzling brightness, as he careered through a cloudless sky; and his rays came glancing back from many an ice-covered lagoon that lay scattered over the face of the ground.

The moan of an expiring northwester was faintly heard from the tops of the magnificent forest pines. Three sportsmen, while it was yet early, met at their trysting place, to perpetrate a *raid* against the deer! They were no novices, those huntsmen; they had won trophies in many a sylvan war, and they now took the field " of malice prepense " with all the appliances of destruction at their beck — practiced drivers of the pack, often proved, and now refreshed by three days' rest. Brief was their interchange of compliment; they felt that such a day was not to be trifled away in talk; and they hallooed their hounds impatiently into the drive — yet not as greenhorns would have done. " Keep clear of the swamps " was the order of the drivers — "leave the close covers — ride not where the ice crackles under the horse's hoof, but look closely into the sheltered knolls, where you will find the deer sunning themselves after the last night's frost." The effect of this order was soon evident, for in the second knoll entered by the hounds a herd of deer were found thawing themselves in the first beams of the ascending sun. Ho! what a burst! with what fury the hounds dash in among them! Now they sweep along the thickets that skirt the drive and climb the summit of that elevated piny ridge — destined one day to become a summer settlement and to bear the name of ———. But not unforeseen or unprovided for was the run which the deer had taken. Frisky Geordy was in their path, and crack went the sound of his gun, and loud and vaunting was the twang of his horn that followed the explosion! And now the frozen earth reëchoed to the tramp of horses' hoofs, as the huntsmen hurried to the call that proclaims that a deer has fallen. There was Geordy, his gun against a pine, his knee upon the still heaving flank of a *pricket buck*, his right hand clenched upon his dripping knife, his left flourishing a horn, which ever and anon was given to his mouth and filled the air with its boastful notes.

"Halloo, Geordy! you have got him fast, I see. Where are the dogs?"

"Gone," said Geordy.

"There's Ruler in the east — what's he after?"

"A deer," says Geordy.

"And Rouser to the south — what's he after?"

"Another deer," says Geordy.

"And Nimrod to the southwest — I need not ask what he's after, for he follows nothing but deer. Your second barrel snapped, of course?"

"I don't say that," says Geordy; "I had *wounded* the six last deer I'd fired at, so I thought I'd *kill* one to-day, and while I looked to see if that was really dead the others slipped by me."

"Done like a sportsman, Geordy; one dead deer is worth a dozen crippled ones. I remember once your powder was too weak; and next, your shot were too small; and next, your aim was somewhat wild; and one went off bored of an ear, and another nicked of a tail. You are bound to set up an infirmary across the river for the dismembered deer you have dispatched there! You have done well to *kill* — let it grow into a habit. Nimrod to the southwest, said you? That rascal is a born economist; and not a foot will he budge in pursuit of a living deer after your horn has told him there is *venison* in the rear! Ruler will drive *his* deer across the river; Rouser, to the marshes. Nimrod's quarry is the only one likely to halt and give us another chance."

And sure enough, there came Nimrod trotting back on his track, his nose cocked up in air as if to indorse and verify the inferences of his *ear*, his tail curled and standing out from his body at an angle of forty-five degrees.

"This is the safe play — hang up the deer — sound your horn till the hounds come in from their several chases — and then for Nimrod's lead! to Chapman's bays, I think!—there are some sheltered nooks in which they will stop and bask when they find themselves unpursued."

"I'll go in with the boys," says Loveleap, with an unconcerned air, but a sly twinkle of the eye, which did not escape his comrades.

"As you like. Geordy and I will mind the stands."

Some time was lost before the hounds could be drawn from their several chases; yet, as emulation did not "prick them on," they came the sooner for being scattered. Loveleap heads the drivers, and it was just what we had anticipated, when, before a single dog had given tongue, we heard him fire; then came a burst, and then a second barrel; but to our great surprise no horn announced the expected success. The report of that gun went unquestioned in our sporting circle; it was in a manner axiomatic in woodcraft mysteries, and passed current with all who heard it for thus much—"a deer is killed." Loveleap did an extraordinary thing that day—*he missed!* But the drivers could not understand and the hounds would not believe it; so they rushed madly away in pursuit, as if it was not possible for the quarry long to escape.

"Push on," says Geordy, "they make for the river!" and away we went. We reined in for a minute at the ford; and finding that they had already outstripped us and were bearing down for Chapman's fort,—a mile to the west of our position, —we struck across for the marshes south of us, where we might, if he was a young deer, intercept him on his return to his accustomed haunts. In an old buck we had no chance; *he* is sure to set a proper value on his life, and seldom stops until he has put a river between his pursuer and himself.

Taking advantage of a road that lay in our way, we soon cleared the woods and entered an old field that skirted the marsh. It was a large waving plain of rank broom grass, chequered here and there by strips of myrtle and marsh mallows.

"So far, Geordy," said I, "we have kept one track; now let us separate. The hounds are out of hearing, and we have little chance of any game but such as we may rouse without their help. How delightfully sheltered is this spot! how completely is it shut in by that semicircle of woods from the sweep of the northwest winds! How genially the sun pours down upon it! Depend upon it, we shall find some luxurious rogues basking in this warm nook, for, next to your Englishman, a deer is the greatest epicure alive! Now, then, by separate tracks let us make across the old field; a blast of the horn will bring us together when we reach the marsh."

By separate tracks then we moved, and had not advanced two hundred yards, when crack went Geordy's gun. I looked in the direction of the report, and his head only was visible above the sea of marsh mallows. The direction of his *face* I could see, and *that* was pointed toward me. Toward me, then, thought I, runs the deer. I reined in my horse and turned his head in that direction. It was such a thickly woven mass of mallows and myrtle — high as my shoulders as I sat in the saddle — that there was little hope of being able to see the game. I trusted to my ear to warn me of his approach, and soon heard the rustling of the leaves and the sharp, quick leap which mark the movement of a deer at speed. I saw him not until he appeared directly under my horse's nose, in act to leap; he vaulted, and would have dropped upon my saddle had he not seen the horse while yet poised in air, and, by an effort like that of the tumbler who throws a somersault, twisted himself suddenly to my right. He grazed my knee in his descent; and as he touched the earth I brought my gun down, pistol-fashion, with a rapid twitch, and sent the whole charge through his backbone. It was so instantaneous — so like a flash of lightning — that I could scarcely credit it when I saw the deer twirling and turning over at my horse's heels. Dismounting to secure him, it was some time before his muscular action was sufficiently overcome to allow me to use my knife. He struggled and kicked; I set down my gun, the better to master him. In the midst of my employment, crack went Geordy's second barrel, nearer than the first, and "*mind! mind!*" followed the discharge. Before I could drop my knife and gain my feet another deer was upon me! He followed directly in the track of the former and passed between my horse and me, so near that I might have bayoneted him! Where was my gun? Lost in the broom grass! What a trial! I looked all around in an instant, and spying it where it lay, caught it eagerly up — the deer had disappeared! It flashed across me that underneath these myrtles the limbs excluded from the sun had decayed, and that in the vistas thus formed a glimpse of the deer might yet be gained. In an instant I am on my knees, darting the most anxious glances along the vista; the flash of a tail is seen — I fire — a struggle is heard — I press forward through the interlacing branches — and to my joy and surprise, *another deer is mine!* Taking him by the legs, I drag him to the spot where the other lay. Then it was *my* turn to sound a "vaunty" peal! Geordy pealed in answer, and soon appeared dragging a deer of his own (having missed one of those that I had killed). Three deer were started — they were all at our feet — and that *without the aid of a dog!* It was the work of five minutes! We piled them in a heap, covered them with branches and myrtle bushes, and tasked our horns to the uttermost to recall the field. One by one the hounds came in, smelt at the myrtle bushes, seemed satisfied, though puzzled, wagged their tails, and coiling themselves each in his proper bed, lay down to sleep. Yet had any stranger approached that myrtle-covered mound every back would have bristled, and a fierce cry of defiance would have broken forth from every tongue, then so mute.

At last came Loveleap, fagged and somewhat fretted by his ill success.

"I have been blowing till I've split my wind, and not a dog has come to my horn. How came you thrown out? and why have you kept such an incessant braying of horns? Why, how is this? the dogs are here?"

"Yes! they have shown their sense in coming to us; there's been butchery hereabouts!"

"One of P————'s cattle killed by the runaways, I suppose."

"Will you lend us your boy to bring a cart?" I said.

"Certainly," says Loveleap; "it will make such a feast for the dogs; but where is the cow?"

"*Here!*" says Geordy, kicking off the myrtle screen and revealing to the sight of his astonished comrade *our three layers of venison*! Oh, you should have seen Loveleap's face!

The cart is brought, and our four deer are soon on their way home. Do you think we accompanied them? No! We were so merciless as to meditate still further havoc. The day was so little spent — and as our hands were in, and there was just in the next drive an overgrown old buck who often had the insolence to baffle us — no! we must take a drive at him! Again the hounds are thrown into cover, headed by our remaining driver; but in the special object of our move we failed — the buck had decamped. Still, *the fortune of the day attended us*; and an inquisitive old turkey gobbler, having ventured to peep at Geordy where he lay in ambush, was sprawled by a shot from his gun and was soon seen dangling from his saddlebow.

This closed our hunt. And now that we have a moment's breathing time, tell me, brother sportsmen who may chance to read this veritable history, has it ever been your fortune, in a single day's hunt and as the spoils of two gunners only, to bring home four deer and a wild turkey? Ye gastronomes! who relish the proceeds of a hunt better than its toils and perils — a glance at that larder, if you please! Look at that fine bird, so carefully hung up by the neck; his spurs are an inch and a half in length, his beard eight inches; what an ample chest! what glossy plumage! — his weight is twenty-five pounds! And see that brave array of haunches! that is a buck of two years, — juicy, tender, but not fat, — capital for steaks! But your eye finds something yet more attractive — the saddle of a four-year-old doe, kidney covered, as you see; a morsel more savoury smokes not upon a monarch's board. How pleasant to eat! Shall I say it? — how much pleasanter to give away! Ah, how such things do win their way to *hearts* — men's and *women's* too! My young sporting friends, a word in your ear: the worst use you can make of your game is to eat it yourselves.

# ROMANCERS AND STORY WRITERS

## EDGAR ALLAN POE

[Edgar Allan Poe was born, it is supposed, in Boston in 1809. His mother and father having died when he was three years old, he was adopted by Mrs. John Allan of Richmond, Virginia. He was educated in England and at the University of Virginia and West Point. In January, 1831, he was dismissed from the Military Academy on account of neglect of duties, and went to New York to embark upon a literary career. His life from this time was very erratic, being passed in various cities — Richmond and Baltimore especially. Poe became connected with several magazines, but on account of the irregularities of his character — especially drinking — and ill health, he was unable to hold any of these positions for any length of time. In May, 1836, he was married to Miss Virginia

EDGAR ALLAN POE

Clemm, his cousin, who at the time of the marriage was but fourteen years old. In 1846, while the Poes were living in a small cottage at Fordham, she died of consumption under distressing conditions of poverty. This bereavement so affected Poe that it is hardly possible to believe that he was himself mentally during the remaining few years of his life. In the early part of October, 1849, he went to Baltimore, and shortly afterwards was found lying senseless in a saloon which was being used as a voting place. He was removed to a hospital where he died on the morning of the 7th of October. The mystery surrounding the circumstances of his death has never been unraveled.

Poe challenges attention in literature because of three notable contributions — critical essays, short stories, and poems. As the critical essays are not represented in this volume, they may be dismissed with the brief statement that in spite of personal bias and jealousies, Poe's criticism is independent and suggestive, and his judgments have in the main proved to be those of posterity. His poetic contribution is discussed in another place in this book. Of his short stories, or " tales," as he called them, it may be said that these are among the best examples of this form of literature in the English language. In range of subject matter Poe was narrow, but on the constructive side of story writing he yields to few writers.]

## THE FALL OF THE HOUSE OF USHER

During the whole of a dull, dark, and soundless day in the autumn of the year, when the clouds hung oppressively low in the heavens, I had been passing alone, on horseback, through a singularly dreary tract of country, and at length found myself, as the shades of the evening drew on, within view of the melancholy House of Usher. I know not how it was — but with the first glimpse of the building a sense of insufferable gloom pervaded my spirit. I say insufferable ; for the feeling was unrelieved by any of that half-pleasurable, because poetic, sentiment with which the mind usually receives even the sternest natural images of the desolate or terrible. I looked upon the scene before me — upon the mere house and the simple landscape features of the domain, upon the bleak walls, upon the vacant eyelike windows, upon a few rank sedges, and upon a few white trunks of decayed trees — with an utter depression of soul which I can compare to no earthly sensation more properly than to the after-dream of the reveler upon opium : the bitter lapse into everyday life, the hideous dropping off of the veil. There was an iciness, a sinking, a sickening of the heart, an unredeemed dreariness of thought which no goading of the imagination could torture into aught of the sublime. What was it — I paused to think — what was it that so unnerved me in the contemplation of the House of Usher? It was a mystery all insoluble; nor could I grapple with the shadowy fancies that crowded upon me as I pondered. I was forced to fall back upon the unsatisfactory conclusion that while, beyond doubt, there *are* combinations of very simple natural objects which have the power of thus affecting us, still the analysis of this power lies among considerations beyond our depth. It was possible, I reflected, that a mere different arrangement of the particulars of the scene, of the details of the picture, would be sufficient to modify, or perhaps to annihilate, its capacity for sorrowful impression; and acting upon this idea, I reined my horse to the precipitous brink of a black and lurid tarn that lay in unruffled luster by the dwelling, and gazed down — but with a shudder even more thrilling than before — upon the remodeled and inverted images of the gray sedge, and the ghastly tree-stems, and the vacant and eyelike windows.

Nevertheless, in this mansion of gloom I now proposed to myself a sojourn of some weeks. Its proprietor, Roderick Usher, had been one of my boon companions in boyhood; but many years had elapsed since our last meeting. A letter, however, had lately reached me in a distant part of the country — a letter from him — which in its wildly importunate nature had admitted of no other than a personal reply. The MS. gave evidence of nervous agitation. The writer spoke of acute bodily illness, of a mental disorder which oppressed him, and of an earnest desire to see me, as his best and indeed his only personal friend, with a view of attempting, by the cheerfulness of my society, some alleviation of his malady. It was the manner in which all this, and much more, was said — it was the apparent *heart* that went with his request — which allowed me no room for hesitation; and I accordingly obeyed forthwith what I still considered a very singular summons.

Although as boys we had been even intimate associates, yet I really knew little of my friend. His reserve had been always excessive and habitual. I was aware, however, that his very ancient family had been noted, time out of mind, for a peculiar sensibility of temperament, displaying itself, through long ages, in many works of exalted art, and manifested of late in repeated deeds of munificent yet unobtrusive charity, as well as in a passionate devotion to the intricacies, perhaps even more than to the orthodox and easily recognizable beauties, of musical science. I had learned, too, the very remarkable fact that the stem of the Usher race, all time-honored as it was, had put forth at no period any enduring branch; in other words, that the entire family lay in the direct line of descent, and had always, with very trifling and very temporary variation, so lain. It was this deficiency, I considered, while running over in thought the perfect keeping of the character of the premises with the accredited character of the people, and while speculating upon the possible influence which the one, in the long lapse of centuries, might have exercised upon the other — it was this deficiency, perhaps, of collateral issue, and the consequent undeviating transmission from sire to son of the patrimony with the name, which had, at length, so identified the two as to merge the original title of the estate in the quaint and equivocal appellation of the "House of Usher," an appellation which seemed to include, in the minds of the peasantry who used it, both the family and the family mansion.

I have said that the sole effect of my somewhat childish experiment, that of looking down within the tarn, had been to deepen the first singular impression. There can be no doubt that the consciousness of the rapid increase of my superstition — for why should I not so term it? — served mainly to accelerate the increase itself. Such, I have long known, is the paradoxical law of all sentiments having terror as a basis. And it might have been for this reason only, that when I again uplifted my eyes to the house itself, from its image in the pool, there grew in my mind a strange fancy — a fancy so ridiculous, indeed, that I but mention it to show the vivid force of the sensations which oppressed me. I had so worked upon my imagination as really to believe that about the whole mansion and domain there hung an atmosphere peculiar to themselves and their immediate vicinity — an atmosphere which had no affinity with the air of heaven, but which had reeked up from decayed trees, and the gray wall, and the silent tarn; a pestilent and mystic vapor, dull, sluggish, faintly discernible, and leaden-hued.

Shaking off from my spirit what *must* have been a dream, I scanned more narrowly the real aspect of the building. Its principal feature seemed to be that of an excessive antiquity. The discoloration of ages had been great. Minute fungi overspread the whole exterior, hanging in a fine tangled webwork from the eaves. Yet all this was apart from any extraordinary dilapidation. No portion of the masonry had fallen; and there appeared to be a wild inconsistency between its still perfect adaptation of parts and the crumbling condition of the individual stones. In this there was much that reminded one of the specious totality of old woodwork which has rotted for long years in some neglected vault, with no disturbance from the breath of the external air. Beyond this indication of extensive decay, however, the fabric gave little token of instability. Perhaps the eye of a scrutinizing observer might have discovered a barely perceptible fissure, which, extending from the roof of the building in front, made its way down the wall in a zigzag direction, until it became lost in the sullen waters of the tarn.

Noticing these things, I rode over a short causeway to the house. A servant in waiting took my horse, and I entered the Gothic archway of the hall. A valet, of stealthy step, thence conducted me, in silence, through many dark and intricate passage in my progress to the studio of his master. Much that I encountered on the way contributed, I know not how, to heighten the vague sentiments of which I have already spoken. While the objects around me — while the carvings of the ceilings, the somber tapestries of the walls, the ebon blackness of the floors, and the phantasmagoric armorial trophies which rattled as I strode — were but matters to which, or to such as which, I had been accustomed from my infancy — while I hesitated not to acknowledge how familiar was all this — I still wondered to find how unfamiliar were the fancies which ordinary images were stirring up. On one of the staircases I met the physician of the family. His countenance, I thought, wore a mingled expression of low cunning and perplexity. He accosted me with trepidation and passed on. The valet now threw open a door and ushered me into the presence of his master.

The room in which I found myself was very large and lofty. The windows were long, narrow, and pointed, and at so vast a distance from the black oaken floor as to be altogether inaccessible from within. Feeble gleams of encrimsoned light made their way through the trellised panes, and served to render sufficiently distinct the more prominent objects around; the eye, however, struggled in vain to reach the remoter angles of the chamber, or the recesses of the vaulted and fretted ceiling. Dark draperies hung upon the walls. The general furniture was profuse, comfortless, antique, and tattered. Many books and musical instruments lay scattered about, but failed to give any vitality to the scene. I felt that I breathed an atmosphere of sorrow. An air of stern, deep, and irredeemable gloom hung over and pervaded all.

Upon my entrance, Usher arose from a sofa on which he had been lying at full length, and greeted me with a vivacious warmth which had much in it, I at first thought, of an over-done cordiality — of the constrained effort of the *ennuyé* man of the world. A glance, however, at his countenance convinced me of his perfect sincerity. We sat down; and for some moments, while he spoke not, I gazed upon him with a feeling half of pity, half of awe. Surely man had never before so terribly altered, in so brief a period, as had Roderick Usher! It was with difficulty that I could bring myself to admit the identity of the wan being before me with the companion of my early boyhood. Yet the character of his face had been at all times remarkable. A cadaverousness of complexion; an eye large, liquid, and luminous beyond comparison; lips somewhat thin and very pallid, but of a surpassingly beautiful curve; a nose of a delicate Hebrew model, but with a breadth of nostril unusual in similar formations; a finely molded chin, speaking, in its want of prominence, of a want of moral energy; hair of a more than weblike softness and tenuity; these features, with an inordinate expansion above the regions of the temple, made up altogether a countenance not easily to be forgotten. And now in the mere exaggeration of the prevailing character of these features, and of the expression they were wont to convey, lay so much of change that I doubted to whom I spoke. The now ghastly pallor of the skin, and the now miraculous luster of the eye, above all things startled and even awed me. The silken hair, too, had been suffered to grow all unheeded, and as, in its wild gossamer texture, it floated rather than fell about the face, I could not, even with effort, connect its arabesque expression with any idea of simple humanity.

In the manner of my friend I was at once struck with an incoherence, an inconsistency; and I soon found this to arise from a series of feeble and futile struggles to overcome an habitual trepidancy, an excessive nervous agitation.  For something of this nature I had indeed been prepared, no less by his letter than by reminiscences of certain boyish traits, and by conclusions deduced from his peculiar physical conformation and temperament.  His action was alternately vivacious and sullen.  His voice varied rapidly from a tremulous indecision (when the animal spirits seemed utterly in abeyance) to that species of energetic concision—that abrupt, weighty, unhurried, and hollow-sounding enunciation—that leaden, self-balanced and perfectly modulated guttural utterance—which may be observed in the lost drunkard, or the irreclaimable eater of opium, during the periods of his most intense excitement.

It was thus that he spoke of the object of my visit, of his earnest desire to see me, and of the solace he expected me to afford him.  He entered, at some length, into what he conceived to be the nature of his malady.  It was, he said, a constitutional and a family evil, and one for which he despaired to find a remedy—a mere nervous affection, he immediately added, which would undoubtedly soon pass off.  It displayed itself in a host of unnatural sensations.  Some of these, as he detailed them, interested and bewildered me; although, perhaps, the terms and the general manner of the narration had their weight.  He suffered much from a morbid acuteness of the senses; the most insipid food was alone endurable; he could wear only garments of certain texture; the odors of all flowers were oppressive; his eyes were tortured by even a faint light; and there were but peculiar sounds, and these from stringed instruments, which did not inspire him with horror.

To an anomalous species of terror I found him a bounden slave.  " I shall perish," said he, " I *must* perish in this deplorable folly.  Thus, thus, and not otherwise, shall I be lost.  I dread the events of the future, not in themselves, but in their results.  I shudder at the thought of any, even the most trivial, incident, which may operate upon this intolerable agitation of soul. I have, indeed, no abhorrence of danger, except in its absolute effect — in terror. In this unnerved — in this pitiable condition, I feel that the period will sooner or later arrive when I must abandon life and reason together in some struggle with the grim phantasm, FEAR."

I learned moreover at intervals, and through broken and equivocal hints, another singular feature of his mental condition. He was enchained by certain superstitious impressions in regard to the dwelling which he tenanted, and whence, for many years, he had never ventured forth — in regard to an influence whose supposititious force was conveyed in terms too shadowy here to be restated — an influence which some peculiarities in the mere form and substance of his family mansion had, by dint of long sufferance, he said, obtained over his spirit — an effect which the physique of the gray walls and turrets, and of the dim tarn into which they all looked down, had, at length, brought about upon the morale of his existence.

He admitted, however, although with hesitation, that much of the peculiar gloom which thus afflicted him could be traced to a more natural and far more palpable origin — to the severe and long-continued illness, indeed to the evidently approaching dissolution, of a tenderly beloved sister — his sole companion for long years, his last and only relative on earth. " Her decease," he said, with a bitterness which I can never forget, " would leave him (him the hopeless and the frail) the last of the ancient race of the Ushers." While he spoke, the lady Madeline (for so was she called) passed slowly through a remote portion of the apartment, and, without having noticed my presence, disappeared. I regarded her with an utter astonishment not unmingled with dread, and yet I found it impossible to account for such feelings. A sensation of stupor oppressed me, as my eyes followed her retreating steps. When a door, at length, closed upon her, my glance sought instinctively and eagerly the countenance of the brother; but he had buried his face in his hands, and I could only perceive that a far more than ordinary wanness had overspread the emaciated fingers through which trickled many passionate tears.

The disease of the lady Madeline had long baffled the skill of her physicians. A settled apathy, a gradual wasting away of the person, and frequent although transient affections of a partially cataleptical character, were the unusual diagnosis. Hitherto she had steadily borne up against the pressure of her malady, and had not betaken herself finally to bed; but on the closing in of the evening of my arrival at the house she succumbed (as her brother told me at night with inexpressible agitation) to the prostrating power of the destroyer; and I learned that the glimpse I had obtained of her person would thus probably be the last I should obtain — that the lady, at least while living, would be seen by me no more.

For several days ensuing, her name was unmentioned by either Usher or myself; and during this period I was busied in earnest endeavors to alleviate the melancholy of my friend. We painted and read together; or I listened, as if in a dream, to the wild improvisations of his speaking guitar. And thus, as a closer and still closer intimacy admitted me more unreservedly into the recesses of his spirit, the more bitterly did I perceive the futility of all attempt at cheering a mind from which darkness, as if an inherent positive quality, poured forth upon all objects of the moral and physical universe, in one unceasing radiation of gloom.

I shall ever bear about me a memory of the many solemn hours I thus spent alone with the master of the House of Usher. Yet I should fail in any attempt to convey an idea of the exact character of the studies, or of the occupations, in which he involved me, or led me the way. An excited and highly distempered ideality threw a sulphureous luster over all. His long improvised dirges will ring forever in my ears. Among other things, I hold painfully in mind a certain singular perversion and amplification of the wild air of the last waltz of Von Weber. From the paintings over which his elaborate fancy brooded, and which grew, touch by touch, into vaguenesses at which I shuddered the more thrillingly because I shuddered knowing not why — from these paintings (vivid as their images now are before me) I would in vain endeavor to educe more than a small portion which should lie within the compass of merely written words. By the utter simplicity, by the nakedness of his designs, he arrested and overawed attention. If ever mortal painted an idea, that mortal was Roderick Usher. For me at least, in the circumstances then surrounding me, there arose, out of the pure abstractions which the hypochondriac contrived to throw upon his canvas, an intensity of intolerable awe, no shadow of which felt I ever yet in the contemplation of the certainly glowing yet too concrete reveries of Fuseli.

One of the phantasmagoric conceptions of my friend, partaking not so rigidly of the spirit of abstraction, may be shadowed forth, although feebly, in words. A small picture presented the interior of an immensely long and rectangular vault or tunnel, with low walls, smooth, white, and without interruption or device. Certain accessory points of the design served well to convey the idea that this excavation lay at an exceeding depth below the surface of the earth. No outlet was observed in any portion of its vast extent, and no torch or other artificial source of light was discernible; yet a flood of intense rays rolled throughout, and bathed the whole in a ghastly and inappropriate splendor.

I have just spoken of that morbid condition of the auditory nerve which rendered all music intolerable to the sufferer, with the exception of certain effects of stringed instruments. It was, perhaps, the narrow limits to which he thus confined himself upon the guitar, which gave birth, in great measure, to the fantastic character of his performances. But the fervid *facility* of his impromptus could not be so accounted for. They must have been, and were, in the notes as well as in the words of his wild fantasias (for he not unfrequently accompanied himself with rhymed verbal improvisations), the result of that intense mental collectedness and concentration to which I have previously alluded as observable only in particular moments of the highest artificial excitement. The words of one of these rhapsodies I have easily remembered. I was, perhaps, the more forcibly impressed with it, as he gave it, because, in the under or mystic current of its meaning, I fancied that I perceived, and for the first time, a full consciousness, on the part of Usher, of the tottering of his lofty reason upon her throne. The verses, which were entitled "The Haunted Palace," ran very nearly, if not accurately, thus:


I

In the greenest of our valleys
    By good angels tenanted,
Once a fair and stately palace —
    Radiant palace — reared its head.
In the monarch Thought's dominion
    It stood there;
Never seraph spread a pinion
    Over fabric half so fair.


II

Banners yellow, glorious, golden,
    On its roof did float and flow,
(This — all this — was in the olden
    Time long ago)

And every gentle air that dallied,
  In that sweet day,
Along the ramparts plumed and pallid,
  A wingéd odor went away.


### III

Wanderers in that happy valley
  Through two luminous windows saw
Spirits moving musically
  To a lute's well-tunéd law,
Round about a throne where, sitting,
  Porphyrogene,
In state his glory well befitting,
  The ruler of the realm was seen.


### IV

And all with pearl and ruby glowing
  Was the fair palace door,
Through which came flowing, flowing, flowing,
  And sparkling evermore,
A troop of Echoes whose sweet duty
  Was but to sing,
In voices of surpassing beauty,
  The wit and wisdom of their king.


### V

But evil things, in robes of sorrow,
  Assailed the monarch's high estate;
(Ah, let us mourn, for never morrow
  Shall dawn upon him, desolate!)
And round about his home the glory
  That blushed and bloomed
Is but a dim-remembered story
  Of the old time entombed.

### VI

And travelers now within that valley
  Through the red-litten windows see
Vast forms that move fantastically
  To a discordant melody;
While, like a ghastly rapid river,
  Through the pale door
A hideous throng rush out forever,
  And laugh — but smile no more.

I well remember that suggestions arising from this ballad led us into a train of thought, wherein there became manifest an opinion of Usher's which I mention not so much on account of its novelty (for other men[1] have thought thus) as on account of the pertinacity with which he maintained it. This opinion, in its general form, was that of the sentience of all vegetable things. But in his disordered fancy the idea had assumed a more daring character, and trespassed, under certain conditions, upon the kingdom of inorganization. I lack words to express the full extent or the earnest *abandon* of his persuasion. The belief, however, was connected (as I have previously hinted) with the gray stones of the home of his forefathers. The conditions of the sentience had been here, he imagined, fulfilled in the method of collocation of these stones — in the order of their arrangement, as well as in that of the many fungi which overspread them, and of the decayed trees which stood around — above all, in the long undisturbed endurance of this arrangement, and in its reduplication in the still waters of the tarn. Its evidence — the evidence of the sentience — was to be seen, he said (and I here started as he spoke), in the gradual yet certain condensation of an atmosphere of their own about the waters and the walls. The result

---

[1] Watson, Dr. Percival, Spallanzani, and especially the Bishop of Landaff. — See " Chemical Essays," Vol. V.

was discoverable, he added, in that silent, yet importunate and terrible, influence which for centuries had molded the destinies of his family, and which made *him* what I now saw him — what he was. Such opinions need no comment, and I will make none.

Our books — the books which, for years, had formed no small portion of the mental existence of the invalid — were, as might be supposed, in strict keeping with this character of phantasm. We pored together over such works as the Ververt and Chartreuse of Gresset; the Belphegor of Machiavelli; the Heaven and Hell of Swedenborg; the Subterranean Voyage of Nicholas Klimm by Holberg; the Chiromancy of Robert Flud, of Jean D'Indaginé, and of De la Chambre; the Journey into the Blue Distance of Tieck; and the City of the Sun of Campanella. One favorite volume was a small octavo edition of the *Directorium Inquisitorum*, by the Dominican Eymeric de Gironne; and there were passages in Pomponius Mela, about the old African Satyrs and Ægipans, over which Usher would sit dreaming for hours. His chief delight, however, was found in the perusal of an exceedingly rare and curious book in quarto Gothic — the manual of a forgotten church — the *Vigiliæ Mortuorum secundum Chorum Ecclesiæ Maguntinæ.*

I could not help thinking of the wild ritual of this work, and of its probable influence upon the hypochondriac, when one evening, having informed me abruptly that the lady Madeline was no more, he stated his intention of preserving her corpse for a fortnight (previously to its final interment) in one of the numerous vaults within the main walls of the building. The worldly reason, however, assigned for this singular proceeding was one which I did not feel at liberty to dispute. The brother had been led to his resolution (so he told me) by consideration of the unusual character of the malady of the deceased, of certain obtrusive and eager inquiries on the part of her medical men, and of the remote and exposed situation of the burial ground of the family. I will not deny that when I called to mind the sinister countenance of the person whom I met upon the staircase, on the day of my arrival at the house, I had no desire to oppose what I regarded as at best but a harmless, and by no means an unnatural, precaution.

At the request of Usher I personally aided him in the arrangements for the temporary entombment. The body having been encoffined, we two alone bore it to its rest. The vault in which we placed it (and which had been so long unopened that our torches, half smothered in its oppressive atmosphere, gave us little opportunity for investigation) was small, damp, and entirely without means of admission for light, lying, at great depth, immediately beneath that portion of the building in which was my own sleeping apartment. It had been used, apparently, in remote feudal times, for the worst purposes of a donjon keep, and in later days as a place of deposit for powder, or some other highly combustible substance, as a portion of its floor, and the whole interior of a long archway through which we reached it, were carefully sheathed with copper. The door, of massive iron, had been, also, similarly protected. Its immense weight caused an unusually sharp, grating sound as it moved upon its hinges.

Having deposited our mournful burden upon tressels within this region of horror, we partially turned aside the yet unscrewed lid of the coffin and looked upon the face of the tenant. A striking similitude between the brother and sister now first arrested my attention; and Usher, divining, perhaps, my thoughts, murmured out some few words from which I learned that the deceased and himself had been twins, and that sympathies of a scarcely intelligible nature had always existed between them. Our glances, however, rested not long upon the dead — for we could not regard her unawed. The

disease which had thus entombed the lady in the maturity of
youth had left, as usual in all maladies of a strictly cataleptical
character, the mockery of a faint blush upon the bosom and
the face, and that suspiciously lingering smile upon the lip
which is so terrible in death. We replaced and screwed down
the lid, and, having secured the door of iron, made our way,
with toil, into the scarcely less gloomy apartments of the upper
portion of the house.

And now, some days of bitter grief having elapsed, an
observable change came over the features of the mental disorder of my friend. His ordinary manner had vanished. His
ordinary occupations were neglected or forgotten. He roamed
from chamber to chamber with hurried, unequal, and objectless
step. The pallor of his countenance had assumed, if possible,
a more ghastly hue — but the luminousness of his eye had
utterly gone out. The once occasional huskiness of his tone
was heard no more; and a tremulous quaver, as if of extreme
terror, habitually characterized his utterance. There were times,
indeed, when I thought his unceasingly agitated mind was
laboring with some oppressive secret, to divulge which he
struggled for the necessary courage. At times, again, I was
obliged to resolve all into the mere inexplicable vagaries of
madness, for I beheld him gazing upon vacancy for long hours,
in an attitude of the profoundest attention, as if listening to
some imaginary sound. It was no wonder that his condition
terrified — that it infected me. I felt creeping upon me, by
slow yet certain degrees, the wild influences of his own fantastic yet impressive superstitions.

It was, especially, upon retiring to bed late in the night of
the seventh or eighth day after the placing of the lady Madeline
within the donjon that I experienced the full power of such feelings. Sleep came not near my couch, while the hours waned
and waned away. I struggled to reason off the nervousness

which had dominion over me. I endeavored to believe that much, if not all, of what I felt was due to the bewildering influence of the gloomy furniture of the room — of the dark and tattered draperies which, tortured into motion by the breath of a rising tempest, swayed fitfully to and fro upon the walls and rustled uneasily about the decorations of the bed. But my efforts were fruitless. An irrepressible tremor gradually pervaded my frame; and at length there sat upon my very heart an incubus of utterly causeless alarm. Shaking this off with a gasp and a struggle, I uplifted myself upon the pillows, and, peering earnestly within the intense darkness of the chamber, hearkened — I know not why, except that an instinctive spirit prompted me — to certain low and indefinite sounds which came, through the pauses of the storm, at long intervals, I knew not whence. Overpowered by an intense sentiment of horror, unaccountable yet unendurable, I threw on my clothes with haste (for I felt that I should sleep no more during the night) and endeavored to arouse myself from the pitiable condition into which I had fallen, by pacing rapidly to and fro through the apartment.

I had taken but few turns in this manner when a light step on an adjoining staircase arrested my attention. I presently recognized it as that of Usher. In an instant afterward he rapped, with a gentle touch, at my door, and entered, bearing a lamp. His countenance was, as usual, cadaverously wan; but, moreover, there was a species of mad hilarity in his eyes, an evidently restrained hysteria in his whole demeanor. His air appalled me — but anything was preferable to the solitude which I had so long endured, and I even welcomed his presence as a relief.

"And you have not seen it?" he said abruptly, after having stared about him for some moments in silence — "you have not then seen it? — but, stay! you shall." Thus speaking, and having carefully shaded his lamp, he hurried to one of the casements and threw it freely open to the storm.

The impetuous fury of the entering gust nearly lifted us from our feet. It was, indeed, a tempestuous yet sternly beautiful night, and one wildly singular in its terror and its beauty. A whirlwind had apparently collected its force in our vicinity; for there were frequent and violent alterations in the direction of the wind; and the exceeding density of the clouds (which hung so low as to press upon the turrets of the house) did not prevent our perceiving the lifelike velocity with which they flew careering from all points against each other, without passing away into the distance. I say that even their exceeding density did not prevent our perceiving this; yet we had no glimpse of the moon or stars, nor was there any flashing forth of the lightning. But the under surfaces of the huge masses of agitated vapor, as well as all terrestrial objects immediately around us, were glowing in the unnatural light of a faintly luminous and distinctly visible gaseous exhalation which hung about and enshrouded the mansion.

"You must not — you shall not behold this!" said I, shudderingly, to Usher, as I led him with a gentle violence from the window to a seat. "These appearances, which bewilder you are merely electrical phenomena not uncommon — or it may be that they have their ghastly origin in the rank miasma of the tarn. Let us close this casement; the air is chilling and dangerous to your frame. Here is one of your favorite romances. I will read, and you shall listen; and so we will pass away this terrible night together."

The antique volume which I had taken up was the "Mad Trist" of Sir Launcelot Canning; but I had called it a favorite of Usher's more in sad jest than in earnest; for, in truth, there is little in its uncouth and unimaginative prolixity which could have had interest for the lofty and spiritual ideality of my friend. It was, however, the only book immediately at hand; and I indulged a vague hope that the excitement which now agitated the hypochondriac might find relief (for the history of mental disorder is full of similar anomalies) even in the extremeness of the folly which I should read. Could I have judged, indeed, by the wild overstrained air of vivacity with which he hearkened, or apparently hearkened, to the words of the tale, I might well have congratulated myself upon the success of my design.

I had arrived at that well-known portion of the story where Ethelred, the hero of the Trist, having sought in vain for peaceable admission into the dwelling of the hermit, proceeds to make good an entrance by force. Here, it will be remembered, the words of the narrative run thus:

"And Ethelred, who was by nature of a doughty heart, and who was now mighty withal, on account of the powerfulness of the wine which he had drunken, waited no longer to hold parley with the hermit, who, in sooth, was of an obstinate and maliceful turn, but, feeling the rain upon his shoulders, and fearing the rising of the tempest, uplifted his mace outright, and with blows made quickly room in the plankings of the door for his gauntleted hand; and now pulling therewith sturdily, he so cracked, and ripped, and tore all asunder, that the noise of the dry and hollow-sounding wood alarumed and reverberated throughout the forest."

At the termination of this sentence I started, and for a moment paused; for it appeared to me (although I at once concluded that my excited fancy had deceived me) — it appeared to me that from some very remote portion of the mansion there came, indistinctly, to my ears, what might have been, in its exact similarity of character, the echo (but a stifled and dull one certainly) of the very cracking and ripping sound which Sir Launcelot had so particularly described. It was, beyond doubt, the coincidence alone which had arrested my attention; for, amid the rattling of the sashes of the casements and the ordinary commingled noises of the still increasing storm, the sound, in itself, had nothing, surely, which should have interested or disturbed me. I continued the story:

"But the good champion Ethelred, now entering within the door, was sore enraged and amazed to perceive no signal of the maliceful hermit; but, in the stead thereof, a dragon of a scaly and prodigious demeanor, and of a fiery tongue, which sate in guard before a palace of gold, with a floor of silver; and upon the wall there hung a shield of shining brass with this legend enwritten —

> Who entereth herein, a conqueror hath bin;
> Who slayeth the dragon, the shield he shall win.

And Ethelred uplifted his mace, and struck upon the head of the dragon, which fell before him, and gave up his pesty breath, with a shriek so horrid and harsh, and withal so piercing, that Ethelred had fain to close his ears with his hands against the dreadful noise of it, the like whereof was never before heard."

Here again I paused abruptly, and now with a feeling of wild amazement; for there could be no doubt whatever that, in this instance, I did actually hear (although from what direction it proceeded I found it impossible to say) a low and apparently distant, but harsh, protracted, and most unusual screaming or grating sound — the exact counterpart of what my fancy had already conjured up for the dragon's unnatural shriek as described by the romancer.

Oppressed, as I certainly was, upon the occurrence of this second and most extraordinary coincidence, by a thousand conflicting sensations, in which wonder and extreme terror were predominant, I still retained sufficient presence of mind to avoid exciting, by any observation, the sensitive nervousness of my companion. I was by no means certain that he had noticed the sounds in question; although, assuredly, a strange alteration had during the last few minutes taken place in his demeanor. From a position fronting my own, he had gradually brought round his chair so as to sit with his face to the door of the chamber; and thus I could but partially perceive his features, although I saw that his lips trembled as if he were murmuring inaudibly. His head had dropped upon his breast — yet I knew that he was not asleep, from the wide and rigid opening of the eye as I caught a glance of it in profile. The motion of his body, too, was at variance with this idea, for he rocked from side to side with a gentle yet constant and uniform sway. Having rapidly taken notice of all this, I resumed the narrative of Sir Launcelot, which thus proceeded:

"And now, the champion, having escaped from the terrible fury of the dragon, bethinking himself of the brazen shield, and of the breaking up of the enchantment which was upon it, removed the carcass from out of the way before him, and approached valorously over the silver pavement of the castle to where the shield was upon the wall; which in sooth tarried not for his full coming, but fell down at his feet upon the silver floor, with a mighty great and terrible ringing sound."

No sooner had these syllables passed my lips than — as if a shield of brass had indeed, at the moment, fallen heavily upon a floor of silver — I became aware of a distinct, hollow, metallic, and clangorous, yet apparently muffled, reverberation. Completely unnerved, I leaped to my feet; but the measured rocking movement of Usher was undisturbed. I rushed to the chair in which he sat. His eyes were bent fixedly before him, and throughout his whole countenance there reigned a stony rigidity. But as I placed my hand upon his shoulder there came a strong shudder over his whole person; a sickly smile quivered about his lips; and I saw that he spoke in a low, hurried, and gibbering murmur, as if unconscious of my presence. Bending closely over him, I at length drank in the hideous import of his words.

" Not hear it ? — yes, I hear it, and *have* heard it. Long —
long — long — many minutes, many hours, many days, have
I heard it — yet I dared not — oh, pity me, miserable wretch
that I am ! — I dared not — I *dared* not speak ! *We have put
her living in the tomb !* Said I not that my senses were acute ?
I *now* tell you that I heard her first feeble movements in the
hollow coffin. I heard them — many, many days ago — yet I
dared not — *I dared not speak !* And now — to-night —
Ethelred — ha ! ha ! — the breaking of the hermit's door, and
the death cry of the dragon, and the clangor of the shield ! —
say, rather, the rending of her coffin, and the grating of the
iron hinges of her prison, and her struggles within the coppered
archway of the vault ! Oh, whither shall I fly ? Will she not
be here anon ? Is she not hurrying to upbraid me for my
haste ? Have I not heard her footstep on the stair ? Do I not
distinguish that heavy and horrible beating of her heart ?
Madman ! " — here he sprang furiously to his feet, and
shrieked out his syllables, as if in the effort he were giving
up his soul — " *Madman ! I tell you that she now stands
without the door !* "

As if in the superhuman energy of his utterance there had
been found the potency of a spell, the huge antique panels to
which the speaker pointed threw slowly back, upon the instant,
their ponderous and ebony jaws. It was the work of the rushing gust — but then without those doors there *did* stand the
lofty and enshrouded figure of the lady Madeline of Usher.
There was blood upon her white robes, and the evidence of
some bitter struggle upon every portion of her emaciated
frame. For a moment she remained trembling and reeling to
and fro upon the threshold — then, with a low moaning cry,
fell heavily inward upon the person of her brother, and, in
her violent and now final death agonies, bore him to the floor
a corpse, and a victim to the terrors he had anticipated.

From that chamber, and from that mansion, I fled aghast. The storm was still abroad in all its wrath as I found myself crossing the old causeway. Suddenly there shot along the path a wild light, and I turned to see whence a gleam so unusual could have issued; for the vast house and its shadows were alone behind me. The radiance was that of the full, setting, and blood-red moon, which now shone vividly through that once barely discernible fissure, of which I have before spoken as extending from the roof of the building, in a zigzag direction, to the base. While I gazed, this fissure rapidly widened — there came a fierce breath of the whirlwind — the entire orb of the satellite burst at once upon my sight — my brain reeled as I saw the mighty walls rushing asunder — there was a long, tumultuous, shouting sound like the voice of a thousand waters — and the deep and dank tarn at my feet closed sullenly and silently over the fragments of the " House of Usher."

## JOHN PENDLETON KENNEDY

[John Pendleton Kennedy was born in Baltimore, Maryland, in 1795. After graduating from a local college he studied law and began to practice his profession. For the rest of his life he divided his attention among law, politics, and literature. In 1852 he became Secretary of the Navy under President Fillmore. He died at Newport, Rhode Island, in 1870.]

## SELECTIONS FROM "SWALLOW BARN"

### SWALLOW BARN, AN OLD VIRGINIA ESTATE

Swallow Barn is an aristocratical old edifice which sits, like a brooding hen, on the southern bank of the James River. It looks down upon a shady pocket or nook, formed by an indentation of the shore, from a gentle acclivity thinly sprinkled with oaks whose magnificent branches afford habitation to sundry friendly colonies of squirrels and woodpeckers.

This time-honored mansion was the residence of the family of Hazards. But in the present generation the spells of love and mortgage have translated the possession to Frank Meriwether, who, having married Lucretia, the eldest daughter of my late Uncle Walter Hazard, and lifted some gentlemanlike en-cumbrances which had been sleeping for years upon the domain, was thus inducted into the proprietary rights. The adjacency of his own estate gave a territorial fea-ture to this alliance, of which the fruits were no less dis-cernible in the multiplication of negroes, cattle, and poul-try than in a flourishing clan of Meriwethers.

JOHN PENDLETON KENNEDY

The main building is more than a century old. It is built with thick brick walls, but one story in height, and surmounted by a double-faced or hipped roof, which gives the idea of a ship bottom upwards. Later buildings have been added to this as the wants or am-bition of the family have expanded. These are all constructed of wood, and seem to have been built in defiance of all laws of congruity, just as convenience required. But they form alto-gether an agreeable picture of habitation, suggesting the idea of comfort in the ample space they fill and in their conspicuous adaptation to domestic uses.

The hall door is an ancient piece of walnut, which has grown too heavy for its hinges and by its daily travel has furrowed the floor in a quadrant, over which it has an uneasy journey. It is shaded by a narrow porch, with a carved pediment upheld by massive columns of wood, somewhat split by the sun. An ample courtyard, inclosed by a semicircular paling, extends in front of the whole pile, and is traversed by a gravel road leading from a rather ostentatious iron gate, which is swung between two pillars of brick surmounted by globes of cut stone. Between the gate and the house a large willow spreads its arched and pendent drapery over the grass. A bridle rack stands within the inclosure, and near it a ragged horse-nibbled plum tree — the current belief being that a plum tree thrives on ill usage — casts its skeleton shadow on the dust.

Some Lombardy poplars, springing above a mass of shrubbery, partially screen various supernumerary buildings at a short distance in the rear of the mansion. Amongst these is to be seen the gable end of a stable, with the date of its erection stiffly emblazoned in black bricks near the upper angle, in figures set in after the fashion of the work on a girl's sampler. In the same quarter a pigeon box, reared on a post and resembling a huge teetotum, is visible, and about its several doors and windows a family of pragmatical pigeons are generally strutting, bridling, and bragging at each other from sunrise until dark.

Appendant to this homestead is an extensive tract of land which stretches some three or four miles along the river, presenting alternately abrupt promontories mantled with pine and dwarf oak, and small inlets terminating in swamps. Some sparse portions of forest vary the landscape, which, for the most part, exhibits a succession of fields clothed with Indian corn, some small patches of cotton or tobacco plants, with the usual varieties of stubble and fallow grounds. These are inclosed by worm fences of shrunken chestnut, where lizards and ground squirrels are perpetually running races along the rails.

A few hundred steps from the mansion a brook glides at a snail's pace towards the river, holding its course through a wilderness of laurel and alder, and creeping around islets covered with green mosses. Across this stream is thrown a rough bridge, which it would delight a painter to see; and not far below it an aged sycamore twists its roots into a grotesque framework to the pure mirror of a spring, which wells up its cool waters from a bed of gravel and runs gurgling to the brook. There it aids in furnishing a cruising ground to a squadron of ducks who, in defiance of all nautical propriety, are incessantly turning up their sterns to the skies. On the grass which skirts the margin of the spring I observe the family linen is usually spread out by some three or four negro women, who chant shrill music over their washtubs, and seem to live in ceaseless warfare with sundry little besmirched and bow-legged blacks, who are never tired of making somersaults and mischievously pushing each other on the clothes laid down to dry.

Beyond the bridge, at some distance, stands a prominent object in the perspective of this picture, — the most venerable appendage to the establishment, — a huge barn with an immense roof hanging almost to the ground and thatched a foot thick with sunburnt straw, which reaches below the eaves in ragged flakes. It has a singularly drowsy and decrepit aspect. The yard around it is strewed knee-deep with litter, from the midst of which arises a long rack resembling a *chevaux-de-frise*, which is ordinarily filled with fodder. This is the customary lounge of half a score of oxen and as many cows, who sustain an imperturbable companionship with a sickly wagon, whose parched tongue and drooping swingletrees, as it stands in the sun, give it a most forlorn and invalid character; whilst some sociable carts under the sheds, with their shafts perched against the walls, suggest the idea of a set of gossiping cronies taking their ease in a tavern porch. Now and then a clownish hobbledehoy colt, with long fetlocks and disordered mane, and a thousand burs in his tail, stalks through this company. But as it is forbidden ground to all his tribe, he is likely very soon to encounter a shower of corncobs from some of the negro men ; upon which contingency he makes a rapid retreat across the bars which imperfectly guard the entrance to the yard, and with an uncouth display of his heels bounds away towards the brook, where he stops and looks back with a saucy defiance ; and after affecting to drink for a moment, gallops away with a braggart whinny to the fields.

## The Master of Swallow Barn

The master of this lordly domain is Frank Meriwether. He is now in the meridian of life — somewhere about forty-five. Good cheer and an easy temper tell well upon him. The first has given him a comfortable, portly figure, and the latter a contemplative turn of mind, which inclines him to be lazy and philosophical.

He has some right to pride himself on his personal appearance, for he has a handsome face, with a dark-blue eye and a fine intellectual brow. His head is growing scant of hair on the crown, which induces him to be somewhat particular in the management of his locks in that locality, and these are assuming a decided silvery hue.

It is pleasant to see him when he is going to ride to the Court House on business occasions. He is then apt to make his appearance in a coat of blue broadcloth, astonishingly glossy, and with an unusual amount of plaited ruffle strutting through the folds of a Marseilles waistcoat. A worshipful finish is given to this costume by a large straw hat, lined with green silk. There is a magisterial fullness in his garments which betokens condition in the world, and a heavy bunch of seals, suspended by a chain of gold, jingles as he moves, pronouncing him a man of superfluities.

[He is too lazy to try to go into politics, but did once make a pretence of studying law in Richmond, and is a somewhat autocratic justice of the peace.]

. . . Having in this way qualified himself to assert and maintain his rights, he came to his estate, upon his arrival at age, a very model of landed gentlemen. Since that time his avocations have had a certain literary tincture; for having settled himself down as a married man, and got rid of his superfluous foppery, he rambled with wonderful assiduity through a wilderness of romances, poems, and dissertations, which are now collected in his library, and, with their battered blue covers, present a lively type of an army of continentals at the close of the war, or a hospital of invalids. These have all, at last, given way to the newspapers—a miscellaneous study very attractive and engrossing to country gentlemen. This line of study has rendered Meriwether a most perilous antagonist in the matter of legislative proceedings.

A landed proprietor, with a good house and a host of servants, is naturally a hospitable man. A guest is one of his daily wants. A friendly face is a necessary of life, without which the heart is apt to starve, or a luxury without which it grows parsimonious. Men who are isolated from society by distance feel these wants by an instinct, and are grateful for the opportunity to relieve them. In Meriwether the sentiment goes beyond this. It has, besides, something dialectic in it. His house is open to everybody, as freely almost as an inn. But to see him when he has had the good fortune to pick up an intelligent, educated gentleman, — and particularly one who listens well! — a respectable, assentatious stranger! All the better if he has been in the Legislature, and better still, if in Congress. Such a person caught within the purlieus of Swallow Barn may set down one week's entertainment as certain, — inevitable, — and as many more as he likes — the more the merrier. He will know something of the quality of Meriwether's rhetoric before he is gone.

Then again, it is very pleasant to see Frank's kind and considerate bearing towards his servants and dependents. His slaves appreciate this and hold him in most affectionate reverence, and, therefore, are not only contented, but happy under his dominion. . . .

He is somewhat distinguished as a breeder of blooded horses; and ever since the celebrated race between Eclipse and Henry has taken to this occupation with a renewed zeal, as a matter affecting the reputation of the state. It is delightful to hear him expatiate upon the value, importance, and patriotic bearing of this employment, and to listen to all his technical lore touching the mystery of horsecraft. He has some fine colts in training, which are committed to the care of a pragmatical old negro, named Carey, who, in his reverence for the occupation, is the perfect shadow of his master. He and Frank hold grave and momentous consultations upon the affairs of the stable, in such a sagacious strain of equal debate that it would puzzle a spectator to tell which was the leading member of the council. Carey thinks he knows a great deal more upon the subject than his master, and their frequent intercourse has begot a familiarity in the old negro which is almost fatal to Meriwether's supremacy. The old man feels himself authorized to maintain his positions according to the freest parliamentary form, and sometimes with a violence of asseveration that compels his master to abandon his ground, purely out of faint-heartedness. Meriwether gets a little nettled by Carey's doggedness, but generally turns it off in a laugh. I was in the stable with him, a few mornings after my arrival, when he ventured to expostulate with the venerable groom upon a professional point, but the controversy terminated in its customary way. "Who sot you up, Master Frank, to tell me how to fodder that 'ere cretur, when I as good as nursed you on my knee?"

"Well, tie up your tongue, you old mastiff," replied Frank, as he walked out of the stable, "and cease growling, since you will have it your own way"; and then, as we left the old man's presence, he added, with an affectionate chuckle, "a faithful old cur, too, that snaps at me out of pure honesty; he has not many years left, and it does no harm to humor him."

## THE MISTRESS OF SWALLOW BARN

Whilst Frank Meriwether amuses himself with his quiddities, and floats through life upon the current of his humor, his dame, my excellent cousin Lucretia, takes charge of the household affairs, as one who has a reputation to stake upon her administration. She has made it a perfect science, and great is her fame in the dispensation thereof!

Those who have visited Swallow Barn will long remember the morning stir, of which the murmurs arose even unto the chambers and fell upon the ears of the sleepers: the dry rubbing of floors, and even the waxing of the same until they were like ice; and the grinding of coffee mills; and the gibber of ducks, and chickens, and turkeys; and all the multitudinous concert of homely sounds. And then, her breakfasts! I do not wish to be counted extravagant, but a small regiment might march in upon her without disappointment; and I would put them for excellence and variety against anything that ever was served upon platter. Moreover, all things go like clockwork. She rises with the lark and infuses an early vigor into the whole household. And yet she is a thin woman to look upon, and a feeble; with a sallow complexion, and a pair of animated black eyes which impart a portion of fire to a countenance otherwise demure from the paths worn across it in the frequent travel of a low-country ague. But, although her life has been somewhat saddened by such visitations, my cousin is too spirited a woman to give up to them; for she is therapeutical in her constitution, and considers herself a full match for any reasonable tertian in the world. Indeed, I have sometimes thought that she took more pride in her leechcraft than becomes a Christian woman; she is even a little vainglorious. For, to say nothing of her skill in compounding simples, she has occasionally brought down upon her head the sober remonstrances of her husband by her pertinacious faith in the efficacy of certain spells in cases of intermittent. But there is no reasoning against her experience. She can enumerate the cases —" and men may say what they choose about its being contrary to reason, and all that: it is their way! But seeing is believing — nine scoops of water in the hollow of the hand, from the sycamore spring, for three mornings, before sunrise, and a cup of strong coffee with lemon juice, will break an ague, try it when you will." In short, as Frank says, " Lucretia will die in that creed."

I am occasionally up early enough to be witness to her morning regimen, which, to my mind, is rather tyrannically enforced against the youngsters of her numerous family, both white and black. She is in the habit of preparing some death-routing decoction for them, in a small pitcher, and administering it to the whole squadron in succession, who severally swallow the dose with a most ineffectual effort at repudiation, and gallop off with faces all rue and wormwood.

Everything at Swallow Barn that falls within the superintendence of my cousin Lucretia is a pattern of industry. In fact, I consider her the very priestess of the American system, for, with her, the protection of manufactures is even more of a passion than a principle. Every here and there, over the estate, may be seen, rising in humble guise above the shrubbery, the rude chimney of a log cabin, where all the livelong day the plaintive moaning of the spinning wheel rises fitfully upon the breeze, like the fancied notes of a hobgoblin, as they are sometimes imitated in the stories with which we frighten children. In these laboratories the negro women are employed in preparing yarn for the loom, from which is produced not only a comfortable supply of winter clothing for the working people but some excellent carpets for the house.

It is refreshing to behold how affectionately vain our good hostess is of Frank, and what deference she shows to his judgment in all matters except those that belong to the home department; for there she is confessedly, and without appeal, the paramount power. It seems to be a dogma with her that he is the very "first man in Virginia," an expression which in this region has grown into an emphatic provincialism. Frank, in return, is a devout admirer of her accomplishments, and although he does not pretend to an ear for music, he is in raptures at her skill on the harpsichord when she plays at night for the children to dance; and he sometimes sets her to singing "The Twins of Latona," and "Old Towler," and "The Rose-Tree in Full Bearing" (she does not study the modern music) for the entertainment of his company. On these occasions he stands by the instrument, and nods his head as if he comprehended the airs.

## TRACES OF THE FEUDAL SYSTEM

The gentlemen of Virginia live apart from each other. They are surrounded by their bondsmen and dependents; and the customary intercourse of society familiarizes their minds to the relation of high and low degree. They frequently meet in the interchange of a large and thriftless hospitality, in which the forms of society are foregone for its comforts, and the business of life thrown aside for the enjoyment of its pleasures. Their halls are large, and their boards ample; and surrounding the great family hearth, with its immense burthen of blazing wood casting a broad and merry glare over the congregated household and the numerous retainers, a social winter party in Virginia affords a tolerable picture of feudal munificence.

Frank Meriwether is a good specimen of the class I have described. He seeks companionship with men of ability, and is a zealous disseminator of the personal fame of individuals who have won any portion of renown in the state. Sometimes I even think he exaggerates a little, when descanting upon the prodigies of genius that have been reared in the Old Dominion; and he manifestly seems to consider that a young man who has astonished a whole village in Virginia by the splendor of his talents must, of course, be known throughout the United States; for he frequently opens his eyes at me with an air of astonishment when I happen to ask him who is the marvel he is speaking of.

I observe, moreover, that he has a constitutional fondness for paradoxes and does not scruple to adopt and republish any apothegm that is calculated to startle one by its novelty. He has a correspondence with several old friends who were with him at college, and who have now risen into an extensive political notoriety in the state; these gentlemen furnish him with many new currents of thought, along which he glides with a happy velocity. He is essentially meditative in his character and somewhat given to declamation; and these traits have communicated a certain measured and deliberate gesticulation to his discourse. I have frequently seen him after dinner stride backward and forward across the room for some moments, wrapped in thought, and then fling himself upon the sofa and come out with some weighty doubt, expressed with a solemn emphasis. In this form he lately began a conversation, or rather a speech, that for a moment quite disconcerted me. "After all," said he, as if he had been talking to me before, although these were the first words he uttered — then making a parenthesis, so as to qualify what he was going to say — "I don't deny that the steamboat is destined to produce valuable results, but after all, I much question (and here he bit his upper lip, and paused an instant) if we are not better without it. I declare, I think it strikes deeper at the supremacy of the states than most persons are willing to allow. This annihilation of space, sir, is not to be desired. Our protection against the evils of consolidation consists in the very obstacles to our intercourse. Splatterthwaite Dubbs of Dinwiddie [or some such name; Frank is famous for quoting the opinions of his contemporaries. This Splatterthwaite, I take it, was some old college chum who had got into the legislature and, I dare say, made pungent speeches] made a good remark — that the home material of Virginia was never so good as when her roads were at their worst." And so Frank went on with quite a harangue, to which none of the company replied one word for fear we might get into a dispute. Everybody seems to understand the advantage of silence when Meriwether is inclined to be expatiatory.

This strain of philosophizing has a pretty marked influence in the neighborhood, for I perceive that Frank's opinions are very much quoted. There is a set of under-talkers about these large country establishments who are very glad to pick up the crumbs of wisdom which fall from a rich man's table; secondhand philosophers, who trade upon other people's stock. Some of these have a natural bias to this venting of upper opinions, by reason of certain dependences in the way of trade and favor; others have it from affinity of blood, which works like a charm over a whole county. Frank stands related, by some tie of marriage or mixture of kin, to an infinite train of connections, spread over the state; and it is curious to learn what a decided hue this gives to the opinions of the district.

We had a notable example of this one morning not long after my arrival at Swallow Barn. Meriwether had given several indications immediately after breakfast of a design to pour out upon us the gathered ruminations of the last twenty-four hours, but we had evaded the storm with some caution, when the arrival of two or three neighbors, — plain, homespun farmers, — who had ridden to Swallow Barn to execute some papers before Frank as a magistrate, furnished him with an occasion that was not to be lost. After dispatching their business he detained them, ostensibly to inquire about their crops and other matters of their vocation, but, in reality, to give them that very flood of politics which we had escaped. We, of course, listened without concern, since we were assured of an auditory that would not flinch. In the course of this disquisition he made use of a figure of speech which savored of some previous study, or, at least, was highly in the oratorical vein. "Mark me, gentlemen," said he, contracting his brow over his fine thoughtful eye and pointing the forefinger of his left hand directly at the face of the person he addressed — "mark me, gentlemen; you and I may not live to see it, but our children will see it, and wail over it — the sovereignty of this Union will be as the rod of Aaron; it will turn into a serpent and swallow up all that struggle with it." Mr. Chub was present at this solemn denunciation and was very much affected by it. He rubbed his hands with some briskness and uttered his applause in a short but vehement panegyric, in which were heard only the detached words — "Mr. Burke — Cicero."

The next day Ned and myself were walking by the schoolhouse and were hailed by Rip from one of the windows, who, in a sly undertone, as he beckoned us to come close to him, told us, "if we wanted to hear a regular preach, to stand fast." We could look into the schoolroom unobserved, and there was our patriotic pedagogue haranguing the boys with a violence of action that drove an additional supply of blood into his face. It was apparent that the old gentleman had got much beyond the depth of his hearers and was pouring out his rhetoric more from oratorical vanity than from any hope of enlightening his audience. At the most animated part of his strain he brought himself, by a kind of climax, to the identical sentiment uttered by Meriwether the day before. He warned his young hearers — the oldest of them was not above fourteen — " to keep a lynx-eyed gaze upon that serpentlike ambition which would convert the government at Washington into Aaron's rod, to swallow up the independence of their native state."

This conceit immediately ran through all the lower circles at Swallow Barn. Mr. Tongue, the overseer, repeated it at the blacksmith's shop in the presence of the blacksmith and Mr. Absalom Bulrush, a spare, ague-and-feverish husbandman who occupies a muddy slip of marshland on one of the river bottoms, which is now under a mortgage to Meriwether; and from these it has spread far and wide, though a good deal diluted, until in its circuit it has reached our veteran groom Carey, who considers the sentiment as importing something of an awful nature. With the smallest encouragement, Carey will put on a tragi-comic face, shake his head very slowly, turn up his eyeballs, and open out his broad, scaly hands, while he repeats with labored voice, " Look out, Master Ned! Aaron's rod a black snake in Old Virginny!" Upon which, as we fall into a roar of laughter, Carey stares with astonishment at our irreverence. But having been set to acting this scene for us once or twice, he now suspects us of some joke and asks " if there isn't a copper for an old negro," which if he succeeds in getting, he runs off, telling us " he is too 'cute to make a fool of himself."

Meriwether does not dislike this trait in the society around him. I happened to hear two carpenters one day, who were making some repairs at the stable, in high conversation. One of them was expounding to the other some oracular opinion of Frank's touching the political aspect of the country, and just at the moment when the speaker was most animated, Meriwether himself came up. He no sooner became aware of the topic in discussion than he walked off in another direction, affecting not to hear it, although I knew he heard every word. He told me afterwards that there was "a wholesome tone of feeling amongst the people in that part of the country."

## The Quarter

Having dispatched these important matters at the stable, we left our horses in charge of the servants and walked towards the cabins, which were not more than a few hundred paces distant. These hovels, with their appurtenances, formed an exceedingly picturesque landscape. They were scattered, without order, over the slope of a gentle hill; and many of them were embowered under old and majestic trees. The rudeness of their construction rather enhanced the attractiveness of the scene. Some few were built after the fashion of the better sort of cottages, but age had stamped its heavy traces upon their exterior; the green moss had gathered upon the roofs, and the coarse weatherboarding had broken, here and there, into chinks. But the more lowly of these structures, and the most numerous, were nothing more than plain log cabins, compacted pretty much on the model by which boys build partridge traps, being composed of the trunks of trees, still clothed with their bark, and knit together at the corners with so little regard to neatness that the timbers, being of unequal lengths, jutted beyond each other, sometimes to the length of a foot. Perhaps none of these latter sort were more than twelve feet square and not above seven in height. A door swung upon wooden hinges, and a small window of two narrow panes of glass were, in general, the only openings in the front. The intervals between the logs were filled with clay, and the roof, which was constructed of smaller timbers, laid lengthwise along it and projecting two or three feet beyond the side or gable walls, heightened, in a very marked degree, the rustic effect. The chimneys communicated even a droll expression to these habitations. They were, oddly enough, built of billets of wood, having a broad foundation of stone, and growing narrower as they rose, each receding gradually from the house to which it was attached, until it reached the height of the roof. These combustible materials were saved from the access of the fire by a thick coating of mud, and the whole structure, from its tapering form, might be said to bear some resemblance to the spout of a teakettle; indeed, this domestic implement would furnish no unapt type of the complete cabin.

From this description, which may serve to illustrate a whole species of habitations very common in Virginia, it will be seen that, on the score of accommodation, the inmates of these dwellings were furnished according to a very primitive notion of comfort. Still, however, there were little garden patches attached to each, where cymblings, cucumbers, sweet potatoes, watermelons, and cabbages flourished in unrestrained luxuriance. Add to this that there were abundance of poultry domesticated about the premises, and it may be perceived that, whatever might be the inconveniences of shelter, there was no want of what, in all countries, would be considered a reasonable supply of luxuries.

Nothing more attracted my observation than the swarms of little negroes that basked on the sunny sides of these cabins and congregated to gaze at us as we surveyed their haunts. They were nearly all in that costume of the golden age which I have heretofore described, and showed their slim shanks and long heels in all varieties of their grotesque natures. Their predominant love of sunshine, and their lazy, listless postures, and apparent content to be silently looking abroad, might well afford a comparison to a set of terrapins luxuriating in the genial warmth of summer on the logs of a mill pond.

And there, too, were the prolific mothers of this redundant brood — a number of stout negro women who thronged the doors of the huts, full of idle curiosity to see us. And, when to these are added a few reverend, wrinkled, decrepit old men, with faces shortened as if with drawing strings, noses that seemed to have run all to nostril, and with feet of the configuration of a mattock, my reader will have a tolerably correct idea of this negro quarter, its population, buildings, external appearance, situation, and extent.

Meriwether, I have said before, is a kind and considerate master. It is his custom frequently to visit his slaves, in order to inspect their condition and, where it may be necessary, to add to their comforts or relieve their wants. His coming amongst them, therefore, is always hailed with pleasure. He has constituted himself into a high court of appeal, and makes it a rule to give all their petitions a patient hearing and to do justice in the premises. This, he tells me, he considers as indispensably necessary. He says that no overseer is entirely to be trusted; that there are few men who have the temper to administer wholesome laws to any population, however small, without some omissions or irregularities, and that this is more emphatically true of those who administer them entirely at their own will. On the present occasion, in almost every house where Frank entered, there was some boon to be asked; and I observed that, in every case, the petitioner was either gratified or refused in such a tone as left no occasion or disposition to murmur. Most of the women had some bargains to offer, of fowls or eggs or other commodities of the household use, and

Meriwether generally referred them to his wife, who, I found, relied almost entirely on this resource for the supply of such commodities, the negroes being regularly paid for whatever was offered in this way.

One old fellow had a special favor to ask — a little money to get a new padding for his saddle, which, he said, "galled his cretur's back." Frank, after a few jocular passages with the veteran, gave him what he desired, and sent him off rejoicing.

"That, sir," said Meriwether, "is no less a personage than Jupiter. He is an old bachelor and has his cabin here on the hill. He is now near seventy and is a kind of King of the Quarter. He has a horse, which he extorted from me last Christmas, and I seldom come here without finding myself involved in some new demand as a consequence of my donation. Now he wants a pair of spurs, which, I suppose, I must give him. He is a preposterous coxcomb, and Ned has administered to his vanity by a present of a *chapeau de bras*, a relic of my military era, which he wears on Sundays with a conceit that has brought upon him as much envy as admiration — the usual condition of greatness."

The air of contentment and good humor and kind family attachment, which was apparent throughout this little community, and the familiar relations existing between them and the proprietor struck me very pleasantly. I came here a stranger, in great degree, to the negro character, knowing but little of the domestic history of these people, their duties, habits, or temper, and somewhat disposed, indeed, from prepossessions, to look upon them as severely dealt with, and expecting to have my sympathies excited towards them as objects of commiseration. I have had, therefore, rather a special interest in observing them. The contrast between my preconceptions of their condition and the reality which I have witnessed, has brought me a most agreeable surprise. I will not say that, in a high state of cultivation and of such self-dependence as they might possibly attain in a separate national existence, they might not become a more respectable people, but I am quite sure they never could become a happier people than I find them here. Perhaps they are destined, ultimately, to that national existence in the clime from which they derive their origin — that this is a transition state in which we see them in Virginia. If it be so, no tribe of people have ever passed from barbarism to civilization whose middle stage of progress has been more secure from harm, more genial to their character, or better supplied with mild and beneficent guardianship, adapted to the actual state of their intellectual feebleness, than the negroes of Swallow Barn. And, from what I can gather, it is pretty much the same on the other estates in this region. I hear of an unpleasant exception to this remark now and then, but under such conditions as warrant the opinion that the unfavorable case is not more common than that which may be found in a survey of any other department of society. The oppression of apprentices, of seamen, of soldiers, of subordinates, indeed, in every relation, may furnish elements for a bead-roll of social grievances quite as striking, if they were diligently noted and brought to view.

## SELECTIONS FROM "HORSESHOE ROBINSON"

### Horseshoe Robinson

It was about two o'clock in the afternoon of a day towards the end of July, 1780, when Captain Arthur Butler, now holding a brevet, some ten days old, of major in the Continental army, and Galbraith Robinson were seen descending the long hill which separates the South Garden from the Cove. They had just left the rich and mellow scenery of the former district, and were now passing into the picturesque valley of the latter.

It was evident from the travel-worn appearance of their horses, as well as from their equipments, that they had journeyed many a mile before they had reached this spot. . . .

Arthur Butler was now in the possession of the vigor of early manhood, with apparently some eight and twenty years upon his head. His frame was well proportioned, light, and active. His face, though distinguished by a smooth and almost beardless cheek, still presented an outline of decided manly beauty. The sun and wind had tanned his complexion, except where a rich volume of black hair upon his brow had preserved the original fairness of a high, broad forehead. A hazel eye sparkled under the shade of a dark lash and indicated, by its alternate playfulness and decision, an adventurous as well as a cheerful spirit. His whole bearing, visage, and figure seemed to speak of one familiar with enterprise and fond of danger; they denoted gentle breeding predominating over a life of toil and privation.

Notwithstanding his profession, which was seen in his erect and peremptory carriage, his dress at this time was, with some slight exceptions, merely civil. He was habited in the costume of a gentleman of the time, with a round hat pretty much of the fashion of the present day — though then but little used except amongst military men — with a white cockade to show his party, while his saddlebow was fortified by a brace of horseman's pistols stowed away in large holsters covered with bearskin; for in those days, when hostile banners were unfurled and men challenged each other upon the highways, these pistols were a part of the countenance (to use an excellent old phrase) of a gentleman.

Galbraith Robinson was a man of altogether rougher mold. Every lineament of his body indicated strength. His stature was rather above six feet; his chest broad; his limbs sinewy, and remarkable for their symmetry. There seemed to be no useless flesh upon his frame to soften the prominent surface of his muscles, and his ample thigh, as he sat upon horseback, showed the working of its texture at each step, as if part of the animal on which he rode. His was one of those iron forms that might be imagined almost bullet-proof. With all these advantages of person there was a radiant, broad good nature upon his face; and the glance of a large, clear, blue eye told of arch thoughts, and of shrewd homely wisdom. A ruddy complexion accorded well with his sprightly but massive features, of which the prevailing expression was such as silently invited friendship and trust. If to these traits be added an abundant shock of yellow, curly hair, terminating in a luxuriant queue, confined by a narrow strand of leather cord, my reader will have a tolerably correct idea of the person I wish to describe.

Robinson had been a blacksmith at the breaking out of the Revolution. He was the owner of a little farm in the Waxhaw settlement on the Catawba, and having pitched his habitation upon a promontory, around whose base the Waxhaw creek swept with a regular but narrow circuit, this locality, taken in connection with his calling, gave rise to a common prefix to his name throughout the neighborhood, and he was therefore almost exclusively distinguished by the sobriquet of Horseshoe Robinson. This familiar appellative had followed him into the army.

The age of Horseshoe was some seven or eight years in advance of that of Butler. On the present occasion his dress was of the plainest and most rustic description: a spherical crowned hat with a broad brim, a coarse gray coatee of mixed cotton and wool, dark linsey-woolsey trousers adhering closely to his leg, hobnailed shoes, and a red cotton handkerchief tied carelessly round his neck with a knot upon his bosom. This costume and a long rifle thrown into the angle of the right arm, with the breech resting on his pommel, and a pouch of deerskin, with a powderhorn attached to it, suspended on his right side, might have warranted a spectator in taking Robinson for a woodsman or hunter from the neighboring mountains.

Such were the two personages who now came "pricking o'er the hill." The period at which I have presented them to my reader was, perhaps, the most anxious one of the whole struggle for independence. Without falling into a long narrative of events which are familiar, at least to every American, I may recall the fact that Gates had just passed southward to take command of the army destined to act against Cornwallis. It was now within a few weeks of that decisive battle which sent the hero of Saratoga "bootless home and weatherbeaten back," to ponder over the mutations of fortune and, in the quiet shades of Virginia, to strike the balance of fame between Northern glory and Southern discomfiture.

[On his way South, Captain Butler passed by Dove Cote, in Virginia, where lived Mildred Lindsay, with whom he was in love. Mildred Lindsay's father was loyal to the king and did not look with favor upon Butler's suit since he had entered the Continental army. Mildred's father favored Tyrrel, who had been sent from England to look after the king's interest. Under these circumstances it was impossible for Butler to do more than to see Mildred secretly on the river bank. At Mrs. Dimock's inn, where Butler and Horseshoe were to spend the night, they met with James Curry, an attendant of Tyrrel, who was carefully watched by Horseshoe under the suspicion that he might be a spy. A quarrel ensued, followed by a fight in which Curry was worsted. The next morning the captain and his companion left early, and after a journey of a week they reached the headquarters of General Gates. Finding no need for his services there, Butler continued his way, according to instructions, to join Colonel Clarke, who was in the mountains of South Carolina raising troops. Horseshoe conducted him by a circuitous route to the house of Wat Adair, a well-known mountaineer, whose good will they wished to obtain. But Adair gave the travelers away to the Tories in spite of the efforts of Mary Musgrove, a mountain girl, to warn Butler. Adair accompanied Horseshoe and Butler on their departure, in order to show them the road.]

## Capture of Butler and Horseshoe

Meantime Butler and Robinson advanced at a wearied pace. The twilight had so far faded as to be only discernible on the western sky. The stars were twinkling through the leaves of the forest, and the light of the firefly spangled the wilderness. The road might be descried, in the most open parts of the wood, for some fifty paces ahead; but where the shrubbery was more dense, it was lost in utter darkness. Our travelers, like most wayfarers towards the end of the day, rode silently along, seldom exchanging a word and anxiously computing the distance which they had yet to traverse before they reached their appointed place of repose. A sense of danger, and the necessity for vigilance, on the present occasion, made them the more silent.

"I thought I heard a wild sort of yell just now — people laughing a great way off," said Robinson, "but there's such a hooting of owls and piping of frogs that I mought have been mistaken. Halt, major. Let me listen — there it is again."

"It is the crying of a panther, sergeant; more than a mile from us, by my ear."

"It is mightily like the scream of drunken men," replied the sergeant; "and there, too! I thought I heard the clatter of a hoof."

The travelers again reined up and listened.

"It is more like a deer stalking through the bushes, Galbraith."

"No," exclaimed the sergeant, "that's the gallop of a horse making down the road ahead of us, as sure as you

MAJOR BUTLER AND HORSESHOE ROBINSON

Reproduction of vignette on title-page of original edition of
"Horseshoe Robinson"

are alive; I heard the shoe strike a stone. You must have hearn it, too."

"I would n't be sure," answered Butler.

"Look to your pistols, major, and prime afresh."

"We seem to have ridden a great way," said Butler, as he concluded the inspection of his pistols and now held one of them ready in his hand. "Can we have lost ourselves? Should we not have reached the Pacolet before this?"

"I have seen no road that could take us astray," replied Robinson, "and, by what we were told just before sundown, I should guess that we could n't be far off the ford. We have n't then quite three miles to Christie's. Well, courage, major! supper and bed were never spoiled by the trouble of getting to them."

"Wat Adair, I think, directed us to Christie's?" said Butler.

"He did; and I had a mind to propose to you, since we caught him in a trick this morning, to make for some other house, if such a thing was possible, or else to spend the night in the woods."

"Perhaps it would be wise, sergeant; and if you think so still, I will be ruled by you."

"If we once got by the riverside, where our horses mought have water, I almost think I should advise a halt there. Although I have made one observation, Major Butler — that running water is lean fare for a hungry man. Howsever, it won't hurt us, and if you say the word we will stop there."

"Then, sergeant, I do say the word."

"Is n't that the glimmering of a light yonder in the bushes?" inquired Horseshoe, as he turned his gaze in the direction of the bivouac, "or is it these here lightning bugs that keep so busy shooting about?"

"I thought I saw the light you speak of, Galbraith; but it has disappeared."

"It is there again, major; and I hear the rushing of the river — we are near the ford. Perhaps this light comes from some cabin on the bank."

"God send that it should turn out so, Galbraith! for I am very weary."

"There is some devilment going on in these woods, major.

I saw a figure pass in front of the light through the bushes. I would be willing to swear it was a man on horseback. Perhaps we have, by chance, fallen on some Tory muster; or, what's not so likely, they may be friends. I think I will ride forward and challenge."

" Better pass unobserved, if you can, sergeant," interrupted Butler. " It will not do for us to run the risk of being separated. Here we are at the river; let us cross, and ride some distance; then, if any one follow us, we shall be more certain of his design."

They now cautiously advanced into the river, which, though rapid, was shallow; and having reached the middle of the stream, they halted to allow their horses water.

"Captain Peter is as thirsty as a man in a fever," said Horseshoe. " He drinks as if he was laying in for a week. Now, major, since we are here in the river, look up the stream. Don't you see, from the image in the water, that there's a fire on the bank? And there, by my soul! there are men on horseback. Look towards the light. Spur, and out on the other side! Quick — quick — they are upon us!"

At the same instant that Horseshoe spoke a bullet whistled close by his ear, and in the next, six or eight men galloped into the river from different points. This was succeeded by a sharp report of firearms from both parties, and the vigorous charge of Robinson, followed by Butler, through the array of the assailants. They gained the opposite bank and now rected all their efforts to outrun their pursuers; but in th crisis of their escape Butler's horse, bounding unde of the spur, staggered a few paces f the ri A bullet had lodged in a vita steed was spent in th stream. Butl he was una' comrade's condition, sprang from his horse and ran to his assistance, and, in the same interval, the ruffian followers gained the spot and surrounded their prisoners. An ineffectual struggle ensued over the prostrate horse and rider, in which Robinson bore down more than one of his adversaries, but was obliged, at last, to yield to the overwhelming power that pressed upon him.

"Bury your swords in both of them to the hilts!" shouted Habershaw; "I don't want to have that work to do to-morrow."

"Stand off!" cried Gideon Blake, as two or three of the gang sprang forward to execute their captain's order; "stand off! the man is on his back, and he shall not be murdered in cold blood"; and the speaker took a position near Butler, prepared to make good his resolve. The spirit of Blake had its desired effect, and the same assailants now turned upon Robinson.

"Hold!" cried Peppercorn, throwing up his sword and warding off the blows that were aimed by these men at the body of the sergeant. "Hold, you knaves! this is my prisoner. I will deal with him to my liking. Would a dozen of you strike one man when he has surrendered? Back, ye cowards; leave him to me. How now, old Horseshoe; are you caught, with your gay master here? Come, come, we know you both. So yield with a good grace, lest, peradventure, I might happen to ~~knock~~ w out your brains."

Silence, fellows! You carrion cro~~ws~~ ~~Haber~~shaw. ~~Reme~~mber the discipline I taught you ~~... you~~r con- ~~... to~~ take the prisoners, since you ~~... art to~~ ~~... the rendez~~vous. And ~~... do you~~ ~~... ab~~out it qui~~ckly ... ha~~nds!" ~~... a~~nd. an~~... com-~~ ~~... w~~o of ~~... nt the~~

shedding of blood. The prisoners were each mounted behind one of the troopers, and in this condition conducted across the river. The saddle and other equipments were stripped from the major's dead steed; and Robinson's horse, Captain Peter, was burdened with the load of two wounded men, whose own horses had escaped from them in the fray. In this guise the band of freebooters, with their prisoners and spoils, slowly and confusedly made their way to the appointed place of re-assembling. In a few moments they were ranged beneath the chestnut, waiting for orders from their self-important and vain commander.

[The next day Horseshoe Robinson managed to escape and bent all his ingenuity to bring about the freedom of Butler. While endeavoring to accomplish this, he meets with the following adventure.]

## HORSESHOE CAPTURES FIVE PRISONERS

David Ramsay's house was situated on a byroad, between five and six miles from Musgrove's mill, and at about the distance of one mile from the principal route of travel between Ninety-Six and Blackstock's. In passing from the military post that had been established at the former place, towards the latter, Ramsay's lay off to the left, with a piece of dense wood intervening. The byway, leading through the farm, diverged from the main road and traversed this wood until it reached the cultivated grounds immediately around Ramsay's dwelling. In the journey from Musgrove's mill to this point of divergence the traveler was obliged to ride some two or three miles upon the great road leading from the British garrison, a road that, at the time of my story, was much frequented by military parties, scouts, and patrols, that were concerned in keeping up the communication between the several posts which were established by the British authorities along that frontier. Amongst the Whig parties, also, there were various occasions which brought them under the necessity of frequent passage through this same district, and which, therefore, furnished opportunities for collision and skirmish with the opposite forces.

On the morning that succeeded the night in which Horseshoe Robinson arrived at Musgrove's, the stout and honest sergeant might have been seen, about eight o'clock, leaving the main road from Ninety-Six, at the point where that leading to David Ramsay's separated from it, and cautiously urging his way into the deep forest by the more private path into which he had entered. The knowledge that Innis was encamped along the Ennoree within a short distance of the mill had compelled him to make an extensive circuit to reach Ramsay's dwelling, whither he was now bent; and he had experienced considerable delay in his morning journey by finding himself frequently in the neighborhood of small foraging parties of Tories whose motions he was obliged to watch for fear of an encounter. He had once already been compelled to use his horse's heels in what he called "fair flight," and once to ensconce himself a full half hour under cover of the thicket afforded him by a swamp. He now, therefore, according to his own phrase, "dived into the little road that scrambled down through the woods towards Ramsay's, with all his eyes about him, looking out as sharply as a fox on a foggy morning"; and with this circumspection he was not long in arriving within view of Ramsay's house. Like a practiced soldier, whom frequent frays has taught wisdom, he resolved to reconnoiter before he advanced upon a post that might be in possession of an enemy. He therefore dismounted, fastened his horse in a fence corner, where a field of corn concealed him from notice, and then stealthily crept forward until he came immediately behind one of the outhouses.

The barking of a house dog brought out a negro boy, to whom Robinson instantly addressed the query,

"Is your master at home?"

"No, sir. He's got his horse, and gone off more than an hour ago."

"Where is your mistress?"

"Shelling beans, sir."

"I didn't ask you," said the sergeant, "what she is doing, but where she is."

"In course, she is in the house, sir," replied the negro with a grin.

"Any strangers there?"

"There was plenty on 'em a little while ago, but they've been gone a good bit."

Robinson, having thus satisfied himself as to the safety of his visit, directed the boy to take his horse and lead him up to the door. He then entered the dwelling.

"Mistress Ramsay," said he, walking up to the dame, who was occupied at a table, with a large trencher before her, in which she was plying that household thrift which the negro described; "luck to you, ma'am, and all your house! I hope you have n't none of these clinking and clattering bullies about you, that are as thick over this country as the frogs in the kneading troughs, that they tell of."

"Good lack, Mr. Horseshoe Robinson," exclaimed the matron, offering the sergeant her hand. "What has brought you here? What news? Who are with you? For patience' sake, tell me!"

"I am alone," said Robinson, "and a little wettish, mistress," he added, as he took off his hat and shook the water from it; "it has just sot up a rain, and looks as if it was going to give us enough on 't. You don't mind doing a little dinner work of a Sunday, I see — shelling of beans, I s'pose, is tantamount to dragging a sheep out of a pond, as the preachers allow on the Sabbath — ha, ha! — Where's Davy?"

"He's gone over to the meetinghouse on Ennoree, hoping to hear something of the army at Camden; perhaps you can tell us the news from that quarter?"

"Faith, that's a mistake, Mistress Ramsay. Though I don't doubt that they are hard upon the scratches by this time. But, at this present speaking, I command the flying artillery. We have but one man in the corps — and that's myself; and all the guns we have got is this piece of ordinance that hangs in this old belt by my side (pointing to his sword), and that I captured from the enemy at Blackstock's. I was hoping I mought find John Ramsay at home — I have need of him as a recruit."

"Ah, Mr. Robinson, John has a heavy life of it over there with Sumpter. The boy is often without his natural rest, or a meal's victuals, and the general thinks so much of him that he can't spare him to come home. I haven't the heart to complain as long as John's service is of any use, but it does seem, Mr. Robinson, like needless tempting of the mercies of Providence. We thought that he might have been here to-day; yet I am glad he didn't come, for he would have been certain to get into trouble. Who should come in this morning, just after my husband had cleverly got away on his horse, but a young cock-a-whoop ensign that belongs to Ninety-Six, and four great Scotchmen with him, all in red coats; they had been out thieving, I warrant, and were now going home again. And who but they! Here they were, swaggering all about my house, and calling for this, and calling for that as if they owned the feesimple of everything on the plantation. And it made my blood rise, Mr. Horseshoe, to see them run out in the yard and catch up my chickens and ducks, and kill as many as they could string about them — and I not daring to say a word, though I did give them a piece of my mind, too."

"Who is at home with you?" inquired the sergeant, eagerly.

"Nobody but my youngest boy, Andrew," answered the dame. "And then the filthy, toping rioters —" she continued, exalting her voice.

"What arms have you in the house?" asked Robinson, without heeding the dame's rising anger:

"We have a rifle, and a horseman's pistol that belongs to John. They must call for drink, too, and turn my house of a Sunday morning into a tavern."

"They took the route towards Ninety-Six, you said, Mistress Ramsay?"

"Yes; they went straight forward upon the road. But, look you, Mr. Horseshoe, you're not thinking of going after them?"

"Isn't there an old field, about a mile from this, on that road?" inquired the sergeant, still intent upon his own thoughts.

"There is," replied the dame; "with the old schoolhouse upon it."

"A lopsided, rickety, log cabin in the middle of the field. Am I right, good woman?"

"Yes."

"And nobody lives in it? It has no door to it?"

"There ha'n't been anybody in it these seven years."

"I know the place very well," said the sergeant, thoughtfully; "there is woods just on this side of it."

"That's true," replied the dame; "but what is it you are thinking about, Mr. Robinson?"

"How long before this rain began was it that they quitted this house?"

"Not above fifteen minutes."

"Mistress Ramsay, bring me the rifle and pistol both — and the powderhorn and bullets."

"As you say, Mr. Horseshoe," answered the dame, as she turned round to leave the room; "but I am sure I can't suspicion what you mean to do."

In a few moments the woman returned with the weapons, and gave them to the sergeant.

"Where is Andy?" asked Horseshoe.

The hostess went to the door and called her son, and almost immediately afterwards a sturdy boy of about twelve or fourteen years of age entered the apartment, his clothes dripping with rain. He modestly and shyly seated himself on a chair near the door, with his soaked hat flapping down over a face full of freckles, and not less rife with the expression of an open, dauntless hardihood of character.

"How would you like a scrummage, Andy, with them Scotchmen that stole your mother's chickens this morning?" asked Horseshoe.

"I'm agreed," replied the boy, "if you will tell me what to do."

"You are not going to take the boy out on any of your desperate projects, Mr. Horseshoe?" said the mother, with the tears starting instantly into her eyes. "You wouldn't take such a child as that into danger?"

"Bless your soul, Mrs. Ramsay, there ar'n't no danger about it! Don't take on so. It's a thing that is either done at a blow, or not done,— and there's an end of it. I want the lad only to bring home the prisoners for me, after I have took them."

"Ah, Mr. Robinson, I have one son already in these wars — God protect him! — and you men don't know how a mother's heart yearns for her children in these times. I cannot give another," she added, as she threw her arms over the shoulders of the youth and drew him to her bosom.

"Oh! it ain't nothing," said Andrew, in a sprightly tone.

"It's only snapping of a pistol, mother,—pooh! If I'm not afraid, you ought n't to be."

"I give you my honor, Mistress Ramsay," said Robinson, "that I will bring or send your son safe back in one hour; and that he sha'n't be put in any sort of danger whatsomedever; come, that's a good woman!"

"You are not deceiving me, Mr. Robinson?" asked the matron, wiping away a tear. "You would n't mock the sufferings of a weak woman in such a thing as this?"

"On the honesty of a sodger, ma'am," replied Horseshoe, "the lad shall be in no danger, as I said before—whatsomedever."

"Then I will say no more," answered the mother. "But Andy, my child, be sure to let Mr. Robinson keep before you."

Horseshoe now loaded the firearms, and having slung the pouch across his body, he put the pistol into the hands of the boy; then, shouldering his rifle, he and his young ally left the room. Even on this occasion, serious as it might be deemed, the sergeant did not depart without giving some manifestation of that light-heartedness which no difficulties ever seemed to have the power to conquer. He thrust his head back into the room, after he had crossed the threshold, and said with an encouraging laugh. "Andy and me will teach them, Mistress Ramsay, Pat's point of war—we will *surround* the ragamuffins."

"Now, Andy, my lad," said Horseshoe, after he had mounted Captain Peter, "you must get up behind me. Turn the lock of your pistol down," he continued, as the boy sprang upon the horse's rump, "and cover it with the flap of your jacket, to keep the rain off. It won't do to hang fire at such a time as this."

The lad did as he was directed, and Horseshoe, having secured his rifle in the same way, put his horse up to a gallop, and took the road in the direction that had been pursued by the soldiers.

As soon as our adventurers had gained a wood, at the distance of about half a mile, the sergeant relaxed his speed, and advanced at a pace a little above a walk.

"Andy," he said, "we have got rather a ticklish sort of a job before us, so I must give you your lesson, which you will understand better by knowing something of my plan. As soon as your mother told me that these thieving villains had left her house about fifteen minutes before the rain came on, and that they had gone along upon this road, I remembered the old field up here, and the little log hut in the middle of it; and it was natural to suppose that they had just got about near that hut when this rain came up; and then, it was the most supposable case in the world that they would naturally go into it, as the dryest place they could find. So now, you see, it's my calculation that the whole batch is there at this very point of time. We will go slowly along, until we get to the other end of this wood, in sight of the old field, and then, if there is no one on the lookout, we will open our first trench; you know what that means, Andy?"

"It means, I s'pose, that we'll go right smack at them," replied Andrew.

"Pretty exactly," said the sergeant. "But listen to me. Just at the edge of the woods you will have to get down and put yourself behind a tree. I'll ride forward, as if I had a whole troop at my heels, and if I catch them, as I expect, they will have a little fire kindled, and, as likely as not, they'll be cooking some of your mother's fowls."

"Yes, I understand," said the boy eagerly, —

"No, you don't," replied Horseshoe, "but you will when you hear what I am going to say. If I get at them onawares, they'll be mighty apt to think they are surrounded, and will bellow, like fine fellows, for quarter. And thereupon, Andy, I'll cry out 'stand fast,' as if I was speaking to my own men, and when you hear that, you must come up full tilt, because it will be a signal to you that the enemy has surrendered. Then it will be your business to run into the house and bring out the muskets, as quick as a rat runs through a kitchen; and when you have done that, why, all 's done. But if you should hear any popping of firearms — that is, more than one shot, which I may chance to let off — do you take that for a bad sign, and get away as fast as you can heel it. You comprehend."

"Oh! yes," replied the lad, "and I 'll do what you want, and more too, maybe, Mr. Robinson."

"*Captain* Robinson, — remember, Andy, you must call me captain, in the hearing of these Scotsmen."

"I 'll not forget that neither," answered Andrew.

By the time that these instructions were fully impressed upon the boy, our adventurous forlorn hope, as it may fitly be called, had arrived at the place which Horseshoe Robinson had designated for the commencement of active operations. They had a clear view of the old field, and it afforded them a strong assurance that the enemy was exactly where they wished him to be, when they discovered smoke arising from the chimney of the hovel. Andrew was soon posted behind a tree, and Robinson only tarried a moment to make the boy repeat the signals agreed on, in order to ascertain that he had them correctly in his memory. Being satisfied from this experiment that the intelligence of his young companion might be depended upon, he galloped across the intervening space, and, in a few seconds, abruptly reined up his steed in the very doorway of the hut. The party within was gathered around a fire at the further end, and, in the corner near the door, were four muskets thrown together against the wall. To spring from his saddle and thrust himself one pace within the door was a movement which the sergeant executed in an instant, shouting at the same time: —

"Halt! File off right and left to both sides of the house,

and wait orders. I demand the surrender of all here," he said, as he planted himself between the party and their weapons. " I will shoot down the first man who budges a foot."

" Leap to your arms," cried the young officer who commanded the little party inside of the house. " Why do you stand ? "

" I don't want to do you or your men any harm, young man," said Robinson, as he brought his rifle to a level, " but, by my father's son, I will not leave one of you to be put upon a muster roll if you raise a hand at this moment."

Both parties now stood, for a brief space, eyeing each other in a fearful suspense, during which there was an expression of doubt and irresolution visible on the countenance of the soldiers, as they surveyed the broad proportions and met the stern glance of the sergeant, whilst the delay, also, began to raise an apprehension in the mind of Robinson that his stratagem would be discovered.

" Shall I let loose upon them, captain ? " said Andrew Ramsay, now appearing, most unexpectedly to Robinson, at the door of the hut. " Come on, boys ! " he shouted, as he turned his face towards the field.

" Keep them outside of the door — stand fast," cried the doughty sergeant, with admirable promptitude, in the new and sudden posture of his affairs caused by this opportune appearance of the boy. " Sir, you see that it's not worth while fighting five to one ; and I should be sorry to be the death of any of your brave fellows ; so take my advice, and surrender to the Continental Congress and this scrap of its army which I command."

During this appeal the sergeant was ably seconded by the lad outside, who was calling out first on one name and then on another, as if in the presence of a troop. The device succeeded, and the officer within, believing the forbearance of Robinson to be real, at length said :

"Lower your rifle, sir. In the presence of a superior force, taken by surprise and without arms, it is my duty to save bloodshed. With the promise of fair usage, and the rights of prisoners of war, I surrender this little foraging party under my command."

"I'll make the terms agreeable," replied the sergeant. "Never doubt me, sir. Right hand file, advance, and receive the arms of the prisoners!"

"I'm here, captain," said Andrew, in a conceited tone, as if it were a near occasion of merriment; and the lad quickly entered the house and secured the weapons, retreating with them some paces from the door.

"Now, sir," said Horseshoe to the ensign, "your sword, and whatever else you mought have about you of the ammunitions of war!"

The officer delivered up his sword and a pair of pocket pistols.

As Horseshoe received these tokens of victory, he asked, with a lambent smile and what he intended to be an elegant and condescending composure, "Your name, sir, if I mought take the freedom?"

"Ensign St. Jermyn, of his Majesty's seventy-first regiment of light infantry."

"Ensign, your servant," added Horseshoe, still preserving this unusual exhibition of politeness. "You have defended your post like an old sodger, although you ha'n't much beard on your chin; but, seeing you have given up, you shall be treated like a man who has done his duty. You will walk out now and form yourselves in line at the door. I'll engage my men shall do you no harm; they are of a marciful breed."

When the little squad of prisoners submitted to this command and came to the door, they were stricken with equal astonishment and mortification to find, in place of the detachment of cavalry which they expected to see, nothing but a man, a boy, and a horse. Their first emotions were expressed in curses, which were even succeeded by laughter from one or two of the number. There seemed to be a disposition on the part of some to resist the authority that now controlled them; and sundry glances were exchanged which indicated a purpose to turn upon their captors. The sergeant no sooner perceived this than he halted, raised his rifle to his breast, and, at the same instant, gave Andrew Ramsay an order to retire a few paces and to fire one of the captured pieces at the first man who opened his lips.

"By my hand," he said, "if I find any trouble in taking you all five safe away from this here house, I will thin your numbers with your own muskets! And that's as good as if I had sworn to it."

"You have my word, sir," said the ensign; "lead on."

"By your leave, my pretty gentleman, you will lead, and I'll follow!" replied Horseshoe. "It may be a new piece of drill to you; but the custom is to give the prisoners the post of honor."

"As you please, sir," answered the ensign. "Where do you take us to?"

"You will march back by the road you came," said the sergeant.

Finding the conqueror determined to execute summary martial law upon the first who should mutiny, the prisoners submitted, and marched in double file from the hut back towards Ramsay's — Horseshoe, with Captain Peter's bridle dangling over his arm, and his gallant young auxiliary Andrew, laden with double the burden of Robinson Crusoe (having all the firearms packed upon his shoulders), bringing up the rear. In this order victors and vanquished returned to David Ramsay's.

"Well, I have brought you your ducks and chickens back, mistress," said the sergeant, as he halted the prisoners at the door; "and what's more, I have brought home a young sodger that's worth his weight in gold."

"Heaven bless my child! my brave boy!" cried the mother, seizing the lad in her arms, unheeding anything else in the present perturbation of her feelings. "I feared ill would come of it; but Heaven has preserved him. Did he behave handsomely, Mr. Robinson? But I am sure he did."

"A little more venturesome, ma'am, than I wanted him to be," replied Horseshoe; "but he did excellent service. These are his prisoners, Mistress Ramsay; I should never have got them if it had n't been for Andy. In these drumming and fifing times the babies suck in quarrel with their mother's milk. Show me another boy in America that's made more prisoners than there was men to fight them with, that's all!"

[This capture of the British ensign Horseshoe Robinson was able to turn to good account as a means of saving Butler. He exacted from the ensign a letter to his British companions telling them of his capture and begging them to be lenient with their prisoner, Major Butler, in order that his life might not be forfeit for any harsh treatment to Butler. This letter reached the British just in time to stay a sentence of death from being pronounced upon Butler. The next day brought the news of a decisive defeat of the Americans under General Gates, and this led the British to think that they might carry out the sentence against Butler without endangering the life of Ensign Jermyn. Accordingly Butler was notified that he would be executed two days hence. Horseshoe, however, brought up a small force of Americans to attack the British camp just in time to save Butler's life, but after the defeat of the British Butler could not be found. James Curry had succeeded in conducting him from the camp at the beginning of the engagement and eventually carried him to Allen Musgrove's mill. Through the aid of

Mary Musgrove, Butler effected his escape, but in a short time was captured by another Tory party.

In the meantime Mildred Lindsay, hearing of Butler's capture through letters brought from him by Horseshoe Robinson, had started from her home at Dove Cote with her brother for Cornwallis' headquarters in the hope of securing her lover's safety. While in Cornwallis' camp she learned of Butler's escape and started on her return to Virginia. On her way she met Mary Musgrove and her father, who had been driven from their home and were fleeing to the North, and learned from them of Butler's recapture. Immediately she turned back to follow and join Butler, accompanied by her brother Henry, Horseshoe Robinson, Mary Musgrove, and Allen Musgrove. This party journeyed toward Gilbert-town unconscious of the fact that military developments were bringing the British troops under Ferguson, whose prisoner Butler was, in the same direction. In the meantime, events had been leading up to the battle of King's Mountain, in which the threads of the story are dramatically brought together into an effective climax.]

## THE BATTLE OF KING'S MOUNTAIN

Towards noon the army reached the neighborhood of King's Mountain. The scouts and parties of the advance had brought information that Ferguson had turned aside from his direct road and taken post upon this eminence, where, it was evident, he meant to await the attack of his enemy. Campbell, therefore, lost no time in pushing forward and was soon rewarded with a view of the object of his pursuit. Some two or three miles distant, where an opening through the forest first gave him a sight of the mass of highland, he could indistinctly discern the array of the adverse army perched on the very summit of the hill.

The mountain consists of an elongated ridge rising out of the bosom of an uneven country to the height of perhaps five hundred feet, and presenting a level line of summit, or crest, from which the earth slopes down, at its southward termination and on each side, by an easy descent; whilst northward it is detached from highlands of inferior elevation by a rugged valley, thus giving it the character of an insulated promontory not exceeding half a mile in length. At the period to which our story refers it was covered, except in a few patches of barren field or broken ground, with a growth of heavy timber, which was so far free from underwood as in no great degree to embarrass the passage of horsemen; and through this growth the eye might distinguish, at a considerable distance, the occasional masses of gray rock that were scattered in huge bowlders over its summit and sides.

The adjacent region lying south from the mountain was partially cleared and in cultivation, presenting a limited range of open ground, over which the march of Campbell might have been revealed in frequent glimpses to the British partisan for some three or four miles. We may suppose, therefore, that the two antagonists watched each other during the advance of the approaching army across this district with emotions of various and deep interest. Campbell drew at length into a ravine which, bounded by low and short hills and shaded by detached portions of the forest, partly concealed his troops from the view of the enemy, who was now not more than half a mile distant. The gorge of this dell, or narrow valley, opened immediately towards the southern termination of the mountain; and the column halted a short distance within, where a bare knoll, or round, low hill, crowned with rock, jutted abruptly over the road and constituted the only impediment that prevented each party from inspecting the array of his opponent.

It was an hour after noon, and the present halt was improved by the men in making ready for battle. Meanwhile the chief officers met together in front and employed their time in surveying the localities of the ground upon which they were soon to be brought to action. The knoll I have described furnished a favorable position for this observation, and thither they had already repaired.

I turn from the graver and more important matters which may be supposed to have occupied the thoughts of the leaders, as they were grouped together on the broad rock, to a subject which was at this moment brought to their notice by the unexpected appearance of two females on horseback, on the road a full half mile in the rear of the army, and who were now approaching at a steady pace. They were attended by a man who, even thus far off, showed the sedateness of age; and a short space behind them rode a few files of troopers in military array.

It was with mingled feelings of surprise and admiration at the courage which could have prompted her at such a time to visit the army that the party recognized Mildred Lindsay and her attendants in the approaching cavalcade. These emotions were expressed by them in the rough and hearty phrase of their habitual and familiar intercourse.

"Let me beg, gentlemen," said Campbell, interrupting them, "that you speak kindly and considerately of yonder lady. By my honor, I have never seen man or woman with a more devoted or braver heart. Poor girl! — she has nobly followed Butler through his afflictions and taken her share of suffering with a spirit that should bring us all to shame. Horseshoe Robinson, who has squired her to our camp, even from her father's house, speaks of a secret between her and our captive friend that tells plainly enough to my mind of sworn faith and long-tried love. As men and soldiers we should reverence it. Williams, look carefully to her comfort and safety. Go, man, at once and meet her on the road. God grant that this day may bring an end to her grief!". . .

It was three o'clock before these arrangements were completed. I have informed my reader that the mountain terminated immediately in front of the outlet from the narrow dell in which Campbell's army had halted, its breast protruding into the plain only some few hundred paces from the head of the column, whilst the valley, that forked both right and left, afforded an easy passage along the base on either side. Ferguson occupied the very summit, and now frowned upon his foe from the midst of a host confident in the strength of their position and exasperated by the pursuit which had driven them into this fastness.

Campbell resolved to assail this post by a spirited attack, at the same moment, in front and on the flanks. With this intent his army was divided into three equal parts. The center was reserved to himself and Shelby; the right was assigned to Sevier and M'Dowell; the left, to Cleveland and Williams. These two latter parties were to repair to their respective sides of the mountain, and the whole were to make the onset by scaling the heights as nearly as possible at the same instant.

The men, before they marched out of the ravine, had dismounted and picketed their horses under the winding shelter of the hills, and, being now separated into detached columns formed in solid order, they were put in motion to reach their allotted posts. The Amherst Rangers were retained on horseback for such duty as might require speed and were stationed close in the rear of Campbell's own division, which now merely marched from behind the shelter of the knoll and halted in the view of the enemy until sufficient delay should be afforded to the flanking divisions to attain their ground.

Mildred, attended by Allen Musgrove and his daughter, still maintained her position on the knoll and from this height surveyed the preparations for combat with a beating heart. The scene within her view was one of intense occupation. The air of stern resolve that sat upon every brow; the silent but onward movement of the masses of men advancing to conflict; the few brief and quick words of command that fell from the distance upon her ear; the sullen beat of the hoof upon the sod, as an occasional horseman sped to and fro between the more remote bodies and the center division, which yet stood in compact phalanx immediately below her at the foot of the hill; then the breathless anxiety of her companions near at hand, and the short note of dread and almost terror that now and then escaped from the lips of Mary Musgrove, as the maiden looked eagerly and fearfully abroad over the plain — all these incidents wrought upon her feelings and caused her to tremble. Yet amidst these novel emotions she was not insensible to a certain lively and even pleasant interest arising out of the picturesque character of the spectacle. The gay sunshine striking aslant these moving battalions, lighting up their fringed and many-colored hunting-shirts and casting a golden hue upon their brown and weather-beaten faces, brought out into warm relief the chief characteristics of this peculiar woodland army. And Mildred sometimes forgot her fears in the fleeting inspiration of the sight, as she watched the progress of an advancing column — at one time moving in close ranks, with the serried thicket of rifles above their heads, and at another deploying into files to pass some narrow path, along which, with trailed arms and bodies bent, they sped with the pace of hunters beating the hillside for game. The tattered and service-stricken banner that shook its folds in the wind above these detached bodies likewise lent its charm of association to the field in the silence and steadfastness of the array in which it was borne, and its constant onward motion, showing it to be encircled by strong arms and stout hearts.

Turning from these, the lady's eye was raised, with a less joyous glance, towards the position of the enemy. On the most prominent point of the mountain's crest she could descry the standard of England fluttering above a concentrated body whose scarlet uniforms, as the sun glanced upon them through the forest, showed that here Ferguson had posted his corps of regulars and held them ready to meet the attack of the center division of the assailants; whilst the glittering of bayonets amidst the dark foliage, at intervals, rearward along the line of the summit, indicated that heavy detachments were stationed in this quarter to guard the flanks. The marching and countermarching of the frequent corps from various positions on the summit, the speeding of officers on horseback, and the occasional movement of small squadrons of dragoons, who were at one moment seen struggling along the sides of the mountain and, at another, descending towards the base or returning to the summit, disclosed the earnestness and activity of the preparation with which a courageous soldier may be supposed to make ready for his foe.

It was with a look of sorrowful concern which brought tears into her eyes that Mildred gazed upon this host and strained her vision in the vain endeavor to catch some evidences of the presence of Arthur Butler. . . .

Meanwhile Campbell and Shelby, each at the head of his men in the center division of the army, steadily commenced the ascent of the mountain. A long interval ensued, in which nothing was heard but the tramp of the soldiers and a few words of almost whispered command, as they scaled the height; and it was not until they had nearly reached the summit that the first peal of battle broke upon the sleeping echoes of the mountain.

Campbell here deployed into line, and his men strode briskly upwards until they had come within musketshot of the British regulars, whose sharp and prolonged volleys, at this instant, suddenly burst forth from the crest of the hill. Peal after peal rattled along the mountain side, and volumes of smoke, silvered by the light of the sun, rolled over and enveloped the combatants.

When the breeze had partially swept away this cloud, and opened glimpses of the battle behind it, the troops of Campbell were seen recoiling before an impetuous charge of the bayonet, in which Ferguson himself led the way. A sudden halt by the retreating Whigs, and a stern front steadfastly opposed to the foe, checked the ardor of his pursuit at an early moment, and, in turn, he was discovered retiring towards his original ground, hotly followed by the mountaineers. Again the same vigorous onset from the royalists was repeated, and again the shaken bands of Campbell rallied and turned back the rush of battle towards the summit. At last, panting and spent with the severe encounter, both parties stood for a space eyeing each other with deadly rage and waiting only to gather breath for the renewal of the strife.

At this juncture the distant firing heard from either flank furnished evidence that Sevier and Cleveland had both come in contact with the enemy. The uprising of smoke above the trees showed the seat of the combat to be below the summit on the mountain sides and that the enemy had there halfway met his foe, whilst the shouts of the soldiers, alternating between the parties of either army, no less distinctly proclaimed the fact that at these remote points the field was disputed with bloody resolution and various success.

It would overtask my poor faculty of description to give my reader even a faint picture of this rugged battlefield. During the pause of the combatants of the center Campbell and Shelby were seen riding along the line and by speech and gesture encouraging their soldiers to still more determined efforts. Little need was there for exhortation ; rage seemed to have refreshed the strength of the men, who, with loud and fierce huzzas, rushed again to the encounter. They were met with a defiance not less eager than their own, and for a time the battle was again obscured under the thick haze engendered by the incessant discharges of firearms. From this gloom a yell of triumph was sometimes heard, as momentary success inspired those who struggled within ; and the frequent twinkle of polished steel glimmering through the murky atmosphere, and the occasional apparition of a speeding horseman, seen for an instant as he came into the clear light, told of the dreadful earnestness and zeal with which the unseen hosts had now joined in conflict. The impression of this contact was various. Parts of each force broke before their antagonists, and in those spots where the array of the fight might be discerned through the shade of the forest or the smoke of battle, both royalists and Whigs were found, at the same instant, to have driven back detached fragments of their opponents. Foemen were mingled hand to hand, through and among their adverse ranks, and for a time no conjecture might be indulged as to the side to which victory would turn.

The flanking detachments seemed to have fallen into the same confusion and might have been seen retreating and advancing upon the rough slopes of the mountain in partisan bodies, separated from their lines, thus giving to the scene an air of bloody riot, more resembling the sudden insurrection of mutineers from the same ranks than the orderly war of trained soldiers.

Through the din and disorder of this fight it is fit that I should take time to mark the wanderings of Galbraith Robinson, whose exploits this day would not ill deserve the pen of Froissart. The doughty sergeant had, for a time, retained his post in the ranks of the Amherst Rangers, and with them had traveled towards the mountain top, close in the rear of Campbell's line. But when the troops had recoiled before the frequent charges of the royalists, finding his station, at best, but that of an inactive spectator, he made no scruple of deserting his companions and trying his fortune on the field in such form of adventure as best suited his temper. With no other weapon than his customary rifle, he stood his ground when others retreated, and saw the ebb and flow of "flight and chase" swell round him, according to the varying destiny of the day. In these difficulties it was his good fortune to escape unhurt, a piece of luck that may, perhaps, be attributed to the coolness with which he either galloped over an adversary or around him, as the emergency rendered most advisable.

In the midst of this busy occupation, at a moment when one of the refluxes of battle brought him almost to the summit, he descried a small party of British dragoons, stationed some distance in the rear of Ferguson's line, whose detached position seemed to infer some duty unconnected with the general fight. In the midst of these he thought he recognized the figure and dress of one familiar to his eye. The person thus singled out by the sergeant's glance stood bareheaded upon a projecting mass of rock, apparently looking with an eager gaze towards the distant combat. No sooner did the conjecture that this might be Arthur Butler flash across his thought than he turned his steed back upon the path by which he had ascended and rode with haste towards the Rangers.

"Stephen Foster," he said, as he galloped up to the lieutenant and drew his attention by a tap of the hand upon his shoulder, "I have business for you, man — you are but wasting your time here — pick me out a half dozen of your best fellows and bring them with you after me. Quick — Stephen— quick!"

The lieutenant of the Rangers collected the desired party and rode after the sergeant, who now conducted this handful of men, with as much rapidity as the broken character of the ground allowed, by a circuit for considerable distance along the right side of the mountain until they reached the top. The point at which they gained the summit brought them between Ferguson's line and the dragoons, who, it was soon perceived, were the party charged with the custody of Butler, and who had been thus detached in the rear for the more safe guardianship of the prisoner. Horseshoe's maneuver had completely cut them off from their friends in front, and they had no resource but to defend themselves against the threatened assault or fly towards the parties who were at this moment engaged with the flanking division of the Whigs. They were taken by surprise, and Horseshoe, perceiving the importance of an immediate attack, dashed onwards along the ridge of the mountain with precipitate speed, calling out to his companions to follow. In a moment the dragoons were engaged in a desperate pell-mell with the Rangers.

"Upon them, Stephen! Upon them bravely, my lads! Huzza for Major Butler! Fling the major across your saddle — the first that reaches him," shouted the sergeant, with a voice that was heard above all the uproar of battle. "What ho — James Curry!" he cried out, as soon as he detected the presence of his old acquaintance in this throng; "stand your ground, if you are a man!"

The person to whom this challenge was directed had made an effort to escape towards a party of his friends whom he was about summoning to his aid, and in the attempt had already ridden some distance into the wood, whither the sergeant had eagerly followed him.

"Ah, ha, old Truepenny, are you there?" exclaimed Curry, turning short upon his pursuer and affecting to laugh as if in scorn. "Horseshoe Robinson, well met!" he added sternly, "I have not seen a better sight to-day than that fool's head of yours upon this hill. No, not even when just now Patrick Ferguson sent your yelping curs back to hide themselves behind the trees."

"Come on, James!" cried Horseshoe, "I have no time to talk. We have an old reckoning to settle, which perhaps you mought remember. I am a man of my word, and, besides, I have set my eye upon Major Butler," he added, with a tone and look that were both impressed with the fierce passion of the scene around him.

"The devil blast you and Major Butler to boot!" exclaimed Curry, roused by Horseshoe's air of defiance. "To it, bully! It shall be short work between us, and bloody," he shouted, as he discharged a pistol shot at the sergeant's breast; which failing to take effect, he flung the weapon upon the ground, brandished his sword, and spurred immediately against his challenger. The sweep of the broadsword fell upon the barrel of Horseshoe's uplifted rifle, and in the next instant the broad hand of our lusty yeoman had seized the trooper by the collar and dragged him from his horse. The two soldiers came to the ground, locked in a mutual embrace, and for a brief moment a desperate trial of strength was exhibited in the effort to gain their feet.

"I have you there," said Robinson, as at length, with a flushed cheek, quick breath, and bloodshot eye, he rose from the earth and shook the dragoon from him, who fell backwards on his knee. "Curse you, James Curry, for a fool and villain! You almost drive me, against my will, to the taking of your life. I don't want your blood. You are beaten, man, and must say so. I grant you quarter upon condition ——"

"Look to yourself! I ask no terms from you," interrupted Curry, as suddenly springing to his feet, he now made a second pass, which was swung with such unexpected vigor at the head of his adversary that Horseshoe had barely time to catch the blow, as before, upon his rifle. The broadsword was broken by the stroke, and one of the fragments of the blade struck the sergeant upon the forehead, inflicting a wound that covered his face with blood. Horseshoe reeled a step or two from his ground and clubbing the rifle, as it is called, by grasping the barrel towards the muzzle, he paused but an instant to dash the blood from his brow with his hand and then with one lusty sweep, to which his sudden anger gave both precision and energy, he brought the piece full upon the head of his foe with such fatal effect as to bury the lock in the trooper's brain, whilst the stock was shattered into splinters. Curry, almost without a groan, fell dead across a ledge of rock at his feet.

"The grudge is done and the fool has met his desarvings," was Horseshoe's brief comment upon the event, as he gazed sullenly, for an instant, upon the dead body. He had no time to tarry. The rest of his party were still engaged with the troopers of the guard, who now struggled to preserve the custody of their prisoner. The bridle rein of Captain Peter had been caught by one of the Rangers, and the good steed was now quickly delivered up to his master, who, flinging himself again into his saddle, rushed into the throng of combatants. The few dragoons, dispirited by the loss of their leader and stricken with panic at this strenuous onset, turned to flight, leaving Butler in the midst of his friends.

"God bless you, major!" shouted Robinson, as he rode up to his old comrade, who, unarmed, had looked upon the struggle with an interest corresponding to the stake he had in the event. "Up, man — here, spring across the pommel. Now, boys, down the mountain, for your lives! Huzza, huzza! we have won him back!" he exclaimed, as, seizing Butler's arm, he lifted him upon the neck of Captain Peter and bounded away at full speed towards the base of the mountain, followed by Foster and his party.

The reader may imagine the poignancy of Mildred's emotions as she sat beside Allen Musgrove and his daughter on the knoll and watched the busy and stirring scene before her. The center division of the assailing army was immediately in her view on the opposite face of the mountain, and no incident of the battle in this quarter escaped her notice. She could distinctly perceive the motions of the Amherst Rangers, to whom she turned her eyes with a frequent and eager glance as the corps with which her brother Henry was associated, and when the various fortune of the fight disclosed to her the occasional retreat of her friends before the vigorous sallies of the enemy or brought to her ear the renewed and angry volleys of musketry, she clenched Mary Musgrove's arm with a nervous grasp and uttered short and anxious ejaculations that showed the terror of her mind.

"I see Mister Henry yet," said Mary, as Campbell's troops rallied from the last shock, and again moved towards the summit. "I see him plainly, ma'am — for I know his green dress and caught the glitter of his brass bugle in the sun. And there now — all is smoke again. Mercy, how stubborn are these men! And there is Mister Henry once more — near the top. He is safe, ma'am."

"How earnestly," said Mildred, unconsciously speaking aloud as she surveyed the scene, "Oh, how earnestly do I wish this battle was done! I would rather, Mr. Musgrove, be in the midst of yonder crowd of angry men, could I but have their recklessness, than here in safety to be tortured with my present feelings."

"In God is our trust, madam," replied the miller. "His arm is abroad over the dangerous paths, for a shield and buckler to them that put their trust in him. Ha! there is Ferguson's white horse rushing, with a dangling rein and empty saddle, down the mountain through Campbell's ranks; the rider has fallen, and there, madam — there, look on it! — is a white flag waving in the hands of a British officer. The fight is done. Hark, our friends are cheering with a loud voice!"

"Thank Heaven — thank Heaven!" exclaimed Mildred, as she sprang upon her feet. "It is even so!"

The loud huzzas of the troops rose upon the air; the firing ceased; the flag of truce fluttered in the breeze; and the confederated bands of the mountaineers, from every quarter of the late battle, were seen hurrying towards the crest of the mountain and mingling amongst the ranks of the conquered foe. Again and again the clamorous cheering of the victors broke forth from the mountain top and echoed along the neighboring valleys.

During this wild clamor and busy movement a party of horsemen were seen, through the occasional intervals of the low wood that skirted the valley on the right, hastening from the field with an eager swiftness towards the spot where Mildred and her companions were stationed.

As they swept along the base of the mountain and approached the knoll they were lost to view behind the projecting angles of the low hills that formed the ravine, through which, my reader is aware, the road held its course. When they reappeared it was in ascending the abrupt acclivity of the knoll and within fifty paces of the party on the top of it.

It was now apparent that the approaching party consisted of Stephen Foster and three or four of the Rangers led by Horseshoe Robinson, with Butler still seated before him as when the sergeant first caught him up in the fight. These were at the same moment overtaken by Henry Lindsay, who had turned back from the mountain at the first announcement of victory to bring the tidings to his sister.

Mildred's cheek grew deadly pale and her frame shook as the cavalcade rushed into her presence.

"There — take him!" cried Horseshoe, with an effort to laugh, but which seemed to be half converted into a quaver by the agitation of his feelings, as, springing to the ground, he swung Butler from the horse, with scarce more effort than he would have used in handling a child; "take him, ma'am. I promised myself to-day that I'd give him to you. And now you've got him. That's a good reward for all your troubles. — God bless us — but I'm happy to-day."

"My husband! — my dear husband!" were the only articulate words that escaped Mildred's lips, as she fell senseless into the arms of Arthur Butler.

## WILLIAM GILMORE SIMMS

[William Gilmore Simms was born at Charleston, South Carolina, in 1806. He received but a limited education, and at the age of twelve became apprenticed to a druggist. But as this occupation did not appeal to him, he began at eighteen the study of law. This profession he abandoned in a short time to become editor of a newly established literary magazine, and from this time on he devoted his entire time to literary work. He was a most prolific writer and not only produced numerous volumes of poetry and fiction but edited one short-lived periodical after another and contributed to various others. The war made the close of his life a sad one. His home was partly burned in 1862, and in 1865 it, together with his fine library, was entirely destroyed. During the years of the war his wife and several of his children died. He found also that the public was beginning to lose its relish for the type of story he wrote. The words of the epitaph he left behind at his death in Charleston in 1870 suggest the essentially brave spirit of the man, "Here lies one who, after a reasonably long life, distinguished chiefly by unceasing labors, has left all his better work undone."

To attempt an enumeration of Simms's many volumes is impossible, the total being, according to one count, above eighty. Suffice it to say that besides fiction he wrote numerous volumes of dramas, criticism, biography, history, and other forms of writing. The result of this literary endeavor is summed up in the words of Professor W. P. Trent: "Although he left behind little that is permanent, he did write half a dozen or more romances of colonial and Revolutionary Carolina that are interesting and valuble for the light they throw upon an important period of Southern history."]

## SELECTION FROM "THE YEMASSEE"

### THE ATTACK ON THE BLOCK HOUSE

[The incidents are supposed to take place in the region of Beaufort, South Carolina, in 1715, when the Yemassee Indians, who had been friendly to the English of South Carolina, joined with the Spaniards in making war upon them.

The story opens with Captain Gabriel Harrison (who is really Governor Craven of South Carolina in disguise) learning of the plans of the Indians and endeavoring to succor the white people from the impending general massacre. Captain Harrison is particularly interested

WILLIAM GILMORE SIMMS

in saving his sweetheart, Bess Matthews, and her father, a Puritan preacher. He urges them either to go to Charleston or to go to the neighboring blockhouse for safety, but the preacher declines to do so, insisting that the Indians intend no mischief. Captain Harrison urges the other frontiersmen to preparations, and the old blockhouse is repaired and made ready for a siege.

When the English try to buy additional land from the Indians, Sanutee, one of the older chiefs, and a few others refuse to assent to the sale, and succeed in having the chiefs who did consent condemned to become outcasts. Among these is Occonestoga, a young chief and the son of Sanutee, who, with the aid of his mother, Matiwan, makes his escape to the whites. Made reckless by drink, Occonestoga consents to return to his people in order to spy upon them for the English. He is caught and condemned to an accursed death. In a thrilling scene his mother kills him in order that he may not die ignominiously.

As Occonestoga had failed to return, Captain Harrison goes himself to spy upon the Indians and is captured. Matiwan, the mother of Occonestoga, aids him to escape from prison because he had shown kindness to her son. Shortly after this the Indians, aided by the Spaniards and certain pirates, begin warfare on the whites and bring torture and devastation upon such of the settlements as had not heeded Captain Harrison's warning. Bess Matthews and her father are saved from the Indians by Chorley, a Spaniard, who has fallen in love with her, though he virtually holds them as his prisoners. The Indians shortly afterwards concentrated their forces on the blockhouse, the attack on which is described in the selection that follows.]

The inmates of the Block House, as we remember, had been warned by Hector of the probable approach of danger, and preparation was the word in consequence. But what was the preparation meant? Under no distinct command, everyone had his own favorite idea of defense, and all was confusion in their councils. The absence of Harrison, to whose direction all parties would most willingly have turned their ears, was now of the most injurious tendency, as it left them unprovided with any head, and just at the moment when a high degree of excitement prevailed against the choice of any substitute. Great bustle and little execution took the place of good order, calm opinion, deliberate and decided action. The men were ready enough to fight, and this readiness was an evil of itself, circumstanced as they were. To fight would have been madness then; to protract the issue and gain time was the object, and few among the defenders of the fortress at that moment were sufficiently collected to see this truth. In reason, there was really but a single spirit in the Block House sufficiently deliberate for the occasion. That spirit was a woman's — the wife of Granger. She had been the child of poverty and privation; the severe school of that best tutor, necessity, had made her equable in mind and intrepid in spirit. She had looked suffering so long in the face that she now regarded it without a tear. Her parents had never been known to her, and the most trying difficulties clung to her from infancy up to womanhood. So exercised, her mind grew strong in proportion to its trials, and she had learned in the end to regard them with a degree of fearlessness far beyond the capacities of any well-bred heir of prosperity and favoring fortune. The same trials attended her after marriage, since the pursuits of her husband carried her into dangers to which even he could oppose far less ability than his wife. Her genius soared infinitely beyond his own, and to her teachings was he indebted for many of those successes which brought him wealth in after years. She counseled his enterprises, prompted or persuaded his proceedings, managed for him wisely and economically, in all respects proved herself unselfish; and, if she did not at any time appear above the way of life they had adopted, she took care to maintain both of them from falling beneath it — a result too often following the exclusive pursuit of gain. Her experience throughout life, hitherto, served her admirably now, when all was confusion among the councils of the men. She descended to the court below, where they made a show of deliberation, and, in her own manner, with a just knowledge of human nature, proceeded to give her aid in their general progress. Knowing that any direct suggestion from a woman, and under circumstances of strife and trial, would necessarily offend the *amour propre* of the nobler animal and provoke his derision, she pursued a sort of management which an experienced woman is usually found to employ as a kind of familiar — a wily little demon, that goes unseen at her bidding and does her business, like another Ariel, the world all the while knowing nothing about it. Calling out from the crowd one of those whom she knew to be not only the most collected, but the one least annoyed by any unnecessary self-esteem, she was in a moment joined by Wat Grayson, and leading him aside, she proceeded to suggest various measures of preparation and defense, certainly the most prudent that had yet been made. This she did with so much unobtrusive modesty that the worthy woodman took it for granted all the while that the ideas were properly his own. She concluded with insisting upon his taking the command.

" But Nichols will have it all to himself. That 's one of our difficulties now."

" What of that? You may easily manage him, Master Grayson."

" How ? " he asked.

" The greater number of the men here are of the ' Green Jackets ' ? "

" Yes — "

" And you are their lieutenant — next in command to Captain Harrison, and their first officer in his absence ? "

" That 's true."

" Command them as your troop exclusively and don't mind the rest."

" But they will be offended."

" And if they are, Master Grayson, is this a time to heed their folly when the enemy's upon us? Let them. You do with your troop without heed to them, and they will fall into your ranks — they will work with you when the time comes."

" You are right," was the reply; and immediately going forward, with a voice of authority, Grayson, calling only the " Green Jackets " around him, proceeded to organize them and put himself in command, as first lieutenant of the only volunteer corps which the parish knew. The corps received the annunciation with a shout, and the majority readily recognized him. Nichols alone grumbled a little, but the minority was too small to offer any obstruction to Grayson's authority, so that he soon submitted with the rest. The command, all circumstances considered, was not improperly given. Grayson, though not overwise, was decisive in action; and, in matters of strife, wisdom itself must be subservient to resolution. Resolution in trial is wisdom. The new commander numbered his force, placed the feeble and the young in the least trying situations, assigned different bodies to different stations, and sent the women and children into the upper and most sheltered apartment. In a few moments things were arranged for the approaching conflict with tolerable precision.

The force thus commanded by Grayson was small enough; the whole number of men in the Block House not exceeding twenty-five. The women and children within its shelter were probably twice that number. The population had been assembled in great part from the entire extent of country lying between the Block House and the Indian settlements. From the Block House downward to Port Royal Island there had been no gathering to this point, the settlers in that section, necessarily, in the event of a like difficulty, seeking a retreat to the fort on the island, which had its garrison already, and was more secure, and in another respect much more safe, as it lay more contiguous to the sea. The greater portion of the country immediately endangered from the Yemassees had been duly warned, and none but the slow, the indifferent, and the obstinate but had taken sufficient heed of the many warnings given them and put themselves in safety. Numbers, however, coming under one or other of these classes had fallen victims to their folly or temerity in the sudden onslaught which followed the first movement of the savages among them, who, scattering themselves over the country, had made their attack so nearly at the same time as to defeat anything like unity of action in the resistance which might have been offered them.

Grayson's first care in his new command was to get the women and children fairly out of the way. The close upper apartment of the Block House had been especially assigned them, and there they had assembled generally. But some few of the old ladies were not to be shut up, and his own good Puritan mother gave the busy commandant no little trouble. She went to and fro, interfering in this, preventing that, and altogether annoying the men to such a degree that it became absolutely necessary to put on a show of sternness which, in a moment of less real danger and anxiety, would have been studiously forborne. With some difficulty, and the assistance of Granger's wife, he at length got her out of the way, and, to the great satisfaction of all parties, she worried herself to sleep in the midst of a Psalm, which she crooned over to the dreariest tune in her whole collection. Sleep had also fortunately seized upon the children generally, and but few in the room assigned to the women were able to withstand the approaches of that subtle magician. The wife of the trader, almost alone, continued watchful — thoughtful in emergency, and with a ready degree of common sense to contend with trial and to prepare against it. The confused cluster of sleeping forms, in all positions and of all sorts and sizes, that hour, in the apartment so occupied, was grotesque enough. One figure alone, sitting in the midst and musing with a concentrated mind, gave dignity to the ludicrous grouping — the majestic figure of Mary Granger, her dark eye fixed upon the silent and sleeping collection in doubt and pity, her black hair bound closely upon her head, and her broad forehead seeming to enlarge and grow with the busy thought at work within it. Her hand, too — strange association — rested upon a hatchet. . . .

The watchers of the fortress, from their several loopholes, looked forth, east and west, yet saw no enemy. All was soft in the picture, all was silent in the deep repose of the forest. The night was clear and lovely, and the vague and dim beauty with which, in the imperfect moonlight, the foliage of the woods spread away in distant shadows or clung and clustered together as in groups, shrinking for concealment from her glances, touched the spirits even of those rude foresters. With them the poetry of the natural world is a matter of feeling ; with the refined it is an instrument of art. Hence it is, indeed, that the poetry of the early ages speaks in the simplest language, while that of civilization, becoming only the agent for artificial enjoyment, is ornate in its dress and complex in its form and structure.

The night wore on, still calm and serene in all its aspects about the Block House. Far away in the distance, like glimpses of a spirit, little sweeps of the river in its crooked windings flashed upon the eye, streaking with a sweet relief the somber foliage of the swampy forest through which it stole. A single note — the melancholy murmur of the chuck-will's-widow, the Carolina whippoorwill — broke fitfully upon the silence, to which it gave an added solemnity. That single note indicated to the keepers of the fortress a watchfulness corresponding with their own, of another living creature. Whether it were human or not — whether it were the deceptive lure and signal of the savage or, in reality, the complaining cry of the solitary and sad night bird which it so resembled, was, however, matter of nice question with those who listened to the strain.

"They are there — they are there, hidden in that wood," cried Grayson; "I 'll swear it. I 've heard them quite too often not to know their cunning now. Hector was right after all, boys."

"What, where?" asked Nichols.

"There, in the bush to the left of the blasted oak — now down to the bluff — and now by the bay on the right. They are all round us."

"By what do you know, Wat?"

"The whippoorwill — that is their cry — their signal."

"It *is* the whippoorwill," said Nichols, — "there is but one of them; you never hear more than one at a time."

"Pshaw!" responded Grayson, — "you may hear half a dozen at a time, as I have done a thousand times. But that is from no throat of bird. It is the Indian. There is but a single note, you perceive, and it rises from three different quarters. Now it is to the Chief's Bluff — and now — it comes immediately from the old grove of scrubby oak. A few shot there would get an answer."

"Good! that is just my thought — let us give them a broadside and disperse the scoundrels," cried Nichols.

"Not so fast, Nichols — you swallow your enemy without asking leave of his teeth. Have you inquired first whether we have powder and shot to throw away upon bushes that may be empty?" now exclaimed the blacksmith, joining in the question.

"A prudent thought, that, Grimstead," said Grayson; "we have no ammunition to spare in that way. But I have a notion that may prove of profit. Where is the captain's straw man — here, Granger, bring out Dugdale's trainer."

The stuffed figure . . . was brought forward, the window looking in the direction of the grove supposed to shelter the savages was thrown open, and the perfectly indifferent head of the automaton thrust incontinently through the opening. The *ruse* was completely successful. The foe could not well resist this temptation, and a flight of arrows, penetrating the figure in every portion of its breast and face, attested the presence of the enemy and the truth of his aim. A wild and shuddering cry rang through the forest at the same instant — that cry, well known as the fearful war whoop, the sound of which made the marrow curdle in the bones of the frontier settler and prompted the mother, with a nameless terror, to hug closer to her bosom the form of her unconscious infant. It was at once answered from side to side, wherever their several parties had been stationed, and it struck terror even into the sheltered garrison which heard it — such terror as the traveler feels by night, when the shrill rattle of the lurking serpent, with that ubiquity of sound which is one of its fearful features, vibrates all around him, leaving him at a loss to say in what quarter his enemy lies in waiting, and teaching him to dread that the very next step which he takes may place him within the coil of death.

" Ay, there they are, sure enough — fifty of them at least, and we shall have them upon us after this monstrous quick, in some way or other," was the speech of Grayson, while a brief silence through all the party marked the deep influence upon them of the summons which they had heard.

" True — and we must be up and doing," said the smith; " we can now give them a shot, [Walter] Grayson, for they will dance out from the cover now, thinking they have killed one of us. The savages — they have thrown away some of *their* powder at least." As Grimstead spoke, he drew three arrows with no small difficulty from the bosom of the figure in which they were buried.

" Better there than in our ribs. But you are right. Stand back for a moment and let me have that loop — I shall waste no shot. Ha! I see — there is one — I see his arm and the edge of his hatchet — it rests upon his shoulder, I reckon, but that is concealed by the brush. He moves — he comes out, and slaps his hands against his thigh. The red devil, but he shall have it. Get ready now, each at his loop, for if I hurt him they will rush out in fury."

The sharp click of the cock followed the words of Grayson, who was an able shot, and the next moment the full report came burdened with a dozen echoes from the crowding woods around. A cry of pain — then a shout of fury and the reiterated whoop followed; and as one of their leaders reeled and sank under the unerring bullet, the band in that station, as had been predicted by Grayson, rushed forth to where he stood, brandishing their weapons with ineffectual fury and lifting their wounded comrade, as is their general custom, to bear him to a place of concealment and preserve him from being scalped, by secret burial in the event of his being dead. They paid for their temerity. Following the direction of their leader, whose decision necessarily commanded their obedience, the Carolinians took quite as much advantage of the exposure of their enemies as the number of the loopholes in that quarter of the building would admit. Five muskets told among the group, and a reiterated shout of fury indicated the good service which the discharge had done and taught the savages a lesson of prudence which, in the present instance, they had been too ready to disregard. They sank back into cover, taking care however to remove their hurt companions, so that, save by the peculiar cry which marks a loss among them, the garrison were unable to determine what had been the success of their discharges. Having driven them back into the brush, however, without loss to themselves, the latter were now sanguine, where, only a moment before, their confined and cheerless position had taught them a feeling of despondency not calculated to improve the comforts of their case.

The Indians had made their arrangements, on the other hand, with no little precaution. But they had been deceived and disappointed. Their scouts, who had previously inspected the fortress, had given a very different account of the defenses and the watchfulness of their garrison, to what was actually the fact upon their appearance. The scouts, however, had spoken truth, and but for the discovery made by Hector, the probability is that the Block House would have been surprised with little or no difficulty. Accustomed to obey Harrison as their only leader, the foresters present never dreamed of preparation for conflict unless under his guidance. The timely advice of the trader's wife, and the confident assumption of command on the part of Walter Grayson, completed their securities. But for this, a confusion of counsels, not less than of tongues, would have neutralized all action and left them an easy prey, without head or direction, to the knives of their insidious enemy. Calculating upon surprise and cunning as the only means by which they could hope to balance the numerous advantages possessed by European warfare over their own, the Indians had relied rather more on the suddenness of their onset and the craft peculiar to their education than on the force of their valor. They felt themselves baffled, therefore, in their main hope, by the sleepless caution of the garrison and now prepared themselves for other means.

They made their disposition of force with no little judgment. Small bodies, at equal distances, under cover, had been stationed all about the fortress. With the notes of the whippoorwill they had carried on their signals and indicated the several stages of their preparation, while, in addition to this, another band,— a sort of forlorn hope, consisting of the more

desperate, who had various motives for signalizing their valor,
— creeping singly from cover to cover, now reposing in the
shadow of a log along the ground, now half buried in a cluster-
ing bush, made their way at length so closely under the walls
of the log house as to be completely concealed from the garrison, which, unless by the window, had no mode of looking
directly down upon them. As the windows were well watched
by their comrades — having once attained their place of concealment — it followed that their position remained entirely
concealed from those within. They lay in waiting for the
favorable moment — silent as the grave, and sleepless — ready,
when the garrison should determine upon a sally, to fall upon
their rear; and, in the meanwhile, quietly preparing dry fuel
in quantity, gathering it from time to time and piling it against
the logs of the fortress, they prepared thus to fire the defenses
that shut them out from their prey.

There was yet another mode of finding entrance, which has
been partially glimpsed at already. The scouts had done their
office diligently in more than the required respects. Finding a
slender pine twisted by a late storm, and scarcely sustained by
a fragment of its shaft, they applied fire to the rich turpentine
oozing from the wounded part of the tree, and carefully directing its fall, as it yielded to the fire, they lodged its extremest
branches, as we have already seen, against the wall of the
Block House and just beneath the window, the only one looking from that quarter of the fortress. Three of the bravest of
their warriors were assigned for scaling this point and securing
their entrance, and the attack was forborne by the rest of the
band while their present design, upon which they built greatly,
was in progress.

Let us then turn to this quarter. We have already seen that
the dangers of this position were duly estimated by Grayson,
under the suggestion of Granger's wife. Unhappily for its

defense, the fate of the ladder prevented that due attention to the subject, at once, which had been imperatively called for; and the subsequent excitement following the discovery of the immediate proximity of the Indians had turned the consideration of the defenders to the opposite end of the building, from whence the partial attack of the enemy, as described, had come. It is true that the workmen were yet busy with the ladder,[1] but the assault had suspended their operations, in the impatient curiosity which such an event would necessarily induce, even in the bosom of fear.

The wife of Grayson [Granger], fully conscious of the danger, was alone sleepless in that apartment. The rest of the women, scarcely apprehensive of attack at all and perfectly ignorant of the present condition of affairs, with all that heedlessness which marks the unreflecting character, had sunk to the repose (without an effort at watchfulness) which previous fatigues had, perhaps, made absolutely unavoidable. She, alone, sat thoughtful and silent — musing over present prospects — perhaps of the past — but still unforgetful of the difficulties and the dangers before her. With a calm temper she awaited the relief which, with the repair of the ladder, she looked for from below.

In the meantime, hearing something of the alarm, together with the distant war whoop, she had looked around her for some means of defense, in the event of any attempt being made upon the window before the aid promised could reach her. But a solitary weapon met her eye, in a long heavy hatchet, a clumsy instrument, rather more like the cleaver of a butcher than the light and slender tomahawk so familiar to the Indians. Having secured this, with the composure of that courage which had been in great part taught her by the necessities

---

[1] The ladder leading up from the floor below to the room where the women were had become broken and another was being constructed. [Editor's note.]

of fortune, she prepared to do without other assistance, and to forego the sentiment of dependence, which is perhaps one of the most marked characteristics of her sex. Calmly looking round upon the sleeping and defenseless crowd about her, she resumed her seat upon a low bench in a corner of the apartment, from which she had risen to secure the hatchet, and, extinguishing the only light in the room, fixed her eye upon the accessible window, while every thought of her mind prepared her for the danger which was at hand. She had not long been seated when she fancied that she heard a slight rustling of the branches of the fallen tree just beneath the window. She could not doubt her senses, and her heart swelled and throbbed with the consciousness of approaching danger. But still she was firm — her spirit grew more confirmed with the coming trial; and, coolly throwing the slippers from her feet, grasping firmly her hatchet at the same time, she softly arose, and keeping close in the shadow of the wall, she made her way to a recess, a foot or so from the entrance, to which it was evident someone was cautiously approaching along the attenuated body of the yielding pine. In a few moments a shadow darkened the opening. She edged more closely to the point and prepared for the intruder. She now beheld the head of the enemy — a fierce and foully painted savage — the war tuft rising up into a ridge, something like a comb, and his face smeared with colors in a style most ferociously grotesque. Still she could not strike, for, as he had not penetrated the window, and as its entrance was quite too small to enable her to strike with any hope of success at any distance through it, she felt that the effort would be wholly without certainty, and failure might be of the worst consequence. Though greatly excited, and struggling between doubt and determination, she readily saw what would be the error of any precipitation. But even as she mused thus apprehensively, the cunning savage laid his hand upon the sill of the window the better to raise himself to its level. That sight tempted her, in spite of her better sense, to the very precipitation she had desired to avoid. In the moment that she saw the hand of the red man upon the sill the hatchet descended, under an impulse scarcely her own. She struck too quickly. The blow was given with all her force and would certainly have separated the hand from the arm had it taken effect. But the quick eye of the Indian caught a glimpse of her movement at the very moment in which it was made, and the hand was withdrawn before the hatchet descended. The steel sank deep into the soft wood — so deeply that she could not disengage it. To try at this object would have exposed her at once to his weapon, and, leaving it where it stuck, she sank back again into shadow.

What now was she to do? To stay where she was would be of little avail, but to cry out to those below, and seek to fly, was equally unproductive of good, besides warning the enemy of the defenselessness of their condition and thus inviting a renewal of the attack. The thought came to her with the danger, and, without a word, she maintained her position in waiting for the progress of events. As the Indian had also sunk from sight, and some moments had now elapsed without his reappearance, she determined to make another effort for the recovery of the hatchet. She grasped it by the handle, and in the next moment the hand of the savage was upon her own. He felt that his grasp was on the fingers of a woman, and in a brief word and something of a chuckle, while he still maintained his hold upon it, he conveyed intelligence of the fact to those below. But it was a woman with a man's spirit with whom he contended, and her endeavor was successful to disengage herself. The same success did not attend her effort to recover the weapon. In the brief struggle with her enemy it had become disengaged from the wood, and while both strove to seize it, it slipped from their mutual hands and, sliding over the sill, in another instant was heard rattling through the intervening bushes. Descending upon the ground below, it became the spoil of those without, whose murmurs of gratulation she distinctly heard. But now came the tug of difficulty. The Indian, striving at the entrance, was necessarily encouraged by the discovery that his opponent was not a man, and assured, at the same time, by the forbearance on the part of those within to strike him effectually down from the tree, he now resolutely endeavored to effect his entrance. His head was again fully in sight of the anxious woman — then his shoulders, and, at length, taking a firm grasp upon the sill, he strove to elevate himself by muscular strength so as to secure him sufficient purchase for the entrance at which he aimed.

What could she do — weaponless, hopeless? The prospect was startling and terrible enough, but she was a strong-minded woman, and impulse served her when reflection would most probably have taught her to fly. She had but one resource, and as the Indian had gradually thrust one hand forward for the hold upon the sill, and raised the other up to the side of the window, she grasped the one nighest to her own. She grasped it firmly with all her might, and to advantage, as, having lifted himself on tiptoe for the purpose of ascent, he had necessarily lost much of the control which a secure hold for his feet must have given him. Her grasp sufficiently assisted him forward to lessen still more greatly the security of his feet, while, at the same time, though bringing him still farther into the apartment, placing him in such a position — half in air — as to defeat much of the muscular exercise which his limbs would have possessed in any other situation. Her weapon now would have been all-important, and the brave woman mentally deplored the precipitancy with which she had acted in the first instance and which had so unhappily deprived her of its use. But self-reproach was unavailing now, and she was satisfied if she could be able to retain her foe in his present position, by which, keeping him out, or in and out, as she did, she necessarily excluded all other foes from the aperture which he so completely filled up. The intruder, though desirous enough of entrance before, was rather reluctant to obtain it now, under existing circumstances. He strove desperately to effect a retreat, but had advanced too far, however, to be easily successful, and in his confusion and disquiet he spoke to those below, in his own language, explaining his difficulty and directing their movement to his assistance. A sudden rush along the tree indicated to the conscious sense of the woman the new danger, in the approach of additional enemies, who must not only sustain but push forward the one with whom she contended. This warned her at once of the necessity of some sudden procedure, if she hoped to do anything for her own and the safety of those around her — the women and the children, whom, amid all the contest, she had never once alarmed. Putting forth all her strength, therefore, though nothing in comparison with that of him whom she opposed (had he been in a condition to exert it), she strove to draw him still farther across the entrance, so as to exclude, if possible, the approach of those coming behind him. She hoped to gain time — sufficient time for those preparing the ladder to come to her relief; and with this hope, for the first time, she called aloud to Grayson and her husband.

The Indian, in the meanwhile, derived the support for his person as well from the grasp of the woman as from his own hold upon the sill of the window. Her effort, necessarily drawing him still farther forward, placed him so completely in the way of his allies that they could do him little service while things remained in this situation, and, to complete the difficulties of his predicament, while they busied themselves in several efforts at his extrication, the branches of the little tree resting

against the dwelling, yielding suddenly to the unusual weight
upon it,— trembling and sinking away at last,— cracked beneath
the burden and, snapping off from its several holds, fell from
under them, dragging against the building in the progress down,
thus breaking their fall but cutting off all their hope from this
mode of entrance and leaving their comrade awkwardly poised
aloft, able neither to enter nor to depart from the window.
The tree finally settled heavily upon the ground, and with it
went the three savages who had so readily ascended to the
assistance of their comrade — bruised and very much hurt;
while he, now without any support but that which he derived
from the sill and what little his feet could secure from the
irregular crevices between the logs of which the house had been
built, was hung in air, unable to advance except at the will of
his woman opponent, and dreading a far worse fall from his
eminence than that which had already happened to his allies.
Desperate with his situation, he thrust his arm, as it was still
held by the woman, still farther into the window, and this en-
abled her with both hands to secure and strengthen the grasp
which she had originally taken upon it. This she did with a
new courage and strength, derived from the voices below, by
which she understood a promise of assistance. Excited and
nerved, she drew the extended arm of the Indian, in spite of
all his struggles, directly over the sill, so as to turn the elbow
completely down upon it. With her whole weight thus employed, bending down to the floor to strengthen herself to the
task, she pressed the arm across the window until her ears
heard the distinct, clear crack of the bone — until she heard
the groan and felt the awful struggles of the suffering wretch,
twisting himself round with all his effort to obtain for the
shattered arm a natural and relaxed position, and, with this
object, leaving his hold upon everything; only sustained, indeed, by the grasp of his enemy. But the movement of the

woman had been quite too sudden, her nerves too firm, and her
strength too great, to suffer him to succeed. The jagged splinters of the broken limb were thrust up, lacerating and tearing
through flesh and skin, while a howl of the acutest agony
attested the severity of that suffering which could extort such
an acknowledgment from the American savage. He fainted
in his pain, and as the weight increased upon the arm of the
woman, the nature of her sex began to resume its sway. With
a shudder of every fiber, she released her hold upon him. The
effort of her soul was over, a strange sickness came upon
her, and she was just conscious of a crashing fall of the heavy
body among the branches of the tree at the foot of the window,
when she staggered back fainting into the arms of her husband,
who just at that moment ascended to her relief.

[Under the leadership of Harrison relief comes to the besieged in the blockhouse, and the Indians are driven off.

After the defeat of the Indians Chorley attempts to carry
Bess Matthews away on his ship, but is shot in his canoe
by Captain Harrison, and Bess Matthews is rescued. Bess
Matthews consents to make her rescuer happy with the hand
which she had hitherto denied him. It is disclosed that Harrison is really the governor of the colony, Charles Craven, and
the story closes with an account of how the colonists drove
the Indians back further from the coast and defeated them in
a final battle.]


## JOHN ESTEN COOKE

[John Esten Cooke was born in Winchester, Virginia, in 1830,
and died in Clarke County, Virginia, in 1886. He left school early
in order to study law, but preferring literature, he devoted himself
largely to writing. He saw service in the Confederate army. When
the war was over he returned to his literary pursuits and continued

to write novels until his death. His novels fall into two groups—those on Colonial and Revolutionary times and those relating to the Civil War. Besides these romances — in all some twenty or more — Cooke wrote a life of Stonewall Jackson and a history of Virginia.]

## SELECTIONS FROM "THE VIRGINIA COMEDIANS"

### MR. CHAMP EFFINGHAM OF EFFINGHAM HALL

On a splendid October afternoon, in the year of our Lord 1763, two persons who will appear frequently in this history were seated in the great dining room of Effingham Hall.

JOHN ESTEN COOKE

But let us first say a few words of this old mansion. Effingham Hall was a stately edifice not far from Williamsburg, which, as everybody knows, was at that period the capital city of the colony of Virginia. The hall was constructed of elegant brick brought over from England; and from the great portico in front of the building a beautiful rolling country of hills and valleys, field and forest, spread itself pleasantly before the eye, bounded far off along the circling belt of woods by the bright waters of the noble river.

Entering the large hall of the old house, you had before you walls covered with deer's antlers, fishing rods, and guns; portraits of cavaliers and dames and children; even carefully painted pictures of celebrated race horses, on whose speed and bottom many thousands of pounds had been staked and lost and won in their day and generation.

On one side of the hall a broad staircase with oaken balustrade led to the numerous apartments above, and on the opposite side a door gave entrance into the great dining room.

The dining room was decorated with great elegance, the carved oak wainscot extending above the mantelpiece in an unbroken expanse of fruits and flowers, hideous laughing faces, and long foamy surges to the cornice. The furniture was in the Louis Quatorze style, which the reader is familiar with, from its reproduction in our own day; and the chairs were the same low-seated affairs, with high carved backs, which are now seen. There were Chelsea figures, and a sideboard full of plate, and a Japan cabinet, and a Kidderminster carpet, and huge andirons. On the andirons crackled a few twigs lost in the great country fireplace.

On the wall hung a dozen pictures of gay gallants, brave warriors, and dames whose eyes outshone their diamonds; and more than one ancestor looked grimly down, clad in a cuirass and armlet and holding in his mailed hand the sword which had done bloody service in its time. The lady portraits, as an invariable rule, were decorated with sunset clouds of yellow lace; the bright locks were powdered, and many little black patches set off the dazzling fairness of the rounded chins. Lapdogs nestled on the satin laps; and not one of the gay dames but seemed to be smiling, with her head bent sidewise fascinatingly on the courtly or warlike figures ranged with them in a long glittering line.

These portraits are worth looking up to, but those which we promised the reader are real.

In one of the carved chairs, if anything more uncomfortable than all the rest, sits, or rather lounges, a young man of about twenty-five. He is very richly clad, and in a costume which would be apt to attract a large share of attention in our own day, when dress seems to have become a mere covering, and the prosaic tendencies of the age are to despise everything but what ministers to actual material pleasure.

The gentleman before us lives fortunately one hundred years before our day and suffers from an opposite tendency in costume. His head is covered with a long flowing peruke, heavy with powder, and the drop curls hang down on his cheeks ambrosially; his cheeks are delicately rouged; and two patches, arranged with matchless art, complete the distinguished *tout ensemble* of the handsome face. At breast a cloud of lace reposes on the rich embroidery of his figured satin waistcoat, reaching to his knees; this lace is *point de Venise* and white, that fashion having come in just one month since. The sleeves of his rich doublet are turned back to his elbows and are as large as a bushel, the opening being filled up, however, with long ruffles, which reach down over the delicate jeweled hand. He wears silk stockings of spotless white, and his feet are cased in slippers of Spanish leather, adorned with diamond buckles. Add velvet garters below the knee, a little muff of leopard skin reposing near at hand upon a chair, not omitting a snuffbox peeping from the pocket, and Mr. Champ Effingham, just from Oxford and his grand tour, is before you with his various surroundings.

He is reading the work which some time since attained to such extreme popularity — Mr. Joseph Addison's serial, " The Spectator," collected now, for its great merits, into bound volumes. Mr. Effingham reads with a languid air (just as he sits) and turns over the leaves with an ivory paper cutter which he brought from Venice with the plate glass yonder on the sideboard near the silver baskets and pitchers. This languor is too perfect to be wholly affected, and when he yawns, as he does frequently, Mr. Effingham applies himself to that task very earnestly.

In one of these paroxysms of weariness the volume slips from his hand to the floor.

"My book," he says to a negro boy, who has just brought in some dishes. The boy hastens respectfully to obey, crossing the whole width of the room for that purpose. Mr. Effingham then continues reading.

[As Effingham rode over to a neighboring estate that afternoon to call on Miss Lee, he met an unknown lady on horseback. Struck by her appearance, he endeavors to make her acquaintance but unsuccessfully.

A few days later Effingham is among those who attend the presentation of "The Merchant of Venice" given by the Virginia Company of Comedians in the Old Theater near the capitol at Williamsburg. He discovers that Portia in the play is none other than the beautiful rider whom he has met. He falls desperately in love with her, but she treats coldly all his attempts to push the acquaintance. A little later, while Beatrice was taking an outing on the James River, her boat was upset by a storm and she was rescued by Charles Waters, a poor fisherman's son. This occurrence marks the beginning of a friendship between these two which ripens rapidly into love. Effingham's infatuation for Beatrice led him to become a member of the Virginia Company of Comedians, in spite of the break with social traditions that such a step involves. Beatrice, however, grows more and more disdainful of his attentions. In the meantime she discovers through the initials " B. W." on a locket she has been wearing, and a letter which comes accidentally into her hands, that her real name is not Beatrice Hallam, but Beatrice Waters, and that she and Charles Waters are cousins. Her father had at his death intrusted her to Hallam, his friend, to carry to his brother, John Waters, who was supposed to be in London. But John Waters had emigrated to Virginia, and Hallam, having been unable to find him, had brought Beatrice up under the impression that she was his daughter. As she is disclosing all this to Charles Waters, Effingham enters the room, and believing his suspicions confirmed of having a rival in Charles Waters, challenges him to a duel. It is under these circumstances that Effingham insists that Beatrice shall keep the promise which he extorted from her some time earlier in the story to accompany him to the Governor's ball.]

## GOVERNOR FAUQUIER'S BALL

The day for the meeting of the House of Burgesses had arrived. . . .

We have already expended some words upon the appearance of the town for days before this important occasion, and can now only add that the bustle was vastly greater, the laughter louder, the crowd larger, and the general excitement a thousand-fold increased on this, the long-expected morning. We have no space to enter into a full description of the appearance which the borough presented; indeed, this narrative is not the proper place for such historic disquisitions, dealing as it does with the fortunes of a few personages who pursued their various careers, and laughed and wept, and loved and hated, almost wholly without the "aid of government." It was scarcely very important to Beatrice, for instance, that his Excellency Governor Fauquier set out from the palace to the sound of cannon, and drawn slowly in his splendid chariot with its six glossy snow-white horses, and its bodyguard of cavalry, went to the capitol, and so delivered there his gracious and vice-regal greeting to the Burgesses, listening in respectful, thoughtful silence. The crowd could not drive away the poor girl's various disquieting thoughts; the smile which his Excellency threw towards the Raleigh, and its throng of lookers-on, scarcely shed any light upon her anxious and fearful heart; she only felt that to-night the crowd at the theater would be noisier and more dense, her duty only more repulsive to her — finally, that all this bustle and confusion was to terminate in a ball, at which she was to pass

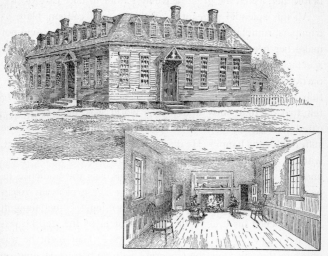

THE RALEIGH TAVERN IN OLD WILLIAMSBURG, AND ITS FAMOUS
APOLLO ROOM

This historic tavern, mentioned constantly in John Esten Cooke's "The Virginia Comedians," was built before 1735 and stood until it was burned in 1859. The Apollo was the room of the tavern used for balls, banquets, political and other gatherings. Few apartments have witnessed as many scenes of brilliant festivity and political excitement

through a fiery ordeal of frowns and comments, even through worse, perhaps more dreadful, trials. She had not dared that morning, when her father told her he should expect her to *keep her promise* and accompany the young man after the theater to the ball — the poor girl had not dared to speak of her secret, or to resist. Then she had *promised* — that was the terrible truth; and so she had only entreated, and cried, and besought her father to have mercy on her; and these entreaties, prayers, and sobs having had no effect, had yielded and gone into her bedchamber and, upon her knees, with Kate's little Bible open before her, asked the great heavenly Father to take care of her.

All this splendid pageant — all this roar of cannon, blare of trumpets, rumbling thunder of the incessant drums — could not make her heart any lighter; her face was still dark. And the spectacle had as little effect upon the other personages of the narrative. Mr. Effingham, seated in his room, smiled scornfully as the music and the people's shouts came to him. He felt that all that noisy and joyous world was alien to him — cared nothing for him — was perfectly indifferent whether he suffered or was happy. He despised the empty fools in his heart, without reflecting that the jar and discord was not in the music and the voices but in himself. And this was the audience he would have to see him play Benedick! — these plebeian voices would have liberty to applaud or hiss him! — the thought nearly opened his eyes to the true character of the step he was about to take. What was he about to do? That night he was going to the palace of the Governor with an actress leaning on his arm — there to defy the whole Colony of Virginia; in effect to say to them, "Look! you laugh at me — I show you that I scorn you!" — then in a day or two his name would be published in a placard, "The part of Benedick, by Champ Effingham, Esq." — to be made the subject of satirical and insulting comment by the very boors and overseers. These two things he was about to do, and he drew back for a moment — for an instant hesitated. But suddenly the interview he had with Hamilton came back to him, and his lip was wreathed with his reckless sneer again. They would not permit him, forsooth! — his appearance at the ball with Miss Hallam would be regarded as a general insult, and a dozen duels spring out of it!—he would do well to avoid the place!—to sneak, to skulk, to swallow all his fine promises and boasts!

"No!" he said aloud, with his teeth clenched; "by heaven! I go there and I act! I love her and I hate her more than ever, and, if necessary, will fight a hundred duels for her with these chivalric gentlemen!"

So the day passed, and evening drew on slowly, and the night came. Let us leave the bustling crowd hurrying toward the theater—leave the taverns overflowing with revelers—let us traverse Gloucester Street, and enter the grounds, through which a fine white graveled walk leads to the palace. On each side of this walk a row of linden trees are ornamented with variegated lanterns, and ere long these lanterns light up lovely figures of fair dames and gallant gentlemen, walking daintily from the carriage portal to the palace. Let us enter. Before us have passed many guests, and the large apartments, with their globe lamps and chandeliers, and portraits of the king and queen, and Chelsea figures, and red damask chairs, and numerous card tables, are already filling with the beauty and grace of that former brilliant and imposing society.

See this group of lovely young girls, with powdered hair brushed back from their tender temples, and snowy necks and shoulders glittering with diamond necklaces; see the queer patches on their chins close by the dimples; see their large falling sleeves, and yellow lace, and bodices with their silken network; see their gowns, looped back from the satin under-skirt, ornamented with flowers in golden thread; their trains and fans and high red-heeled shoes, and all their puffs and furbelows and flounces; see, above all, their gracious smiles, as they flirt their fans and dart their fatal glances at the magnificently clad gentlemen in huge ruffles and silk stockings, and long, broad-flapped waistcoats and embroidered coats, with sleeves turned back to the elbow and profusely laced; see how they ogle, and speak with dainty softness under their breath, and sigh and smile, and ever continue playing on the hapless cavaliers the dangerous artillery of their brilliant eyes.

Or see this group of young country gentlemen, followers of the fox, with their ruddy faces and laughing voices; their queues secured by plain black ribbon; their strong hands, accustomed to heavy buckskin riding gloves; their talk of hunting, crops, the breed of sheep and cattle, and the blood of horses.

Or pause a moment near that group of dignified gentlemen, with dresses plain though rich, and lordly brows and clear bright eyes, strong enough to look upon the sun of royalty, and, undazzled, see the spots disfiguring it. Hear them converse calmly, simply, like giants knowing their strength; how slow and clear and courteous their tones! how plain their manners!

Lastly, see the motley throng of the humbler planters, some of the tradesmen, factors as they were called, mingled with the yeoman; see their wives and daughters, fair and attractive, but so wholly outshone by the little powdered damsels; last of all, though not least, see his bland Excellency Governor Fauquier gliding among the various groups and smiling on everybody.

Let us endeavor to catch some of the words uttered by these various personages, now so long withdrawn from us in the far past — that silent, stern, inexorable past, which swallows up so many noble forms, and golden voices, and high deeds, and which in turn will obliterate us and our little or great actions, as it has effaced — though Heaven be thanked, not wholly! — what illustrated and adorned those times which we are now trying to depict. And first let us listen to this group of quiet, calm-looking men; fame has spoken loudly of them all.

"Your reverend opponent really got the better of you, I think, sir," says a quiet, plain, simple gentleman, with a fine face and eye. "The Twopenny-Act made out too clear a case, in mere point of law, to need the afterclap."

"True, sir," his friend replies, smiling so pleasantly that his very name seemed to indicate his character, "but I would willingly be unhorsed again by the Reverend Mr. Camm, in a cause so good. Everything concerning Virginia, you know, is dear to me. I believe some of my friends consider me demented on the subject — or at least call me the 'Virginia Antiquary.'"

"I consider it a very worthy designation, sir; and in spite of my opinion that 'The Colonel's Dismounted' is an appropriate title, — I cannot be otherwise than frank ever, — I am fully convinced that equity was with you. But here comes our noble Roman."

As he speaks, a tall, fine-looking gentleman approaches, with an eagle eye, a statuesque head, inclined forward as though listening courteously, a smile upon his lips, his right hand covered with a black bandage.

"What news from Westmoreland, pray, seigneur of Chantilly?" asks the opponent of the Reverend Mr. Camm. "Do they think of testing the Twopenny-Act by suits for damages?"

"No, sir," says the newcomer, very courteously; "I believe, however, that in Hanover County the Reverend Mr. Maury has brought suit against the collector."

"Ah, then we shall get some information from our friend from Caroline! See, here he is. Good day, sir!"

He who now approaches has the same calm, benignant expression as the rest — an expression, indeed, which seems to have dwelt always on those serene noble faces of that period, so full of stirring events and strong natures. The face was not unlike that which we fancy Joseph Addison's must have been; a quiet, serene smile, full of courtesy and sweetness, illuminated it, attracting people of all ages and conditions. When he speaks, it is in the *vox argentea* of Cicero — a gentle stream of sound, rippling in the sunlight.

"What from Caroline, pray?" asks the 'dismounted Colonel,' pressing the hand held out to him with great warmth. "Do the clergy speak of bringing suit to recover damages at once, for the acts of '55 and '58?"

"I believe not," the gentleman from Caroline replies, courteously, in his soft voice; "but have you not heard the news from Hanover?"

"No, sir; pray let us hear —"

"In the action brought by the Reverend Mr. Maury against the collector, a young man of that county has procured a triumphant verdict for the collector."

"For the collector?"

"Yes!"

"Against the clergy?"

"Yes!"

"You said a triumphant verdict?"

"One penny damages."

An expression of extreme delight diffuses itself over the face of the gentleman receiving this reply.

"And what is the name of the young man who has worked this wonder?"

"Mr. Patrick Henry."

"I have no acquaintance with him."

"I think you will have, however, sir. His speech is said to have been something wonderful; the people carried him on their shoulders, the parsons fled from the bench — I found the county, as I passed through, completely crazy with delight. But what is that small volume, peeping from your pocket, sir?" adds the speaker, with a smile at the abstracted and delighted expression of his interlocutor.

"An Anacreon, from Glasgow, sir," says the other, almost forgetting his delight at the issue of the parsons' cause, as he takes the book from his pocket and opens it. It is a small thin volume, with an embossed back, covered with odd gilt figures; and the Greek type is of great size, and very black and heavy.

"Greek?" says the gentleman from Caroline, smiling serenely. "Ah, I fear it is Hebrew to me! I may say, however, that from what I have heard, this young Mr. Henry is a fair match for a former orator of that language — Demosthenes!"

"Well, sir," says the Roman, "if he is Demosthenes, yonder is our valiant Alexander!"

"Who is he?"

"Is that fine face not familiar?"

"Ah, Col. Washington! I know him but slightly; yet, assuredly, his countenance gives promise of a noble nature; he has certainly already done great service to the government, and I wonder his Majesty has not promoted him. His promotion will, however, await further services, I fancy."

"Ah, gentlemen, you are welcome!" says a courteous voice; "Mr. Wythe, Colonel Bland, Mr. Lee, Mr. Pendleton, I rejoice to see you all: welcome, welcome!" And his Excellency Governor Fauquier, with courtly urbanity, presses the hands of his guests.

"You will find card tables in the next room, should you fancy joining in the fascinating amusements of tictac and spadille," he adds, blandly smiling as he passes on.

The next group which we approach is quite large, and all talk at once, with hearty laughter and rough frankness; and this talk concerns itself with plantation matters — the blood of horses, breeds of cattle, and the chase. Let us listen, even if in the uproar we can catch nothing very connected, and at the risk of finding ourselves puzzled by the jumble of questions and replies.

" The three-field system, I think, sir, has the advantage over all others of — "

" Oh, excellent, sir ! I never saw a finer leaf, and when we cut it — "

" Suddenly the blood rushed over his frill, and we found he had broken his collar bone ! "

" The finest pack, I think, in all Prince George — "

" By George ! — "

" He's a fine fellow, and has, I think, cause to congratulate himself on his luck. His wife is the loveliest girl I ever saw, and — "

" Trots like lightning ! "

" Well, well, nothing astonishes me ! The world must be coming to an end — "

" On Monday forenoon — "

" On the night before — "

" They say the races near Jamestown will be more crowded this year than ever. I announced — "

" The devil ! — "

" Good evening, sir ; I hope your mare will be in good condition for the race — "

" To destruction, sir — I tell you such a black act would ruin the ministry — even Granville — "

" Loves his pipe — "

" The races — "

" Hedges — "

" Distanced — "

" I know his pedigree ; you are mistaken — by Sir Archy, dam — "

" The odds ? I close with you. Indeed, I think I could afford — "

" Ah, gentlemen ! " a courteous voice interposes, amid the

uproar, "talking of races? Mr. Hamilton, Mr. Lane, welcome to my poor house! You will find card tables in the adjoining room." And his bland Excellency passes on.

Space fails us or we might set down for the reader's amusement some of the quiet and pleasant talk of the well-to-do factors and humbler planters and their beautiful wives and daughters. We must pass on; but let us pause a moment yet to hear what this group of magnificently dressed young dames and their gay gallants are saying.

" Really, Mr. Alston, your compliments surpass any which I have received for a very long time," says a fascinating little beauty, in a multiplicity of furbelows and with a small snow-storm on her head,— flirting her fan, all covered with Corydons and Chloes, as she speaks; "what verses did you allude to, when you said that 'Laura was the very image of myself'? I am dying with curiosity to know!"

"Those written by our new poet yonder; have you not heard them?"

"No, sir, upon my word! But the author is —"

"The Earl of Dorset, yonder."

"The Earl of Dorset!"

"Ah, charming Miss Laura! permit the muse to decorate herself with a coronet, and promenade, in powdered wig and ruffles, without questioning her pedigree."

A little laugh greets these *petit maître* words.

"Well, sir, the verses," says Laura, with a fatal glance.

The gallant bows low, and draws from his pocket a manuscript, secured with blue ribbon and elegantly written in the round, honest-looking characters of the day.

"Here it is," he says.

And all the beautiful girls who have listened to the colloquy gather around the reader, to drink in the fascinating rimes of the muse, in an earl's coronet and powder.

"First comes the prologue, as I may say," the reader commences; "it is an address to his pen:

> Wilt thou, advent'rous pen, describe
> The gay, delightful silken tribe,
>     That maddens all our city;
> Nor dread lest while you foolish claim
> A near approach to beauty's flame,
>     Icarus' fate may hit ye!"

The speaker pauses, and a great fluttering of fans ensues, with many admiring comments on the magnificent simile of Icarus.

The reader continues, daintily arranging his snowy frill. "Mark the fate of the bard," he says, and reads:

> "With singèd pinions tumbling down,
> The scorn and laughter of the town,
>     Thou 'lt rue thy daring flight.
> While every Miss, with cool contempt,
> Affronted by the bold attempt,
>     Will, tittering, view thy plight."

"Tittering—observe the expressive phrase," says the reader. They all cry out at this.

"Tittering!"

"Ladies do not titter!"

"Really!"

"Tittering!"

The serene reader raises his hand, and, adjusting his wig, says:

"Mere poetic license, ladies; merely imagination; not fact. True, very true! ladies never *titter*—an abominable imputation. But, listen."

And he continues:

> "Myrtilla's beauties who can paint,
> The well-turned form, the glowing teint,
>     May deck a common creature;

> But who can make th' expressive soul,
> With lively sense inform the whole,
>     And light up every feature?"

"A bad rime 'teint,' and a somewhat aristocratic allusion to 'common creatures,'" says the reader.

"Oh, it is beautiful!" says a pretty little damsel, enthusiastically.

"I am glad you like your portrait, my dear madam," says the gallant, "I assure you that Myrtilla was designed for you."

"Oh!" murmurs Myrtilla, covering her face with her fan. . . .

Some more verses are read, and they are received with a variety of comment.

"Listen now, to the last," says the engaging reader.

> "With pensive look and head reclined,
> Sweet emblem of the purest mind,
>     Lo! where Cordelia sits!
> On Dion's image dwells the fair —
> Dion, the thunderbolt of war —
>     The prince of modern wits!
>
> "At length fatigued with beauty's blaze,
> The feeble muse no more essays,
>     Her picture to complete.
> The promised charms of younger girls,
> When nature the gay scene unfurls,
>     Some happier bard shall treat!"

There is a silence for some moments after these words — the manuscript having passed from the gallant's hands to another group.

"Who is Cordelia? let me think," says Laura, knitting her brows, and raising to her lips a fairy hand covered with diamonds, absently.

"And Dion — who can he be?" says Isadora, twisting her satin sleeve between her fingers abstractedly.

"It is! — no, it is not!"

"I know, now! — but that don't suit!"

"Permit me to end your perplexity, ladies," says the oracle, "Cordelia is Miss Clare Lee, and Dion is Mr. Champ Effingham!"

A general exclamation of surprise from all the ladies. They say:

"It suits him, possibly, but —"

"He may be the prince of wits; still it does not follow —"

"Certainly not, that —"

"Clare is not such a little saint!"

"Let me defend her," says a gentleman, smiling; "I grant you that 't is extravagant to call Mr. Effingham a thunderbolt —"

"Laughable."

"Amusing," say the gentlemen.

"Or the prince of modern wits," continues the counsel for the defense.

"Preposterous!"

"Unjust!" they add.

"But I must be permitted to say," goes on the chivalric defender of the absent, "that Miss Clare Lee fully deserves her character; the comparison of that lovely girl, ladies, to Cordelia — Cordelia, the sweetest of all Shakespeare's characters — seems to me nothing more than justice."

The gentlemen greet this with enthusiastic applause, for our little, long-lost-sight of heroine had subdued all hearts.

"As regards Mr. Effingham," adds Clare's knight, "I shall be pardoned for not saying anything, since he is not present."

"Then I will say something," here interposes a small gentleman, with a waistcoat reaching to his knees and profusely

laced, like all the rest of his clothes, — indeed, the richness
of his costume was distressing, — "but I will say, sir, that
Mr. Effingham's treatment of that divine creature, Miss Clare
Lee, is shameful."

"How?" ask the ladies, agitating their fans and scenting a
delicious bit of scandal.

"Why," says the gentleman in the long waistcoat, squaring
himself, so to speak, and greatly delighted at the sudden acces-
sion to his importance — the general opinion being that he was
somewhat insignificant, "why, ladies, he has been running after
that little jade, Miss Hallam!"

"Miss Hallam!" cry the ladies, in virtuous ignorance, though
nothing was more notorious than the goings-on of our friend
Mr. Effingham, "Miss Hallam!"

"Precisely, ladies."

"The actress?"

"Yes."

"A playing girl!" exclaims a lady, of say thirty, and covering her face as she spoke.

"Falling in love with her!"

"Possible?"

"Have n't you heard all about it?"

This home question causes a flutter and a silence.

"I 'll tell you, then," continues the gentleman in the long
waistcoat, "I 'll tell you all about the doings of 'Dion, the
thunderbolt of war, and prince of modern wits.' *He*, the thunderbolt of war? — preposterous! *He*, the prince of wits? —
ludicrous! He may be the king of coxcombs, the coryphæus
of dandies — but that is all."

The gentlemen standing around listen to these words with
some amusement and more disgust. It is plain that some secret
spite actuates the gentleman in the long waistcoat.

"Well, let us hear Mr. Effingham's crimes," says Laura.

"By all means," adds Isadora.

"Of course," says Myrtilla.

"He has been making himself ridiculous about that actress," continues the chronicler, "and, I have even heard, designs to marry her."

The ladies make a movement to express surprise and indignation but, after a moment's reflection, suppress this somewhat ambiguous exhibition of their feelings.

"He's been at the Raleigh Tavern, making love to her for a month," continues the narrator.

"At the tavern?"

"Yes, in town here."

"Did anyone ever!" says the lady of uncertain age.

"Never! never!" chime in the virtuous little damsels, shaking their heads solemnly.

"He has left his family," the gentleman in the long waistcoat goes on, indignantly, "and they are dying of grief."

"Oh, can it be!"

"Certainly, madam. Why are they not here to-night?"

"Very true."

"Why is Clare Lee, the victim of his insincerity, away, pray tell me! They are not here — they are not coming, madam."

At the same moment, the usher announces the squire, Miss Alethea, and Miss Clare Lee — Master Willie and Kate being too small to be seen, which the squire had warned them of. The squire is as bluff as ever, and makes his salutation to his Excellency with great cordiality — Clare is pale and absent, presenting thus a singular contrast to Henrietta, who enters a moment afterwards, brilliant, imposing, and smiling, like a queen receiving the homage of the nobility around her throne. She sweeps on, leaning on the arm of honest Jack Hamilton, and the party are swallowed in the crowd.

Let us return to the group, whose conversation the new arrivals had interrupted.

"Well, I was mistaken," says the gentleman in the long waistcoat, "but anyone may see that Clare Lee is dying slowly!"

At which affecting observation the young ladies sigh and shake their heads.

"And just think what that man has thrown this divine creature away for," continues the *censor morum* : "for a common actress! — an ordinary playing girl, tolerably pretty she may be, but vastly overrated — a mere thing of stage paint and pearl powder, strutting through her parts and ranting like an Amazon!"

"I think her quite pretty," says Laura, "but it is too bad."

"Dreadful!"

"Awful!"

"Horrible!"

"Shocking!"

These are some of the comments on Mr. Effingham's conduct, from the elegant little dames.

"He is ashamed to show himself anywhere," continues the gentleman in the long waistcoat, "and only yesterday met me on the street and, in passing, turned away his head, plainly afraid that I would not speak in return had he addressed me!"

At which words the gentlemen are observed to smile — knowing as they do something of Mr. Champ Effingham's personal character and habits.

"He actually was afraid to look at me," says the censor, "and I am told keeps his room all day or passes his time in the society of that Circe, yes, that siren who is only too fond of him, I am afraid — and I predict will make him marry her at last."

The ladies sigh and agitate their fans with diamond-sparkling hands. They feel themselves very far above this shameless creature attempting to catch — as we now say — Mr. Effingham. They pity her, for such a thing never has occurred to them — no gentleman has ever been attractive enough for them to have designs upon his heart. And so they pity and despise Beatrice for wishing to run away with her admirer.

"He is heartily ashamed of his infatuation, and I saw him last night in the theater, positively afraid to look at the audience — but staring all the time at her," continues the small gentleman.

"But that is easy to understand, as he is in love," says Myrtilla, with a strong inclination to take the part of the reprobate against his enemy.

"No, no, madam," exclaims the censor, "he was really ashamed to look at the people, and took not the least notice of their frowns : he does not visit anywhere ; he knows he would not be received — he is afraid to show his face."

It seemed that the gentleman in the long waistcoat was doomed to have all his prophecies falsified; for at that moment, the usher announced in a loud voice, which attracted the attention of the whole company :

"Mr. Effingham and Miss Hallam !"

Mr. Effingham entered under the full light of the central chandelier, with Beatrice on his arm. He carried his head proudly erect, his eye was clear and steady, his lip calm and only slightly sarcastic ; his whole carriage displayed perfect and unaffected self-possession. The thousand eyes bent on him vainly sought in his eyes, or lips, anything going to show that he felt conscious of the dreadful, the awful, social enormity which he was committing.

Mr. Effingham was dressed with extraordinary richness. He was always elegant in his costume ; on that night he was splendid. His coat of rich cut velvet was covered with embroidery and sparkled with a myriad of chased-gold buttons; his lace ruffles at breast and wrist were point-de-Venise, his fingers were brilliant with rings, and his powdered hair waved from his clear, pale temples like a stream of silver dust. He looked like a courtier of the days of Louis XIV, dressed for a royal reception.

And how did Beatrice compare with this brilliant star of fashion — this thunderbolt of war and prince of modern wits, as the muse in powdered hair and ruffles had characterized him? Poor Beatrice was quite eclipsed by her cavalier. Her simple, unassuming dress of pearl color, looped back with plain ribbon and without a single flower or any ornament whatever, looked strangely out of place thrown in contrast with the brilliant silks and velvets and gold buttons and diamonds of her companion; her modest, tender face and drooping head, with its unpretending coiffure, looked quite insignificant beside the bold, defiant countenance of Mr. Effingham, which returned look for look and gaze for gaze, with an insulting nonchalance and easy hauteur. We know how reluctantly Beatrice had come thither — rather how bitter a trial it was to her — and we may understand why she looked pale and troubled and — spite of the fact that she had just encountered the gaze of a curious and laughing audience without any emotion — now felt her spirit die within her. It was not because she shrunk from comment half so much as from the fact that each moment she expected to see opposite to her the cold, pale face and sick, reproachful eyes of Clare Lee — of Clare, who had thrown aside the prejudices of class, even forgot the jealousy of a wronged and wretched rival, to press in her arms the rival who had made all her woe, and that rival a common actress. It was the dread of her eye which made poor Beatrice tremble — this alone made her lip quiver and her brow droop.

His excellency Governor Fauquier came forward to welcome his guests, but started at the sight of Beatrice, and almost uttered an exclamation. For a moment he was staggered and said nothing. This soon passed, however, and by the time Mr. Effingham had accomplished his easy bow, the Governor was himself again and, like the elegant gentleman he was, made a low inclination before Beatrice. Then he made a pleasant allusion to the weather — that much-abused subject, which has extricated so many perishing conversations — and so, smiling agreeably, passed on.

Mr. Effingham advanced through the opening, on each side of which extended a row of brilliant forms, sparkling with lace and jewels, without any apparent consciousness that he and his companion were the observed of all observers — without being conscious, one would have said, of those murmured comments which greeted on every side the strange and novel scene. His manner to Beatrice, as he bent down to speak to her, was full of respectful and chivalric feeling; his eye was soft, his lip smiling; the highest lady of the land· might well have felt an emotion of pleasure in so elegant and noble an exhibition of regard. And this was not affected by Mr. Effingham. By no means. We have failed to convey a truthful impression of this young gentleman's character if the reader has not, before this time, perceived that with all his woeful faults and failings Mr. Champ Effingham had much in his character of the bold gentleman — the ancient knight. With those thousand satirical or scornful eyes bent on her, Beatrice was dearer to him than she had ever been before. Those elegant ladies and gallant gentlemen were saying with disdain, " a common actress ! " Well, he would espouse the cause of that girl they scorned against them all and treat her like a queen ! Never had she had more complete possession of his heart ; never had his heart thrilled so deliciously at the contact of her hand, resting upon his arm.

As we have said, all drew back from the newcomers, and they entered through an open space, like a king leading in his queen. Mr. Effingham looked round with a cool and easy smile, and led the young girl to a seat near some elderly dowagers in turbans and diamonds, who had enthroned themselves in state to watch their daughters and see that those inexperienced creatures did not give too much encouragement to ineligible personages. As Beatrice sank into one of the red damask chairs, the surrounding chairs suddenly retreated on their rollers, and the turbans agitated themselves indignantly. Mr. Effingham smiled, with his easy, mocking expression, and observing that one of the diamond-decorated dowagers had dropped her fan, picked it up and presented it to her with a bow. The indignant lady turned away her head with a frown.

" Ah," said Mr. Effingham, politely, " I was mistaken."

And fanning himself for a moment negligently, he placed the richly feathered instrument in the hand of Beatrice.

" My fan, if you please, sir," said the owner, suddenly flushing with indignant fire.

" Your fan, madam?" asked Mr. Effingham, with polite surprise.

" Yes, sir! you picked it up, sir!"

" A thousand pardons!" returned the young gentleman, with a courteous smile; "did I?"

" Yes, sir! that is it, sir! In the hands of that —."

" Oh, I understand," returned Mr. Effingham; and with a low inclination to Beatrice, he said, holding out his hand, " Will you permit me?"

The fan was restored by the young girl, just as she had taken it — unconsciously, and the dowager received it with the tips of her fingers, as if it had been contaminated. At the same moment the band struck up a minuet, and two couples began to dance. . . .

"Come!" said he to Beatrice; and taking her hand, he raised her, and led her forward.

"Not so fast," he said, with a gesture of his hand, to the musicians; "I cannot dance a minuet to a gavotte tune."

And he entered into the broad, open space with Beatrice the mark of a thousand eyes. . . .

The entrance of Mr. Effingham into the open space, to dance the second minuet of the evening, had caused an awful sensation. As he glided through the stately dance to the slow-rolling music, bowing profoundly, with his tender, lordly smile, touching the young girl's hand with chivalric respect, pressing his cocked hat to his heart at each inclination of his handsome and brilliant head, all eyes had been bent upon him, all tongues busy with him. And these eyes and tongues had taken equal note of Beatrice. The young girl moved through the old stately dance with that exquisite grace and ease with which she performed every evolution, and her tender, agitated face, as we have seen, tempered the wrath of many an indignant damsel. After the first burst of surprise and anger, the gentlemen too began to take the part — as Virginia gentlemen always have done and always will do — of the lonely girl environed by so many hostile eyes and slighting comments. They forgot the prepossessions of rank, the prejudices of class — no longer remembered that the young actress occupied upon the floor a position to which she was not entitled; they only saw a woman who had all the rest against her, and their sympathy was nearly powerful enough to make them lose sight of Mr. Effingham's defiance.

A murmur rose as the music stopped, and he led her to a seat; and then a species of undulation in the crowd, near the entrance into the next room, attracted attention. Mr. Effingham had his back turned, however, and did not observe this incident. He was talking to Beatrice in a low tone.

"You see," he said, with his calm, nonchalant voice — "you see, Beatrice, that this superb society, which you fancied you would find yourself so much out of place in, is not so very extraordinary after all. I think that I hazard nothing in saying that the second minuet was better than the first; you are, indeed, far more beautiful than that little dame whose ancestors, I believe, came over with the conqueror — Captain Smith."

And his cynical smile grew soft as he gazed on the tender, anxious face.

"It was not so dreadful an ordeal," he added, "though I must say we were the subject of much curiosity. I observed a group criticizing me, which pleased me. There was a fiery young gentleman in a long waistcoat, whom I offended by not returning his bow some months since — and I believe he was the orator of the occasion."

With which words, Mr. Effingham's lip curled.

"See! the very same group — everybody, in fact, is gazing at us. Let them! you are lovelier than them all."

And Mr. Effingham raised his head proudly and looked around like an emperor. But Beatrice felt her heart die within her. That minuet had exhausted her strength; each moment she expected to see the pale cold face of Clare looking at her. Mr. Effingham observed how faint she was, and leaning over took a smelling bottle from the hand of the old dowager who had dropped the fan — bowing and smiling.

He presented it to Beatrice, but she put it away with the back of her hand, whereupon Mr. Effingham, with a second bow, restored it to the dowager, who, aghast at his impudence, beaten by his superior coolness, and overwhelmed with rage, took it without knowing what she did. Mr. Effingham thereupon turned, smiling, to Beatrice again:

"There seems to be something going on yonder," he said, leaning on her chair, and directing the young girl's attention to the flashing waves of the crowd, which moved to and fro like foaming billows, in the light of the brilliant chandeliers. Beatrice felt an indefinable and vague fear take possession of her heart. At the same moment, Master Willie came pushing and elbowing through the crowd.

"Cousin Clare is sick!" he said; "you'd better go and see her, brother Champ. She liked to fainted just now!"

Beatrice understood all.

"Oh, sir! let me go!" she cried, "go out with me! I shall die here! — oh, I cannot — that dance nearly killed me — and now! — Oh, sir, have pity, give me your arm!".

And rising with a hurried movement, she placed her hand on Mr. Effingham's arm. That gentleman smiled bitterly.

"Yes," he said, "this is the tragedy after the comedy! I understand this fainting."

"Oh, sir, have pity — I must go!" cried Beatrice, "I will go alone!"

Mr. Effingham held her back and hesitated. At last he said,

"Well, madam — as you please — I have had a pleasant minuet — I will go."

And with the same cold, defiant ease, he led the young girl across the room and issued forth into the open air.

[When Effingham is subsequently rejected most positively by Beatrice Hallam, he becomes desperate and tries to kidnap her. While he is carrying her away in a sailboat down the James River, Charles Waters rescues her, and she eventually becomes his wife.[1]]

---

[1] Since Book II of "The Virginia Comedians" carries on virtually an independent story, it has not been deemed necessary to extend the summary to include these further incidents.

# HUMORISTS

## AUGUSTUS BALDWIN LONGSTREET

[Augustus Baldwin Longstreet was born in Augusta, Georgia, in 1790. He graduated at Yale in 1813 and practiced law in Georgia, becoming a district judge in 1822. In addition to the practice of law, he did editorial work in Augusta, where he established the *Sentinel*. In 1838 he became a Methodist minister, and was thereafter largely connected with educational institutions, being in turn president of Emory College, Georgia, of Centenary College, Louisiana, of the University of Mississippi, and of South Carolina College. He died in Oxford, Mississippi, in 1870. His fame as a writer rests upon a single book, " Georgia Scenes," consisting of realistic sketches of Georgia country life, written originally as contributions to newspapers and later gathered into book form.]

### THE HORSE SWAP

During the session of the Supreme Court, in the village of ——, about three weeks ago, when a number of people were collected in the principal street of the village, I observed a young man riding up and down the street, as I supposed, in a violent passion. He galloped this way, then that, and then the other; spurred his horse to one group of citizens, then to another; then dashed off at half speed, as if fleeing from danger; and, suddenly checking his horse, returned first in a pace, then in a trot, and then in a canter. While he was performing these various evolutions, he cursed, swore, whooped, screamed, and tossed himself in every attitude which man could assume on horseback. In short, he *cavorted* most magnanimously (a term which, in our tongue, expresses all that I have described, and a little more), and seemed to be setting all creation at defiance. As I like to see all that is passing, I determined to take a position a little nearer to him, and to ascertain, if possible, what it was that affected him so sensibly. Accordingly, I approached a crowd before which he had stopped for a moment,

BLOSSOM AND HIS HORSE, BULLET

Reproduction of one of the original illustrations of "Georgia Scenes"

and examined it with the strictest scrutiny. But I could see nothing in it that seemed to have anything to do with the cavorter. Every man appeared to be in good humor, and all minding their own business. Not one so much as noticed the principal figure. Still he went on. After a semicolon pause, which my appearance seemed to produce (for he eyed me closely as I approached), he fetched a whoop and swore that he could outswap any live man, woman, or child that ever walked these hills, or that ever straddled horseflesh since the days of old daddy Adam. "Stranger," said he to me, "did you ever see the *Yellow Blossom* from Jasper?"

"No," said I, "but I have often heard of him."

"I'm the boy," continued he; "perhaps a *leetle*, jist a *leetle*, of the best man at a horse swap that ever trod shoe leather."

I began to feel my situation a little awkward, when I was relieved by a man somewhat advanced in years, who stepped up and began to survey the Yellow Blossom's horse with much apparent interest. This drew the rider's attention, and he turned the conversation from me to the stranger.

"Well, my old coon," said he, "do you want to swap *hosses*?"

"Why, I don't know," replied the stranger; "I believe I've got a beast I'd trade with you for that one, if you like him."

"Well, fetch up your nag, my old cock; you're jist the lark I wanted to get hold of. I am perhaps a *leetle*, jist a *leetle*, of the best man at a horse swap that ever stole *cracklins* out of his mammy's fat gourd. Where's your *hoss*?"

"I'll bring him presently, but I want to examine your horse a little."

"Oh! look at him," said the Blossom, alighting and hitting him a cut; "look at him. He's the best piece of *hoss*flesh in the thirteen united univarsal worlds. There's no sort o' mistake in little Bullet. He can pick up miles on his feet and fling 'em behind him as fast as the next man's *hoss*, I don't care where he comes from. And he can keep at it as long as the sun can shine without resting."

During this harangue little Bullet looked as if he understood it all, believed it, and was ready at any moment to verify it. He was a horse of goodly countenance, rather expressive of vigilance than fire, though an unnatural appearance of fierceness was thrown into it by the loss of his ears, which had been cropped pretty close to his head. Nature had done but little for Bullet's head and neck, but he managed, in a great measure, to hide their defects by bowing perpetually. He had obviously suffered severely for corn, but if his ribs and hip bones had not disclosed the fact, *he* never would have done it, for he was in all respects as cheerful and happy as if he commanded all the corn cribs and fodder stacks in Georgia. His height was about twelve hands, but as his shape partook somewhat of that of the giraffe, his haunches stood much lower. They were short, straight, peaked, and concave. Bullet's tail, however, made amends for all his defects. All that the artist could do to beautify it had been done, and all that horse could do to compliment the artist, Bullet did. His tail was nicked in superior style and exhibited the line of beauty in so many directions that it could not fail to hit the most fastidious taste in some of them. From the root it drooped into a graceful festoon, then rose in a handsome curve, then resumed its first direction, and then mounted suddenly upward like a cypress knee to a perpendicular of about two and a half inches. The whole had a careless and bewitching inclination to the right. Bullet obviously knew where his beauty lay and took all occasions to display it to the best advantage. If a stick cracked, or if anyone moved suddenly about him, or coughed, or hawked, or spoke a little louder than common, up went Bullet's tail like lightning, and if the *going up* did not please, the *coming down* must of necessity, for it was as different from the other movement as was its direction. The first was a bold and rapid flight upward, usually to an angle of forty-five degrees. In this position he kept his interesting appendage until he satisfied himself that nothing in particular was to be done, when he commenced dropping it by half inches, in second beats, then in triple time, then faster and shorter, and faster and shorter still, until it finally died away imperceptibly into its natural position. If I might compare sights to sounds I should say its *settling* was more like the note of a locust than anything else in nature.

Either from native sprightliness of disposition, from uncontrollable activity, or from an unconquerable habit of removing flies by the stamping of the feet, Bullet never stood still, but always kept up a gentle fly-scaring movement of his limbs, which was peculiarly interesting.

"I tell you, man," proceeded the Yellow Blossom, "he's the best live hoss that ever trod the grit of Georgia. Bob Smart knows the hoss. Come here, Bob, and mount this hoss, and show Bullet's motions." Here Bullet bristled up, and looked as if he had been hunting for Bob all day long and had just found him. Bob sprang on his back. "Boo-oo-oo!" said Bob, with a fluttering noise of the lips; and away went Bullet, as if in a quarter race, with all his beauties spread in handsome style.

"Now fetch him back," said Blossom. Bullet turned and came in pretty much as he went out.

"Now trot him by." Bullet reduced his tail to "customary," sidled to the right and left airily, and exhibited at least three varieties of trot in the short space of fifty yards.

"Make him pace!" Bob commenced twitching the bridle and kicking at the same time. These inconsistent movements obviously (and most naturally) disconcerted Bullet; for it was impossible for him to learn, from them, whether he was to proceed or stand still. He started to trot and was told that wouldn't do. He attempted a canter and was checked again. He stopped and was urged to go on. Bullet now rushed into the wild field of experiment and struck out a gait of his own that completely turned the tables upon his rider and certainly deserved a patent. It seemed to have derived its elements from the jig, the minuet, and the cotillon. If it was not a pace, it certainly had *pace* in it, and no man could venture to call it anything else; so it passed off to the satisfaction of the owner.

"Walk him!" Bullet was now at home again, and he walked as if money was staked on him.

The stranger, whose name, I afterwards learned, was Peter Ketch, having examined Bullet to his heart's content, ordered his son Neddy to go and bring up Kit. Neddy soon appeared upon Kit, a well-formed sorrel of the middle size and in good order. His *tout ensemble* threw Bullet entirely in the shade, though a glance was sufficient to satisfy anyone that Bullet had decided advantage of him in point of intellect.

"Why, man," said Blossom, "do you bring such a hoss as that to trade for Bullet? Oh, I see you're no notion of trading."

"Ride him off, Neddy!" said Peter. Kit put off at a handsome lope.

"Trot him back!" Kit came in at a long sweeping trot, and stopped suddenly at the crowd.

"Well," said Blossom, "let me look at him; maybe he'll do to plow."

"Examine him!" said Peter, taking hold of the bridle close to the mouth, "he's nothing but a tacky. He ain't as *pretty* a horse as Bullet, I know, but he'll do. Start 'em together for a hundred and fifty *mile*; and if Kit an't twenty mile ahead of him at the coming out, any man may take Kit for nothing. But he's a monstrous mean horse, gentlemen, any man may see that. He's the scariest horse, too, you ever saw. He won't do to hunt on, nohow. Stranger, will you let Neddy have your rifle to shoot off him? Lay the rifle between his ears, Neddy, and shoot at the blaze in that stump. Tell me when his head is high enough."

Ned fired and hit the blaze, and Kit did not move a hair's breadth.

"Neddy, take a couple of sticks and beat on that hogshead at Kit's tail."

Ned made a tremendous rattling, at which Bullet took fright, broke his bridle, and dashed off in grand style, and would have stopped all farther negotiations by going home in disgust had not a traveler arrested him and brought him back: but Kit did not move.

"I tell you, gentlemen," continued Peter, "he's the scariest horse you ever saw. He an't as gentle as Bullet, but he won't do any harm if you watch him. Shall I put him in a cart, gig, or wagon for you, stranger? He'll cut the same capers there he does here. He's a monstrous mean horse."

During all this time Blossom was examining him with the nicest scrutiny. Having examined his frame and limbs, he now looked at his eyes.

"He's got a curious look out of his eyes," said Blossom.

"Oh, yes, sir," said Peter, "just as blind as a bat. Blind horses always have clear eyes. Make a motion at his eyes, if you please, sir."

Blossom did so, and Kit threw up his head rather as if something pricked him under the chin than as if fearing a blow. Blossom repeated the experiment, and Kit jerked back in considerable astonishment.

"Stone blind, you see, gentlemen," proceeded Peter; "but he's just as good to travel of a dark night as if he had eyes."

"Blame my buttons," said Blossom, "if I like them eyes."

"No," said Peter, "nor I neither. I'd rather have 'em made of diamonds; but they'll do, if they don't show as much white as Bullet's."

"Well," said Blossom, "make a pass at me."

"No," said Peter; "you made the banter, now make your pass."

"Well, I'm never afraid to price my hosses. You must give me twenty-five dollars boot."

"Oh, certainly; say fifty, and my saddle and bridle in. Here, Neddy, my son, take away daddy's horse."

"Well," said Blossom, "I've made my pass, now you make yours."

"I'm for short talk in a horse swap and therefore always tell a gentleman at once what I mean to do. You must give me ten dollars."

Blossom swore absolutely, roundly, and profanely that he never would give boot.

"Well," said Peter, "I didn't care about trading, but you cut such high shines that I thought I'd like to back you out, and I've done it. Gentlemen, you see I've brought him to a hack."

"Come, old man," said Blossom, "I've been joking with you. I begin to think you do want to trade, therefore give me five dollars and take Bullet. I'd rather lose ten dollars any time than not make a trade, though I hate to fling away a good hoss."

"Well," said Peter, "I'll be as clever as you are; just put the five dollars on Bullet's back and hand him over, it's a trade."

Blossom swore again, as roundly as before, that he would not give boot; and, said he, "Bullet wouldn't hold five dollars on his back, nohow. But as I bantered you, if you say an even swap, here's at you."

"I told you," said Peter, "I'd be as clever as you, therefore here goes two dollars more, just for trade sake. Give me three dollars and it's a bargain."

Blossom repeated his former assertion; and here the parties stood for a long time, and the bystanders (for many were now collected) began to taunt both parties. After some time, however, it was pretty unanimously decided that the old man had backed Blossom out.

At length Blossom swore he " never would be backed out for three dollars after bantering a man," and accordingly they closed the trade.

" Now," said Blossom, as he handed Peter the three dollars, " I'm a man that when he makes a bad trade, makes the most of it until he can make a better. I'm for no rues and after claps."

" That's just my way," said Peter ; " I never goes to law to mend my bargains."

" Ah, you're the kind of boy I love to trade with. Here's your hoss, old man. Take the saddle and bridle off him, and I'll strip yours ; but lift up the blanket easy from Bullet's back, for he's a mighty tender-backed hoss."

The old man removed the saddle, but the blanket stuck fast. He attempted to raise it, and Bullet bowed himself, switched his tail, danced a little, and gave signs of biting.

" Don't hurt him, old man," said Blossom, archly ; " take it off easy. I am, perhaps, a leetle of the best man at a horse swap that ever catched a coon."

Peter continued to pull at the blanket more and more roughly, and Bullet became more and more *cavortish*, insomuch that when the blanket came off he had reached the *kicking* point in good earnest.

The removal of the blanket disclosed a sore on Bullet's backbone that seemed to have defied all medical skill. It measured six full inches in length and four in breadth and had as many features as Bullet had motions. My heart sickened at the sight, and I felt that the brute who had been riding him in that situation deserved the halter.

The prevailing feeling, however, was that of mirth. The laugh became loud and general at the old man's expense, and rustic witticisms were liberally bestowed upon him and his late purchase. These Blossom continued to provoke by various remarks. He asked the old man "if he thought Bullet would let five dollars lie on his back." He declared most seriously that he had owned that horse three months and had never discovered before that he had a sore back, "or he never should have thought of trading him," etc.

The old man bore it all with the most philosophic composure. He evinced no astonishment at his late discovery and made no replies. But his son Neddy had not disciplined his feelings quite so well. His eyes opened wider and wider from the first to the last pull of the blanket, and, when the whole sore burst upon his view, astonishment and fright seemed to contend for the mastery of his countenance. As the blanket disappeared, he stuck his hands in his breeches pockets, heaved a deep sigh, and lapsed into a profound revery, from which he was only roused by the cuts at his father. He bore them as long as he could, and when he could contain himself no longer he began, with a certain wildness of expression which gave a peculiar interest to what he uttered: "His back's mighty bad off, but . . . old Kit's both blind and *deef*. . . . You walk him, and see if he *eint*. His eyes don't look like it; but he'd *jist as leve go agin* the house with you, or in a ditch, as anyhow. Now you go try him." The laugh was now turned on Blossom; and many rushed to test the fidelity of the little boy's report. A few experiments established its truth beyond controversy.

"Neddy," said the old man, "you ought n't to try and make people discontented with their things. Stranger, don't mind what the little boy says. If you can only get Kit rid of them little failings, you'll find him all sorts of a horse. You are a *leetle* the best man at a horse swap that ever I got hold of; but don't fool away Kit. Come, Neddy, my son, let's be moving; the stranger seems to be getting snappish."

## THE TURN OUT

In the good old days of *fescues*, *abisselfas*, and *anpersants*, terms which used to be familiar in this country during the Revolutionary War, and which lingered in some of our county schools for a few years afterward, I visited my friend Captain Griffin, who resided about seven miles to the eastward of Wrightsborough, then in Richmond, but now in Columbia County. I reached the captain's hospitable home on Easter, and was received by him and his good lady with a *Georgia welcome* of 1790. It was warm from the heart, and taught me in a moment that the obligations of the visit were upon their side, not mine. Such receptions were not peculiar at that time to the captain and his family; they were common throughout the state. Where are they now! and where the generous hospitalities which invariably followed them! I see them occasionally at the contented farmer's door and at his festive board, but when they shall have taken leave of these, Georgia will know them no more.

The day was consumed in the interchange of news between the captain and myself (though, I confess, it might have been better employed), and the night found us seated round a temporary fire, which the captain's sons had kindled up for the purpose of dyeing eggs. It was a common custom of those days with boys to dye and peck eggs on Easter Sunday and for a few days afterward. They were colored according to the fancy of the dyer — some yellow, some green, some purple, and some with a variety of colors, borrowed from a piece of calico. They were not unfrequently beautified with a taste and skill which would have extorted a compliment from Hezekiah Niles, if he had seen them a year ago, in the hands of the " young operatives," in some of the northern manufactories. No sooner was the work of dyeing finished, than our young operatives sallied forth to stake the whole proceeds of their " domestic industry" upon a peck. Egg was struck against egg, point to point, and the egg that was broken was given up as lost to the owner of the one which came whole from the shock.

While the boys were busily employed in the manner just mentioned, the captain's youngest son, George, gave us an anecdote highly descriptive of the Yankee and Georgia character, even in their buddings, and at this early date. "What you think, pa," said he, "Zeph Pettibone went and got his Uncle Zach to turn him a wooden egg, and he won a whole hatful o' eggs from all us boys 'fore we found it out; but when we found it out maybe John Brown did n't smoke him for it, and took away all his eggs and give 'em back to us boys; and you think he did n't go then and git a guinea egg, and win most as many more, and John Brown would o' give it to him agin if all we boys had n't said we thought it was fair. I never see such a boy as that Zeph Pettibone in all my life. He don't mind whipping no more 'an nothing at all, if he can win eggs."

This anecdote, however, only fell in by accident, for there was an all-absorbing subject which occupied the minds of the boys during the whole evening, of which I could occasionally catch distant hints in undertones and whispers, but of which I could make nothing until they were afterward explained by the captain himself. Such as "I'll be bound Pete Jones and Bill Smith stretches him." "By Jockey, soon as they seize him you'll see me down upon him like a duck upon a June bug." "By the time he touches the ground he'll think he's got into a hornet's nest," etc.

"The boys," said the captain, as they retired, "are going to turn out the schoolmaster to-morrow, and you can perceive they think of nothing else. We must go over to the schoolhouse and witness the contest, in order to prevent injury to preceptor or pupils; for, though the master is always, upon such occasions, glad to be turned out, and only struggles long enough to present his patrons a fair apology for giving the children a holiday, which he desires as much as they do, the boys always conceive a holiday gained by a 'turn out' as the sole achievement of their valor; and, in their zeal to distinguish themselves upon such memorable occasions, they sometimes become too rough, provoke the master to wrath, and a very serious conflict ensues. To prevent these consequences, to bear witness that the master was *forced* to yield before he would withhold a day of his promised labor from his employers, and to act as a mediator between him and the boys in settling the articles of peace, I always attend; and you must accompany me to-morrow." I cheerfully promised to do so.

The captain and I rose before the sun, but the boys had risen and were off to the schoolhouse before the dawn. After an early breakfast, hurried by Mrs. G. for our accommodation, my host and myself took up our line of march towards the schoolhouse. We reached it about half an hour before the master arrived, but not before the boys had completed its fortifications. It was a simple log pen, about twenty feet square, with a doorway cut out of the logs, to which was fitted a rude door, made of clapboards, and swung on wooden hinges. The roof was covered with clapboards also, and retained in their places by heavy logs placed on them. The chimney was built of logs, diminishing in size from the ground to the top, and overspread inside and out with red-clay mortar. The classic hut occupied a lovely spot, overshadowed by majestic hickories, towering poplars, and strong-armed oaks. The little plain on which it stood was terminated, at the distance of about fifty paces from its door, by the brow of a hill, which descended rather abruptly to a noble spring that gushed joyously forth from among the roots of a stately beech at its foot. The stream from this fountain scarcely burst into view before it hid itself beneath the dark shade of a field of cane which overspread the dale through which it flowed and marked its windings until it turned from the sight among vine-covered hills, at a distance far beyond that to which the eye could have traced it without the help of its evergreen belt. A remark of the captain's, as we viewed the lovely country around us, will give the reader my apology for the minuteness of the foregoing description. "These lands," said he, "will never wear out. Where they lie level, they will be as good fifty years hence as they are now." Forty-two years afterward I visited the spot on which he stood when he made the remark. The sun poured his whole strength upon the bald hill which once supported the sequestered schoolhouse; many a deep-washed gully met at a sickly bog where gushed the limpid fountain; a dying willow rose from the soil which nourished the venerable beech; flocks wandered among the dwarf pines, and cropped a scanty meal from the vale where the rich cane bowed and rustled to every breeze, and all around was barren, dreary, and cheerless. But to return.

As I before remarked, the boys had strongly fortified the schoolhouse, of which they had taken possession. The door was barricaded with logs, which I should have supposed would have defied the combined powers of the whole school. The chimney too was nearly filled with logs of goodly size, and these were the only passways to the interior. I concluded if a *turn out* was all that was necessary to decide the contest in favor of the boys, they had already gained the victory. They had, however, not as much confidence in their outworks as I had, and therefore had armed themselves with long sticks — not for the purpose of using them upon the master if the battle should come to close quarters, for this was considered unlawful warfare, but for the purpose of guarding their *works* from his approaches, which it was considered perfectly lawful to protect by all manner of jabs and punches through the cracks. From the early assembling of the girls it was very obvious that they had been let into the conspiracy, though they took no part in the active operations. They would, however, occasionally drop a word of encouragement to the boys, such as "I wouldn't turn out the master, but if I did turn him out, I'd die before I'd give up." These remarks doubtless had an emboldening effect upon "the young freeborns," as Mrs. Trollope would call them, for I never knew the Georgian of any age who was indifferent to the smiles and praises of the ladies — before his marriage.

At length Mr. Michael St. John, the schoolmaster, made his appearance. Though some of the girls had met him a quarter of a mile from the schoolhouse and told him all that had happened, he gave signs of sudden astonishment and indignation when he advanced to the door and was assailed by a whole platoon of sticks from the cracks. "Why, what does all this mean?" said he, as he approached the captain and myself, with a countenance of two or three varying expressions.

"Why," said the captain, "the boys have turned you out, because you have refused to give them an Easter holiday."

"Oh," returned Michael, "that's it, is it? Well, I'll see whether their parents are to pay me for letting their children play when they please." So saying, he advanced to the schoolhouse and demanded, in a lofty tone, of its inmates an unconditional surrender.

"Well, give us holiday then," said twenty little urchins within, "and we'll let you in."

"Open the door of the academy" (Michael would allow nobody to call it a schoolhouse) — "Open the door of the academy this instant," said Michael, "or I'll break it down."

"Break it down," said Pete Jones and Bill Smith, "and we'll break you down."

During this colloquy I took a peep into the fortress to see how the garrison were affected by the parley. The little ones were obviously panic-struck at the first words of command; but their fears were all chased away by the bold, determined reply of Pete Jones and Bill Smith, and they raised a whoop of defiance.

Michael now walked round the academy three times, examining all its weak points with great care. He then paused, reflected for a moment, and wheeled off suddenly towards the woods, as though a bright thought had just struck him. He passed twenty things which I supposed he might be in quest of, such as huge stones, fence rails, portable logs, and the like, without bestowing the least attention upon them. He went to one old log, searched it thoroughly; then to another; then to a hollow stump, peeped into it with great care; then to a hollow log, into which he looked with equal caution, and so on.

"What is he after?" inquired I.

"I'm sure I don't know," said the captain, "but the boys do. Don't you notice the breathless silence which prevails in the schoolhouse, and the intense anxiety with which they are eying him through the cracks?"

At this moment Michael had reached a little excavation at the root of a dogwood and was in the act of putting his hand into it, when a voice from the garrison exclaimed, with most touching pathos, "Lo'd o' messy, he's found my eggs! boys, let's give up."

"I won't give up," was the reply from many voices at once.

"Rot your cowardly skin, Zeph Pettibone, you wouldn't give a wooden egg for all the holidays in the world."

If these replies did not reconcile Zephaniah to his apprehended loss, it at least silenced his complaints. In the meantime Michael was employed in relieving Zeph's storehouse of its provisions; and, truly, its contents told well for Zeph's skill in egg-pecking. However, Michael took out the eggs with great care and brought them within a few paces of the schoolhouse and laid them down with equal care in full view of the besieged. He revisited the places which he had searched and to which he seemed to have been led by intuition, for from nearly all of them did he draw eggs, in greater or less numbers. These he treated as he had done Zeph's, keeping each pile separate. Having arranged the eggs in double files before the door, he marched between them with an air of triumph and once more demanded a surrender, under pain of an entire destruction of the garrison's provisions.

"Break 'em just as quick as you please," said George Griffin; "our mothers 'll give us a plenty more, won't they, pa?"

"I can answer for yours, my son," said the captain; "she would rather give up every egg upon the farm than see you play the coward or traitor to save your property."

Michael, finding that he could make no impression upon the fears or the avarice of the boys, determined to carry their fortifications by storm. Accordingly he procured a heavy fence rail and commenced the assault upon the door. It soon came to pieces, and the upper logs fell out, leaving a space of about three feet at the top. Michael boldly entered the breach, when, by the articles of war, sticks were thrown aside as no longer lawful weapons. He was resolutely met on the half-demolished rampart by Peter Jones and William Smith, supported by James Griffin. These were the three largest boys in the school, the first about sixteen years of age, the second about fifteen, and the third just eleven. Twice was Michael repulsed by these young champions, but the third effort carried him fairly into the fortress. Hostilities now ceased for awhile, and the captain and I, having leveled the remaining logs at the door, followed Michael into the house. A large three-inch plank (if it deserve that name, for it was wrought from the half of a tree's trunk entirely with the ax), attached to the logs by means of wooden pins, served the whole school for a writing desk. At a convenient distance below it, and on a line with it, stretched a smooth log resting upon the logs of the house, which answered for the writers' seat. Michael took his seat upon the desk, placed his feet on the seat, and was sitting very composedly,

MICHAEL ST. JOHN, THE SCHOOLMASTER, EFFECTING AN
ENTRANCE BY STORM

Reproduction of one of the original illustrations of "Georgia Scenes"

when, with a simultaneous movement, Pete and Bill seized each a leg, and marched off with it in quick time. The consequence is obvious; Michael's head first took the desk, then the seat, and finally the ground (for the house was not floored), with three sonorous thumps of most doleful portent. No sooner did he touch the ground than he was completely buried with boys. The three elder laid themselves across his head, neck,

and breast, the rest arranging themselves *ad libitum*. Michael's
equanimity was considerably disturbed by the first thump, became restive with the second, and took flight with the third.
His first effort was to disengage his legs, for without them he
could not rise, and to lie in his present position was extremely
inconvenient and undignified. Accordingly, he drew up his
right, and kicked at random. This movement laid out about
six in various directions upon the floor. Two rose crying.
"Ding his old red-headed skin," said one of them, "to go
and kick me right in my sore belly, where I fell down and
raked it running after that fellow that cried 'school-butter.'"

"Drot his old snaggle-tooth picture," said the other, "to go
and hurt my sore toe, where I knocked the nail off going to
the spring to fetch a gourd of *warter* for him, and not for
myself n 'other."

"Hut!" said Captain Griffin, "young Washingtons mind
these trifles! At him again."

The name of Washington cured their wounds and dried up
their tears in an instant, and they legged him *de novo*. The left
leg treated six more as unceremoniously as the right had those
just mentioned; but the talismanic name had just fallen upon
their ears before the kick, so they were invulnerable. They
therefore returned to the attack without loss of time. The
struggle seemed to wax hotter and hotter for a short time after
Michael came to the ground, and he threw the children about
in all directions and postures, giving some of them thumps
which would have placed the *ruffle-shirted* little darlings of the
present day under the discipline of paregoric and opodeldoc for
a week; but these hardy sons of the forest seemed not to feel
them. As Michael's head grew easy, his limbs, by a natural
sympathy, became more quiet, and he offered one day's holiday
as the price. The boys demanded a week; but here the
captain interposed, and, after the common but often unjust

custom of arbitrators, split the difference. In this instance the terms were equitable enough, and were immediately acceded to by both parties. Michael rose in a good humor, and the boys were, of course.

## WILLIAM TAPPAN THOMPSON

[William Tappan Thompson was born at Ravenna, Ohio, in 1812. After going South he was chiefly engaged in journalistic work, mainly in connection with the Savannah *Morning News*, with which he was associated until his death, in 1882. He first came into prominence as a humorous writer through his amusing " Major Jones Letters," contributed to his paper, *The Miscellany*, published at Madison, Georgia, from 1840 to 1845. This has remained his most famous book, but in addition to it he published several other volumes of humorous sketches.]

## MAJOR JONES'S COURTSHIP

PINEVILLE, December 27, 1842

To MR. THOMPSON : *Dear Sir* — Crismus is over, and the thing is ded. You know I told you in my last letter I was gwine to bring Miss Mary up to the chalk a Crismus. Well, I done it, slick as a whistle, though it come mighty nigh bein a serious undertakin. But I 'll tell you all about the whole circumstance.

The fact is, I's made my mind up more 'n twenty times to jest go and come rite out with the whole bisness ; but whenever I got whar she was, and whenever she looked at me with her witchin eyes, and kind o' blushed at me, I always felt sort o' skeered and fainty, and all what I made up to tell her was forgot, so I could n't think of it to save me. But you 's a married man, Mr. Thompson, so I could n't tell you nothin about popin the question, as they call it. It 's a mighty grate favor to ax of a rite pretty gall, and to people as ain't used to it, it goes monstrous hard, don't it? They say widders don't mind it no more'n nothin. But I'm makin a transgression, as the preacher ses.

Crismus eve I put on my new suit, and shaved my face as slick as a smoothin iron, and after tea went over to old Miss Stallinses. As soon as I went into the parler whar they was all settin round the fire, Miss Carline and Miss Kesiah both laughed rite out.

"There, there," ses they, "I told you so, I knew it would be Joseph."

"What's I done, Miss Carline?" ses I.

"You come under little sister's chicken bone, and I do blieve she knew you was comin when she put it over the dore."

"No, I didn't — I didn't no such thing, now," ses Miss Mary, and her face blushed red all over.

"Oh, you needn't deny it," ses Miss Kesiah; "you b'long to Joseph now, jest as sure as ther's any charm in chicken bones."

I know'd that was a first-rate chance to say something, but the dear little creater looked so sorry and kep blushin so, I couldn't say nothin zactly to the pint, so I tuck a chair and reached up and tuck down the bone and put it in my pocket.

"What are you gwine to do with that old bone now, Majer?" ses Miss Mary.

"I'm gwine to keep it as long as I live," ses I, "as a Crismus present from the handsomest gall in Georgia."

When I sed that, she blushed worse and worse.

"Ain't you shamed, Majer?" ses she.

"Now you ought to give *her* a Crismus gift, Joseph, to keep all *her* life," sed Miss Carline.

"Ah," ses old Miss Stallins, "when I was a gall we used to hang up our stockins — "

"Why, mother!" ses all of 'em, "to say stockins rite afore —"

Then I felt a little streaked too, cause they was all blushin as hard as they could.

"Highty-tity!" ses the old lady —"what monstrous 'fine-ment. I'd like to know what harm ther is in stockins. People nowadays is gittin so mealy-mouthed they can't call nothin by its rite name, and I don't see as they's any better than the old-time people was. When I was a gall like you, child, I used to hang up my stockins and git 'em full of presents."

The galls kep laughin.

"Never mind," ses Miss Mary, "Majer's got to give me a Crismus gift, — won't you, Majer?"

"Oh, yes," ses I; "you know I promised you one."

"But I did n't mean *that*," ses she.

"I've got one for you, what I want you to keep all your life, but it would take a two-bushel bag to hold it," ses I.

"Oh, that's the kind," ses she.

"But will you keep it as long as you live?" ses I.

"Certainly, I will, Majer."

"Monstrous 'finement nowadays — old people don't know nothin bout perliteness," said old Miss Stallins, jest gwine to sleep with her nittin in her hand.

"Now you hear that, Miss Carline," ses I. "She ses she'll keep it all her life."

"Yes, I will," ses Miss Mary —"but what is it?"

"Never mind," ses I, "you hang up a bag big enuff to hold it and you'll find out what it is, when you see it in the mornin."

Miss Carline winked at Miss Kesiah, and then whispered to her — then they both laughed and looked at me as mischievous as they could. They spicioned something.

"You'll be sure to give it to me now, if I hang up a bag?" ses Miss Mary.

"And promise to keep it," ses I.

"Well, I will, cause I know that you wouldn't give me nothin that wasn't worth keepin."

They all agreed they would hang up a bag for me to put Miss Mary's Crismus present in, in the back porch; and bout nine o'clock I told 'em good evenin and went home.

I sot up till midnight, and when they was all gone to bed I went softly into the back gate, and went up to the porch, and thar, shore enuff, was a grate big meal bag hangin to the jice. It was monstrous unhandy to git to it, but I was tarmined not to back out. So I sot some chairs on top of a bench and got hold of the rope and let myself down into the bag; but jest as I was gittin in, the bag swung agin the chairs, and down they went with a terrible racket. But nobody didn't wake up but old Miss Stallinses grate big cur dog, and here he cum rippin and tearin through the yard like rath, and round and round he went tryin to find what was the matter. I sot down in the bag and didn't breathe louder nor a kitten for fear he'd find me out, and after a while he quit barkin. The wind begun to blow bominable cold, and the old bag kep turnin round and swinging so it made me seasick as the mischief. I was fraid to move for fear the rope would break and let me fall, and thar I sot with my teeth rattlin like I had a ager. It seemed like it would never come daylight, and I do blieve if I didn't love Miss Mary so powerful I would froze to death; for my hart was the only spot that felt warm, and it didn't beat moren two licks a minit, only when I thought how she would be sprised in the mornin, and then it went in a canter. Bimeby the cussed old dog come up on the porch and begun to smell about the bag, and then he barked like he thought he'd treed something. "Bow! wow! wow!" ses he. Then he'd smell agin and try to git up to the bag. "Git out!" ses I, very low, for fear they would hear me. "Bow! wow! wow!" ses he. "Be gone!

you bominable fool!" ses I, and I felt all over in spots, for I spected every minit he 'd nip me, and what made it worse, I did n't know wharabouts he 'd take hold. " Bow! wow! wow!" Then I tried coaxin — " Come here, good feller," ses I, and whistled a little to him, but it was n't no use. Thar he stood and kep up his eternal whinin and barkin, all night. I could n't tell when daylight was breakin, only by the chickens crowin, and I was monstrous glad to hear 'em, for if I'd had to stay thar one hour more, I don't blieve I'd ever got out of that bag alive.

Old Miss Stallins come out fust, and as soon as she saw the bag, ses she: "What upon yeath has Joseph went and put in that bag for Mary? I 'll lay it 's a yearlin or some live animal, or Bruin would n't bark at it so."

She went in to call the galls, and I sot thar, shiverin all over so I could n't hardly speak if I tried to,—but I did n't say nothin. Bimeby they all come runnin out.

" My Lord, what is it?" ses Miss Mary.

" Oh, it 's alive!" ses Miss Kesiah. " I seed it move."

" Call Cato, and make him cut the rope," ses Miss Carline, "and let 's see what it is. Come here, Cato, and git this bag down."

" Don't hurt it for the world," ses Miss Mary.

Cato untied the rope that was round the jice and let the bag down easy on the floor, and I tumbled out all covered with corn meal from head to foot.

" Goodness gracious!" ses Miss Mary, "if it ain't the Majer himself!"

" Yes," ses I, "and you know you promised to keep my Crismus present as long as you lived."

The galls laughed themselves almost to deth, and went to brushin off the meal as fast as they could, sayin they was gwine to hang that bag up every Crismus till they got husbands, too. Miss Mary — bless her bright eyes — she blushed as butiful as a mornin-glory, and sed she'd stick to her word. She was rite out of bed, and her hair wasn't komed, and her dress wasn't fix't at all, but the way she looked pretty was rale distractin. I do blieve if I was froze stiff, one look at her charmin face, as she stood lookin down to the floor with her rogish eyes and her bright curls fallin all over her snowy neck, would fotch'd me too. I tell you what, it was worth hangin in a meal bag from one Crismus to another to feel as happy as I have ever sense.

I went home after we had the laugh out, and set by the fire till I got thawed. In the forenoon all the Stallinses come over to our house and we had one of the greatest Crismus dinners that ever was seed in Georgia, and I don't blieve a happier company ever sot down to the same table. Old Miss Stallins and mother settled the match, and talked over everything that ever happened in ther families, and laughed at me and Mary, and cried bout ther ded husbands, cause they wasn't alive to see ther children married.

It's all settled now, 'cept we hain't sot the weddin day. I'd like to have it all over at once, but young galls always like to be engaged awhile, you know, so I spose I must wait a month or so. Mary (she ses I mustn't call her Miss Mary now) has been a good deal of trouble and botheration to me; but if you could see her you wouldn't think I ought to grudge a little sufferin to git sich a sweet little wife.

You must come to the weddin if you possibly kin. I'll let you know when. No more from    Your frend, till deth,

Jos. Jones

## JOSEPH GLOVER BALDWIN

[Joseph Glover Baldwin was born in Virginia, near Winchester, in 1815. In early manhood he went into the lower South, finally settling in Sumter County, Alabama. He practiced law in Alabama, with some political recognition, until he moved in 1854 to California. In 1858 he was elected to the supreme court of California, but resigned the position after three years and returned to the practice of law. He died in San Francisco in 1864. He obtains his position in literature through two volumes: the humorous sketches, originally contributed to the *Southern Literary Messenger*, published in book form in 1853 as "Flush Times in Alabama and Mississippi," and a volume entitled "Party Leaders," published in 1855, in which he sketched with considerable ability the careers of several prominent political leaders in the South.]

### OVID BOLUS, ESQ.

And what history of that halcyon period, ranging from the year of grace 1835 to 1837, that golden era when shinplasters were the sole currency, when bank bills were "as thick as autumn leaves in Vallombrosa," and credit was a franchise — what history of those times would be complete that left out the name of Ovid Bolus? As well write the biography of Prince Hal and forbear all mention of Falstaff. In law phrase the thing would be a "deed without a name," and void; a most unpardonable *casus omissus*. . . .

I have had a hard time of it in endeavoring to assign to Bolus his leading vice. I have given up the task in despair, but I have essayed to designate that one which gave him, in the end, most celebrity. I am aware that it is invidious to make comparisons and to give preëminence to one over other rival qualities and gifts, where all have high claims to distinction; but then, the stern justice of criticism in this case requires a discrimination which to be intelligible and definite must be relative and comparative. I therefore take the responsibility of saying, after due reflection, that, in my opinion, Bolus's reputation stood higher for lying than for anything else; and in thus assigning preëminence to this poetic property, I do it without any desire to derogate from other brilliant characteristics belonging to the same general category, which have drawn the wondering notice of the world.

Some men are liars from interest; not because they have no regard for truth, but because they have less regard for it than for gain. Some are liars from vanity; because they would rather be well thought of by others than have reason for thinking well of themselves. Some are liars from a sort of necessity, which overbears, by the weight of temptation, the sense of virtue. Some are enticed away by allurements of pleasure or seduced by evil example and education. Bolus was none of these; he belonged to a higher department of the fine arts and to a higher class of professors of this sort of *belles-lettres*. Bolus was a natural liar, just as some horses are natural pacers, and some dogs natural setters. What he did in that walk was from the irresistible promptings of instinct and a disinterested love of art. His genius and his performances were free from the vulgar alloy of interest or temptation. Accordingly, he did not labor a lie. He lied with a relish; he lied with a coming appetite, growing with what it fed on; he lied from the delight of invention and the charm of fictitious narrative. It is true he applied his art to the practical purposes of life, but in so far did he glory the more in it, just as an ingenious machinist rejoices that his invention, while it has honored science, has also supplied a common want.

Bolus's genius for lying was encyclopedical; it was what German criticism calls many-sided. It embraced all subjects without distinction or partiality. It was equally good upon all, "from grave to gay, from lively to severe."

Bolus's lying came from his greatness of soul and his comprehensiveness of mind. The truth was too small for him. Fact was too dry and commonplace for the fervor of his genius. Besides, great as was his memory, — for he even remembered the outlines of his chief lies, — his invention was still larger. He had a great contempt for history and historians. He thought them tame and timid cobblers — mere tinkers on other peoples' wares; simple parrots and magpies of other men's sayings or doings; borrowers of and acknowledged debtors for others' chattels, got without skill; they had no separate estate in their ideas; they were bailees of goods which they did not pretend to hold by adverse title; buriers of talents in napkins, making no usury; barren and unprofitable nonproducers in the intellectual vineyard — *nati consumere fruges*.

He adopted a fact occasionally to start with, but, like a Sheffield razor and the crude ore, the workmanship, polish, and value were all his own. A Tibet shawl could as well be credited to the insensate goat that grew the wool, as the author of a fact that Bolus honored with his artistical skill could claim to be the inventor of the story. . . .

There was nothing narrow, sectarian, or sectional in Bolus's lying. It was, on the contrary, broad and catholic. It had no respect to times or places. It was as wide, illimitable, as elastic and variable, as the air he spent in giving it expression. It was a generous, gentlemanly, whole-souled faculty. It was often employed on occasions of thrift, but no more and no more zealously on these than on others of no profit to himself. He was an egotist, but a magnificent one; he was not a liar because an egotist, but an egotist because a liar. He usually made himself the hero of the romantic exploits and adventures he narrated; but this was not so much to exalt himself as because it was more convenient to his art. He had nothing malignant or invidious in his nature. If he exalted himself, it was seldom or never to the disparagement of others, unless, indeed, those others were merely imaginary persons or too far off to be hurt. He would as soon lie for you as for himself. It was all the same, so there was something doing in his line of business, except on those cases in which his necessities required to be fed at your expense.

He did not confine himself to mere lingual lying; one tongue was not enough for all the business he had on hand. He acted lies as well. Indeed, sometimes his very silence was a lie. He made nonentity fib for him, and performed wondrous feats by a "masterly inactivity." . . .

In lying, Bolus was not only a successful but he was a very able practitioner. Like every other eminent artist he brought all his faculties to bear upon his art. Though quick of perception and prompt of invention, he did not trust himself to the inspirations of his genius for *improvising* a lie when he could well premeditate one. He deliberately built up the substantial masonry, relying upon the occasion and its accessories chiefly for embellishment and collateral supports, as Burke excogitated the more solid parts of his great speeches and left unprepared only the illustrations and fancy work. . . .

Bolus's manner was, like every truly great man's, his own. It was excellent. He did not come blushing up to a lie, as some otherwise very passable liars do, as if he was making a mean compromise between his guilty passion or morbid vanity and a struggling conscience. He and it were on very good terms — at least, if there was no affection between the couple, there was no fuss in the family; or, if there were any scenes or angry passages, they were reserved for strict privacy and never got out. My own opinion is that he was as destitute of the article as an ostrich. Thus he came to his work bravely, cheerfully, and composedly. The delights of composition, invention, and narration did not fluster his style or agitate his delivery. He knew how, in the tumult of passion, to assume the "temperance to give it smoothness." A lie never ran away with him, as it is apt to do with young performers; he could always manage and guide it, and to have seen him fairly mounted would have given you some idea of the polished elegance of D'Orsay and the superb *manage* of Murat. There is a tone and manner of narration different from those used in delivering ideas just conceived, just as there is difference between the sound of the voice in reading and in speaking. Bolus knew this and practiced on it. When he was narrating he put the facts in order and seemed to speak them out of his memory, but not formally or as if by rote. He would stop himself to correct a date; recollect he was wrong — he was at that year at the White Sulphur or Saratoga, etc.; having got the date right the names of persons present would be incorrect, etc., and these he corrected in turn. A stranger hearing him would have feared the marring of a good story by too fastidious a conscientiousness in the narrator.

## HOW THE FLUSH TIMES SERVED THE VIRGINIANS

Superior to many of the settlers in elegance of manners and general intelligence, it was the weakness of the Virginian to imagine he was superior too in the essential art of being able to hold his hand and make his way in a new country, and especially *such* a country and at *such* a time. What a mistake that was! The times were out of joint. It was hard to say whether it were more dangerous to stand still or to move. If the emigrant stood still, he was consumed, by no slow degrees, by expenses; if he moved, ten to one he went off in a galloping consumption by a ruinous investment. Expenses then — necessary articles about three times as high, and extra articles still more extra-priced — were a different thing in the new country from what they were in the old. In the old country, a jolly

Virginia, starting the business of free living on a capital of a plantation, and fifty or sixty negroes, might reasonably calculate, if no ill luck befell him, by the aid of a usurer, and the occasional sale of a negro or two, to hold out without declared insolvency, until a green old age. His estate melted like an estate in chancery, under the gradual thaw of expenses; but in the fast country, it went by the sheer cost of living — some *poker* losses included — like the fortune of the confectioner in California, who failed for one hundred thousand dollars in the six months' keeping of a candy shop. But all the habits of his life, his taste, his associations, his education — everything — the trustingness of his disposition — his want of business qualification — his sanguine temper — all that was Virginian in him, made him the prey, if not of imposture, at least of unfortunate speculations. Where the keenest jockey often was bit, what chance had *he*? About the same that the verdant Moses had with the venerable old gentleman, his father's friend, at the fair, when he traded the Vicar's pony for the green spectacles. But how could he believe it? How *could* he believe that the stuttering, grammarless Georgian, who had never heard of the resolutions of '98, could beat him in a land trade? "Have no money dealings with my father," said the friendly Martha to Lord Nigel, "for, idiot though he seems, he will make an ass of thee." What pity some monitor, equally wise and equally successful with old Trapbois' daughter, had not been at the elbow of every Virginia! "'T wad frae monie a blunder freed him — an' foolish notion."

If he made a bad bargain, how could he expect to get rid of it? *He* knew nothing of the elaborate machinery of ingenious chicane — such as feigning bankruptcy, fraudulent conveyances, making over to his wife, running property — and had never heard of such tricks of trade as sending out coffins to the graveyard, with negroes inside, carried off by sudden spells of imaginary disease, to be "resurrected" in due time grinning on the banks of the Brazos.

The new philosophy too had commended itself to his speculative temper. He readily caught at the idea of a new spirit of the age having set in, which rejected the saws of Poor Richard as being as much out of date as his almanacs. He was already, by the great rise of property, compared to his condition under the old-time prices, rich; and what were a few thousands of debt, which two or three crops would pay off, compared to the value of his estate? (He never thought that the value of property might come down, while the debt was a fixed fact.) He lived freely, for it was a liberal time, and liberal fashions were in vogue, and it was not for a Virginian to be behind others in hospitality and liberality. He required credit and security, and, of course, had to stand security in return. When the crash came, and no "accommodations" could be had, except in a few instances, and in those on the most ruinous terms, he fell an easy victim. They broke by neighborhoods. They usually indorsed for each other, and when one fell — like the child's play of putting bricks on end at equal distances, and dropping the first in line against the second, which fell against the third, and so on to the last — all fell; each got broke as security, and yet few or none were able to pay their own debts! . . .

There was one consolation — if the Virginian involved himself like a fool, he suffered himself to be sold out like a gentleman. When his card house of visionary projects came tumbling about his ears, the next question was, the one Webster plagiarized, "Where am I to go?" Those who had fathers, uncles, aunts, or other *dernier resorts* in Virginia limped back, with feathers molted and crestfallen, to the old stamping ground, carrying the returned Californian's fortune of ten thousand dollars — six bits in money, and the balance in experience.

Those who were in the condition of the prodigal (barring the father, the calf — the fatted one I mean — and the fiddle) had to turn their accomplishments to account; and many of them, having lost all by eating and drinking, sought the retributive justice from meat and drink, which might at least support them in poverty. Accordingly they kept tavern and made a barter of hospitality, a business the only disagreeable part of which was receiving the money, and the only one I know for which a man can eat and drink himself into qualification. And while I confess I never knew a Virginian, out of the state, to keep a bad tavern, I never knew one to draw a solvent breath from the time he opened house until death or the sheriff closed it.

Others again got to be not exactly overseers but some nameless thing, the duties of which were nearly analogous, for some more fortunate Virginian, who had escaped the wreck and who had got his former boon companion to live with him on board, or other wages, in some such relation that the friend was not often found at table at the dinings given to the neighbors, and had got to be called Mr. Flournoy instead of Bob, and slept in an outhouse in the yard, and only read the *Enquirer* of nights and Sundays.

Some of the younger scions that had been transplanted early and stripped of their foliage at a tender age, had been turned into birches for the corrective discipline of youth. Yes; many who had received academical or collegiate educations, disregarding the allurements of the highway, turning from the gala-day exercise of ditching, scorning the effeminate relaxation of splitting rails, heroically led the Forlorn Hope of the battle of life, the corps of pedagogues of country schools — *academies*, I beg pardon for *not* saying; for, under the Virginia economy, every crossroad log cabin, where boys were flogged from B–a–k–e–r to Constantinople, grew into the dignity of a sort of runt college; and the teacher vainly endeavored to hide the meanness of the calling beneath the sonorous *sobriquet* of Professor. . . .

I had a friend on whom this catastrophe descended. Tom Edmundson was buck of the first head — gay, witty, dashing, vain, proud, handsome, and volatile, and, withal, a dandy and lady's man to the last intent in particular. He had graduated at the University, and had just settled with his guardian, and received his patrimony of ten thousand dollars in money. Being a young gentleman of enterprise, he sought the alluring fields of Southwestern adventure, and found them in this state. Before he well knew the condition of his exchequer, he had made a permanent investment of one half of his fortune in cigars, champagne, trinkets, buggies, horses, and current expenses, including some small losses at poker, which game he patronized merely for amusement; and found that it diverted him a good deal, but diverted his cash much more. He invested the balance, on private information kindly given him, in "Choctaw Floats," a most lucrative investment it would have turned out but for the facts: 1. That the Indians never had any title; 2. The white man who kindly interposed to act as guardian for the Indians did not have the Indian title; 3. The land, left subject to entry if the "Floats" had been good, was not worth entering. "These imperfections off its head," I know of no fancy stock I would prefer to a "Choctaw Float." "Brief, brave, and glorious" was "Tom's young career." When Thomas found, as he did shortly, that he had bought five thousand dollars' worth of moonshine and had no title to it, he honestly informed his landlord of the state of his "fiscality," and that worthy kindly consented to take a new buggy, at half price, in payment of the old balance. The horse, a nick-tailed trotter, Tom had raffled off, but omitting to require cash, the process of collection resulted in his getting the price of one chance — the winner of the horse magnanimously paying his subscription. The rest either had gambling offsets, else were not prepared just at any one particular given moment to pay up, though always ready generally and in a general way.

Unlike his namesake, Tom and his landlady were not — for a sufficient reason — very gracious; and so, the only common bond, Tom's money, being gone, Tom received "notice to quit" in regular form.

In the hurly-burly of the times I lost sight of Tom for a considerable period. One day, as I was traveling over the hills in Greene, by a crossroad leading me near a country mill, I stopped to get water at a spring at the bottom of the hill. Clambering up the hill, after remounting, the summit of it brought me to a view, on the other side, through the bushes, of a log country schoolhouse, the door being wide open, and who did I see but Tom Edmundson, dressed as fine as ever, sitting back in an armchair, one thumb in his waistcoat armhole, the other hand brandishing a long switch, or rather pole. As I approached a little nearer I heard him speak out: "Sir — Thomas Jefferson, of Virginia, was the author of the Declaration of Independence — mind that. I thought everybody knew that — even the Georgians." Just then he saw me coming through the bushes and entering the path that led by the door. Suddenly he broke from the chair of state, and the door was slammed to, and I heard some one of the boys, as I passed the door, say, "Tell him he can't come in — the master's sick." This was the last I ever saw of Tom. I understand he afterwards moved to Louisiana, where he married a rich French widow, having first, however, to fight a duel with one of her sons, whose opposition could n't be appeased until some such expiatory sacrifice to the manes of his worthy father was attempted; which failing, he made rather a *lame* apology for his zealous indiscretion, — the poor fellow could make no other, — for Tom had unfortunately fixed him for visiting his mother on crutches the balance of his life.

One thing I will say for the Virginians — I never knew one of them, under any pressure, to extemporize a profession. The

TOM EDMUNDSON AS SCHOOLMASTER

Reproduction of one of the original illustrations of "Flush Times in Alabama and Mississippi"

sentiment of reverence for the mysteries of medicine and law was too large for deliberate quackery; as to the pulpit, a man might as well do his starving without the hypocrisy. But others were not so nice. I have known them to rush, when the wolf was after them, from the countinghouse or the plantation into a doctor's shop or a law office, as if those places were the sanctuaries from the avenger; some pretended to be doctors that did not know a liver from a gizzard, administering medicine by the guess, without knowing enough of pharmacy to tell whether the stuff exhibited in the big-bellied blue, red, and green bottles at the show windows of the apothecary's shop was given by the drop or the half pint.

Divers left, but what became of them, I never knew any more than they know what becomes of the sora after frost. Many were the instances of suffering; of pitiable misfortune, involving and crushing whole families; of pride abased; of honorable sensibilities wounded; of the provision for old age destroyed; of hopes of manhood overcast; of independence dissipated and the poor victim, without help, or hope, or sympathy, forced to petty shifts for a bare subsistence, and a ground-scuffle for what in happier days he threw away. But there were too many examples of this sort for the expenditure of a useless compassion; just as the surgeon after a battle grows case-hardened from an excess of objects of pity.

# POETS

## ST. GEORGE TUCKER

[St. George Tucker was born in Bermuda in 1752. He came early to Virginia and was educated at William and Mary College, after which he was called to the bar. Tucker served in the Virginia legislature, but won his chief distinction as professor of law in William and Mary College. In addition to composing fugitive poems, of which the one here given is the best known, he wrote several political and legal works of note. He died in 1828.]

## RESIGNATION

Days of my youth,
   Ye have glided away;
Hairs of my youth,
   Ye are frosted and gray;
Eyes of my youth,
   Your keen sight is no more;
Cheeks of my youth,
   Ye are furrowed all o'er;
Strength of my youth,
   All your vigor is gone;
Thoughts of my youth,
   Your gay visions are flown.

Days of my youth,
   I wish not your recall;
Hairs of my youth,
   I'm content ye should fall;

Eyes of my youth,
    You much evil have seen;
Cheeks of my youth,
    Bathed in tears have you been;
Thoughts of my youth,
    You have led me astray;
Strength of my youth,
    Why lament your decay?

Days of my age,
    Ye will shortly be past;
Pains of my age,
    Yet awhile ye can last;
Joys of my age,
    In true wisdom delight;
Eyes of my age,
    Be religion your light;
Thoughts of my age,
    Dread ye not the cold sod;
Hopes of my age,
    Be ye fixed on your God.

## FRANCIS SCOTT KEY

[Francis Scott Key was born in Frederick County, Maryland, in 1780. After being educated at St. John's College, Annapolis, he began the practice of law in Washington, where he died in 1843. After his death a volume of his poems was published, but as it consists largely of occasional pieces not originally intended for publication, it has added little to his fame, and "The Star-Spangled Banner" remains his best-known production.]

FRANCIS SCOTT KEY

## THE STAR-SPANGLED BANNER

O say, can you see, by the dawn's early light,
　What so proudly we hail'd at the twilight's last gleaming,
Whose broad stripes and bright stars, through the perilous fight,
　O'er the ramparts we watched were so gallantly streaming?

And the rocket's red glare, the bomb bursting in air,
Gave proof through the night that our flag was still there;
O! say, does that star-spangled banner yet wave
O'er the land of the free, and the home of the brave?

On the shore, dimly seen through the mists of the deep,
   Where the foe's haughty host in dread silence reposes,
What is that, which the breeze, o'er the towering steep
   As it fitfully blows, half conceals, half discloses?
Now it catches the gleam of the morning's first beam
In full glory reflected, now shines on the stream;
'T is the star-spangled banner; O! long may it wave
O'er the land of the free, and the home of the brave!

And where is that band who so vauntingly swore
   That the havoc of war and the battle's confusion
A home and a country should leave us no more?
   Their blood has wash'd out their foul footsteps' pollution.
No refuge could save the hireling and slave
From the terror of flight, or the gloom of the grave;
And the star-spangled banner in triumph doth wave
O'er the land of the free, and the home of the brave.

O! thus be it ever! when freemen shall stand
   Between their lov'd homes and the war's desolation!
Blest with vict'ry and peace, may the heav'n-rescued land
   Praise the power that hath made and preserved us a nation.
Then conquer we must, when our cause it is just,
And this be our motto — *In God is our trust*,
And the star-spangled banner in triumph shall wave
O'er the land of the free, and the home of the brave.

## RICHARD HENRY WILDE

[Richard Henry Wilde was born in Dublin, Ireland, in 1789, and died in New Orleans in 1847. When he was a boy his family came to America and settled in Baltimore. Upon the death of his father he removed to Georgia, where he studied law and entered politics, eventually becoming for several terms a member of Congress. During a stay in Europe from 1835 to 1840 he did considerable study in Dante and Tasso, and helped to discover Giotto's portrait of the first-named poet. On his return he settled in New Orleans, where he became professor of law in the University of Louisiana. Meanwhile he had made a reputation for himself as a poet by poems contributed to newspapers and magazines, which he did not collect during his life into book form.]

### MY LIFE IS LIKE THE SUMMER ROSE

My life is like the summer rose,
    That opens to the morning sky,
But, ere the shades of evening close,
    Is scattered on the ground — to die!
Yet on the rose's humble bed
The sweetest dews of night are shed,
As if she wept the waste to see —
But none shall weep a tear for me!

My life is like the autumn leaf
    That trembles in the moon's pale ray:
Its hold is frail — its date is brief,
    Restless — and soon to pass away!
Yet, ere that leaf shall fall and fade,
The parent tree will mourn its shade,
The winds bewail the leafless tree —
But none shall breathe a sigh for me!

My life is like the prints, which feet
    Have left on Tampa's desert strand;
Soon as the rising tide shall beat,
    All trace will vanish from the sand;
Yet, as if grieving to efface
All vestige of the human race,
On that lone shore loud moans the sea —
But none, alas! shall mourn for me!


## TO THE MOCKING-BIRD

Winged mimic of the woods! thou motley fool!
    Who shall thy gay buffoonery describe?
Thine ever-ready notes of ridicule
    Pursue thy fellows still with jest and gibe.
    Wit, sophist, songster, Yorick of thy tribe,
Thou sportive satirist of Nature's school,
    To thee the palm of scoffing we ascribe,
Arch-mocker and mad Abbot of Misrule!
    For such thou art by day — but all night long
Thou pourest a soft, sweet, pensive, solemn strain,
    As if thou didst in this thy moonlight song
Like to the melancholy Jacques complain,
    Musing on falsehood, folly, vice, and wrong,
And sighing for thy motley coat again.


## EDWARD COATE PINKNEY

[Edward Coate Pinkney was born in London in 1802, while his
father was United States Commissioner to Great Britain. On his return to America, he was put to school in Baltimore, and later entered
the navy as midshipman. He resigned from the navy to engage in
the practice of law, but his health failed and he died in Baltimore

in 1828, at the age of twenty-six. His small volume of poetry published in 1825 contained a few pieces which not only won him considerable praise in his lifetime but are sure of immortality among American lyrics.]

### SONG

We break the glass, whose sacred wine
    To some beloved health we drain,
Lest future pledges, less divine,
    Should e'er the hallowed toy profane;
And thus I broke a heart, that poured
    Its tide of feeling out for thee,
In drafts, by after-times deplored,
    Yet dear to memory.

But still the old impassioned ways
    And habits of my mind remain,
And still unhappy light displays
    Thine image chambered in my brain,
And still it looks as when the hours
    Went by like flights of singing birds,
Or that soft chain of spoken flowers,
    And airy gems, thy words.

### A SERENADE

Look out upon the stars, my love,
    And shame them with thine eyes,
On which, than on the lights above,
    There hang more destinies.
Night's beauty is the harmony
    Of blending shades and light;
Then, Lady, up, — look out, and be
    A sister to the night! —

Sleep not! — thine image wakes for aye,
  Within my watching breast:
Sleep not! — from her soft sleep should fly,
  Who robs all hearts of rest.
Nay, Lady, from thy slumbers break,
  And make this darkness gay,
With looks, whose brightness well might make
  Of darker nights a day.


## A HEALTH

I fill this cup to one made up
  Of loveliness alone,
A woman, of her gentle sex
  The seeming paragon;
To whom the better elements
  And kindly stars have given
A form so fair, that, like the air,
  'T is less of earth than heaven.

Her every tone is music's own,
  Like those of morning birds,
And something more than melody
  Dwells ever in her words;
The coinage of her heart are they,
  And from her lips each flows
As one may see the burthened bee
  Forth issue from the rose.

Affections are as thoughts to her,
  The measures of her hours;
Her feelings have the fragrancy,
  The freshness, of young flowers;

And lovely passions, changing oft,
    So fill her, she appears
The image of themselves by turns, —
    The idol of past years!

Of her bright face one glance will trace
    A picture on the brain,
And of her voice in echoing hearts
    A sound must long remain;
But memory such as mine of her
    So very much endears,
When death is nigh, my latest sigh
    Will not be life's, but hers.

I fill this cup to one made up
    Of loveliness alone,
A woman, of her gentle sex
    The seeming paragon —
Her health! and would on earth there stood
    Some more of such a frame,
That life might be all poetry,
    And weariness a name.

## MIRABEAU BUONAPARTE LAMAR

[Mirabeau Buonaparte Lamar was born in Georgia in 1798 and died in 1859 at Richmond, Texas. After several years of farming and business life, Lamar became, in 1828, editor of the *Columbus Independent*. In 1835 he emigrated to Texas, and for the remainder of his days lived a picturesque life in that state. He served in the Texan war for independence, and in the Mexican War. Later in life he received diplomatic appointments to Argentina, Costa Rica, and Nicaragua. His volume of poems entitled "Verse Memorials" was published in 1857.]

## THE DAUGHTER OF MENDOZA

O lend to me, sweet nightingale,
   Your music by the fountains,
And lend to me your cadences,
   O river of the mountains!
That I may sing my gay brunette,
A diamond spark in coral set,
Gem for a prince's coronet —
.  The daughter of Mendoza.

How brilliant is the morning star!
   The evening star, how tender!
The light of both is in her eye,
   Their softness and their splendor.
But for the lash that shades their light
They were too dazzling for the sight;
And when she shuts them, all is night —
   The daughter of Mendoza.

O! ever bright and beauteous one,
   Bewildering and beguiling,
The lute is in thy silvery tones,
   The rainbow in thy smiling.
And thine is, too, o'er hill and dell,
The bounding of the young gazelle,
The arrow's flight and ocean's swell —
   Sweet daughter of Mendoza!

What though, perchance, we meet no more? —
   What though too soon we sever?
Thy form will float like emerald light,
   Before my vision ever.

For who can see and then forget
The glories of my gay brunette?
Thou art too bright a star to set —
    Sweet daughter of Mendoza!


## ALBERT PIKE

[Albert Pike was a New Englander, born in Boston in 1809, who settled in the Southwest. The larger part of the time he lived in Arkansas, where he was editor, lawyer, and soldier. After the Civil War, in which he served on the Southern side, he moved to Washington, where he practiced law. There he died in 1891.]


## TO THE MOCKING BIRD

Thou glorious mocker of the world! I hear
    Thy many voices ringing through the glooms
Of these green solitudes; and all the clear,
Bright joyance of their song enthralls the ear,
    And floods the heart. Over the spherèd tombs
Of vanished nations rolls thy music-tide:
    No light from History's starlit page illumes
The memory of these nations; they have died:
    None care for them but thou; and thou mayst sing
    O'er me, perhaps, as now thy clear notes ring
Over their bones by whom thou once wast deified.

Glad scorner of all cities! Thou dost leave
    The world's mad turmoil and incessant din,
Where none in others' honesty believe,
Where the old sigh, the young turn gray and grieve,
    Where misery gnaws the maiden's heart within.
Thou fleest far into the dark green woods,
    Where, with thy flood of music, thou canst win

Their heart to harmony, and where intrudes
    No discord on thy melodies.  Oh, where,
    Among the sweet musicians of the air,
Is one so dear as thou to these old solitudes?


Ha! what a burst was that! The Æolian strain
    Goes floating through the tangled passages
Of the still woods; and now it comes again,
A multitudinous melody, like a rain
    Of glassy music under echoing trees,
Close by a ringing lake.  It wraps the soul
    With a bright harmony of happiness,
Even as a gem is wrapped when round it roll
    Thin waves of crimson flame, till we become,
    With the excess of perfect pleasure, dumb,
And pant like a swift runner clinging to the goal.


I cannot love the man who doth not love,
    As men love light, the song of happy birds;
For the first visions that my boy-heart wove,
To fill its sleep with, were that I did rove
    Through the fresh woods, what time the snowy herds
Of morning clouds shrunk from the advancing sun,
    Into the depths of Heaven's blue heart, as words
From the poet's lips float gently, one by one,
    And vanish in the human heart; and then
    I reveled in such songs, and sorrowed, when,
With noon-heat overwrought, the music-gush was done.


I would, sweet bird, that I might live with thee,
    Amid the eloquent grandeur of these shades,
Alone with Nature! — but it may not be:
I have to struggle with the stormy sea

Of human life until existence fades
Into death's darkness. Thou wilt sing and soar
Through the thick woods and shadow-checkered glades,
While pain and sorrow cast no dimness o'er
The brilliance of thy heart; but I must wear,
As now, my garments of regret and care,
As penitents of old their galling sackcloth wore.

Yet, why complain? What though fond hopes deferred
Have overshadowed Life's green paths with gloom?
Content's soft music is not all unheard:
There is a voice sweeter than thine, sweet bird,
To welcome me, within my humble home;
There is an eye, with love's devotion bright,
The darkness of existence to illume.
Then why complain? When Death shall cast his blight
Over the spirit, my cold bones shall rest
Beneath these trees; and from thy swelling breast,
Over them pour thy song, like a rich flood of light.

## PHILIP PENDLETON COOKE

[Philip Pendleton Cooke was born in Martinsburg, Virginia, in 1816. After graduating from Princeton he began the practice of law with his father, but spent most of his time in his two delights — hunting and literary pursuits. He was a man with lyrical talent who failed of full development through failure to take his poetic gift seriously, habits of procrastination, and frail health. He died in 1850.]

### FLORENCE VANE

I loved thee long and dearly,
Florence Vane;
My life's bright dream, and early,
Hath come again;

I renew, in my fond vision,
        My heart's dear pain,
My hope, and thy derision,
        Florence Vane.


The ruin lone and hoary,
        The ruin old,
Where thou didst hark my story,
        At even told, —
That spot — the hues Elysian
        Of sky and plain —
I treasure in my vision,
        Florence Vane.


Thou wast lovelier than the roses
        In their prime;
Thy voice excelled the closes
        Of sweetest rime;
Thy heart was as a river
        Without a main.
Would I had loved thee never,
        Florence Vane!


But, fairest, coldest wonder!
        Thy glorious clay
Lieth the green sod under —
        Alas the day!
And it boots not to remember
        Thy disdain—
To quicken love's pale ember,
        Florence Vane.

The lilies of the valley
    By young graves weep,
The pansies love to dally
    Where maidens sleep;
May their bloom, in beauty vying,
    Never wane
Where thine earthly part is lying,
    Florence Vane!

## LIFE IN THE AUTUMN WOODS

Summer has gone!
And fruitful autumn has advanced so far,
That there is warmth, not heat, in the broad sun,
And you may look with steadfast gaze upon
    The ardors of his car;
The stealthy frosts, whom his spent looks embolden,
    Are making the green leaves golden.

What a brave splendor
Is in the October air! How rich and clear —
How life-full, and all joyous! We must render
Love to the springtime, with its sproutings tender,
    As to a child quite dear —
But autumn is a noon, prolonged, of glory —
    A manhood not yet hoary.

I love the woods
In this best season of the liberal year;
I love to haunt their whispering solitudes,
And give myself to melancholy moods,
    With no intruder near;
And find strange lessons, as I sit and ponder,
    In every natural wonder.

But not alone
As Shakespeare's melancholy courtier loved Ardennes,
Love I the autumn forest ; and I own
I would not oft have mused as he, but flown
    To hunt with Amiens —
And little recked, as up the bold deer bounded,
    Of the sad creature wounded.


    That gentle knight,
Sir William Wortley, weary of his part,
In painted pomps, which he could read aright,
Built Warncliffe lodge — for that he did delight
    To hear the belling hart.
It was a gentle taste, but its sweet sadness
    Yields to the hunter's madness.


    What passionate
And wild delight is in the proud swift chase !
Go out what time the lark, at heaven's red gate,
Soars joyously singing — quite infuriate
    With the high pride of his place ;
What time the unrisen sun arrays the morning
    In its first bright adorning.


    Hark the shrill horn —
As sweet to hear as any clarion —
Piercing with silver call the ear of morn ;
And mark the steeds, stout Curtal, and Topthorn,
    And Greysteil, and the Don —
Each one of them his fiery mood displaying
    With pawing and with neighing.

Urge your swift horse
After the crying hounds in this fresh hour—
Vanquish high hills—stem perilous streams perforce—
Where the glades ope give free wings to your course—
And you will know the power
Of the brave chase—and how of griefs the sorest,
A cure is in the forest.


Or stalk the deer:
The same red fires of dawn illume the hills,
The gladdest sounds are crowding on your ear,
There is a life in all the atmosphere—
Your very nature fills
With the fresh hour, as up the hills aspiring,
You climb with limbs untiring.


It is a fair
And pleasant sight, to see the mountain stag,
With the long sweep of his swift walk, repair
To join his brothers; or the plethoric bear
Lying on some high crag,
With pinky eyes half closed, but broad head shaking,
As gadflies keep him waking.


And these you see,
And, seeing them, you travel to their death,
With a slow stealthy step from tree to tree—
Noting the wind, however faint it be;
The hunter draws a breath
In times like these, which he will say repays him
For all the care that waylays him.

A strong joy fills —
A rapture far beyond the tongue's cold power —
My heart in golden autumn fills and thrills!
And I would rather stalk the breezy hills —
    Descending to my bower
Nightly by the bold spirit of health attended —
    Than pine where life is splendid.


## THEODORE O'HARA

[Theodore O'Hara was born of Irish parentage at Danville, Kentucky, in 1820. Upon graduating from St. Joseph's College, at Bardstown, Kentucky, he studied law. After serving in the Mexican War, he was editor of a paper in Frankfort, Kentucky, and later of one in Mobile, Alabama. He participated in the Civil War, and, after its close, he engaged in farming in Alabama, where he died in 1867. O'Hara has left, so far as is known, but two poems, " The Bivouac of the Dead " and " The Old Pioneer."]


### THE BIVOUAC OF THE DEAD

The muffled drum's sad roll has beat
    The soldier's last tattoo:
No more on Life's parade shall meet
    That brave and fallen few.
On Fame's eternal camping-ground
    Their silent tents are spread,
And Glory guards, with solemn round,
    The bivouac of the dead.

No rumor of the foe's advance
    Now swells upon the wind;
No troubled thought at midnight haunts
    Of loved ones left behind;

No vision of the morrow's strife
    The warrior's dream alarms;
No braying horn nor screaming fife
    At dawn shall call to arms.


Their shivered swords are red with rust,
    Their plumèd heads are bowed;
Their haughty banner, trailed in dust,
    Is now their martial shroud.
And plenteous funeral tears have washed
    The red stains from each brow,
And the proud forms, by battle gashed,
    Are free from anguish now.


The neighboring troop, the flashing blade,
    The bugle's stirring blast,
The charge, the dreadful cannonade,
    The din and shout, are past;
Nor war's wild note nor glory's peal
    Shall thrill with fierce delight
Those breasts that nevermore may feel
    The rapture of the fight.


Like the fierce northern hurricane
    That sweeps his great plateau,
Flushed with the triumph yet to gain,
    Came down the serried foe.
Who heard the thunder of the fray
    Break o'er the field beneath,
Knew well the watchword of that day
    Was " Victory or Death."

Long had the doubtful conflict raged
　O'er all that stricken plain,
For never fiercer fight had waged
　The vengeful blood of Spain;
And still the storm of battle blew,
　Still swelled the gory tide;
Not long, our stout old chieftain knew,
　Such odds his strength could bide.


'T was in that hour his stern command
　Called to a martyr's grave
The flower of his beloved land,
　The nation's flag to save.
By rivers of their fathers' gore
　His first-born laurels grew,
And well he deemed the sons would pour
　Their lives for glory too.


Full many a norther's breath has swept
　O'er Angostura's plain,
And long the pitying sky has wept
　Above its moldered slain.
The raven's scream, or eagle's flight,
　Or shepherd's pensive lay,
Alone awakes each sullen height
　That frowned o'er that dread fray.


Sons of the Dark and Bloody Ground,
　Ye must not slumber there,
Where stranger steps and tongues resound
　Along the heedless air.

Your own proud land's heroic soil
    Shall be your fitter grave:
She claims from war his richest spoil —
    The ashes of her brave.


Thus 'neath their parent turf they rest,
    Far from the gory field,
Borne to a Spartan mother's breast
    On many a bloody shield;
The sunshine of their native sky
    Smiles sadly on them here,
And kindred eyes and hearts watch by
    The heroes' sepulcher.


Rest on, embalmed and sainted dead!
    Dear as the blood ye gave;
No impious footstep here shall tread
    The herbage of your grave;
Nor shall your glory be forgot
    While Fame her record keeps,
Or Honor points the hallowed spot
    Where valor proudly sleeps.


Yon marble minstrel's voiceless stone
    In deathless song shall tell,
When many a vanished age hath flown,
    The story how ye fell;
Nor wreck, nor change, nor winter's blight,
    Nor Time's remorseless doom,
Shall dim one ray of glory's light
    That gilds your deathless tomb.

## ALEXANDER BEAUFORT MEEK

[Alexander Beaufort Meek was born in Columbia, South Carolina, in 1814. At an early age he removed with his parents to Alabama, where he became lawyer, politician, editor. After the Civil War he removed to Columbus, Mississippi, where he died, in 1865. Besides poetry, he published a volume of orations and sketches.]

### A SONG

The bluebird is whistling in Hillibee grove, —
  *Terra-re! Terra-re!*
His mate is repeating the tale of his love, —
  *Terra-re!*
  But never that song,
  As its notes fleet along,
So sweet and so soft in its raptures can be,
As thy low-whispered words, young chieftain, to me.

Deep down in the dell is a clear crystal stream,
  *Terra-re! Terra-re!*
Where, scattered like stars, the white pebbles gleam,
  *Terra-re!*
  But deep in my breast,
  Sweet thoughts are at rest,
No eye but my own in their beauty shall see;
They are dreams, happy dreams, young chieftain, of thee.

The honey-bud blooms when the springtime is green,
  *Terra-re! Terra-re!*
And the fawn with the roe, on the hilltop is seen,
  *Terra-re!*

But 't is spring all the year,
When my loved one is near,
And his smiles are like bright beaming blossoms to me,
Oh! to rove o'er the hilltop, young chieftain, with thee.

## LAND OF THE SOUTH

Land of the South! — imperial land! —
  How proud thy mountains rise! —
How sweet thy scenes on every hand!
  How fair thy covering skies!
But not for this, — oh, not for these,
  I love thy fields to roam, —
Thou hast a dearer spell to me, —
  Thou art my native home!

Thy rivers roll their liquid wealth,
  Unequaled to the sea, —
Thy hills and valleys bloom with health,
  And green with verdure be!
But, not for thy proud ocean streams,
  Not for thine azure dome, —
Sweet, sunny South! — I cling to thee, —
  Thou art my native home!

I 've stood beneath Italia's clime,
  Beloved of tale and song, —
On Helvyn's hills, proud and sublime,
  Where nature's wonders throng;
By Tempe's classic sunlit streams,
  Where gods, of old, did roam, —
But ne'er have found so fair a land
  As thou — my native home!

And thou hast prouder glories too,
   Than nature ever gave, —
Peace sheds o'er thee, her genial dew,
   And Freedom's pinions wave, —
Fair science flings her pearls around,
   Religion lifts her dome, —
These, these endear thee, to my heart, —
   My own, loved native home!

And " heaven's best gift to man " is thine,
   God bless thy rosy girls! —
Like sylvan flowers, they sweetly shine, —
   Their hearts are pure as pearls!
And grace and goodness circle them,
   Where'er their footsteps roam, —
How can I then, whilst loving them,
   Not love my native home!

Land of the South! — imperial land! —
   Then here's a health to thee, —
Long as thy mountain barriers stand,
   May'st thou be blessed and free! —
May dark dissension's banner ne'er
   Wave o'er thy fertile loam, —
But should it come, there's one will die,
   To save his native home!

## THE MOCKING BIRD

From the vale, what music ringing,
   Fills the bosom of the night;
On the sense, entranced, flinging
   Spells of witchery and delight!

O'er magnolia, lime and cedar,
　From yon locust top, it swells,
Like the chant of serenader,
　Or the rimes of silver bells!
　　Listen! dearest, listen to it!
　　　Sweeter sounds were never heard!
　　'T is the song of that wild poet —
　　　Mime and minstrel — Mocking Bird.

See him, swinging in his glory,
　On yon topmost bending limb!
Caroling his amorous story,
　Like some wild crusader's hymn!
Now it faints in tones delicious
　As the first low vow of love!
Now it bursts in swells capricious,
　All the moonlit vale above!
　　Listen! dearest, etc.

Why is 't thus, this sylvan Petrarch
　Pours all night his serenade?
'T is for some proud woodland Laura,
　His sad sonnets all are made!
But he changes now his measure —
　Gladness bubbling from his mouth —
Jest, and gibe, and mimic pleasure —
　Winged Anacreon of the South!
　　Listen! dearest, etc.

Bird of music, wit and gladness,
　Troubadour of sunny climes,
Disenchanter of all sadness, —
　Would thine art were in my rimes.

O'er the heart that's beating by me,
   I would weave a spell divine;
Is there aught she could deny me,
    Drinking in such strains as thine?
      Listen! dearest, etc.

## HENRY ROOTES JACKSON

[Henry Rootes Jackson was born of English parentage in Athens, Georgia, in 1820, and died in Savannah in 1898. After graduating from Yale he practiced law in Georgia. He saw service in both the Mexican War and the Civil War. In 1853 he accepted a diplomatic appointment to Austria; in 1885 he was honored with a similar appointment to Mexico. His contribution to Southern poetry is a single volume of poems.]

### THE RED OLD HILLS OF GEORGIA

The red old hills of Georgia!
   So bald, and bare, and bleak —
Their memory fills my spirit
   With thoughts I cannot speak.
They have no robe of verdure,
   Stript naked to the blast;
And yet, of all the varied earth,
   I love them best at last.

The red old hills of Georgia!
   My heart is on them now;
Where, fed from golden streamlets,
   Oconee's waters flow!
I love them with devotion,
   Though washed so bleak and bare; —
Oh! can my spirit e'er forget
   The warm hearts dwelling there?

I love them for the living, —
　　The generous, kind, and gay ;
And for the dead who slumber
　　Within their breasts of clay.
I love them for the bounty,
　　Which cheers the social hearth ;
I love them for their rosy girls —
　　The fairest on the earth !


The red old hills of Georgia !
　　Oh ! where, upon the face
Of earth, is freedom's spirit
　　More bright in any race ? —
In Switzerland and Scotland
　　Each patriot breast it fills,
But oh ! it blazes brighter yet
　　Among our Georgia hills !


And where, upon their surface,
　　Is heart to feeling dead ? —
Oh ! when has needy stranger
　　Gone from those hills unfed ?
There bravery and kindness,
　　For aye, go hand in hand,
Upon your washed and naked hills,
　　" My own, my native land ! "


The red old hills of Georgia
　　I never can forget ;
Amid life's joys and sorrows,
　　My heart is on them yet ; —

And when my course is ended,
　　When life her web has wove,
Oh! may I then, beneath those hills,
　　Lie close to them I love!


## MY WIFE AND CHILD

The tattoo beats; — the lights are gone; —
　　The camp around in slumber lies; —
The night, with solemn pace, moves on; —
　　The shadows thicken o'er the skies; —
But sleep my weary eyes hath flown,
　　And sad, uneasy thoughts arise.


I think of thee, oh! dearest one!
　　Whose love mine early life hath blest; —
Of thee and him — our baby son —
　　Who slumbers on thy gentle breast; —
God of the tender, frail, and lone,
　　Oh! guard that little sleeper's rest!


And hover, gently hover near
　　To her, whose watchful eye is wet —
The mother, wife, the doubly dear,
　　In whose young heart have freshly met
Two streams of love so deep and clear —
　　And cheer her drooping spirit yet!


Now, as she kneels before thy throne,
　　Oh! teach her, Ruler of the skies!
That while, by thy behest alone,

Earth's mightiest powers fall or rise,
No tear is wept to thee unknown,
  Nor hair is lost, nor sparrow dies!


That thou canst stay the ruthless hand
  Of dark disease, and soothe its pain;
That only by thy stern command
  The battle's lost, the soldier's slain;
That from the distant sea or land
  Thou bring'st the wanderer home again!


And when upon her pillow lone
  Her tear-wet cheek is sadly pressed,
May happier visions beam upon
  The brightening currents of her breast, —
Nor frowning look, nor angry tone,
  Disturb the sabbath of her rest!


Whatever fate those forms may throw,
  Loved with a passion almost wild —
By day, by night — in joy, or woe —
  By fears oppressed, or hopes beguiled —
From every danger, every foe,
  Oh! God! protect my wife and child!


## JAMES MATTHEWS LEGARÉ

[James Matthews Legaré was born in Charleston, South Carolina, in 1823. Very little is known of him beyond the fact that he invented several appliances which failing health prevented him from perfecting, and that he contributed poetry to the magazines. His single volume of verse, "Orta-Undis, and Other Poems," was published in 1848. He died in Aiden, South Carolina, in 1859.]

## TO A LILY

Go bow thy head in gentle spite,
Thou lily white.
For she who spies thee waving here,
With thee in beauty can compare
As day with night.

Soft are thy leaves and white : her arms
Boast whiter charms.
Thy stem prone bent with loveliness
Of maiden grace possesseth less :
Therein she charms.

Thou in thy lake dost see
Thyself : so she
Beholds her image in her eyes
Reflected.  Thus did Venus rise
From out the sea.

Inconsolate, bloom not again,
Thou rival vain
Of her whose charms have thine outdone :
Whose purity might spot the sun,
And make thy leaf a stain.

## HAW BLOSSOMS

While yesterevening, through the vale
Descending from my cottage door
I strayed, how cool and fresh a look
All nature wore.

The calmias and goldenrods,
And tender blossoms of the haw,
Like maidens seated in the wood,
Demure, I saw.

The recent drops upon their leaves
Shone brighter than the bluest eyes,
And filled the little sheltered dell
Their fragrant sighs.

Their pliant arms they interlaced,
As pleasant canopies they were:
Their blossoms swung against my cheek
Like braids of hair.

And when I put their boughs aside
And stooped to pass, from overhead
The little agitated things
A shower shed

Of tears. Then thoughtfully I spoke;
Well represent ye maidenhood,
Sweet flowers. Life is to the young
A shady wood.

And therein some like goldenrods,
For grosser purposes designed,
A gay existence lead, but leave
No germ behind.

And others like the calmias,
On cliff-sides inaccessible,
Bloom paramount, the vale with sweets
Yet never fill.

But underneath the glossy leaves,
When, working out the perfect law,
The blossoms white and fragrant still
Drop from the haw ;

Like worthy deeds in silence wrought
And secret, through the lapse of years,
In clusters pale and delicate
The fruit appears.

In clusters pale and delicate
But waxing heavier each day,
Until the many-colored leaves
Drift from the spray.

Then pendulous, like amethysts
And rubies, purple ripe and red,
Wherewith God's feathered pensioners
In flocks are fed.

Therefore, sweet reader of this rime,
Be unto thee examples high
Not calmias and goldenrods
That scentless die :

But the meek blossoms of the haw,
That fragrant are wherever wind
The forest paths, and perishing
Leave fruits behind.

## WILLIAM GILMORE SIMMS

[For the details of Simms's life see the sketch given (page 104) in connection with selections from his prose romances. In poetry he was prolific, but his hand was too heavy for verse, and his poetic work ranks distinctly lower than his prose writings.]

### OH, THE SWEET SOUTH!

Oh, the sweet South! the sunny, sunny South!
    Land of true feeling, land forever mine!
I drink the kisses of her rosy mouth,
    And my heart swells as with a draft of wine;
She brings me blessings of maternal love;
    I have her smile which hallows all my toil;
Her voice persuades, her generous smiles approve,
    She sings me from the sky and from the soil!
Oh! by her lonely pines, that wave and sigh —
    Oh! by her myriad flowers, that bloom and fade —
By all the thousand beauties of her sky,
    And the sweet solace of her forest shade,
        She's mine — she's ever mine —
        Nor will I aught resign
Of what she gives me, mortal or divine:
        Will sooner part
        With life, hope, heart —
Will die — before I fly!

Oh! love is hers — such love as ever glows
    In souls where leaps affection's living tide;
She is all fondness to her friends — to foes
    She glows a thing of passion, strength, and pride;
She feels no tremors when the danger's nigh,
    But the fight over, and the victory won,

WOODLANDS, THE COUNTRY ESTATE OF WILLIAM GILMORE SIMMS

How, with strange fondness, turns her loving eye,
    In tearful welcome, on each gallant son!
Oh! by her virtues of the cherished past —
    By all her hopes of what the future brings —
I glory that my lot with her is cast,
    And my soul flushes, and exultant sings:
        She's mine — she's ever mine —
        For her I will resign
All precious things — all placed upon her shrine;
        Will freely part
        With life, hope, heart, —
Will die — do aught but fly!


## THE SWAMP FOX

We follow where the Swamp Fox guides,
    His friends and merry men are we;
And when the troop of Tarleton rides,
    We burrow in the cypress tree.
The turfy hammock is our bed,
    Our home is in the red deer's den,
Our roof, the tree top overhead,
    For we are wild and hunted men.


We fly by day and shun its light,
    But, prompt to strike the sudden blow,
We mount and start with early night,
    And through the forest track our foe.
And soon he hears our chargers leap,
    The flashing saber blinds his eyes,
And ere he drives away his sleep,
    And rushes from his camp, he dies.

Free bridle bit, good gallant steed,
  That will not ask a kind caress
To swim the Santee at our need,
  When on his heels the foemen press, —
The true heart and the ready hand,
  The spirit stubborn to be free,
The twisted bore, the smiting brand, —
  And we are Marion's men, you see.


Now light the fire and cook the meal,
  The last, perhaps, that we shall taste;
I hear the Swamp Fox round us steal,
  And that's a sign we move in haste.
He whistles to the scouts, and hark!
  You hear his order calm and low.
Come, wave your torch across the dark,
  And let us see the boys that go.


We may not see their forms again,
  God help 'em, should they find the strife!
For they are strong and fearless men,
  And make no coward terms for life;
They'll fight as long as Marion bids,
  And when he speaks the word to shy,
Then, not till then, they turn their steeds,
  Through thickening shade and swamp to fly.


Now stir the fire and lie at ease, —
  The scouts are gone, and on the brush
I see the Colonel bend his knees,
  To take his slumbers too.  But hush!

He's praying, comrades; 'tis not strange;
 The man that's fighting day by day
May well, when night comes, take a change,
 And down upon his knees to pray.


Break up that hoecake, boys, and hand
 The sly and silent jug that's there;
I love not it should idly stand
 When Marion's men have need of cheer.
'Tis seldom that our luck affords
 A stuff like this we just have quaffed,
And dry potatoes on our boards
 May always call for such a draft.


Now pile the brush and roll the log;
 Hard pillow, but a soldier's head
That's half the time in brake and bog
 Must never think of softer bed.
The owl is hooting to the night,
 The cooter crawling o'er the bank,
And in that pond the flashing light
 Tells where the alligator sank.


What! 'tis the signal! start so soon,
 And through the Santee swamp so deep,
Without the aid of friendly moon,
 And we, Heaven help us! half asleep!
But courage, comrades! Marion leads,
 The Swamp Fox takes us out to-night;
So clear your swords and spur your steeds,
 There's goodly chance, I think, of fight.

We follow where the Swamp Fox guides,
    We leave the swamp and cypress tree,
Our spurs are in our coursers' sides,
    And ready for the strife are we.
The Tory camp is now in sight,
    And there he cowers within his den ;
He hears our shouts, he dreads the fight,
    He fears, and flies from Marion's men.


## EDGAR ALLAN POE

[For sketch of Poe's life see page 27.]


### TO HELEN

Helen, thy beauty is to me
    Like those Nicéan barks of yore,
That gently, o'er a perfumed sea,
    The weary, wayworn wanderer bore
    To his own native shore.


On desperate seas long wont to roam,
    Thy hyacinth hair, thy classic face,
Thy Naiad airs have brought me home
    To the glory that was Greece,
And the grandeur that was Rome.


Lo ! in yon brilliant window niche
    How statue-like I see thee stand,
    The agate lamp within thy hand !
Ah, Psyche, from the regions which
    Are Holy-Land !

POE'S ROOM AT THE UNIVERSITY OF VIRGINIA, NO. 13 WEST RANGE

*Upper picture*, the doorway of the room with the memorial tablet above it; *middle picture*, the arcade in which the room is located; *lower picture*, the interior of the room as it is at present with various relics relating to Poe

## ISRAFEL

In Heaven a spirit doth dwell
  "Whose heart-strings are a lute";
None sing so wildly well
As the angel Israfel,
And the giddy stars (so legends tell),
Ceasing their hymns, attend the spell
  Of his voice, all mute.

Tottering above
  In her highest noon,
  The enamored moon
Blushes with love,
  While, to listen, the red levin
  (With the rapid Pleiads, even,
  Which were seven,)
  Pauses in Heaven.

And they say (the starry choir
  And the other listening things)
That Israfeli's fire
Is owing to that lyre
  By which he sits and sings —
The trembling living wire
  Of those unusual strings.

But the skies that angel trod,
Where deep thoughts are a duty —
Where Love's a grown-up God —
  Where the Houri glances are
Imbued with all the beauty
  Which we worship in a star.

Therefore, thou art not wrong,
    Israfeli, who despisest
An unimpassioned song ;
To thee the laurels belong,
    Best bard, because the wisest !
Merrily live, and long !

The ecstasies above
    With thy burning measures suit —
Thy grief, thy joy, thy hate, thy love,
    With the fervor of thy lute —
    Well may the stars be mute !

Yes, Heaven is thine ; but this
    Is a world of sweets and sours ;
    Our flowers are merely — flowers,
And the shadow of thy perfect bliss
    Is the sunshine of ours.

If I could dwell
Where Israfel
    Hath dwelt, and he where I,
He might not sing so wildly well
    A mortal melody,
While a bolder note than this might swell
    From my lyre within the sky.


THE RAVEN

Once upon a midnight dreary, while I pondered, weak and
    weary,
Over many a quaint and curious volume of forgotten lore —
While I nodded, nearly napping, suddenly there came a tapping,

As of someone gently rapping, rapping at my chamber door.
"'Tis some visitor," I muttered, "tapping at my chamber
    door —
        Only this and nothing more."

Ah, distinctly I remember it was in the bleak December;
And each separate dying ember wrought its ghost upon the floor.
Eagerly I wished the morrow; — vainly I had sought to borrow
From my books surcease of sorrow — sorrow for the lost
    Lenore —
For the rare and radiant maiden whom the angels name
    Lenore —
        Nameless *here* forevermore.

And the silken, sad, uncertain rustling of each purple curtain
Thrilled me — filled me with fantastic terrors never felt before;
So that now, to still the beating of my heart, I stood repeating
"'Tis some visitor entreating entrance at my chamber door —
Some late visitor entreating entrance at my chamber door;
        This it is and nothing more."

Presently my soul grew stronger; hesitating then no longer,
"Sir," said I, "or Madam, truly your forgiveness I implore;
But the fact is I was napping, and so gently you came rapping,
And so faintly you came tapping, tapping at my chamber door,
That I scarce was sure I heard you" — here I opened wide
    the door; —
        Darkness there and nothing more.

Deep into that darkness peering, long I stood there wondering,
    fearing,
Doubting, dreaming dreams no mortal ever dared to dream
    before;

But the silence was unbroken, and the stillness gave no token,
And the only word there spoken was the whispered word,
    " Lenore ! "
This I whispered, and an echo murmured back the word,
    " Lenore ! "
            Merely this and nothing more.

Back into the chamber turning, all my soul within me burning,
Soon again I heard a tapping somewhat louder than before.
" Surely," said I, " surely that is something at my window
    lattice ;
Let me see, then, what thereat is, and this mystery explore —
Let my heart be still a moment and this mystery explore ; —
          'Tis the wind and nothing more."

Open here I flung the shutter, when, with many a flirt and flutter,
In there stepped a stately Raven of the saintly days of yore.
Not the least obeisance made he ; not a minute stopped or
    stayed he ;
But, with mien of lord or lady, perched above my chamber
    door —
Perched upon a bust of Pallas just above my chamber door —
          Perched, and sat, and nothing more.

Then this ebony bird beguiling my sad fancy into smiling,
By the grave and stern decorum of the countenance it wore,
" Though thy crest be shorn and shaven, thou," I said, " art
    sure no craven,
Ghastly grim and ancient Raven wandering from the Nightly
    shore —
Tell me what thy lordly name is on the Night's Plutonian
    shore ! "
          Quoth the Raven, " Nevermore."

Much I marveled this ungainly fowl to hear discourse so plainly,
Though its answer little meaning — little relevancy bore ;
For we cannot help agreeing that no living human being
Ever yet was blessed with seeing bird above his chamber door —
Bird or beast upon the sculptured bust above his chamber door,
            With such name as " Nevermore."

But the Raven, sitting lonely on the placid bust, spoke only
That one word, as if his soul in that one word he did outpour,
Nothing further then he uttered — not a feather then he
    fluttered —
Till I scarcely more than muttered, — " Other friends have
    flown before —
On the morrow *he* will leave me, as my Hopes have flown
    before."
            Then the bird said, " Nevermore."

Startled at the stillness broken by reply so aptly spoken,
" Doubtless," said I, " what it utters is its only stock and store,
Caught from some unhappy master whom unmerciful Disaster
Followed fast and followed faster till his songs one burden
    bore —
Till the dirges of his Hope that melancholy burden bore
            Of ' Never — nevermore.' "

But the Raven still beguiling all my fancy into smiling,
Straight I wheeled a cushioned seat in front of bird, and bust
    and door ;
Then, upon the velvet sinking, I betook myself to linking
Fancy unto fancy, thinking what this ominous bird of yore —
What this grim, ungainly, ghastly, gaunt, and ominous bird
    of yore
            Meant in croaking " Nevermore."

This I sat engaged in guessing, but no syllable expressing
To the fowl whose fiery eyes now burned into my bosom's
    core;
This and more I sat divining, with my head at ease reclining
On the cushion's velvet lining that the lamplight gloated o'er,
But whose velvet violet lining with the lamplight gloating o'er,
        *She* shall press, ah, nevermore!


Then, methought, the air grew denser, perfumed from an
    unseen censer
Swung by seraphim whose footfalls tinkled on the tufted floor.
"Wretch," I cried, "thy God hath lent thee — by these angels
    he hath sent thee
Respite — respite and nepenthe from thy memories of Lenore;
Quaff, oh quaff this kind nepenthe and forget this lost Lenore!"
        Quoth the Raven, "Nevermore."


"Prophet!" said I, "thing of evil! prophet still, if bird or
    devil! —
Whether Tempter sent, or whether tempest tossed thee here
    ashore,
Desolate yet all undaunted, on this desert land enchanted —
On this home by Horror haunted — tell me truly, I implore —
Is there — *is* there balm in Gilead? — tell me — tell me, I
    implore!"
        Quoth the Raven, "Nevermore."


"Prophet!" said I, "thing of evil! — prophet still, if bird or
    devil!
By that Heaven that bends above us — by that God we both
    adore —
Tell this soul with sorrow laden if, within the distant Aidenn,

It shall clasp a sainted maiden whom the angels name Lenore —
Clasp a rare and radiant maiden whom the angels name Lenore!"
          Quoth the Raven, " Nevermore."


" Be that word our sign of parting, bird or fiend!" I shrieked,
          upstarting —
" Get thee back into the tempest and the Night's Plutonian
     shore !
Leave no black plume as a token of that lie thy soul hath spoken!
Leave my loneliness unbroken!—quit the bust above my door!
Take thy beak from out my heart, and take thy form from off
     my door!"
          Quoth the Raven, " Nevermore."


And the Raven, never flitting, still is sitting, *still* is sitting
On the pallid bust of Pallas just above my chamber door ;
And his eyes have all the seeming of a demon's that is dreaming,
And the lamplight o'er him streaming throws his shadow on
     the floor ;
And my soul from out that shadow that lies floating on the floor
          Shall be lifted — nevermore !


## ULALUME

          The skies they were ashen and sober ;
               The leaves they were crispèd and sere,
               The leaves they were withering and sere ;
          It was night in the lonesome October
               Of my most immemorial year ;
          It was hard by the dim lake of Auber,
               In the misty mid region of Weir :
          It was down by the dank tarn of Auber,
               In the ghoul-haunted woodland of Weir.

Here once, through an alley Titanic
    Of cypress, I roamed with my Soul —
    Of cypress, with Psyche, my Soul.
These were days when my heart was volcanic
    As the scoriac rivers that roll,
    As the lavas that restlessly roll
Their sulphurous currents down Yaanek
    In the ultimate climes of the pole,
That groan as they roll down Mount Yaanek
    In the realms of the boreal pole.


Our talk had been serious and sober,
    But our thoughts they were palsied and sere,
    Our memories were treacherous and sere,
For we knew not the month was October,
    And we marked not the night of the year,
    (Ah, night of all nights in the year!)
We noted not the dim lake of Auber
    (Though once we had journeyed down here),
Remembered not the dank tarn of Auber
    Nor the ghoul-haunted woodland of Weir.


And now, as the night was senescent
    And star-dials pointed to morn,
    As the star-dials hinted of morn,
At the end of our path a liquescent
    And nebulous luster was born,
Out of which a miraculous crescent
    Arose with a duplicate horn,
Astarte's bediamonded crescent
    Distinct with its duplicate horn.

And I said — " She is warmer than Dian :
    She rolls through an ether of sighs,
    She revels in a region of sighs :
She has seen that the tears are not dry on
    These cheeks, where the worm never dies,
And has come past the stars of the Lion
    To point us the path to the skies,
    To the Lethean peace of the skies :
Come up, in despite of the Lion,
    To shine on us with her bright eyes :
Come up through the lair of the Lion,
    With love in her luminous eyes."


But Psyche, uplifting her finger,
    Said — " Sadly this star I mistrust,
    Her pallor I strangely mistrust :
Oh, hasten ! — oh, let us not linger !
    Oh, fly ! — let us fly ! — for we must."
In terror she spoke, letting sink her
    Wings until they trailed in the dust ;
In agony sobbed, letting sink her
    Plumes till they trailed in the dust,
    Till they sorrowfully trailed in the dust.


I replied — " This is nothing but dreaming :
    Let us on by this tremulous light !
    Let us bathe in this crystalline light !
Its sibyllic splendor is beaming
    With hope and in beauty to-night :
    See, it flickers up the sky through the night !
Ah, we safely may trust to its gleaming,

And be sure it will lead us aright:
We safely may trust to a gleaming
  That cannot but guide us aright,
  Since it flickers up to Heaven through the night.''


Thus I pacified Psyche and kissed her,
  And tempted her out of her gloom,
  And conquered her scruples and gloom;
And we passed to the end of the vista,
  But were stopped by the door of a tomb,
  By the door of a legended tomb;
And I said — '' What is written, sweet sister,
  On the door of this legended tomb ? ''
  She replied — '' Ulalume — Ulalume —
  'T is the vault of thy lost Ulalume ! ''


Then my heart it grew ashen and sober
  As the leaves that were crispèd and sere,
  As the leaves that were withering and sere,
And I cried — '' It was surely October
  On this very night of last year
  That I journeyed — I journeyed down here,
  That I brought a dread burden down here:
  On this night of all nights in the year,
  Ah, what demon has tempted me here ?
Well I know, now, this dim lake of Auber,
  This misty mid region of Weir:
Well I know, now, this dank tarn of Auber,
  This ghoul-haunted woodland of Weir.''

## ANNABEL LEE

It was many and many a year ago,
    In a kingdom by the sea,
That a maiden there lived whom you may know
    By the name of Annabel Lee;
And this maiden she lived with no other thought
    Than to love and be loved by me.

I was a child and she was a child,
    In this kingdom by the sea,
But we loved with a love that was more than love —
    I and my Annabel Lee —
With a love that the wingèd seraphs of heaven
    Coveted her and me.

And this was the reason that, long ago,
    In this kingdom by the sea,
A wind blew out of a cloud, chilling
    My beautiful Annabel Lee;
So that her highborn kinsmen came
    And bore her away from me,
To shut her up in a sepulcher
    In this kingdom by the sea.

The angels, not half so happy in heaven,
    Went envying her and me —
Yes! — that was the reason (as all men know,
    In this kingdom by the sea)
That the wind came out of the cloud by night,
    Chilling and killing my Annabel Lee.

But our love it was stronger by far than the love
　　　Of those who were older than we —
　　　Of many far wiser than we —
And neither the angels in heaven above,
　　　Nor the demons down under the sea,
Can ever dissever my soul from the soul
　　　Of the beautiful Annabel Lee:

For the moon never beams, without bringing me dreams
　　　Of the beautiful Annabel Lee;
And the stars never rise, but I feel the bright eyes
　　　Of the beautiful Annabel Lee:
And so, all the nighttide, I lie down by the side
Of my darling — my darling — my life and my bride,
　　　In the sepulcher there by the sea —
　　　In her tomb by the sounding sea.

## ELDORADO

Gayly bedight,
A gallant knight,
In sunshine and in shadow,
Had journeyed long,
Singing a song,
In search of Eldorado.

But he grew old,
This knight so bold,
And o'er his heart a shadow
Fell as he found
No spot of ground
That looked like Eldorado.

And, as his strength
Failed him at length,
He met a pilgrim shadow:
" Shadow," said he,
" Where can it be,
This land of Eldorado?"


" Over the Mountains
Of the Moon,
Down the Valley of the Shadow,
Ride, boldly ride,"
The shade replied,
" If you seek for Eldorado!"

# PART II. POETRY OF THE CIVIL WAR

## JAMES RYDER RANDALL

[James Ryder Randall was born in Baltimore, Maryland, in 1839. After being educated at Georgetown College he entered business in Baltimore, but finally drifted into teaching and became professor of literature at Poydras College in Louisiana. In his latter years he was connected with *The Chronicle* of Augusta, Georgia, where he died in 1908. During the war he wrote several excellent war poems, and after the war he continued to write verse in connection with his newspaper work.]

### MY MARYLAND

The despot's heel is on thy shore,
      Maryland!
His torch is at thy temple door,
      Maryland!
Avenge the patriotic gore
That flecked the streets of Baltimore,
And be the battle-queen of yore,
      Maryland, my Maryland!

Hark to an exiled son's appeal,
      Maryland!
My Mother State, to thee I kneel,
      Maryland!
For life and death, for woe and weal,
Thy peerless chivalry reveal,
And gird thy beauteous limbs with steel,
      Maryland, my Maryland!

Thou wilt not cower in the dust,
        Maryland!
Thy beaming sword shall never rust,
        Maryland!
Remember Carroll's sacred trust,
Remember Howard's warlike thrust,
And all thy slumberers with the just,
        Maryland, my Maryland!

Come! 't is the red dawn of the day,
        Maryland!
Come with thy panoplied array,
        Maryland!
With Ringgold's spirit for the fray,
With Watson's blood at Monterey,
With fearless Lowe and dashing May,
        Maryland, my Maryland!

Dear Mother, burst the tyrant chain,
        Maryland!
Virginia should not call in vain,
        Maryland!
She meets her sisters on the plain, —
" *Sic semper!* " 't is the proud refrain
That baffles minions back amain,
        Maryland!
Arise in majesty again,
        Maryland, my Maryland!

Come! for thy shield is bright and strong,
        Maryland!
Come! for thy dalliance does thee wrong,
        Maryland!

Come to thine own heroic throng
Stalking with Liberty along,
And chant thy dauntless slogan-song,
    Maryland, my Maryland !

I see the blush upon thy cheek,
    Maryland !
For thou wast ever bravely meek,
    Maryland !
But lo ! there surges forth a shriek,
From hill to hill, from creek to creek,
Potomac calls to Chesapeake,
    Maryland, my Maryland !

Thou wilt not yield the Vandal toll,
    Maryland !
Thou wilt not crook to his control,
    Maryland !
Better the fire upon thee roll,
Better the shot, the blade, the bowl,
Than crucifixion of the soul,
    Maryland, my Maryland !

I hear the distant thunder hum,
    Maryland !
The Old Line bugle, fife, and drum,
    Maryland !
She is not dead, nor deaf, nor dumb ;
Huzza ! she spurns the Northern scum !
She breathes ! She burns ! She 'll come ! She 'll come !
    Maryland, my Maryland !

## JOHN PELHAM

Just as the spring came laughing through the strife,
    With all its gorgeous cheer,
In the bright April of historic life
    Fell the great cannoneer.


The wondrous lulling of a hero's breath
    His bleeding country weeps;
Hushed, in the alabaster arms of Death,
    Our young Marcellus sleeps.


Nobler and grander than the child of Rome,
    Curbing his chariot steeds,
The knightly scion of a Southern home
    Dazzled the land with deeds.


Gentlest and bravest in the battle-brunt —
    The Champion of the Truth —
He bore his banner to the very front
    Of our immortal youth.


A clang of sabers mid Virginian snow,
    The fiery pang of shells, —
And there's a wail of immemorial woe
    In Alabama dells:


The pennon droops, that led the sacred band
    Along the crimson field;
The meteor blade sinks from the nerveless hand,
    Over the spotless shield.

We gazed and gazed upon that beauteous face,
  While, round the lips and eyes,
Couched in their marble slumber, flashed the grace
  Of a divine surprise.

O mother of a blessed soul on high,
  Thy tears may soon be shed!
Think of thy boy, with princes of the sky,
  Among the Southern dead.

How must he smile on this dull world beneath,
  Fevered with swift renown, —
He, with the martyr's amaranthine wreath,
  Twining the victor's crown!

## ALBERT PIKE

[For sketch of Pike see page 198.]

### DIXIE

Southrons, hear your country call you!
Up, lest worse than death befall you!
  To arms! To arms! To arms, in Dixie!
Lo! all the beacon fires are lighted, —
Let all hearts be now united!
  To arms! To arms! To arms, in Dixie!
    Advance the flag of Dixie!
      Hurrah! hurrah!
  For Dixie's land we take our stand,
    And live or die for Dixie!
  To arms! To arms!
    And conquer peace for Dixie!
  To arms! To arms!
    And conquer peace for Dixie!

Hear the Northern thunders mutter!
Northern flags in South winds flutter!
Send them back your fierce defiance!
Stamp upon the accursed alliance!

Fear no danger! Shun no labor!
Lift up rifle, pike, and saber!
Shoulder pressing close to shoulder,
Let the odds make each heart bolder!

How the South's great heart rejoices
At your cannons' ringing voices!
For faith betrayed, and pledges broken,
Wrong inflicted, insults spoken.

Strong as lions, swift as eagles,
Back to their kennels hunt these beagles!
Cut the unequal bonds asunder!
Let them hence each other plunder!

Swear upon your country's altar
Never to submit or falter,
Till the spoilers are defeated,
Till the Lord's work is completed.

## HARRY McCARTHY

[Harry McCarthy was an Irish actor who enlisted in the Confederate army from Arkansas. After a time he was granted a discharge and continued his career as an actor in Richmond and other places. Little is known of his subsequent career. He wrote other war poems, but none attained the popularity of " The Bonnie Blue Flag."]

## THE BONNIE BLUE FLAG

We are a band of brothers, and native to the soil,
Fighting for our liberty, with treasure, blood, and toil;
    And when our rights were threatened, the cry rose near
      and far:
    Hurrah for the Bonnie Blue Flag that bears a Single Star!

*Chorus*

    Hurrah! Hurrah! for Southern rights, Hurrah!
    Hurrah for the Bonnie Blue Flag that bears a Single Star!

As long as the Union was faithful to her trust,
Like friends and like brethren kind were we and just;
    But now when Northern treachery attempts our rights to mar,
    We hoist on high the Bonnie Blue Flag that bears a Single
      Star. — *Chorus*

First gallant South Carolina nobly made the stand;
Then came Alabama, who took her by the hand;
    Next, quickly Mississippi, Georgia, and Florida,
    All raised on high the Bonnie Blue Flag that bears a Single
      Star. — *Chorus*

Ye men of valor, gather round the banner of the right,
Texas and fair Louisiana, join us in the fight:
    Davis, our loved President, and Stephens, statesman rare,
    Now rally round the Bonnie Blue Flag that bears a Single
      Star. — *Chorus*

And here's to brave Virginia! The Old Dominion State
With the young Confederacy at length has linked her fate;
    Impelled by her example, now other States prepare
    To hoist on high the Bonnie Blue Flag that bears a Single
      Star. — *Chorus*

Then cheer, boys, cheer, raise the joyous shout,
For Arkansas and North Carolina now have both gone out;
   And let another rousing cheer for Tennessee be given —
   The Single Star of the Bonnie Blue Flag has grown to be
      eleven. — *Chorus*

Then, here's to our Confederacy; strong we are and brave,
Like patriots of old we'll fight our heritage to save;
   And rather than submit to shame, to die we would prefer —
   So cheer again for the Bonnie Blue Flag that bears a Single
      Star!

### Chorus

Hurrah! Hurrah! for Southern rights, Hurrah!
Hurrah! for the Bonnie Blue Flag has gained the Eleventh
   Star.

## JOHN ESTEN COOKE

[For biographical note in regard to John Esten Cooke see page 123.]

### THE BAND IN THE PINES

*Heard after Pelham died*

Oh, band in the pine wood cease!
   Cease with your splendid call;
The living are brave and noble,
   But the dead are bravest of all!

They throng to the martial summons,
   To the loud triumphant strain,
And the dear bright eyes of long dead friends
   Come to the heart again!

They come with the ringing bugle,
 And the deep drums' mellow roar;
Till the soul is faint with longing
 For the hands we clasp no more!

Oh, band in the pine wood cease!
 Or the heart will melt with tears,
For the gallant eyes and the smiling lips,
 And the voices of old years.

## JOHN REUBEN THOMPSON

[John Reuben Thompson was born in Richmond, Virginia, in 1823. After graduating from the University of Virginia, he studied law and settled in Richmond. His interest in literary pursuits caused him, however, to turn aside from law in 1847 to the editorship of the *Southern Literary Messenger*. In 1859 he moved to Augusta, Georgia, to become editor of *The Southern Field and Fireside*. Being incapacitated by frail health for military service, Thompson went during the Civil War to London, where he wrote articles for English magazines in defense of the Confederacy. In 1866 he became literary editor of the New York *Evening Post*, and is said to have been one of the two most distinguished occupants of that position. He died in New York in 1873. His poems have unfortunately never been collected in book form.]

JOHN REUBEN THOMPSON

## ASHBY

To the brave all homage render!
   Weep, ye skies of June!
With a radiance pure and tender,
   Shine, O saddened moon;
" *Dead upon the field of glory!* " —
Hero fit for song and story —
   Lies our bold dragoon!

Well they learned, whose hands have slain him,
   Braver, knightlier foe
Never fought 'gainst Moor nor Paynim —
   Rode at Templestowe:
With a mien how high and joyous,
'Gainst the hordes that would destroy us,
   Went he forth, we know.

Nevermore, alas! shall saber
   Gleam around his crest —
Fought his fight, fulfilled his labor,
   Stilled his manly breast —
All unheard sweet Nature's cadence,
Trump of fame and voice of maidens,
   Now he takes his rest.

Earth, that all too soon hath bound him,
   Gently wrap his clay!
Linger lovingly around him,
   Light of dying day!
Softly fall the summer showers —
Birds and bees among the flowers
   Make the gloom seem gay!

There, throughout the coming ages,
　　When his sword is rust,
And his deeds in classic pages —
　　Mindful of her trust,
Shall Virginia, bending lowly,
Still a ceaseless vigil holy
　　Keep above his dust!


## MUSIC IN CAMP

Two armies covered hill and plain,
　　Where Rappahannock's waters
Ran deeply crimsoned with the stain
　　Of battle's recent slaughters.

The summer clouds lay pitched like tents
　　In meads of heavenly azure;
And each dread gun of the elements
　　Slept in its hid embrasure.

The breeze so softly blew, it made
　　No forest leaf to quiver;
And the smoke of the random cannonade
　　Rolled slowly from the river.

And now, where circling hills looked down
　　With cannon grimly planted,
O'er listless camp and silent town
　　The golden sunset slanted.

When on the fervid air there came
　　A strain — now rich, now tender;
The music seemed itself aflame
　　With day's departing splendor.

A Federal band, which, eve and morn,
   Played measures brave and nimble,
Had just struck up, with flute and horn
   And lively clash of cymbal.

Down flocked the soldiers to the banks,
   Till, margined by its pebbles,
One wooded shore was blue with " Yanks,"
   And one was gray with " Rebels."

Then all was still, and then the band,
   With movement light and tricksy,
Made stream and forest, hill and strand,
   Reverberate with " Dixie."

The conscious stream with burnished glow
   Went proudly o'er its pebbles,
But thrilled throughout its deepest flow
   With yelling of the Rebels.

Again a pause, and then again
   The trumpets pealed sonorous,
And " Yankee Doodle " was the strain
   To which the shore gave chorus.

The laughing ripple shoreward flew,
   To kiss the shining pebbles ;
Loud shrieked the swarming Boys in Blue
   Defiance to the Rebels.

And yet once more the bugles sang
   Above the stormy riot ;
No shout upon the evening rang —
   There reigned a holy quiet.

The sad, slow stream its noiseless flood
   Poured o'er the glistening pebbles;
All silent now the Yankees stood,
   And silent stood the Rebels.

No unresponsive soul had heard
   That plaintive note's appealing,
So deeply " Home, Sweet Home " had stirred
   The hidden founts of feeling.

Or Blue or Gray, the soldier sees,
   As by the wand of fairy,
The cottage 'neath the live-oak trees,
   The cabin by the prairie.

Or cold or warm, his native skies
   Bend in their beauty o'er him;
Seen through the tear-mist in his eyes,
   His loved ones stand before him.

As fades the iris after rain,
   In April's tearful weather,
The vision vanished, as the strain
   And daylight died together.

But memory, waked by music's art
   Expressed in simplest numbers,
Subdued the sternest Yankee's heart,
   Made light the Rebel's slumbers.

And fair the form of music shines,
   That bright, celestial creature,
Who still, 'mid war's embattled lines,
   Gave this one touch of Nature.

## THE BURIAL OF LATANE

The combat raged not long, but ours the day;
   And through the hosts that compassed us around
Our little band rode proudly on its way,
   Leaving one gallant comrade, glory-crowned,
Unburied on the field he died to gain,
Single of all his men amid the hostile slain.

One moment on the battle's edge he stood,
   Hope's halo like a helmet round his hair,
The nest beheld him, dabbled in his blood,
   Prostrate in death, and yet in death how fair!
Even thus he passed through the red gate of strife,
From earthly crowns and psalms to an immortal life.

A brother bore his body from the field
   And gave it unto stranger's hands that closed
The calm, blue eyes on earth forever sealed,
   And tenderly the slender limbs composed:
Strangers, yet sisters, who with Mary's love,
Sat by the open tomb and weeping looked above.

A little child strewed roses on his bier,
   Pale roses, not more stainless than his soul,
Nor yet more fragrant than his life sincere
   That blossomed with good actions, brief, but whole:
The aged matron and the faithful slave
Approached with reverent feet the hero's lowly grave.

No man of God might say the burial rite
   Above the " rebel " — thus declared the foe
That blanched before him in the deadly fight,

But woman's voice, in accents soft and low,
Trembling with pity, touched with pathos, read
Over his hallowed dust the ritual for the dead.

" 'T is sown in weakness, it is raised in power,"
    Softly the promise floated on the air,
And the sweet breathings of the sunset hour
    Came back responsive to the mourner's prayer;
Gently they laid him underneath the sod,
And left him with his fame, his country, and his God.

Let us not weep for him whose deeds endure,
    So young, so brave, so beautiful, he died;
As he had wished to die; the past is sure,
    Whatever yet of sorrow may betide
Those who still linger by the stormy shore,
Change cannot harm him now nor fortune touch him more.

And when Virginia, leaning on her spear,
    *Victrix et vidua*, the conflict done,
Shall raise her mailed hand to wipe the tear
    That starts as she recalls each martyred son,
No prouder memory her breast shall sway,
Than thine, our early-lost, lamented Latane.

## WILLIAM GORDON McCABE

[William Gordon McCabe was born at Richmond, Virginia, in 1841. During the war he served in the artillery of the Army of Northern Virginia. After the war he established at Petersburg, Virginia, a boys' preparatory school, which after some years was moved to Richmond. Mr. McCabe has published not only poems but textbooks, literary reviews, and historical articles.]

## DREAMING IN THE TRENCHES

I picture her there in the quaint old room,
　　Where the fading firelight starts and falls,
Alone in the twilight's tender gloom
　　With the shadows that dance on the dim-lit walls.


Alone, while those faces look silently down
　　From their antique frames in a grim repose —
Slight scholarly Ralph in his Oxford gown,
　　And stanch Sir Alan, who died for Montrose.


There are gallants gay in crimson and gold,
　　There are smiling beauties with powdered hair,
But she sits there, fairer a thousandfold,
　　Leaning dreamily back in her low armchair.


And the roseate shadows of fading light
　　Softly clear steal over the sweet young face,
Where a woman's tenderness blends to-night
　　With the guileless pride of a knightly race.


Her small hands lie clasped in a listless way
　　On the old *Romance* — which she holds on her knee —
*Of Tristram*, the bravest of knights in the fray,
　　*And Iseult*, who waits by the sounding sea.


And her proud, dark eyes wear a softened look
　　As she watches the dying embers fall:
Perhaps she dreams of the knight in the book,
　　Perhaps of the pictures that smile on the wall.

What fancies I wonder are thronging her brain,
  For her cheeks flush warm with a crimson glow!
Perhaps — ah! me, how foolish and vain!
  But I'd give my life to believe it so!


Well, whether I ever march home again
  To offer my love and a stainless name,
Or whether I die at the head of my men, —
  I'll be true to the end all the same.


## CHRISTMAS NIGHT OF '62

The wintry blast goes wailing by,
  The snow is falling overhead;
  I hear the lonely sentry's tread,
And distant watch fires light the sky.


Dim forms go flitting through the gloom;
  The soldiers cluster round the blaze
  To talk of other Christmas days,
And softly speak of home and home.


My saber swinging overhead
  Gleams in the watch fire's fitful glow,
  While fiercely drives the blinding snow,
And memory leads me to the dead.


My thoughts go wandering to and fro,
  Vibrating 'twixt the Now and Then;
  I see the low-browed home again,
The old hall wreathed with mistletoe.

And sweetly from the far-off years
    Comes borne the laughter faint and low,
    The voices of the Long Ago!
My eyes are wet with tender tears.

I feel again the mother-kiss,
    I see again the glad surprise
    That lighted up the tranquil eyes
And brimmed them o'er with tears of bliss,

As, rushing from the old hall door,
    She fondly clasped her wayward boy —
    Her face all radiant with the joy
She felt to see him home once more.

My saber swinging on the bough
    Gleams in the watch fire's fitful glow,
    While fiercely drives the blinding snow
Aslant upon my saddened brow.

Those cherished faces all are gone!
    Asleep within the quiet graves
    Where lies the snow in drifting waves, —
And I am sitting here alone.

There's not a comrade here to-night
    But knows that loved ones far away
    On bended knees this night will pray:
" God bring our darling from the fight."

But there are none to wish me back,
    For me no yearning prayers arise.
    The lips are mute and closed the eyes —
My home is in the bivouac.

## JOHN PEGRAM

What shall we say now of our gentle knight?
  Or how express the measure of our woe
For him who rode the foremost in the fight,
  Whose good blade flashed so far amid the foe?

Of all his knightly deeds what need to tell —
  That good blade now lies fast within its sheath —
What can we do but point to where he fell,
  And, like a soldier, met a soldier's death.

We sorrow not as those who have no hope,
  For he was pure in heart as brave in deed —
God pardon us, if blind with tears we grope,
  And love be questioned by the hearts that bleed.

And yet — O foolish and of little faith! —
  We cannot choose but weep our useless tears —
We loved him so! we never dreamed that Death
  Would dare to touch him in his brave young years.

Ah! dear bronzed face, so fearless and so bright!
  As kind to friend as thou wast stern to foe —
No more we'll see thee radiant in the fight,
  The eager eyes — the flush on cheek and brow.

No more we'll greet the lithe, familiar form
  Amid the surging smoke with deaf'ning cheer —
No more shall soar above the iron storm
  Thy ringing voice in accents sweet and clear.

Aye! he has fought the fight and passed away —
   Our grand young leader smitten in the strife,
So swift to seize the chances of the fray,
   And careless only of his noble life.

He is not dead but sleepeth! Well we know
   The form that lies to-day beneath the sod
Shall rise what time the golden bugles blow
   And pour their music through the courts of God.

And there amid our great heroic dead,
   The war-worn sons of God whose work is done!—
His face shall shine, as they with stately tread
   In grand review sweep past the jasper throne.

Let not our hearts be troubled! Few and brief
   His days were here, yet rich in love and faith;
Lord, we believe, help Thou our unbelief,
   And grant Thy servants such a life and death!

## JOHN WILLIAMSON PALMER

[John Williamson Palmer was born in Baltimore, Maryland, in 1825. After studying medicine, he began the practice of his profession in San Francisco. After 1870 he resided in New York and engaged in general literary work. For a time he was editorially connected with the Century Dictionary. His collected poems were published in 1901 under the title "For Charlie's Sake, and Other Ballads and Lyrics. He died in 1906."]

### STONEWALL JACKSON'S WAY

Come, stack arms, men: pile on the rails;
   Stir up the camp fire bright!
No growling if the canteen fails:
   We'll make a roaring night.

Here Shenandoah brawls along,
There burly Blue Ridge echoes strong
To swell the Brigade's rousing song,
   Of Stonewall Jackson's Way.


We see him now — the queer slouched hat,
   Cocked over his eye askew:
The shrewd, dry smile; the speech so pat,
   So calm, so blunt, so true.
The " Blue-light Elder " knows 'em well:
Says he, " That 's Banks: he 's fond of shell.
Lord save his soul: we 'll give him — ": well,
   That 's Stonewall Jackson's Way.


Silence!  Ground arms!  Kneel all!  Caps off!
   Old Massa 's going to pray.
Strangle the fool that dares to scoff:
   Attention! — it 's his way.
Appealing from his native sod,
*In forma pauperis* to God,
" Lay bare Thine arm!  Stretch forth Thy rod:
   Amen! "  That 's Stonewall's Way.


He 's in the saddle now.  Fall in!
   Steady!  the whole brigade.
Hill 's at the ford, cut off; we 'll win
   His way out, ball and blade.
What matter if our shoes are worn?
What matter if our feet are torn?
Quick step!  we 're with him before morn
   That 's Stonewall Jackson's Way.

The sun's bright lances rout the mists
    Of morning ; and, By George !
Here 's Longstreet, struggling in the lists,
    Hemmed in an ugly gorge.
Pope and his Dutchmen ! whipped before.
" Bay'nets and grape ! " hear Stonewall roar.
Charge, Stuart ! Pay off Ashby's score,
    In Stonewall Jackson's Way.


Ah, Maiden ! wait, and watch, and yearn,
    For news of Stonewall's band.
Ah, Widow ! read, with eyes that burn,
    That ring upon thy hand.
Ah, Wife ! sew on, pray on, hope on !
Thy life shall not be all forlorn.
The foe had better ne'er been born,
    That gets in Stonewall's Way.


## HENRY LYNDEN FLASH

[Henry Lynden Flash was born in Cincinnati, Ohio, in 1835. He was an officer in the Confederate army and after the war made his home in New Orleans until 1886, when he removed to Los Angeles, California. In 1860 he published a volume entitled " Poems," but his reputation rests chiefly upon several pieces written in war time.]


### STONEWALL JACKSON

Not midst the lightning of the stormy fight,
    Nor in the rush upon the vandal foe,
Did kingly Death, with his resistless might,
    Lay the great leader low.

His warrior soul its earthly shackles broke
  In the full sunshine of a peaceful town;
When all the storm was hushed, the trusty oak
  That propped our cause went down.


Though his alone the blood that flecks the ground,
  Recalling all his grand heroic deeds,
Freedom herself is writhing in the wound,
  And all the country bleeds.


He entered not the Nation's Promised Land
  At the red belching of the cannon's mouth,
But broke the House of Bondage with his hand—
  The Moses of the South!


O gracious God! not gainless is the loss:
  A glorious sunbeam gilds thy sternest frown;
And while his country staggers 'neath the Cross,
  He rises with the Crown!


## THADDEUS OLIVER

[Thaddeus Oliver was born in Twiggs County, Georgia, in 1826.
He was an eloquent lawyer and a gifted man. He died in a hospital
at Charleston, South Carolina, in 1864.]


### ALL QUIET ALONG THE POTOMAC TO-NIGHT

"All quiet along the Potomac," they say,
  "Except now and then a stray picket
Is shot, as he walks on his beat, to and fro,
  By a rifleman hid in the thicket.

'T is nothing — a private or two, now and then,
    Will not count in the news of the battle ;
Not an officer lost — only one of the men,
    Moaning out, all alone, the death rattle."


All quiet along the Potomac to-night,
    Where the soldiers lie peacefully dreaming ;
Their tents in the rays of the clear autumn moon,
    Or the light of the watch fires, are gleaming.
A tremulous sigh, as the gentle night wind
    Through the forest leaves softly is creeping ;
While stars up above, with their glittering eyes,
    Keep guard — for the army is sleeping.


There's only the sound of the lone sentry's tread,
    As he tramps from the rock to the fountain,
And thinks of the two in the low trundle-bed
    Far away in the cot on the mountain.
His musket falls slack — his face, dark and grim,
    Grows gentle with memories tender,
As he mutters a prayer for the children asleep —
    For their mother — may Heaven defend her !


The moon seems to shine just as brightly as then,
    That night, when the love yet unspoken
Leaped up to his lips — when low-murmured vows
    Were pledged to be ever unbroken.
Then drawing his sleeve roughly over his eyes,
    He dashes off tears that are welling,
And gathers his gun closer up to its place
    As if to keep down the heart-swelling.

He passes the fountain, the blasted pine tree —
　　The footstep is lagging and weary;
Yet onward he goes, through the broad belt of light,
　　Toward the shades of the forest so dreary.
Hark! was it the night wind that rustled the leaves?
　　Was it moonlight so wondrously flashing?
It looked like a rifle — "Ah! Mary, good-by!"
　　And the lifeblood is ebbing and plashing.

All quiet along the Potomac to-night,
　　No sound save the rush of the river;
While soft falls the dew on the face of the dead —
　　The picket's off duty forever.


## MARIE RAVENEL DE LA COSTE

[Marie Ravenel de la Coste was born of French parents in
Savannah, Georgia, where the greater part of her early life was
spent. Her life has been devoted to teaching French, and the
writing of poetry has been merely an incidental matter with her.
Owing to her reticence about herself, it is not possible to give fuller
biographical details.]


### SOMEBODY'S DARLING

Into a ward of the whitewashed walls
　　Where the dead and the dying lay,
Wounded by bayonets, shells, and balls,
　　Somebody's darling was borne one day.
Somebody's darling, so young and brave,
　　Wearing still on his pale, sweet face —
Soon to be hid by the dust of the grave —
　　The lingering light of his boyhood's grace.

Matted and damp are the curls of gold
   Kissing the snow of that fair young brow;
Pale are the lips of delicate mold,
   Somebody's darling is dying now.
Back from the beautiful blue-veined brow
   Brush every wandering silken thread,
Cross his hands on his bosom now —
   Somebody's darling is still and dead!

Kiss him once for somebody's sake;
   Murmur a prayer both soft and low;
One bright curl from its fair mates take —
   They were somebody's pride, you know.
Somebody's hand has rested there;
   Was it a mother's soft and white?
Or have the lips of a sister fair
   Been baptized in those waves of light?

God knows best! He was somebody's love;
   Somebody's heart enshrined him there —
Somebody wafted his name above,
   Night and morn, on the wings of prayer.
Somebody wept when he marched away,
   Looking so handsome, brave, and grand;
Somebody's kiss on his forehead lay,
   Somebody clung to his parting hand.

Somebody's watching and waiting for him,
   Yearning to hold him again to her heart;
And there he lies — with his blue eyes dim,
   And the smiling, childlike lips apart.

Tenderly bury the fair young dead,
  Pausing to drop on his grave a tear;
Carve on the wooden slab o'er his head,
  "Somebody's darling slumbers here."

## CAROLINE AUGUSTA BALL

[Caroline A. Ball was born in Charleston, South Carolina, in 1823. She spent the early years of her life in the North, but in her young womanhood she returned to Charleston. Here she married Mr. Isaac Ball and bore a conspicuous part in the social life of Charleston. She published in 1866 her small volume of poetry under the title "The Jacket of Gray, and Other Poems."]

### THE JACKET OF GRAY

Fold it up carefully, lay it aside,
Tenderly touch it, look on it with pride;
For dear must it be to our hearts evermore,
The jacket of gray our loved soldier boy wore.

Can we ever forget when he joined the brave band,
Who rose in defense of dear Southern land;
And in his bright youth hurried on to the fray;
How proudly he donned it, — the jacket of gray?

His fond mother blessed him and looked up above,
Commending to Heaven the child of her love;
What anguish was hers mortal tongue may not say,
When he passed from her sight in the jacket of gray.

But her country had called him, she would not repine,
Though costly the sacrifice placed on its shrine;
Her heart's dearest hopes on its altar she lay,
When she sent out her boy in his jacket of gray!

Months passed, and war's thunders rolled over the land,
Unsheathed was the sword and lighted the brand;
We heard in the distance the noise of the fray,
And prayed for our boy in the jacket of gray.

Ah! vain all — all vain were our prayers and our tears,
The glad shout of victory rang in our ears;
But our treasured one on the cold battlefield lay,
While the lifeblood oozed out on the jacket of gray.

His young comrades found him and tenderly bore
His cold, lifeless form to his home by the shore;
Oh, dark were our hearts on that terrible day
When we saw our dead boy in the jacket of gray.

Ah! spotted and tattered and stained now with gore
Was the garment which once he so proudly wore.
We bitterly wept as we took it away,
And replaced with death's white robe the jacket of gray.

We laid him to rest in his cold, narrow bed,
And graved on the marble we placed o'er his head,
As the proudest of tributes our sad hearts could pay, —
" He never disgraced the dear jacket of gray."

Then fold it up carefully, lay it aside,
Tenderly touch it, look on it with pride;
For dear must it be to our hearts evermore,
The jacket of gray our loved soldier boy wore.

## MARGARET JUNKIN PRESTON

[Mrs. Margaret Junkin Preston was born in Milton, Pennsylvania, in 1820. In 1848 her father became President of Washington College (now Washington and Lee University), and Lexington, Virginia, became thereafter the home of the family. In 1857 she married Professor T. L. Preston, of the Virginia Military Institute at Lexington. The rest of her life was spent in Lexington, with the exception of a few years toward the end in Baltimore. It was in the latter city that she died, in 1897.]

### GONE FORWARD [1]

Yes, " Let the tent be struck " : Victorious morning
   Through every crevice flashes in a day
Magnificent beyond all earth's adorning :
    The night is over ; wherefore should he stay ?
    And wherefore should our voices choke to say,
        " The General has gone forward " ?

Life's foughten field not once beheld surrender ;
   But with superb endurance, present, past,
Our pure Commander, lofty, simple, tender,
    Through good, through ill, held his high purpose fast,
    Wearing his armor spotless, — till at last,
        Death gave the final, " *Forward.*"

All hearts grew sudden palsied : Yet what said he
   Thus summoned ? — " *Let the tent be struck !* " — For when
Did call of duty fail to find him ready
    Nobly to do his work in sight of men,
    For God's and for his country's sake — and then,
        To watch, wait, or go forward ?

[1] The selections from Margaret Junkin Preston are reprinted through the courtesy of the holder of the copyright, the Houghton Mifflin Company.

We will not weep, — we dare not! Such a story
 As his large life writes on the century's years,
Should crowd our bosoms with a flush of glory,
 That manhood's type, supremest that appears
 To-day, *he* shows the ages.  Nay, no tears
   Because he has gone forward!


Gone forward? — Whither? — Where the marshal'd legions,
 Christ's well-worn soldiers, from their conflicts cease ; —
Where Faith's true Red-Cross knights repose in regions
 Thick-studded with the calm, white tents of peace, —
 Thither, right joyful to accept release,
   The General has gone forward!



## THE SHADE OF THE TREES

 What are the thoughts that are stirring his breast?
  What is the mystical vision he sees?
 " *Let us pass over the river and rest*
  *Under the shade of the trees.*"


 Has he grown sick of his toils and his tasks?
  Sighs the worn spirit for respite or ease?
 Is it a moment's cool halt that he asks
  Under the shade of the trees?


 Is it the gurgle of waters whose flow
  Ofttime has come to him, borne on the breeze,
 Memory listens to, lapsing so low,
  Under the shade of the trees?

Nay — though the rasp of the flesh was so sore,
  Faith, that had yearnings far keener than these,
Saw the soft sheen of the Thitherward Shore,
  Under the shade of the trees ; —

Caught the high psalms of ecstatic delight, —
  Heard the harps harping, like soundings of seas, —
Watched earth's assoilèd ones walking in white
  Under the shade of the trees.

O, was it strange he should pine for release,
  Touched to the soul with such transports as these, —
He who so needed the balsam of peace,
  Under the shade of the trees ?

Yea, it was noblest for *him* — it was best,
  (Questioning naught of our Father's decrees),
*There* to pass over the river and rest
  Under the shade of the trees !

## ANONYMOUS

### THE SOLDIER BOY

I give my soldier boy a blade,
  In fair Damascus fashioned well ;
Who first the glittering falchion swayed,
  Who first beneath its fury fell,
I know not : but I hope to know
  That for no mean or hireling trade,
To guard no feeling, base or low,
  I give my soldier boy a blade.

Cool, calm, and clear the lucid flood
  In which its tempering work was done;
As calm, as cool, as clear of mood
  Be thou whene'er it sees the sun;
For country's claim, at honor's call,
  For outraged friend, insulted maid,
At mercy's voice to bid it fall,
  I give my soldier boy a blade.

The eye which marked its peerless edge,
  The hand that weighed its balanced poise,
Anvil and pincers, forge and wedge,
  Are gone with all their flame and noise;
And still the gleaming sword remains.
  So when in dust I low am laid,
Remember by these heartfelt strains
  I give my soldier boy a blade.

## "THE BRIGADE MUST NOT KNOW, SIR!"

"Who've ye got there?"  "Only a dying brother,
  Hurt in the front just now."
"Good boy! he'll do.  Somebody tell his mother
  Where he was killed, and how."

"Whom have you there?"  "A crippled courier, Major,
  Shot by mistake, we hear.
He was with Stonewall."  "Cruel work they've made here;
  Quick with him to the rear!"

"Well, who comes next?"  "Doctor, speak low, speak low, sir;
  Don't let the men find out!
It's Stonewall!"  "God!"  "The brigade must not know, sir,
  While there's a foe about!"

Whom have we here — shrouded in martial manner,
    Crowned with a martyr's charm?
A grand dead hero, in a living banner,
    Born of his heart and arm:

The heart whereon his cause hung — see how clingeth
    That banner to his bier!
The arm wherewith his cause struck — hark! how ringeth
    His trumpet in their rear!

What have we left? His glorious inspiration,
    His prayers in council met;
Living, he laid the first stones of a nation;
    And dead, he builds it yet.

## THE CONFEDERATE FLAG

No more o'er human hearts to wave,
    Its tattered folds forever furled:
We laid it in an honored grave,
    And left its memories to the world.

The agony of long, long years,
    May, in a moment, be compressed,
And with a grief too deep for tears,
    A heart may be oppressed.

Oh! there are those who die too late
    For faith in God, and Right, and Truth, —
The cold mechanic grasp of Fate
    Hath crushed the roses of their youth.

More blessed are the dead who fell
    Beneath it in unfaltering trust,
Than we, who loved it passing well,
    Yet lived to see it trail in dust.


It hath no future which endears,
    And this farewell shall be our last:
Embalm it in a nation's tears,
    And consecrate it to the past!


To moldering hands that to it clung,
    And flaunted it in hostile faces,
To pulseless arms that round it flung,
    The terror of their last embraces —


To our dead heroes — to the hearts
    That thrill no more to love or glory,
To those who acted well their parts,
    Who died in youth and live in glory —


With tears forever be it told,
    Until oblivion covers all:
Until the heavens themselves wear old,
    And totter slowly to their fall.


## LINES ON A CONFEDERATE NOTE

Representing nothing on God's earth now,
    And naught in the waters below it,
As the pledge of a nation that's dead and gone,
    Keep it, dear friend, and show it.

Show it to those who will lend an ear
   To the tale that this paper can tell
Of Liberty born of the patriot's dream,
   Of a storm-cradled nation that fell.

Too poor to possess the precious ores,
   And too much of a stranger to borrow,
We issued to-day our promise to pay,
   And hoped to repay on the morrow.
The days rolled by and weeks became years,
   But our coffers were empty still;
Coin was so rare that the treasury 'd quake
   If a dollar should drop in the till.

But the faith that was in us was strong, indeed,
   And our poverty well we discerned,
And this little check represented the pay
   That our suffering veterans earned.
We knew it had hardly a value in gold,
   Yet as gold each soldier received it;
It gazed in our eyes with a promise to pay,
   And each Southern patriot believed it.

But our boys thought little of price or of pay,
   Or of bills that were overdue;
We knew if it brought us our bread to-day,
   'T was the best our poor country could do.
Keep it, it tells all our history o'er,
   From the birth of our dream till the last;
Modest, and born of the angel Hope,
   Like our hope of success, it passed.

## ABRAM JOSEPH RYAN

[Abram Joseph Ryan was born in Norfolk, Virginia, in 1839. He entered the Roman Catholic priesthood in 1861 and was a chaplain in the Confederate army. After the war his service to his church took him into almost every Southern state, his longest stay in any one place being twelve years in Mobile, Alabama. During this part of his life he busied himself with preaching, lecturing, editing religious periodicals, and writing verse. Father Ryan died in Louisville, Kentucky, in 1886.]

### THE CONQUERED BANNER

Furl that Banner, for 't is weary;
Round its staff 't is drooping dreary;
   Furl it, fold it, it is best;
For there 's not a man to wave it,
And there 's not a sword to save it,
And there 's not one left to lave it
In the blood which heroes gave it;
And its foes now scorn and brave it;
   Furl it, hide it — let it rest!

Take that Banner down! 't is tattered;
Broken is its staff and shattered;
And the valiant hosts are scattered
   Over whom it floated high.
Oh! 't is hard for us to fold it;
Hard to think there 's none to hold it;
Hard that those who once unrolled it
   Now must furl it with a sigh.

Furl that Banner! furl it sadly!
Once ten thousands hailed it gladly,
And ten thousands wildly, madly,
   Swore it should forever wave;

Swore that foeman's sword should never
Hearts like theirs entwined dissever,
Till that flag should float forever
   O'er their freedom or their grave!

Furl it! for the hands that grasped it,
And the hearts that fondly clasped it,
   Cold and dead are lying low;
And that Banner — it is trailing!
While around it sounds the wailing
   Of its people in their woe.

For, though conquered, they adore it!
Love the cold, dead hands that bore it!
Weep for those who fell before it!
Pardon those who trailed and tore it!
But, oh! wildly they deplore it,
   Now who furl and fold it so.

Furl that Banner! True, 't is gory,
Yet 't is wreathed around with glory,
And 't will live in song and story,
   Though its folds are in the dust:
For its fame on brightest pages,
Penned by poets and by sages,
Shall go sounding down the ages —
   Furl its folds though now we must.

Furl that Banner, softly, slowly!
Treat it gently — it is holy —
   For it droops above the dead.
Touch it not — unfold it never,
Let it droop there, furled forever,
   For its people's hopes are dead!

## THE SWORD OF ROBERT LEE

Forth from its scabbard, pure and bright,
    Flashed the sword of Lee!
Far in the front of the deadly fight,
High o'er the brave in the cause of Right,
Its stainless sheen, like a beacon light,
    Led us to Victory.

Out of its scabbard, where, full long,
    It slumbered peacefully,
Roused from its rest by the battle's song,
Shielding the feeble, smiting the strong,
Guarding the right, avenging the wrong,
    Gleamed the sword of Lee.

Forth from its scabbard, high in air
    Beneath Virginia's sky —
And they who saw it gleaming there,
And knew who bore it, knelt to swear
That where that sword led they would dare
    To follow — and to die.

Out of its scabbard! Never hand
    Waved sword from stain as free,
Nor purer sword led braver band,
Nor braver bled for a brighter land,
Nor brighter land had a cause so grand,
    Nor cause a chief like Lee!

Forth from its scabbard! how we prayed
    That sword might victor be;
And when our triumph was delayed,

And many a heart grew sore afraid,
We still hoped on while gleamed the blade
    Of noble Robert Lee.

Forth from its scabbard all in vain
    Forth flashed the sword of Lee;
'T is shrouded now in its sheath again,
It sleeps the sleep of our noble slain,
Defeated, yet without a stain,
    Proudly and peacefully.

## HENRY TIMROD

[Henry Timrod was born in Charleston, South Carolina, in 1829. On his father's side he was of German descent, and on his mother's,

HENRY TIMROD

of English. He was educated in Charleston schools and in the University of Georgia, but was compelled to leave college before taking his degree on account of poverty. Returning to Charleston, he prepared himself for the practice of law, but finding this distasteful, he began to fit himself for a college professorship. Failing to secure the position he sought, he taught private classes for about ten years. In the meantime he was writing poetry and contributing his verse to the *Southern Literary Messenger* and *Russell's Magazine*. A volume of Timrod's verses was published in Boston in 1860, but in the excitement of those times did not attract widespread attention. At the outbreak of the war

Timrod enlisted, but finding his constitution too weak to undergo the hardships of camp life, he contented himself with service as army correspondent. In 1864 he accepted an appointment as editor of the *South Carolinian* at Columbia. Feeling now settled, he married Miss Kate Goodwin, an English girl resident in Charleston. But his happiness was of brief duration. Disease was making inroads upon his frail body, the death of his young son added to his sorrows, and the desolation of war rendered him destitute of property. Consumption eventually overcame him, and in 1867 he was laid to rest. Timrod wrote some beautiful and enduring lyrics dealing with love and nature, but he most deeply stirred his generation by his martial and patriotic poems. Hence his sobriquet, "The Laureate of the Confederacy."]

## CAROLINA [1]

The despot treads thy sacred sands,
Thy pines give shelter to his bands,
Thy sons stand by with idle hands,
            Carolina!
He breathes at ease thy airs of balm,
He scorns the lances of thy palm;
Oh! who shall break thy craven calm,
            Carolina!
Thy ancient fame is growing dim,
A spot is on thy garment's rim;
Give to the winds thy battle hymn,
            Carolina!


Call on thy children of the hill,
Wake swamp and river, coast and rill,
Rouse all thy strength and all thy skill,
            Carolina!

Cite wealth and science, trade and art,
Touch with thy fire the cautious mart,
And pour thee through the people's heart,
          Carolina!
Till even the coward spurns his fears,
And all thy fields and fens and meres
Shall bristle like thy palm with spears,
          Carolina!


Hold up the glories of thy dead;
Say how thy elder children bled,
And point to Eutaw's battle-bed,
          Carolina!
Tell how the patriot's soul was tried,
And what his dauntless breast defied;
How Rutledge ruled and Laurens died,
          Carolina!
Cry! till thy summons, heard at last,
Shall fall like Marion's bugle blast
Reëchoed from the haunted Past,
          Carolina!


I hear a murmur as of waves
That grope their way through sunless caves,
Like bodies struggling in their graves,
          Carolina!
And now it deepens; slow and grand
It swells, as, rolling to the land,
An ocean broke upon thy strand,
          Carolina!

Shout! let it reach the startled Huns!
And roar with all thy festal guns!
It is the answer of thy sons,
         Carolina!


They will not wait to hear thee call;
From Sachem's Head to Sumter's wall
Resounds the voice of hut and hall,
         Carolina!
No! thou hast not a stain, they say,
Or none save what the battle-day
Shall wash in seas of blood away,
         Carolina!
Thy skirts indeed the foe may part,
Thy robe be pierced with sword and dart,
They shall not touch thy noble heart,
         Carolina!


Ere thou shalt own the tyrant's thrall
Ten times ten thousand men must fall;
Thy corpse may hearken to his call,
         Carolina!
When, by thy bier, in mournful throngs
The women chant thy mortal wrongs,
'T will be their own funereal songs,
         Carolina!
From thy dead breast by ruffians trod
No helpless child shall look to God;
All shall be safe beneath thy sod,
         Carolina!

Girt with such wills to do and bear,
Assured in right, and mailed in prayer,
Thou wilt not bow thee to despair,
             Carolina!
Throw thy bold banner to the breeze!
Front with thy ranks the threatening seas
Like thine own proud armorial trees,
             Carolina!
Fling down thy gauntlet to the Huns,
And roar the challenge from thy guns;
Then leave the future to thy sons,
             Carolina!


## A CRY TO ARMS

Ho! woodsmen of the mountain side!
    Ho! dwellers in the vales!
Ho! ye who by the chafing tide
    Have roughened in the gales!
Leave barn and byre, leave kin and cot,
    Lay by the bloodless spade;
Let desk, and case, and counter rot,
    And burn your books of trade.


The despot roves your fairest lands;
    And till he flies or fears,
Your fields must grow but armed bands,
    Your sheaves be sheaves of spears!
Give up to mildew and to rust
    The useless tools of gain;
And feed your country's sacred dust
    With floods of crimson rain!

Come, with the weapons at your call —
  With musket, pike, or knife;
He wields the deadliest blade of all
  Who lightest holds his life.
The arm that drives its unbought blows
  With all a patriot's scorn,
Might brain a tyrant with a rose,
  Or stab him with a thorn.


Does any falter? let him turn
  To some brave maiden's eyes,
And catch the holy fires that burn
  In those sublunar skies.
Oh! could you like your women feel,
  And in their spirit march,
A day might see your lines of steel
  Beneath the victor's arch.


What hope, O God! would not grow warm
  When thoughts like these give cheer?
The Lily calmly braves the storm,
  And shall the Palm-tree fear?
No! rather let its branches court
  The rack that sweeps the plain;
And from the Lily's regal port
  Learn how to breast the strain!


Ho! woodsmen of the mountain side!
  Ho! dwellers in the vales!
Ho! ye who by the roaring tide
  Have roughened in the gales!

Come! flocking gayly to the fight,
　　From forest, hill, and lake;
We battle for our Country's right,
　　And for the Lily's sake!


## CHARLESTON

Calm as that second summer which precedes
　　The first fall of the snow,
In the broad sunlight of heroic deeds,
　　The City bides the foe.


As yet, behind their ramparts stern and proud,
　　Her bolted thunders sleep—
Dark Sumter, like a battlemented cloud,
　　Looms o'er the solemn deep.


No Calpe frowns from lofty cliff or scar
　　To guard the holy strand;
But Moultrie holds in leash her dogs of war
　　Above the level sand.


And down the dunes a thousand guns lie couched,
　　Unseen, beside the flood—
Like tigers in some Orient jungle crouched
　　That wait and watch for blood.


Meanwhile, through streets still echoing with trade,
　　Walk grave and thoughtful men,
Whose hands may one day wield the patriot's blade
　　As lightly as the pen.

And maidens, with such eyes as would grow dim
   Over a bleeding hound,
Seem each one to have caught the strength of him
   Whose sword she sadly bound.


Thus girt without and garrisoned at home,
   Day patient following day,
Old Charleston looks from roof, and spire, and dome,
   Across her tranquil bay.


Ships, through a hundred foes, from Saxon lands
   And spicy Indian ports,
Bring Saxon steel and iron to her hands,
   And Summer to her courts.


But still, along yon dim Atlantic line,
   The only hostile smoke
Creeps like a harmless mist above the brine,
   From some frail, floating oak.


Shall the Spring dawn, and she still clad in smiles,
   And with an unscathed brow,
Rest in the strong arms of her palm-crowned isles,
   As fair and free as now?


We know not; in the temple of the Fates
   God has inscribed her doom;
And, all untroubled in her faith, she waits
   The triumph or the tomb.

## SPRING

Spring, with that nameless pathos in the air
Which dwells with all things fair,
Spring, with her golden suns and silver rain,
Is with us once again.

Out in the lonely woods the jasmine burns
Its fragrant lamps, and turns
Into a royal court with green festoons
The banks of dark lagoons.

In the deep heart of every forest tree
The blood is all aglee,
And there's a look about the leafless bowers
As if they dreamed of flowers.

Yet still on every side we trace the hand
Of Winter in the land,
Save where the maple reddens on the lawn,
Flushed by the season's dawn;

Or where, like those strange semblances we find
That age to childhood bind,
The elm puts on, as if in Nature's scorn,
The brown of Autumn corn.

As yet the turf is dark, although you know
That, not a span below,
A thousand germs are groping through the gloom,
And soon will burst their tomb.

Already, here and there, on frailest stems
Appear some azure gems,
Small as might deck, upon a gala day,
The forehead of a fay.

In gardens you may note amid the dearth
The crocus breaking earth;
And near the snowdrop's tender white and green,
The violet in its screen.

But many gleams and shadows need must pass
Along the budding grass,
And weeks go by, before the enamored South
Shall kiss the rose's mouth.

Still there's a sense of blossoms yet unborn
In the sweet airs of morn;
One almost looks to see the very street
Grow purple at his feet.

At times a fragrant breeze comes floating by,
And brings, you know not why,
A feeling as when eager crowds await
Before a palace gate

Some wondrous pageant; and you scarce would start,
If from a beech's heart,
A blue-eyed Dryad, stepping forth, should say,
" Behold me! I am May! "

Ah! who would couple thoughts of war and crime
With such a blessèd time!
Who in the west wind's aromatic breath
Could hear the call of Death!

Yet not more surely shall the Spring awake
The voice of wood and brake,
Than she shall rouse, for all her tranquil charms,
A million men to arms.

There shall be deeper hues upon her plains
Than all her sunlit rains,
And every gladdening influence around,
Can summon from the ground.

Oh! standing on this desecrated mold,
Methinks that I behold,
Lifting her bloody daisies up to God,
Spring kneeling on the sod,

And calling, with the voice of all her rills,
Upon the ancient hills
To fall and crush the tyrants and the slaves
Who turn her meads to graves.

### THE COTTON BOLL

While I recline
At ease beneath
This immemorial pine,
Small sphere!
(By dusky fingers brought this morning here
And shown with boastful smiles),
I turn thy cloven sheath,
Through which the soft white fibers peer,
That, with their gossamer bands,
Unite, like love, the sea-divided lands,
And slowly, thread by thread,

Draw forth the folded strands,
Than which the trembling line,
By whose frail help yon startled spider fled
Down the tall spear grass from his swinging bed,
Is scarce more fine ;
And as the tangled skein
Unravels in my hands,
Betwixt me and the noonday light,
A veil seems lifted, and for miles and miles
The landscape broadens on my sight,
As, in the little boll, there lurked a spell
Like that which, in the ocean shell,
With mystic sound,
Breaks down the narrow walls that hem us round,
And turns some city lane
Into the restless main,
With all his capes and isles !

Yonder bird,
Which floats, as if at rest,
In those blue tracts above the thunder, where
No vapors cloud the stainless air,
And never sound is heard,
Unless at such rare time
When, from the City of the Blest,
Rings down some golden chime,
Sees not from his high place
So vast a cirque of summer space
As widens round me in one mighty field,
Which, rimmed by seas and sands,
Doth hail its earliest daylight in the beams
Of gray Atlantic dawns ;
And, broad as realms made up of many lands,

Is lost afar
Behind the crimson hills and purple lawns
Of sunset, among plains which roll their streams
Against the Evening Star!
And lo!
To the remotest point of sight,
Although I gaze upon no waste of snow,
The endless field is white;
And the whole landscape glows,
For many a shining league away,
With such accumulated light
As Polar lands would flash beneath a tropic day!
Nor lack there (for the vision grows,
And the small charm within my hands —
More potent even than the fabled one,
Which oped whatever golden mystery
Lay hid in fairy wood or magic vale,
The curious ointment of the Arabian tale —
Beyond all mortal sense
Doth stretch my sight's horizon, and I see,
Beneath its simple influence,
As if with Uriel's crown,
I stood in some great temple of the Sun,
And looked, as Uriel, down!)
Nor lack there pastures rich and fields all green
With all the common gifts of God,
For temperate airs and torrid sheen
Weave Edens of the sod;
Through lands which look one sea of billowy gold
Broad rivers wind their devious ways;
A hundred isles in their embraces fold
A hundred luminous bays;
And through yon purple haze

Vast mountains lift their plumed peaks cloud-crowned ;
And, save where up their sides the plowman creeps,
An unhewn forest girds them grandly round,
In whose dark shades a future navy sleeps !
Ye Stars, which, though unseen, yet with me gaze
Upon this loveliest fragment of the earth !
Thou Sun, that kindlest all thy gentlest rays
Above it, as to light a favorite hearth !
Ye Clouds, that in your temples in the West
See nothing brighter than its humblest flowers !
And you, ye Winds, that on the ocean's breast
Are kissed to coolness ere ye reach its bowers !
Bear witness with me in my song of praise,
And tell the world that, since the world began,
No fairer land hath fired a poet's lays,
Or given a home to man !

But these are charms already widely blown !
His be the meed whose pencil's trace
Hath touched our very swamps with grace,
And round whose tuneful way
All Southern laurels bloom ;
The Poet of " The Woodlands," unto whom
Alike are known
The flute's low breathing and the trumpet's tone,
And the soft west wind's sighs ;
But who shall utter all the debt,
O land wherein all powers are met
That bind a people's heart,
The world doth owe thee at this day,
And which it never can repay,
Yet scarcely deigns to own !
Where sleeps the poet who shall fitly sing
The source wherefrom doth spring

That mighty commerce which, confined
To the mean channels of no selfish mart,
Goes out to every shore
Of this broad earth, and throngs the sea with ships
That bear no thunders; hushes hungry lips
In alien lands;
Joins with a delicate web remotest strands;
And gladdening rich and poor,
Doth gild Parisian domes,
Or feed the cottage smoke of English homes,
And only bounds its blessings by mankind!
In offices like these, thy mission lies,
My Country! and it shall not end
As long as rain shall fall and Heaven bend
In blue above thee; though thy foes be hard
And cruel as their weapons, it shall guard
Thy hearth-stones as a bulwark; make thee great
In white and bloodless state;
And haply, as the years increase —
Still working through its humbler reach
With that large wisdom which the ages teach —
Revive the half-dead dream of universal peace!
As men who labor in that mine
Of Cornwall, hollowed out beneath the bed
Of ocean, when a storm rolls overhead,
Hear the dull booming of the world of brine
Above them, and a mighty muffled roar
Of winds and waters, yet toil calmly on,
And split the rock, and pile the massive ore,
Or carve a niche, or shape the archèd roof;
So I, as calmly, weave my woof
Of song, chanting the days to come,
Unsilenced, though the quiet summer air

Stirs with the bruit of battles, and each dawn
Wakes from its starry silence to the hum
Of many gathering armies.  Still,
In that we sometimes hear,
Upon the Northern winds, the voice of woe
Not wholly drowned in triumph, though I know
The end must crown us, and a few brief years
Dry all our tears,
I may not sing too gladly.  To thy will
Resigned, O Lord! we cannot all forget
That there is much even Victory must regret.
And, therefore, not too long
From the great burthen of our country's wrong
Delay our just release!
And, if it may be, save
These sacred fields of peace
From stain of patriot or of hostile blood!
Oh, help us, Lord! to roll the crimson flood
Back on its course, and, while our banners wing
Northward, strike with us! till the Goth shall cling
To his own blasted altar stones, and crave
Mercy; and we shall grant it, and dictate
The lenient future of his fate
There, where some rotting ships and crumbling quays
Shall one day mark the Port which ruled the Western seas.

## THE LILY CONFIDANTE

Lily! lady of the garden!
    Let me press my lip to thine!
Love must tell its story, Lily!
    Listen thou to mine.

Two I choose to know the secret —
　　Thee, and yonder wordless flute;
Dragons watch me, tender Lily,
　　And thou must be mute.

There's a maiden, and her name is —
　　Hist! was that a rose-leaf fell?
See, the rose is listening, Lily,
　　And the rose may tell.

Lily-browed and lily-hearted,
　　She is very dear to me;
Lovely? yes, if being lovely
　　Is — resembling thee.

Six to half a score of summers
　　Make the sweetest of the " teens " —
Not too young to guess, dear Lily,
　　What a lover means.

Laughing girl and thoughtful woman,
　　I am puzzled how to woo —
Shall I praise, or pique her, Lily?
　　Tell me what to do.

" Silly lover, if thy Lily
　　Like her sister lilies be,
Thou must woo, if thou wouldst wear her,
　　With a simple plea.

" Love's the lover's only magic,
　　Truth the very subtlest art.;
Love that feigns, and lips that flatter,
　　Win no modest heart.

" Like the dewdrop in my bosom,
　　Be thy guileless language, youth;
Falsehood buyeth falsehood only,
　　Truth must purchase truth.

" As thou talkest at the fireside,
　　With the little children by —
As thou prayest in the darkness,
　　When thy God is nigh —

" With a speech as chaste and gentle,
　　And such meanings as become
Ear of child, or ear of angel,
　　Speak, or be thou dumb.

" Woo her thus, and she shall give thee
　　Of her heart the sinless whole,
All the girl within her bosom,
　　And her woman's soul."

## MAGNOLIA CEMETERY ODE

Sleep sweetly in your humble graves,
　　Sleep, martyrs of a fallen cause;
Though yet no marble column craves
　　The pilgrim here to pause.

In seeds of laurel in the earth
　　The blossom of your fame is blown,
And somewhere, waiting for its birth,
　　The shaft is in the stone!

Meanwhile, behalf the tardy years
　　Which keep in trust your storied tombs,
Behold! your sisters bring their tears,
　　And these memorial blooms.

Small tributes! but your shades will smile
   More proudly on these wreaths to-day,
Than when some cannon-molded pile
   Shall overlook this bay.

Stoop, angels, hither from the skies!
   There is no holier spot of ground
Than where defeated valor lies,
   By mourning beauty crowned!

## FRANCIS ORRAY TICKNOR

[Francis Orray Ticknor was born in Fortville, Georgia, in 1822. After studying medicine in New York and Philadelphia, he settled

FRANCIS ORRAY TICKNOR

From a sketch by his granddaughter, Michelle Cunliffe Ticknor

first at Shell Creek, Lumpkin County, Georgia, and later on a farm called "Torch Hill" near Columbus, Georgia, and there for the rest of his life led the life of a country physician. His special passions were the cultivating of fruits and flowers, music, and the writing of poetry. His poems secured for him some local reputation, but as he wrote verse only for the pleasure of his friends, he made no collection of them for publication. Five years after his death in 1874, an incomplete edition was published, which has been supplanted by a later edition prepared by the poet's granddaughter, Michelle Cunliffe Ticknor.]

## LITTLE GIFFEN [1]

Out of the focal and foremost fire,
Out of the hospital's walls as dire;
Smitten of grape-shot and gangrene —
Eighteenth battle and *he* sixteen —
Specter! — such as you seldom see,
Little Giffen of Tennessee.


"Take him and welcome!" the surgeons said,
"Little the doctor can help the dead!" —
So we took him and brought him where
The balm was sweet in the summer air,
And we laid him down on a wholesome bed, —
Utter Lazarus, heel to head!


And we watched the war with abated breath, —
Skeleton boy against skeleton Death!
Months of torture, how many such!
Weary weeks of the stick and crutch;
And still a glint in the steel-blue eye
Told of a spirit that would n't die.


And did n't! — Nay, more! in Death's despite
The crippled skeleton learned to write —
"Dear Mother"! at first, of course, and then
"Dear Captain"! — inquiring about the men!
Captain's answer: "Of eighty and five,
Giffen and I are left alive!"

[1] The selections from Ticknor are reprinted through the courtesy of the holder of the copyright, The Neale Publishing Company.

Word of gloom from the war, one day :
Johnston pressed at the front they say,
Little Giffen was up and away ! —
A tear, his first, as he bade good-by,
Dimmed the glint of his steel-blue eye ; —
" I 'll write, if spared ! " — there was news of the fight
But none of Giffen ! — He did not write !

I sometimes fancy that were I king
Of the princely knights of Golden Ring,
With the song of the minstrel in mine ear
And the tender legend that trembles here,
I'd give the best on his bended knee,
The whitest soul of my chivalry,
For Little Giffen of Tennessee.

## THE VIRGINIANS OF THE VALLEY

The knightliest of the knightly race,
That since the days of old,
Have kept the lamp of chivalry
Alight in hearts of gold.
The kindliest of the kindly band
That, rarely hating ease,
Yet rode with Spotswood round the land,
With Raleigh around the seas.

Who climbed the blue embattled hills
Against embattled foes,
And planted there, in valleys fair,
The lily and the rose !

Whose fragrance lives in many lands,
Whose beauty stars the earth,
And lights the hearths of happy homes
With loveliness and worth !


We thought they slept ! — the sons who kept
The names of noble sires,
And slumbered, while the darkness crept
Around their vigil fires !
But aye ! the " Golden Horse-shoe " Knights
Their Old Dominion keep,
Whose foes have found enchanted ground
But not a knight asleep.


## UNKNOWN

The prints of feet are worn away,
    No more the mourners come ;
The voice of wail is mute to-day
    As his whose life is dumb.


The world is bright with other bloom ;
    Shall the sweet summer shed
Its living radiance o'er the tomb
    That shrouds the doubly dead ?


Unknown !  Beneath our Father's face
    The starlit hillocks lie ;
Another rosebud ! lest His grace
    Forget us when we die.

## PAGE BROOK

There is dust on the doorway, there is mold on the wall—
There's a chill at the hearthstone—a hush through the hall;
And the stately old mansion stands darkened and cold
By the leal, loving hearts that it sheltered of old.

No light at the lattice, no smile at the door;
No cheer at its table, no dance on its floor;
But "Glory departed," and silence alone;
"Dust unto dust" upon pillar and stone!

No laughter of childhood, no shout on the lawn;
No footstep to echo the feet that are gone:
Feet of the beautiful, forms of the brave—
Failing in other lands, gone to the grave.

No carol at morning, no hymn rising clear,
Nor song at the bridal, nor chant at the bier!
All the chords of its symphonies scattered and riven,
Its altar in ashes, its incense in Heaven.

'T is an ache at the heart, thus lonely to stand
By the wreck of a home once the pride of the land;
Its chambers unfilled as its children depart,
The melody stilled in its desolate heart.

Yet softly the sunlight still rests on the grass
And lightly and swiftly the cloud-shadows pass,
And still the wide meadow exults in the sheen
With its foam crest of snow, and its billows of green!

And the verdure shall creep to the moldering wall
And the sunshine shall sleep in the desolate hall —
And the foot of the pilgrim shall find to the last
Some fragrance of home, at this shrine of the Past.


## LOYAL

The Douglas — in the days of old —
    The gentle minstrels sing,
Wore at his heart, incased in gold,
    The heart of Bruce, his king.


Through Paynim lands to Palestine,
    Befall what peril might,
To lay that heart on Christ, his shrine,
    His knightly word he plight.


A weary way, by night and day,
    Of vigil and of fight,
Where never rescue came by day
    Nor ever rest by night.


And one by one the valiant spears,
    They faltered from his side;
And one by one his heavy tears
    Fell for the Bruce who died.


All fierce and black, around his track,
    He saw the combat close,
And counted but a single sword
    Against uncounted foes.

He drew the casket from his breast,
　He bared his solemn brow,
Oh, kingliest and knightliest,
　Go first in battle, now !


Where leads my Lord of Bruce, the sword
　Of Douglas shall not stay !
Forward — and to the feet of Christ
　I follow thee, to-day.


The casket flashed ! — The battle clashed,
　Thundered and rolled away.
And dead above the heart of Bruce
　The heart of Douglas lay.


" Loyal ! " — Methinks the antique mold
　Is lost ! — or theirs alone,
Who sheltered Freedom's heart of gold,
　Like Douglas with their own.

# PART III. THE NEW SOUTH IN LITERATURE

## HUMORISTS

### RICHARD MALCOLM JOHNSTON

[Richard Malcolm Johnston was born in Hancock County, Georgia, in 1822. After graduating from Mercer University, he entered upon the practice of law, but in 1857 became professor of English literature at the University of Georgia. After the war he established a boarding school for boys at Sparta, Georgia, and afterward near Baltimore, Maryland. It was in Baltimore that he died, in 1898. His racy character studies, entitled " Dukesborough Tales," which had appeared in the *Southern Magazine*, were first collected into book form in 1871, but did not attract general attention until published again nine years later. This initial volume was followed by several volumes of fiction, — novels and collections of tales, — as well as of literary and social papers.]

### THE GOOSEPOND SCHOOLMASTER

It was the custom of the pupils in the Goosepond, as in most of the other country schools of those times, to study aloud. Whether the teachers thought that the mind could not act unless the tongue was going, or that the tongue going was the only evidence that the mind was acting, it never did appear. Such had been the custom, and Mr. Meadows did not aspire to be an innovator. It was his rule, however, that there should be perfect silence on his arrival, in order to give him an opportunity of saying or doing anything he might wish. This morning there did not seem to be anything heavy on his mind which required to be lifted off. He, however, looked at Brinkly Glisson with an expression of some disappointment. He had beaten him the morning before for not having gotten there in time, though the boy's excuse was that he had gone a mile out of his way on an errand for his mother. He looked at him as if he had expected to have had some business with him, which now unexpectedly had to be postponed. He then looked around over the school, and said: "Go to studyin'."

He had been in the habit of speaking but to command, and of commanding but to be obeyed. Instantaneously was heard, then and there, that unintelligible tumult, the almost invariable incident of the country schools of that generation. There were spellers and readers, geographers, and arithmeticians, all engaged in their several pursuits, in the most inexplicable confusion. Sometimes the spellers would have the heels of the others, and sometimes the readers. The geographers were always third, and the arithmeticians always behind. It was very plain to be seen that these last never would catch the others. The faster they added or subtracted, the oftener they had to rub out and commence anew. It was always but a short time before they found this to be the case, and so they generally concluded to adopt the maxim of the philosopher, of being slow in making haste. The geographers were a little faster and a little louder. But the spellers and readers had it, I tell you. Each speller and each reader went through the whole gamut of sounds, from low up to high, and from high down to low again; sometimes by regular ascension and descension, one note at a time, sounding what musicians call the diatonic intervals; at other times, going up and coming down upon the perfect fifths only. It was refreshing to see the passionate eagerness which these urchins manifested for the acquisition of knowledge! To have heard them for the first time, one might possibly have been reminded of the Apostles' preaching at Pentecost, when were spoken the languages of the Parthians and Medes, Elamites and the dwellers in Mesopotamia, and in Judea and Cappadocia; in Pontus and Asia, Phrygia and Pamphylia; in Egypt and in the parts of Syria about Cyrene; and Strangers of Rome, Jews and Proselytes, Cretes and Arabians. Sometimes these jarring tongues subsided a little, when half a dozen or so would stop to blow; but in the next moment the chorus would swell again in a new and livelier *accrescendo*. When this process had gone on for half an hour, Mr. Meadows lifted his voice and shouted, "Silence!" and all was still.

Now were to commence the recitations, during which stillness like that of death was required. For as great a help to study as this jargon was, Mr. Meadows found that it did not contribute any aid to the doing of *his* work.

He now performed an interesting feat. He put his hand behind the lapel of his coat collar, and then, after withdrawing it, and holding it up, his thumb and forefinger joined together, he said: "There is too much fuss here. I'm going to drop this pin, and I shall whip every single one of you little boys that don't hear it when it falls. Thar!"

"I heerd it, Mr. Meadows! I heerd it, Mr. Meadows!" exclaimed, simultaneously, five or six little fellows.

"Come up here, you little rascals. You are a liar!" said he to each one. "I never drapped it; I never had nary one to drap. It just shows what liars you are. Set down and wait awhile; I'll show you how to tell *me* lies."

The little liars slunk to their seats, and the recitations commenced. Memory was the only faculty of mind that got development at this school. Whoever could say exactly what the book said was adjudged to know his lesson. About half of the pupils on this morning were successful. The other half were found to be delinquent. Among these was Asa Boatright. That calculating young gentleman knew *his* words and felt safe. The class had spelled around three or four times when lo! the contingency which Allen Thigpen had suggested did come to pass. Betsy Wiggins missed her word; Heneritter Bangs (in the language of Allen) hern; and Mandy Grizzle hern; and thus responsibilities were suddenly cast upon Asa which he was wholly unprepared to meet and which, from the look of mighty reproach that he gave each of these young ladies as she handed over her word, he evidently thought it the height of injustice that he should have been called upon to meet. Mr. Meadows, closing his book, tossed it to Asa, who, catching it as it was falling at his feet, turned and, his eyes swimming with tears, went back to his seat. As he passed Allen Thigpen, the latter whispered: "What did I tell you? You heerd the pin drap, too!"

Now Allen was in no plight to have given this taunt to Asa. He had not given five minutes' study to his arithmetic during the whole morning. But Mr. Meadows made a rule (this one for himself, though all the pupils knew it better than any rule he had) never to allow Allen to miss a lesson; and as he had kindly taken this responsibility upon himself, Allen was wont to give himself no trouble about the matter.

Brinkly Glisson was the last to recite. Brinkly was no great hand at pronunciation. He had been reading but a short time when Mr. Meadows advanced him into geography, with the purpose, as Brinkly afterward came to believe, of getting the half-dollar extra tuition. This morning he thought he knew his lesson; and he did, as he understood it. When called to recite, he went up with a countenance expressive of mild happiness, handed the book to Mr. Meadows, and, putting his hands in his pockets, awaited the questions. And now it was an interesting sight to see Mr. Meadows smile as Brinkly talked of is-lands and promonitaries, thismuses and hemispheries. The lad misunderstood that smile, and his heart was glad for the unexpected reception of a little complacency from the master. But he was not long in error.

" Is-lands, eh? Thismuses, eh? Take this book and see if you can find any is-lands and promonitaries, and then bring them to me. I want to see them things, I do. Find 'em, if you please."

Brinkly took the book, and it would have melted the heart of any other man to see the deep despair of his heart as he looked on it and was spelling over to himself the words as he came to them.

" Mr. Meadows," he said in pleading tones, " I thought it was is-land. Here it is, I-s-is-l-a-n-d-land, Is-land"; and he looked into his face beseechingly.

" Is-land, eh? *Is-land!* Now, thismuses and promonitaries and hemispheries — "

" Mr. Meadows, I did not know how to pronounce them words. I asked you how to pronounce 'em and you would n't tell me; and I asked Allen, and he told me the way I said them."

" I believe that to be a lie." Brinkly's face reddened, and his breathing was fast and hard. He looked at the master as but once or twice before during the term, but made no answer.

At that moment Allen leaned carelessly on his desk, his elbows resting on it, and chin on his hands, and said dryly, " Yess, I did tell him so."

The man reddened a little. After a moment's pause, however, he said: " How often have I got to tell you not to ask anybody but me how to pronounce words? That 'll do, sir; sit down, sir."

## GEORGE WILLIAM BAGBY

[George William Bagby was born in Buckingham County, Virginia, in 1828. After graduating from the medical school of the University of Pennsylvania he made his residence in Richmond. He became a journalist and wrote some very witty letters under the pen name of "Mozis Addums." He also made a reputation as a humorous lecturer. So sympathetically did he treat the humorous aspects of Virginia life that he won for himself the title of "the Virginia Elia." He died in 1883.]

## JUD BROWNIN'S ACCOUNT OF RUBINSTEIN'S PLAYING

"Jud, they say you heard Rubinstein play when you were in New York."

"I did, in the cool."

"Well, tell us about it."

"What? me? I might 's well tell you about the creation of the world."

"Come, now; no mock modesty. Go ahead."

"Well, sir, he had the blaemedest, biggest, cattycornedest pianner you ever laid eyes on; somethin' like a distractid billiard table on three legs. The lid was heisted, and mighty well it was. If it had n't been, he 'd tore the intire insides clean out, and scattered 'em to the four winds of heaven."

"Played well, did he?"

"You bet he did; but don't interrup' me. When he first set down he 'peared to keer mighty little 'bout playin', and wished he had n' come. He tweedle-leedled a little on the trible, and twoodle-oodle-oodled some on the base — just foolin' and boxin' the thing's jaws for bein' in his way. And I says to a man settin' next to me, s' I, 'What sort of fool playin' is that?' And he says, 'Heish!' But presently his hands commenced chasin' one 'nother up and down the keys, like a passel of rats scamperin' through a garret very swift. Parts of it was sweet, though, and reminded me of a sugar squirrel turnin' the wheel of a candy cage. ' Now,' I says to my neighbor, ' he's showin' off. He thinks he's a-doin' of it; but he ain't got no idee, no plan of nuthin'. If he'd play me up a tune of some kind or other, I'd — '

" But my neighbor says, ' Heish ! ' very impatient.

" I was just about to git up and go home, bein' tired of that foolishness, when I heard a little bird wakin' up away off in the woods, and callin' sleepy-like to his mate, and I looked up and I see that Ruben was beginnin' to take interest in his business, and I set down agin. It was the peep of day. The light come faint from the east, the breeze blowed gentle and fresh, some more birds waked up in the orchard, then some more in the trees near the house, and all begun singin' together. People begun to stir, and the gal opened the shutters. Just then the first beam of the sun fell upon the blossoms ; a leetle more and it techt the roses on the bushes, and the next thing it was broad day ; the sun fairly blazed ; the birds sang like they'd split their little throats ; all the leaves was movin', and flashin' diamonds of dew, and the whole wide world was bright and happy as a king. Seemed to me like there was a good breakfast in every house in the land, and not a sick child or woman anywhere. It was a fine mornin'.

" And I says to my neighbor, ' That's music, that is.'

" But he glared at me like he'd like to cut my throat.

" Presently the wind turned ; it begun to thicken up, and a kind of gray mist come over things ; I got low-spirited d'rectly. Then a silver rain begun to fall ; I could see the drops touch the ground ; some flashed up like long pearl earrings ; and the rest rolled away like round rubies. It was pretty, but melancholy. Then the pearls gathered themselves into long strands and necklaces, and then they melted into thin silver streams running between golden gravels, and then the streams joined each other at the bottom of the hill, and made a brook that flowed silent except that you could kinder see the music specially when the bushes on the banks moved as the music went along down the valley. I could smell the flowers in the meadows. But the sun did n't shine, nor the birds sing; it was a foggy day, but not cold. Then the sun went down, it got dark, the wind moaned and wept like a lost child for its dead mother, and I could a-got up then and there and preached a better sermon than any I ever listened to. There was n't a thing in the world left to live for, not a blame thing, and yet I did n't want the music to stop one bit. It was happier to be miserable than to be happy without being miserable. I could n't understand it. . . . Then, all of a sudden, old Ruben changed his tune. He ripped and he rar'd, he tipped and he tar'd, he pranced and he charged like the grand entry at a circus. 'Peared to me like all the gas in the house was turned on at once, things got so bright, and I hilt up my head, ready to look any man in the face, and not afeared of nothin'. It was a circus, and a brass band, and a big ball, all goin' on at the same time. He lit into them keys like a thousand of brick, he gave 'em no rest, day nor night; he set every living joint in me agoin', and not bein' able to stand it no longer, I jumpt spang onto my seat, and jest hollered: '*Go it, my Rube!*'

"Every blamed man, woman, and child in the house riz on me, and shouted, 'Put him out! Put him out!'

"With that some several p'licemen run up, and I had to simmer down. But I would a-fit any fool that laid hands on me, for I was bound to hear Ruby out or die.

"He had changed his tune agin. He hopt-light ladies and tiptoed fine from eend to eend of the keyboard. He played soft, and low, and solemn. I heard the church bells over the hills. The candles in heaven was lit, one by one. I saw the stars rise. The great organ of eternity began to play from the world's end to the world's end, and all the angels went to prayers. Then the music changed to water, full of feeling that could n't be thought, and began to drop — drip, drop, drip, drop — clear and sweet, like tears of joy fallin' into a lake of glory.

"He stopt a minute or two, to fetch breath. Then he got mad. He run his fingers through his hair, he shoved up his sleeves, he opened his coat-tails a leetle further, he drug up his stool, he leaned over, and, sir, he just went for that old pianner. He slapt her face, he boxed her jaws, he pulled her nose, he pinched her ears, and he scratched her cheeks, till she farly yelled. He knockt her down and he stompt on her shameful. She bellowed like a bull, she bleated like a calf, she howled like a hound, she squealed like a pig, she shrieked like a rat, and then he would n't let her up. He run a quarter-stretch down the low grounds of the bass, till he got clean into the bowels of the earth, and you heard thunder galloping after thunder, through the hollows and caves of perdition; and then he fox-chased his right hand with his left till he got away out of the trible into the clouds, whar the notes was finer than the pints of cambric needles, and you could n't hear nothin' but the shadders of 'em. And then he would n't let the old pianner go. He fetcht up his right wing, he fetcht up his left wing, he fetcht up his center, he fetcht up his reserves. He fired by file, he fired by platoons, by company, by regiments, and by brigades. He opened his cannon, siege-guns down thar, Napoleons here, twelve-pounders yonder, big guns, little guns, middle-sized guns, round shot, shell, shrapnel, grape, canister, mortars, mines, and magazines, every livin' battery and bomb a-goin' at the same time. The house trembled, the lights danced, the walls shuk, the floor come up, the ceilin' come down, the sky split, the ground rockt — BANG!

"With that *bang!* he lifted hisself bodily into the ar', and he come down with his knees, his ten fingers, his ten toes, his elbows, and his nose, strikin' every single solitary key on that pianner at the same time. The thing busted and went off into seventeen hundred and fifty-seven thousand five hundred and forty-two hemi-demi-semi-quivers, and I know'd no mo'."

# NOVELISTS AND STORY WRITERS

## GEORGE WASHINGTON CABLE

[George Washington Cable was born in New Orleans, Louisiana, in 1844. Though very young when the Civil War began, he served in the Fourth Mississippi Cavalry. After the war he was for some years a surveyor and then a clerk in a cotton factor's office. He gave up this position to become a reporter on the New Orleans *Picayune*, for which he had been writing sketches. Reporting was, however, not to his taste, and finding that the stories he had had time to write between his newspaper duties were acceptable to *Scribner's Magazine* and other periodicals, he decided in 1879 to devote himself to literature as a profession. In 1886 he moved to Northampton, Massachusetts, where he still resides. While engaged in newspaper work he began to write sketches of New Orleans

GEORGE WASHINGTON CABLE

life. These he later gathered into his book "Old Creole Days," published in 1879. Since then he has written several novels and collections of short stories, nearly all of which have his distinctive background of Louisiana Creole life. Becoming interested in philanthropic enterprises, he has given much time and energy to the promotion of societies for social betterment, such as the Home Culture Clubs, founded in 1887, now the Northampton People's Institute. In addition to the writing of books, he has lectured on literary and philanthropic subjects and has given readings from his own stories.]

## THE DANCE IN PLACE CONGO[1]

### I. CONGO SQUARE

Whoever has been to New Orleans with eyes not totally abandoned to buying and selling will, of course, remember St. Louis Cathedral, looking southeastward — riverward — across quaint Jackson Square, the old Place d'Armes. And if he has any feeling for flowers, he has not forgotten the little garden behind the cathedral, so antique and unexpected, named for the beloved old priest Père Antoine.

The old Rue Royale lies across the sleeping garden's foot. On the street's farther side another street lets away at right angles, northwestward, straight, and imperceptibly downward from the cathedral and garden toward the rear of the city. It is lined mostly with humble ground-floor-and-garret houses of stuccoed brick, their wooden doorsteps on the brick sidewalks. This is Orleans Street, so named when the city was founded.

Its rugged round-stone pavement is at times nearly as sunny and silent as the landward side of a coral reef. Thus for about half a mile; and then Rampart Street, where the palisade wall of the town used to run in Spanish days, crosses it, and a public square just beyond draws a grateful canopy of oak and sycamore boughs. That is the Place. One may shut his buff umbrella there, wipe the beading sweat from the brow, and fan himself with his hat. Many 's the bullfight has taken place on that spot Sunday afternoons of the old time. That is Congo Square.

The trees are modern. So are the buildings about the four sides, for all their aged looks. So are all the grounds' adornments. Trémé market, off beyond, toward the swamp, is not

[1] Owing to inability to secure permission from the publishers of Mr. Cable's works to include a selection from his short stories or his novels, I have availed myself of this vivid sketch of a characteristic feature of the old life of New Orleans. The article was originally contributed to the *Century Magazine*, Vol. XXXI, page 517.

so very old, and the scowling, ill-smelling prison on the right, so Spanish-looking and dilapidated, is not a third the age it seems; not fifty-five. In that climate every year of a building's age counts for ten. Before any of these M. Cayetano's circus and menagerie were here. Cayetane the negroes called him. He was the Barnum of that region and day.

> Miché Cayetane, qui sortie de l'Havane,
> Avec so chouals et somacaques.

That is, " who came from Havana with his horses and baboons."

Up at the other end of Orleans Street, hid only by the old padre's garden and the cathedral, glistens the ancient Place d'Armes. In the early days it stood for all that was best; the place for political rallying, the retail quarter of all fine goods and wares, and at sunset and by moonlight the promenade of good society and the haunt of true lovers; not only in the military, but also in the most unwarlike sense the place of arms, and of hearts and hands, and of words tender as well as words noble.

The Place Congo, at the opposite end of the street, was at the opposite end of everything. One was on the highest ground; the other on the lowest. The one was the rendezvous of the rich man, the master, the military officer — of all that went to make up the ruling class; the other of the butcher and baker, the raftsman, the sailor, the quadroon, the painted girl, and the negro slave. No meaner name could be given the spot. The negro was the most despised of human creatures and the Congo the plebeian among negroes. The white man's plaza had the army and navy on its right and left, the courthouse, the council-hall and the church at its back, and the world before it. The black man's was outside the rear gate, the poisonous wilderness on three sides and the proud man's contumely on its front.

Before the city overgrew its flimsy palisade walls, and closing in about this old stamping-ground gave it set bounds, it was known as Congo Plains. There was wide room for much field sport, and the Indian villagers of the town's outskirts and the lower class of white Creoles made it the ground of their wild ball game of *raquette*. Sunday afternoons were the time for it. Hence, beside these diversions there was, notably, another.

The hour was the slave's term of momentary liberty, and his simple, savage, musical and superstitious nature dedicated it to amatory song and dance tinctured with his rude notions of supernatural influences.

## II. Grand Orchestra

The booming of African drums and blast of huge wooden horns called to the gathering. It was these notes of invitation, reaching beyond those of other outlandish instruments, that caught the Ethiopian ear, put alacrity into the dark foot, and brought their owners, male and female, trooping from all quarters. The drums were very long, hollowed, often from a single piece of wood, open at one end and having a sheep or goat skin stretched across the other. One was large, the other much smaller. The tight skin heads were not held up to be struck; the drums were laid along on the turf and the drummers bestrode them, and beat them on the head madly with fingers, fists, and feet, — with slow vehemence on the great drum, and fiercely and rapidly on the small one. Sometimes an extra performer sat on the ground behind the larger drum, at its open end, and "beat upon the wooden sides of it with two sticks." The smaller drum was often made from a joint or two of very large bamboo, in the West Indies where such could be got, and this is said to be the origin of its name; for it was called the *Bamboula*.

In stolen hours of night or the basking-hour of noon the black man contrived to fashion these rude instruments and others. The drummers, I say, bestrode the drums; the other musicians sat about them in an arc, cross-legged on the ground. One important instrument was a gourd partly filled with pebbles or grains of corn, flourished violently at the end of a stout staff with one hand and beaten upon the palm of the other. Other performers rang triangles, and others twanged from jew's-harps an astonishing amount of sound. Another instrument was the jawbone of some ox, horse, or mule, and a key rattled rhythmically along its weather-beaten teeth. At times the drums were reënforced by one or more empty barrels or casks beaten on the head with the shank bones of cattle.

A queer thing that went with these when the affair was pretentious — full dress, as it were — at least it was so in the West Indies, whence Congo Plains drew all inspirations — was the Marimba brett, a union of reed and string principles. A single strand of wire ran lengthwise of a bit of wooden board, sometimes a shallow box of thin wood, some eight inches long by four or five in width, across which, under the wire, were several joints of reed about a quarter of an inch in diameter and of graduated lengths. The performer, sitting cross-legged, held the board in both hands and plucked the ends of the reeds with his thumb-nails. The result was called — music.

But the grand instrument at last, the first violin, as one might say, was the banjo. It had but four strings, not six: beware of the dictionary. It is not the "favorite musical instrument of the negroes of the Southern States of America." Uncle Remus says truly that that is the fiddle; but for the true African dance, a dance not so much of legs and feet as of the upper half of the body, a sensual, devilish thing tolerated only by Latin-American masters, there was wanted the dark inspiration of African drums and the banjo's thrump and strum.

And then there was that long-drawn human cry of tremendous volume, richness, and resound, to which no instrument within their reach could make the faintest approach:

> Eh! pou' la belle Layotte ma mourri 'nocent,
> Oui 'nocent ma mourri!

all the instruments silent while it rises and swells with mighty energy and dies away distantly, " Yea-a-a-a-a-a! " — then the crash of savage drums, horns, and rattles —

> For the fair Layotte I must crazy die!
> Yes, crazy I must die!

To all this there was sometimes added a Pan's-pipe of but three reeds, made from single joints of the common brake cane, and called by English-speaking negroes " the quills." . . .

Such was the full band. All the values of contrast that discord can furnish must have been present, with whatever there is of ecstasy in maddening repetition, for of this the African can never have too much.

And yet there was entertaining variety. Where? In the dance! There was constant, exhilarating novelty — endless invention — in the turning, bowing, arm-swinging, posturing, and leaping of the dancers. Moreover, the music of Congo Plains was not tamed to mere monotone. Monotone became subordinate to many striking qualities. The strain was wild. Its contact with French taste gave it often great tenderness of sentiment. It grew in fervor, and rose and sank, and rose again, with the play of emotion in the singers and dancers.

### III. THE GATHERING

It was a weird one. The negro of colonial Louisiana was a most grotesque figure. He was nearly naked. Often his neck and arms, thighs, shanks, and splay feet were shrunken, tough,

GEORGE WASHINGTON CABLE          319

sinewy like a monkey's. Sometimes it was scant diet and cruel labor that had made them so. Even the requirement of law was only that he should have not less than a barrel of corn — nothing else — a month, nor get more than thirty lashes to the twenty-four hours. The whole world was crueler those times than now ; we must not judge them by our own.

Often the slave's attire was only a cotton shirt, or a pair of pantaloons hanging in indecent tatters to his naked waist. The bondwoman was well clad who had on as much as a coarse chemise and petticoat. To add a *tignon* — a Madras handkerchief twisted into a turban — was high gentility, and the number of kerchiefs beyond that one was the measure of absolute wealth. Some were rich in *tignons*; especially those who served within the house, and pleased the mistress, or even the master — there were Hagars in those days. However, Congo Plains did not gather the house servants so much as the "field-hands."

These came in troops. See them ; wilder than gypsies ; wilder than the Moors and Arabs whose strong blood and features one sees at a glance in so many of them ; gangs, — as they were called, — gangs and gangs of them, from this and that and yonder direction ; tall, well-knit Senegalese from Cape Verde, black as ebony, with intelligent, kindly eyes and long, straight, shapely noses ; Mandingoes, from the Gambia River, lighter of color, of cruder form, and a cunning that shows in the countenance ; whose enslavement seems specially a shame, their nation the "merchants of Africa," dwelling in towns, industrious, thrifty, skilled in commerce and husbandry, and expert in the working of metals, even to silver and gold ; and Fulahs, playfully miscalled "*Poulards*," — fat chickens, — of goodly stature, and with a perceptible rose tint in the cheeks ; and Sosos, famous warriors, dexterous with the African targe ; and in contrast to these, with small ears, thick eyebrows, bright eyes, flat, upturned noses, shining skin, wide mouths and white teeth, the negroes of Guinea, true and unmixed, from the Gold Coast, the Slave Coast, and the Cape of Palms — not from the Grain Coast; the English had that trade. See them come! Popoes, Cotocolies, Fidas, Socoes, Agwas, short, copper-colored Mines — what havoc the slavers did make! — and from interior Africa others equally proud and warlike: fierce Nagoes and Fonds; tawny Awassas; Iboes, so light-colored that one could not tell them from mulattoes but for their national tattooing; and the half-civilized and quick-witted but ferocious Arada, the original Voudoo worshiper. And how many more! For here come, also, men and women from all that great Congo coast, — Angola, Malimbe, Ambrice, etc., — small, good-natured, sprightly "boys," and gay, garrulous "gals," thick-lipped but not tattooed; chattering, chaffering, singing, and guffawing as they come: these are they for whom the dance and the place are named, the most numerous sort of negro in the colonies, the Congoes and Franc-Congoes, and though serpent worshipers, yet the gentlest and kindliest natures that came from Africa. Such was the company. Among these *bossals* — that is, native Africans — there was, of course, an ever-growing number of negroes who proudly called themselves Creole negroes, that is, born in America; [1] and at the present time there is only here and there an old native African to be met with, vain of his singularity and trembling on his staff.

## IV. THE BAMBOULA

The gathering throng closed in around, leaving unoccupied the circle indicated by the crescent of musicians. The short, harsh turf was the dancing floor. The crowd stood. Fancy the

---

[1] This broader use of the term is very common. The Creole "dialect" is the broken English *of the Creoles*, while the Creole *patois* is the corrupt French, not of the Creoles, but rather of the former slave race in the country of the Creoles. So of Creole negroes and Creole dances and songs. [Author's note.]

picture. The pack of dark, tattered figures touched off every here and there with the bright colors of a Madras *tignon*. The squatting, cross-legged musicians. The low-roofed, embowered town off in front, with here and there a spire lifting a finger of feeble remonstrance; the flat, grassy plain stretching around and behind, dotted with black stumps; in the distance the pale-green willow undergrowth, behind it the *cyprière* — the cypress swamp — and in the pale, seven-times-heated sky the sun, only a little declined to south and westward, pouring down its beams.

With what particular musical movements the occasion began does not now appear. May be with very slow and measured ones; they had such that were strange and typical. I have heard the negroes sing one — though it was not of the dance-ground but of the cane-field — that showed the emphatic barbarism of five bars to the line, and was confined to four notes of the open horn.

But I can only say that with some such slow and quiet strain the dance may have been preluded. It suits the Ethiopian fancy for a beginning to be dull and repetitious; the bottom of the ladder must be on the ground.

The singers almost at the first note are many. At the end of the first line every voice is lifted up. The strain is given the second time with growing spirit. Yonder glistening black Hercules, who plants one foot forward, lifts his head and bare, shining chest, and rolls out the song from a mouth and throat like a cavern, is a *candio*, a chief, or was before he was overthrown in battle and dragged away, his village burning behind him, from the mountains of High Soudan. That is an African amulet that hangs about his neck — a *greegree*. He is of the Bambaras, as you may know by his solemn visage and the long tattoo streaks running down from the temples to the neck, broadest in the middle, like knife-gashes. See his play of restrained enthusiasm catch from one bystander to another. They swing and bow to right and left, in slow time to the piercing treble of the Congo women. Some are responsive! others are competitive. Hear that bare foot slap the ground! one sudden stroke only, as it were the foot of a stag. The musicians warm up at the sound. A smiting of breasts with open hands begins very softly and becomes vigorous. The women's voices rise to a tremulous intensity. Among the chorus of Franc-Congo singing-girls is one of extra good voice, who thrusts in, now and again, an improvisation. This girl here, so tall and straight, is a Yaloff. You see it in her almost Hindu features, and hear it in the plaintive melody of her voice. Now the chorus is more piercing than ever. The women clap their hands in time, or standing with arms akimbo receive with faint courtesies and head-liftings the low bows of the men, who deliver them swinging this way and that.

See! Yonder brisk and sinewy fellow has taken one short, nervy step into the ring, chanting with rising energy. Now he takes another, and stands and sings and looks here and there, rising upon his broad toes and sinking and rising again, with what wonderful lightness! How tall and lithe he is. Notice his brawn shining through his rags. He too is a *candio*, and by the three long rays of tattooing on each side of his face, a Kiamba. The music has got into his feet. He moves off to the farther edge of the circle, still singing, takes the prompt hand of an unsmiling Congo girl, leads her into the ring, and, leaving the chant to the throng, stands her before him for the dance.

Will they dance to that measure? Wait! A sudden frenzy seizes the musicians. The measure quickens, the swaying, attitudinizing crowd starts into extra activity, the female voices grow sharp and staccato, and suddenly the dance is the furious Bamboula.

Now for the frantic leaps! Now for frenzy! Another pair are in the ring! The man wears a belt of little bells, or, as a substitute, little tin vials of shot, "bram-bram sonnette!" And still another couple enter the circle. What wild — what terrible delight! The ecstasy rises to madness; one — two — three of the dancers fall — *bloucoutoum! boum!* — with foam on their lips and are dragged out by arms and legs from under the tumultuous feet of crowding newcomers. The musicians know no fatigue; still the dance rages on:

> Quand patate la cuite na va mangé li!

And all to that one nonsense line meaning only,

> When that 'tater 's cooked don't you eat it up!

It was a frightful triumph of body over mind, even in those early days when the slave was still a genuine pagan; but as his moral education gave him some hint of its enormity, and it became a forbidden fruit monopolized by those of reprobate will, it grew everywhere more and more gross. No wonder the police stopped it in Congo Square. . . .

It is odd that such fantastical comicality of words should have been mated to such fierce and frantic dancing, but so it was. The reeking faces of the dancers, moreover, always solemnly grave. So we must picture it now if we still fancy ourselves spectators on Congo Plains. The bamboula still roars and rattles, twangs, contorts, and tumbles in terrible earnest, while we stand and talk. So, on and on.

## JOEL CHANDLER HARRIS

[Joel Chandler Harris was born in Eatonton, Georgia, in 1848. He left school at the age of twelve to go to the farm of a Mr.

JOEL CHANDLER HARRIS

Turner, nine miles from Eatonton, to learn the printer's trade in connection with the publication of a newspaper. Most of his training for his future work was obtained from the books of Mr. Turner's library and from the negroes on the plantation, from whom he stored his mind with their folklore. In 1876 Harris became a member of the editorial staff of the *Atlanta Constitution*. For this paper he wrote the negro folk tales which were gathered into the volume "Uncle Remus : his Songs and Sayings," published in 1880. This book at once gave the author a national reputation, which has been sustained by his further volumes dealing with negro folklore and the life of Georgia country people. He died at his home, "Sign of the Wren's Nest," in a suburb of Atlanta, Georgia, in 1908.]

## BRER RABBIT GROSSLY DECEIVES BRER FOX

When the little boy, whose nights with Uncle Remus are as entertaining as those Arabian ones of blessed memory, had finished supper the other evening and hurried out to sit with his venerable patron, he found the old man in great glee. Indeed, Uncle Remus was talking and laughing to himself at such a rate that the little boy was afraid he had company. The truth is, Uncle Remus had heard the child coming, and when the rosy-cheeked chap put his head in the door, was engaged in a monologue, the burden of which seemed to be:

> Ole Molly Ha'r
> W'at you doin' d'ar
> Settin' in de cornder
> Smokin' yo' seegyar?

As a matter of course, this vague allusion reminded the little boy of the fact that the wicked Fox was still in pursuit of the Rabbit, and he immediately put his curiosity in the shape of a question.

"Uncle Remus, did the Rabbit have to go clean away when he got loose from the Tar-baby?"

"Bless grashus, honey, dat he did n't. Who? Him? You dunno nuthin' 'tall 'bout Brer Rabbit ef dat 's de way you put-tin' 'em down. W'at he gwine 'way fer? He mouter stayed sorter close 'twell de pitch rub off'n his ha'r, but 'twan't menny days 'fo' he waz lopin' up en down de naberhood same ez ever, en I dunno ef he were n't mo' sassier den befo'.

"Seem like dat de tale 'bout how he got mixt up wid de Tar-baby got 'roun' 'mongst de nabers. Leas'ways, Miss Meadows en de gals got win' un it, en de nex' time Brer Rabbit paid um a visit, Miss Meadows tackled 'im 'bout it, en de gals sot up a monst'us gigglement. Brer Rabbit, he sot up des ez cool ez a cowcumber, he did, en let 'em run on."

"Who was Miss Meadows, Uncle Remus?" inquired the little boy.

"Don' ax me, honey. She was in de tale, en de tale I give you like hit were gun ter me. Brer Rabbit, he sot dar, he did, sorter lam'like, en den bimeby he cross his legs, he did, en wink his eye slow en up en say, sezee:

"'Ladies, Brer Fox wuz my daddy's ridin' hoss fer thirty year; maybe mo', but thirty year dat I knows un!' sezee, en den he paid 'em his 'spects, en tip his beaver, en march off, he did, des ez stiff en ez stuck up ez a fire-stick.

"Nex' day, Brer Fox cum callin', en w'en he gun fer ter laff 'bout Brer Rabbit, Miss Meadows en de gals, dey ups en tells 'im 'bout w'at Brer Rabbit said. Den Brer Fox grit his toof sho' nuff, he did, en he look mighty dumpy, but w'en he riz fer ter go, he up en say, sezee:

"'Ladies, I ain't 'sputin' w'at you say, but I'll make Brer Rabbit chaw up his words en spit um out right here whar you kin see 'im,' sezee, en wid dat off Brer Fox marcht.

"En w'en he got in de big road, he shuck de dew off'n his tail, en made a straight shoot fer Brer Rabbit's house. W'en he got dar, Brer Rabbit wuz 'spectin' un 'im, en de do' was shet fas'. Brer Fox knock. Nobody never ans'er. Brer Fox knock. Nobody ans'er. Den he knock ag'in — blam, blam. Den Brer Rabbit holler out mighty weak:

"'Is dat you, Brer Fox? I want you to run fer ter fetch de doctor. Dat bait er pusly w'at I et dis mawnin' is gittin' 'way wid me. Do please run quick, Brer Fox,' sez Brer Rabbit, sezee.

"'I come atter you, Brer Rabbit,' sez Brer Fox, sezee. 'Dere's gwineter be a party over at Miss Meadows's,' sezee. 'All de gals 'll be dere, en I promus' dat I'd fetch you. De gals, dey 'lowed dat hit would n't be no party 'ceppin' I fotch you,' sez Brer Fox, sezee.

"Den Brer Rabbit say he was too sick, en Brer Fox say he wuzzent, en dar dey had it up and down, 'sputin' en contendin'. Brer Rabbit say he could n't walk. Brer Fox say he'd tote 'im. Brer Rabbit say how? Brer Fox say in his arms. Brer Rabbit say he'd drap 'im. Brer Fox 'low he would n't. Bimeby, Brer Rabbit say he'd go ef Brer Fox tote 'im on his back. Brer Fox

say he would. Brer Rabbit say he could n't ride widout a
saddle. Brer Fox say he 'd git de saddle. Brer Rabbit say he
could n't set in de saddle less he had bridle fer ter hol' by. Brer
Fox say he 'd git de bridle. Brer Rabbit say he could n't ride
widout bline-bridle, kaze Brer Fox 'd be shyin' at stumps 'long
de road, en fling 'im off. Brer Fox say he 'd git de bline-bridle.
Den Brer Rabbit say he 'd go. Den Brer Fox say he 'd ride
Brer Rabbit mos' up ter Miss Meadows's en den he could git
down en walk de balance er de way. Brer Rabbit 'greed, en
den Brer Fox lipt out atter de saddle en bridle.

"Co'se Brer Rabbit know'd de game dat Brer Fox wuz fixin'
fer ter play, en he 'termined fer ter outdo 'im, en by de time he
koam his ha'r en twis' his mustash, en sorter rig up, here come
Brer Fox, saddle en bridle on, en lookin' ez peart ez a circus
pony. He trot up ter de do' en stood dar pawin' de groun' en
chompin' de bit same like sho' nuff hoss, en Brer Rabbit he
mounted, he did, en dey amble off. Brer Fox could n't see
behine wid de bline-bridle on, but bimeby he feel Brer Rabbit
raise one er his foots.

"'W'at you doin't now, Brer Rabbit?' sezee.

"'Short'nin' de lef' stir'p, Brer Fox,' sezee.

"Bimeby, Brer Rabbit raise up de udder foot.

"'W'at you doin't now, Brer Rabbit?' sezee.

"'Pullin' down my pants, Brer Fox,' sezee.

"All de time, bless grashus, honey, Brer Rabbit were puttin'
on his spurrers en w'en dey got close to Miss Meadows's, whar
Brer Rabbit wuz to git off, en Brer Fox made a motion fer ter
put on brakes, Brer Rabbit slap de spurrers inter Brer Fox's
flanks, en you better b'leeve he got over groun'. W'en dey got
ter de house, Miss Meadows en all de gals wuz er settin' on de
peazzer, en 'stidder stoppin' at de gate, Brer Rabbit rid on by,
he did, en come gallopin' down de road en up ter de hoss rack,
w'ich he hitch Brer Fox at, en den he santer inter de house,

he did, en shake han's wid de gals en set dar smokin' his seegyar same ez town man. Bimeby, he draw in long puff en den let hit out in er cloud, en squar' hisse'f back, en holler out, he did:

"'Ladies, ain't I done tell you Brer Fox wuz de ridin' hoss fer our fambly? He's sorter losin' his gait now, but I 'speck I kin fetch 'im all right in a mont' er so,' sezee.

"En den Brer Rabbit smile, he did, en de gals giggle, en Miss Meadows, she praise up de pony, en dar wuz Brer Fox hitch fas' ter de rack en could n't he'p hisse'f."

"Is that all, Uncle Remus?" asked the little boy as the old man paused.

"Dat ain't all, honey, but 't won't do fer to give out too much cloff fer ter cut one pa'r pants," replied the old man sententiously.

### THE CUNNING FOX IS AGAIN VICTIMIZED

When "Miss Sally's" little boy went to Uncle Remus the next night to hear the conclusion of the adventure in which the Rabbit made a riding horse of the Fox to the great enjoyment and gratification of Miss Meadows and the girls, he found the old man in a bad humor.

"I ain't tellin' no tales ter bad chilluns," said Uncle Remus, curtly.

"But, Uncle Remus, I ain't bad," said the little boy, plaintively.

"Who dat chunkin' dem chickens dis mawnin'? Who dat knockin' out fokes's eyes wid dat Yaller-bammer sling des 'fo' dinner? Who dat sickin' dat pinter puppy atter my pig? Who dat scatterin' my ingun sets? Who dat flingin' rocks on top er my house, w'ich a little mo' en one un um would er drapt spang on my head?"

"Well, now, Uncle Remus, I did n't go to do it. I won't do so any more. Please, Uncle Remus, if you will tell me I 'll run in the house and bring you some tea-cakes."

"Seein 's better 'n hearin' tell un um," replied the old man, the severity of his countenance relaxing into a smile; but the little boy darted out and in a few minutes came running back with his pockets full and his hands full.

"I lay yo' mammy 'll 'spishun dat de rats' stummucks is widenin' in dis naberhood, w'en she come fer ter count up 'er cakes," said Uncle Remus, with a chuckle. "Deze," he continued, dividing the cakes into two equal parts, "deze I 'll tackle now, en deze I 'll lay by fer Sunday.

"Lemme see. I mos' dis'member wharbouts Brer Fox en Brer Rabbit wuz."

"The Rabbit rode the Fox to Miss Meadows's and hitched him to the horse rack," said the little boy.

"W'y co'se he did," said Uncle Remus, "co'se he did. Well, Brer Rabbit rid Brer Fox up, he did, en tied 'im to de rack, en sot out in de peazzer wid de gals smokin' er his seegyar wid mo' proudness dan w'at you mos' ever see. Dey talk, en dey sing, en dey play on de peanner, de gals did, twell bimeby hit come time fer Brer Rabbit fer to be gwine, en he tell um all good-bye, en strut out to de hoss rack same 's ef he wuz de king er de patter-rollers, en den he mounted Brer Fox and rid off.

"Brer Fox ain't sayin' nothin' 'tall. He des rack off en keep his mouf shet, en Brer Rabbit know'd der wuz bizness cookin' up fer him, en he feel monst'us skittish. Brer Fox amble on twell he got in de long land outer sight er Miss Meadows's house, en den he turn loose, he did. He rip en he r'ar en he cuss en he swar; he snort en he cavort."

"What was he doing that for, Uncle Remus?" the little boy inquired.

"He wuz tryin' fer ter fling Brer Rabbit, bless yo' soul. But he des might ez well er rastled wid his own shadder. Ev'y time he hump hisse'f, Brer Rabbit slap de spurrers in 'im, en dar dey had it up en down. Brer Fox fa'rly to' up de groun', he did, en he jump so high en he jump so quick dat he mighty nigh snatch his own tail off. Dey kep' on gwine on dis way twell bimeby Brer Fox lay down en roll over, he did, en dis sorter unsettle Brer Rabbit, but by de time Brer Fox got back on his footses ag'in, Brer Rabbit wuz gwine thoo de underbresh mo' samer dan a race hoss. Brer Fox, he lit out atter 'im, he did, en he push Brer Rabbit so close dat it wuz 'bout all he could do fer ter git in a holler tree. Hole too little fer Brer Fox fer ter git in, en he hatter lay down en res' en gedder his mine tergedder.

"While he wuz layin' dar Mr. Buzzard come floppin' 'long en seein' Brer Fox stretch out on de groun' he lit en view de premusses. Den Mr. Buzzard sorter shake his wing, en put his head on one side, en say to hisse'f like, sezee:

"'Brer Fox dead, en I so sorry,' sezee.

"'No I ain't dead nudder,' sez Brer Fox, sezee. 'I got ole man Rabbit pent up in here,' sezee, 'en I'm gwineter git 'im dis time ef it takes twell Chris'mus,' sezee.

"Den atter some mo' palaver, Brer Fox make a bargain dat Mr. Buzzard wuz ter watch de hole en keep Brer Rabbit dar w'ilst Brer Fox went atter his axe. Den Brer Fox, he lope off, he did, en Mr. Buzzard, he tuck up his stan' at de hole. Bimeby, w'en all got still, Brer Rabbit sorter scramble down close ter de hole, he did, en holler out:

"'Brer Fox! oh, Brer Fox!'

"Brer Fox done gone, en nobody say nuthin'. Den Brer Rabbit squall out like he wuz mad, sezee:

"'You need n't talk les' you wanter,' sezee. 'I knows youer dar, en I ain't keerin',' sezee. 'I des wanter tell you dat I wish mighty bad Brer Turkey Buzzard wuz here,' sezee.

" Den Mr. Buzzard try to talk like Brer Fox :

" ' W'at you want wid Mr. Buzzard ? ' sezee.

" ' Oh, nothin' 'tickler, 'cep' dere 's de fattes' gray squir'l in yer dat I ever see,' sezee, ' en ef Brer Turkey Buzzard was 'roun' he 'd be mighty glad fer ter git 'im,' sezee.

" ' How Mr. Buzzard gwine ter git 'im ? ' sez de Buzzard, sezee.

" ' Well, dar 's a little hole 'roun' on de udder side er de tree,' sez Brer Rabbit, sezee, ' en ef Brer Turkey Buzzard wuz here so he could take up his stan' dar,' sezee, ' I could drive de squir'l out,' sezee.

" Den Brer Rabbit kick up a racket like he wer' drivin' sumpin' out, en Mr. Buzzard he rush 'roun' fer ter ketch de squir'l, en Brer Rabbit, he dash out, he did, en he des fly fer home."

At this point, Uncle Remus took one of the tea-cakes, held his head back, opened his mouth, dropped the cake in with a sudden motion, looked at the little boy with an expression of astonishment, and then closed his eyes and began to chew, mumbling as an accompaniment the plaintive tune of " Don't you grieve atter me."

The séance was over ; but before the little boy went into the " big house," Uncle Remus laid his rough hand tenderly on the child's shoulder and remarked in a confidential tone :

" Honey, you mus' git up soon Chris'mus mawnin' en open de do' ; kaze I'm gwineter bounce in on Marse John en Miss Sally, en holler ' Chris'mus gif',' des like I useter endurin' de fahmin' days 'fo' de war, w'en ole Miss wuz 'live. I boun' dey don't fergit de ole nigger, nudder. W'en you hear me callin' de pigs, honey, you des hop up en onfassen de do'. I lay I 'll give Marse John wunner deze yer 'sprize parties."

## MARY NOAILLES MURFREE ("CHARLES EGBERT CRADDOCK")

[Mary Noailles Murfree, known in literature as Charles Egbert Craddock, was born near Murfreesboro, Tennessee, in 1850. Being

left slightly lame from a stroke of paralysis when a child, she devoted herself largely to reading and study. For many years she spent her summers in the mountains of East Tennessee, and thus she became familiar with the material that appears in her stories — the beauty of the mountains and the primitive life of the mountaineers. In 1884 she collected her earliest stories into a volume entitled "In the Tennessee Mountains." This has been followed by other volumes about the mountaineers, novels of life in other sections of the South, and various magazine articles. For a number of years after the war the Murfree family lived in St. Louis, returning in 1890 to Murfreesboro, which has since been the novelist's home.]

MARY NOAILLES MURFREE

### THE "HARNT" THAT WALKS CHILHOWEE [1]

The breeze freshened, after the sun went down, and the hop and gourd vines were all astir as they clung about the little porch where Clarsie was sitting now, idle at last. The rain-clouds had disappeared, and there bent over the dark, heavily wooded ridges a pale blue sky, with here and there the crystalline sparkle of a star. A halo was shimmering in the east,

[1] Reprinted from "In the Tennessee Mountains" by special arrangement with the holders of the copyright, Houghton Mifflin Company.

where the mists had gathered about the great white moon, hanging high above the mountains. Noiseless wings flitted through the dusk; now and then the bats swept by so close as to wave Clarsie's hair with the wind of their flight. What an airy, glittering, magical thing was that gigantic spider-web suspended between the silver moon and her shining eyes! Ever and anon there came from the woods a strange, weird, long-drawn sigh, unlike the stir of the wind in the trees, unlike the fret of the water on the rocks. Was it the voiceless sorrow of the sad earth? There were stars in the night besides those known to astronomers: the stellular fire-flies gemmed the black shadows with a fluctuating brilliancy; they circled in and out of the porch, and touched the leaves above Clarsie's head with quivering points of light. A steadier and an intenser gleam was advancing along the road, and the sound of languid footsteps came with it; the aroma of tobacco graced the atmosphere, and a tall figure walked up to the gate.

"Come in, come in," said Peter Giles, rising, and tendering the guest a chair. "Ye air Tom Pratt, ez well ez I kin make out by this light. Waal, Tom, we hain't furgot ye sence ye done been hyar."

As Tom had been there on the previous evening, this might be considered a joke, or an equivocal compliment. The young fellow was restless and awkward under it, but Mrs. Giles chuckled with great merriment. . . .

"Waal," said Peter Giles, "what 's the news out yer way, Tom? Ennything a-goin' on?"

"Thar war a shower yander on the Backbone; it rained toler'ble hard fur a while, an' sot up the corn wonderful. Did ye git enny hyar?"

"Not a drap."

"'Pears ter me ez I kin see the clouds a-circlin' round Chilhowee, an' a-rainin' on everybody's cornfield 'ceptin' ourn," said Mrs. Giles. "Some folks is the favored of the Lord, an' t'others hev ter work fur everything an' git nuthin'. Waal, waal; we-uns will see our reward in the nex' worl'. Thar's a better worl' than this, Tom."

"That's a fac'," said Tom, in orthodox assent.

"An' when we leaves hyar once, we leaves all trouble an' care behind us, Tom; fur we don't come back no more." Mrs. Giles was drifting into one of her pious moods.

"I dunno," said Tom. "Thar hev been them ez hev."

"Hev what?" demanded Peter Giles, startled.

"Hev come back ter this hyar yearth. Thar's a harnt that walks Chilhowee every night o' the worl'. I know them ez hev seen him."

Clarsie's great dilated eyes were fastened on the speaker's face. There was a dead silence for a moment, more eloquent with these looks of amazement than any words could have been.

"I reckons ye remember a puny, shriveled little man, named Reuben Crabb, ez used ter live yander, eight mile along the ridge ter that thar big sulphur spring," Tom resumed, appealing to Peter Giles. "He war born with only one arm."

"I 'members him," interpolated Mrs. Giles, vivaciously. "He war a mighty porely, sickly little critter, all the days of his life. 'T war a wonder he war ever raised ter be a man, — an' a pity, too. An' 't war powerful comical, the way of his takin' off; a stunted, one-armed little critter a-ondertakin' ter fight folks an' shoot pistols. He hed the use o' his one arm, sure."

"Waal," said Tom, "his house ain't thar now, 'kase Sam Grim's brothers burned it ter the ground fur his a-killin' of Sam. That war n't all that war done ter Reuben fur killin' of Sam. The sheriff run Reuben Crabb down this hyar road 'bout a mile from hyar, — mebbe less, — an' shot him dead in the road, jes' whar it forks. Waal, Reuben war in company with another evil-doer, — *he* war from the Cross-Roads, an' I furgits what he hed done, but he war a-tryin' ter hide in the mountings, too; an' the sheriff lef' Reuben a-lyin' thar in the road, while he tries ter ketch up with the t'other; but his horse got a stone in his hoof, an' he los' time, an' hed ter gin it up. An' when he got back ter the forks o' the road whar he had lef' Reuben a-lyin' dead, thar war nuthin' thar 'ceptin' a pool o' blood. Waal, he went right on ter Reuben's house, an' them Grim boys hed burnt it ter the ground; but he seen Reuben's brother Joel. An' Joel, he tole the sheriff that late that evenin' he hed tuk Reuben's body out 'n the road an' buried it, 'kase it hed been lyin' thar in the road ever sence early in the mornin', an' he could n't leave it thar all night, an' he hed n't no shelter fur it, sence the Grim boys hed burnt down the house. So he war obleeged ter bury it. An' Joel showed the sheriff a new-made grave, an' Reuben's coat whar the sheriff's bullet hed gone in at the back an' kem out 'n the breast. The sheriff 'lowed ez they 'd fine Joel fifty dollars fur a-buryin' of Reuben afore the cor'ner kem; but they never done it, ez I knows on. The sheriff said that when the cor'ner kem the body would be tuk up fur a 'quest. But thar hed been a powerful big frishet, an' the river 'twixt the cor'ner's house an' Chilhowee could n't be forded fur three weeks. The cor'ner never kem, an' so thar it all stayed. That war four year ago."

"Waal," said Peter Giles, dryly, "I ain't seen no harnt yit. I knowed all that afore."

Clarsie's wondering eyes upon the young man's moonlit face had elicited these facts, familiar to the elders, but strange, he knew, to her.

"I war jes' a-goin' on ter tell," said Tom, abashed. "Waal, ever sence his brother Joel died, this spring, Reuben's harnt walks Chilhowee." . . .

"My Lord!" exclaimed Peter Giles. "I 'low I could n't live a minit ef I war ter see that thar harnt that walks Chilhowee!"

" I know *I* could n't," said his wife.

" Nor me, nuther," murmured Clarsie. . . .

" 'Pears ter me," said Mrs. Giles, " ez many mountings ez thar air round hyar, he mought hev tuk ter walkin' some o' them, stiddier Chilhowee."

[When the young man had taken his leave, and the household had retired, Clarsie, finding herself unable to sleep, arose and stole from the house to try a method of telling fortunes she knew in order to determine whether she was really going to marry Sam Burney. While she was engaged in these procedures, she became aware of a stirring in the laurel bushes.]

Her eyes were fixed upon the dense growth with a morbid fascination, as she moved away ; but she was once more rooted to the spot when the leaves parted and in the golden moonlight the ghost stood before her. She could not nerve herself to run past him, and he was directly in her way homeward. His face was white, and lined, and thin ; that pitiful quiver was never still in the parted lips ; he looked at her with faltering, beseeching eyes. Clarsie's merciful heart was stirred. " What ails ye, ter come back hyar, an' foller me ? " she cried out abruptly. And then a great horror fell upon her. Was not one to whom a ghost should speak doomed to death, sudden and immediate ?

The ghost replied in a broken, shivering voice, like a wail of pain, " I war a-starvin', — I war a-starvin'," with despairing iteration.

It was all over, Clarsie thought. The ghost had spoken, and she was a doomed creature. She wondered that she did not fall dead in the road. While those beseeching eyes were fastened in piteous appeal on hers, she could not leave him. " I never hearn that 'bout ye," she said, reflectively. " I knows ye hed awful troubles while ye war alive, but I never knowed ez ye war starved."

Surely that was a gleam of sharp surprise in the ghost's prominent eyes, succeeded by a sly intelligence.

"Day is nigh ter breakin'," Clarsie admonished him, as the lower rim of the moon touched the silver mists of the west. "What air ye a-wantin' of me?" . . .

"Ye do ez ye air bid, or it'll be the worse for ye," said the "harnt," in the same quivering, shrill tone. "Thar's hunger in the nex' worl' ez well ez in this, an' ye bring me some vittles hyar this time ter-morrer, an' don't ye tell nobody ye hev seen me, nuther, or it'll be the worse for ye."

There was a threat in his eyes as he disappeared in the laurel, and left the girl standing in the last rays of moonlight. . . .

The next morning, before the moon sank, Clarsie, with a tin pail in her hand, went to meet the ghost at the appointed place. She understood now why the terrible doom that falls upon those to whom a spirit may chance to speak had not descended upon her, and that fear was gone; but the secrecy of her errand weighed heavily. She had been scrupulously careful to put into the pail only such things as had fallen to her share at the table, and which she had saved from the meals of yesterday. "A gal that goes a-robbin' fur a hongry harnt," was her moral reflection, "oughter be throwed bodaciously off'n the bluff."

She found no one at the forks of the road. In the marshy dip were only the myriads of mountain azaleas, only the masses of feathery ferns, only the constellated glories of the laurel blooms. A sea of shining white mist was in the valley, with glinting golden rays striking athwart it from the great cresset of the sinking moon; here and there the long, dark, horizontal line of a distant mountain's summit rose above the vaporous shimmer, like a dreary, somber island in the midst of enchanted waters. Her large, dreamy eyes, so wild and yet so gentle, gazed out through the laurel leaves upon the floating gilded flakes of light, as in the deep coverts of the mountain, where the fulvous-tinted deer were lying, other eyes, as wild and as gentle, dreamily watched the vanishing moon. Overhead, the filmy, lacelike clouds, fretting the blue heavens, were tinged with a faint rose. Through the trees she caught a glimpse of the red sky of dawn, and the glister of a great lucent, tremulous star. From the ground, misty blue exhalations were rising, alternating with the long lines of golden light yet drifting through the woods. It was all very still, very peaceful, almost holy. One could hardly believe that these consecrated solitudes had once reverberated with the echoes of man's death-dealing ingenuity, and that Reuben Crabb had fallen, shot through and through, amid that wealth of flowers at the forks of the road. She heard suddenly the far-away baying of a hound. Her great eyes dilated, and she lifted her head to listen. Only the solemn silence of the woods, the slow sinking of the noiseless moon, the voiceless splendor of that eloquent day-star.

Morning was close at hand, and she was beginning to wonder that the ghost did not appear, when the leaves fell into abrupt commotion, and he was standing in the road, beside her. He did not speak, but watched her with an eager, questioning intentness, as she placed the contents of the pail upon the moss at the roadside. " I'm a-comin' agin ter-morrer," she said gently. He made no reply, quickly gathered the food from the ground, and disappeared in the deep shades of the woods.

She had not expected thanks, for she was accustomed only to the gratitude of dumb beasts; but she was vaguely conscious of something wanting, as she stood motionless for a moment, and watched the burnished rim of the moon slip down behind the western mountains. Then she slowly walked along her misty way in the dim light of the coming dawn. There was a footstep in the road behind her; she thought it was the ghost once more. She turned, and met Simon Burney, face to face. His rod was on his shoulder, and a string of fish was in his hand.

"Ye air a-doin' wrongful, Clarsie," he said sternly. "It air agin the law fur folks ter feed an' shelter them ez is a-runnin' from jestice. An' ye'll git yerself inter trouble. Other folks will find ye out, besides me, an' then the sheriff'll be up hyar arter ye."

The tears rose to Clarsie's eyes. This prospect was infinitely more terrifying than the awful doom which follows the horror of a ghost's speech.

"I can't holp it," she said, however, doggedly swinging the pail back and forth. "I can't gin my consent ter starvin' of folks, even ef they air a-hidin' an' a-runnin' from jestice." . . .

He left her walking on toward the rising sun, and retraced his way to the forks of the road. The jubilant morning was filled with the song of birds; the sunlight flashed on the dew; all the delicate enameled bells of the pink and white azaleas were swinging tremulously in the wind; the aroma of ferns and mint rose on the delicious fresh air. Presently he checked his pace, creeping stealthily on the moss and grass beside the road rather than in the beaten path. He pulled aside the leaves of the laurel with no more stir than the wind might have made, and stole cautiously through its dense growth, till he came suddenly upon the puny little ghost, lying in the sun at the foot of a tree. The frightened creature sprang to his feet with a wild cry of terror, but before he could move a step he was caught and held fast in the strong grip of the stalwart mountaineer beside him. "I hev kem hyar ter tell ye a word, Reuben Crabb," said Simon Burney. "I hev kem hyar ter tell ye that the whole mounting air a-goin' ter turn out ter sarch fur ye; the sheriff air a-ridin' now, an' ef ye don't come along with me they 'll hev ye afore night, 'kase thar air two hunderd dollars reward fur ye."

What a piteous wail went up to the smiling blue sky, seen through the dappling leaves above them! What a horror, and despair, and prescient agony were in the hunted creature's face! The ghost struggled no longer; he slipped from his feet down upon the roots of the tree, and turned that woful face, with its starting eyes and drawn muscles and quivering parted lips, up toward the unseeing sky.

"God A'mighty, man!" exclaimed Simon Burney, moved to pity. "Why n't ye quit this hyar way of livin' in the woods like ye war a wolf? Why n't ye come back an' stand yer trial? From all I 've hearn tell, it 'pears ter me ez the jury air obleeged ter let ye off, an' I 'll take keer of ye agin them Grims."

"I hain't got no place ter live in," cried out the ghost, with a keen despair.

Simon Burney hesitated. Reuben Crabb was possibly a murderer, — at the best could but be a burden. The burden, however, had fallen in his way, and he lifted it.

"I tell ye now, Reuben Crabb," he said, "I ain't a-goin' ter holp no man ter break the law an' hender jestice; but ef ye will go an' stand yer trial, I 'll take keer of ye agin them Grims ez long ez I kin fire a rifle. An' arter the jury hev done let ye off, ye air welcome ter live along o' me at my house till ye die. Ye air no 'count ter work, I know, but I ain't a-goin' ter grudge ye fur a livin' at my house."

And so it came to pass that the reward set upon the head of the harnt that walked Chilhowee was never claimed.

With his powerful ally, the forlorn little specter went to stand his trial, and the jury acquitted him without leaving the box. Then he came back to the mountains to live with Simon Burney. The cruel gibes of his burly mockers that had beset his feeble life from his childhood up, the deprivation and loneliness and despair and fear that had filled those days when he walked Chilhowee, had not improved the harnt's temper. He was a helpless creature, not able to carry a gun or hold a plow, and the years that he spent smoking his cob pipe in Simon Burney's door were idle years and unhappy. But Mrs. Giles said she thought he was "a mighty lucky little critter: fust, he hed Joel ter take keer of him an' feed him, when he tuk ter the woods ter pertend he war a harnt; an' they do say now that Clarsie Pratt, afore she war married, used ter kerry him vittles, too; an' then old Simon Burney tuk him up 'an' fed him ez plenty ez ef he war a good workin' hand, an' gin him clothes an' house-room, an' put up with his jawin' jes' like he never hearn a word of it. But law! some folks dunno when they air well off."

There was only a sluggish current of peasant blood in Simon Burney's veins, but a prince could not have dispensed hospitality with a more royal hand. Ungrudgingly he gave of his best; valiantly he defended his thankless guest at the risk of his life; with a moral gallantry he struggled with his sloth, and worked early and late, that there might be enough to divide. There was no possibility of a recompense for him, not even in the encomiums of discriminating friends, nor the satisfaction of tutored feelings and a practiced spiritual discernment; for he was an uncouth creature, and densely ignorant.

The grace of culture is, in its way, a fine thing, but the best that art can do — the polish of a gentleman — is hardly equal to the best that Nature can do in her higher moods.

## THOMAS NELSON PAGE

[Thomas Nelson Page was born in Hanover County, Virginia, in 1853. He was educated at Washington and Lee University. He then

studied law at the University of Virginia, and between 1875 and 1893 he practiced his profession in Richmond. Since 1893 Mr. Page has lived in Washington and has given himself entirely to .literary work. Like other Southern writers of his time he began his literary career by writing stories and sketches for the newspapers and magazines. His first stories were collected in 1887 and published under the title " In Ole Virginia." His later writings have included, in addition to several volumes of short stories, novels and collections of essays. Since 1893 Mr. Page has

THOMAS NELSON PAGE

lived in Washington and given himself entirely to literary work. In 1913 he was appointed by President Wilson Ambassador to Italy.]

### MARSE CHAN (SUMMARY)[1]

The narrator is an old darky, who is pictured in the beginning of the story as standing with a hoe and a watering pot in his hand, waiting at the "worm-fence" for the advent down the path of a noble-looking old setter, gray with age and over-round from too abundant feeding. The setter, like some old-time planter, sauntered slowly, and in lordly oblivion of the negro, up to the fence, while the latter began to take down the rails, talking meanwhile to the dog in a pretended tone of

[1] This summary, giving a good idea of the story " Marse Chan," is reprinted with some adaptations from H. E. Fiske's " Provincial Types in American Fiction."

criticism : "Now, I got to pull down de gap, I suppose ! Yo' so sp'ilt yo' kyahn hardly walk. Jes' ez able to git over it as I is ! Jes' like white folks — think 'cuz you 's white and I 's black, I got to wait on yo' all de time. Ne'm mine, I ain' gwi' do it !" As his dogship marched sedately through the "gap" and down the road, the negro suddenly discovered a stranger looking on, and hastened to remark somewhat apologetically : "He know I don' mean nothin' by what I sez. He 's Marse Chan's dawg, an' he 's so ole he kyahn git long no pearter. He know I 'se jes' prodjickin' wid 'im."

The darky explained to the stranger that " Marse Chan " (or Channin') was his young master, that the place with "de rock gate-pos's " which the stranger had just passed was " ole Cun'l Chamb'lin's," and that since the war " our place " had been acquired by certain "unknowns" who were probably "half-strainers."

At the request of the stranger to tell him all about "Marse Chan " the old negro recalled, "jes' like 't wuz yistiddy," how "ole marster" (Marse Chan's father), smiling " wus 'n a 'possum," came out on the porch with his new-born son in his arms, and catching sight of Sam (the narrator, who was then but eight years old), called him up on the porch and put the baby in his arms, with the solemn injunction that Sam was to be the young master's body servant as long as he lived. "Yo' jes' ought to a-heard de folks sayin', 'Lawd ! marster, dat boy 'll drap dat chile !' 'Naw, he won't,' sez marster ; 'I kin trust 'im.' " And then the old master walked after Sam carrying the young master, until Sam entered the house and laid his precious burden on the bed.

Sam recalled, too, how Marse Chan, when in school, once carried Miss Anne, Colonel Chamberlin's little daughter, on his shoulders across a swollen creek, and how the next day, when his father gave him a pony to show his pleasure over his son's chivalry, Marse Chan came walking home from school, having given his pony to Miss Anne. "'Yes,' sez ole marster, laughin', 'I s'pose you's already done giv' her yo'se'f, an' nex' thing I know you'll be givin' her this plantation and all my niggers.'" It was only a fortnight later that Colonel Chamberlin invited the "ole marster" and his whole family over to dinner, — expressly naming Marse Chan in the note, — and after dinner two ponies stood at the door, the one Marse Chan had given Miss Anne, and the other a present to Marse Chan from the Colonel. And after a "gre't" speech by the Colonel, the two young lovers went off to ride, while the "grown folks" laughed and chatted and smoked their cigars.

To the eye of Sam's endearing memory those were the good old times, — "de bes' Sam ever see! Dey wuz, in fac'! Niggers did n' hed nothin' 't all to do — jes' hed to 'ten' to de feedin' an' cleanin' de horses, an' doin' what de marster tell 'em to do; an' when dey wuz sick, dey had things sont 'em out de house, an' de same doctor come to see 'em whar 'ten' to de white folks when dey wuz po'ly. Dyar warn' no trouble nor nothin'."

The considerate affection shown for the young Sam by Marse Chan was illustrated by the little incident of the punishment inflicted on both of them by the "ole marster" for sliding down the straw-stacks against orders. The master first whipped young Marse Chan and then began on Sam, who was using his lungs to lighten the severity of his punishment. Marse Chan took his own whipping without a murmur; "but soon ez he commence warmin' me an' I begin to holler, Marse Chan he bu'st out cryin', an' stept right in befo' old marster, an' ketchin' de whup, sed: "'Stop, seh! Yo' sha'n't whup 'im; he b'longs to me, an' ef you hit 'im another lick I'll set 'im free!' . . .

"Marse Chan he war n' mo' 'n eight years ole, an' dyah dey wuz — ole marster standin' wid he whup raised up, an' Marse Chan red an' cryin', hol'in' on to it, an' sayin' I b'longs to 'im.

"Ole marster, he raise' de whup, an' den he drapt it, an' broke out in a smile over he face, an' he chuck Marse Chan onder de chin, an' tu'n right roun' an' went away, laughin' to hisse'f; an' I heah 'im tellin' ole missis dat evenin', an' laughin' 'bout it."

Sam's vivid memory saw again the picture of the dawn-light on the river when Marse Chan and old Colonel Chamberlin fought their famous duel that grew out of the unfounded charges against Marse Chan's father made by the Colonel in a political speech. Sam could see again the early morning light on his young master's face, and could hear the ominous voice of one of the seconds saying, "Gentlemen, are you ready?"

"An' he sez, 'Fire, one, two' — an' ez he said 'one' ole Cun'l Chamb'lin raised he pistil an' shot right at Marse Chan. De ball went th'oo' his hat. I seen he hat sort o' settle on he head ez de bullit hit it, an' *he* jes' tilted his pistil up in de a'r an' shot — *bang*; an' ez de pistil went *bang*, he sez to Cun'l Chamb'lin, 'I mek you a present to yo' fam'ly, seh!' . . .

"But ole Cun'l Chamb'lin he nuver did furgive Marse Chan, an' Miss Anne she got mad too. Wimmens is mons'us onreasonable nohow. Dey's jes' like a catfish: you can n' tek hole on 'em like udder folks, an' when you gits 'm yo' can n' always hole 'em."

In sympathetic and picturesque language the old darky recounted the last meeting between Marse Chan and Miss Anne, as they stood together in the moonlight, and Sam overheard the fateful words of the implacable Southern woman, "'But I don' love yo'.' (Jes' dem th'ee wuds!) De wuds fall right slow — like dirt falls out a spade on a coffin when yo's buryin' anybody, an' seys, 'Uth to uth.' Marse Chan he jes' let her hand drap, an' he stiddy hisse'f 'g'inst de gate-pos', an' he did n' speak torekly."

Sam's account of how Marse Chan went to the war, of how in the tent he knocked down Mr. Ronny for speaking contemptuously of Colonel Chamberlin and his daughter, and of the effect on Marse Chan's face of the letter of reconciliation and love he received from Miss Anne, — brings the vivid narrative to Marse Chan's splendid charge on the field at the head of the regiment, carrying its fallen flag up the hill, and inspiring it by his dauntless leadership. "I seen 'im when he went, de sorrel four good lengths ahead o' ev'ry urr hoss, jes' like he use' to be in a fox-hunt, an' de whole rigimint right arfter him." But suddenly the sorrel came galloping back, the rein hanging down on one side to his knee, — and poor Sam knew that Marse Chan was killed. He found his master among the dead, still holding in his hand the flag. "I tu'n 'im over an' call 'im, 'Marse Chan!' but 't wan' no use, he wuz done gone home, sho' 'nuff. I pick' 'im up in my arms wid de fleg still in he han's, an' toted 'im back jes' like I did dat day when he wuz a baby, an' ole marster gin 'im to me in my arms, an' sez he could trus' me, an' tell me to tek keer on 'im long ez he lived."

And when Sam reached home with the body in the ambulance and had gone over to let Miss Anne know the awful news that "Marse Chan he done got he furlough," and she had ridden back and prostrated herself before Marse Chan's old mother, there is the close of the tragic story as told by the old negro in these words:

"Ole missis stood for 'bout a minit lookin' down at her, an' den she drapt down on de flo' by her, an' took her in bofe her arms.

"I could n' see, I wuz cryin' so myse'f, an' ev'ybody wuz cryin'. But dey went in arfter a while in de parlor, an' shet de do'; an' I heahd 'em say, Miss Anne she tuk de coffin in her arms an' kissed it, an' kissed Marse Chan, an' call 'im by his name, an' her darlin', an' ole missis lef' her cryin' in dyar tell some one on 'em went in, an' found her done faint on de flo'." And it was not long before Miss Anne, broken by nursing in the hospitals and by fever and sorrow, was laid beside the body of Marse Chan.

## THE TRAINING OF THE OLD VIRGINIA LAWYER

His training was not always that of the modern law-class; but it was more than a substitute for it; and it was of its own kind complete. He "read law under" some old lawyer, some friend of his father or himself, who, although not a professor, was, without professing it, an admirable teacher. He associated with him constantly, in season and out of season; he saw him in his every mood; he observed him in intercourse with his clients, with his brothers of the bar, with the outside world; he heard him discourse of law, of history, of literature, of religion, of philosophy; he learned from him to ponder every manifestation of humanity; to consider the great underlying principles into which every proposition was resolvable; he found in him an exemplification of much that he inculcated, and a frank avowal of that wherein he failed. He learned to accept Lord Coke's dictum, "*melior est petere fontes quam sectari rivulos*" — to look to the sources rather than to tap the streams; he fed upon the strong meat of the institutes and the commentaries with the great leading cases which stand now as principles; he received by absorption the traditions of the profession. On these, like a healthy child, he grew strong without taking note. Thus in due time when his work came he was fully equipped. His old tutor had not only taught him law; he had taught him that the law was a science, and a great, if not the greatest, science. He had impressed him with the principles which he himself held, and they were sound; he had stamped upon his mind the conviction, that he, his tutor, was the greatest lawyer of his time, a conviction which no subsequent observation or experience ever served to remove.

He had made his mark, perhaps unexpectedly, in some case in which the force of his maturing intellect had suddenly burst forth, astonishing alike the bar and the bench and enrapturing the public. Perhaps it was a criminal case; perhaps one in which equity might be on his side, with the law dead against him; and which was regarded by older men with the conservatism of age as impossible until, by his brilliant effort, he unexpectedly won it. As like as not he rode forty miles that night to give a flower to his sweetheart.

From this time his reputation, his influence, and his practice increased. His professional position was henceforth assured. He had risen from a tyro to be an old lawyer.

## JAMES LANE ALLEN

[James Lane Allen was born near Lexington, Kentucky, in 1849. He attended Transylvania University, and after teaching school for several years he accepted the chair of Latin and higher English in Bethany College, West Virginia. After two years he resigned this position and has since devoted himself to literature, residing the greater part of the time in New York City. His earlier sketches of Kentucky life were published in 1891 under the title "Flute and Violin." This was followed by the short novels "A Kentucky Cardinal," and its sequel "Aftermath," and "A Summer in Arcady." With "The Choir Invisible" Mr. Allen began to work in the longer form of fiction, the novel, which has since chiefly occupied his time.]

### TWO GENTLEMEN OF KENTUCKY [1]

[Under the new conditions resulting from the Civil War and his altered fortunes, Colonel Romulus Fields, representing "the flower of that social order which had bloomed in rank perfection over the blue-grass plains of Kentucky during the final decades of the old régime," determined to sell his place and move to town. Of the Colonel's former slaves, one remained inseparable from his person. This was "an old gentleman — for such he was — named Peter Cotton." "In early

[1] These extracts from the story entitled "Two Gentlemen of Kentucky" are reprinted from "Flute and Violin" by special arrangement with the publishers of Mr. Allen's works, the Macmillan Company.

manhood Peter had been a woodchopper; but he had one day had his leg broken by the limb of a falling tree, and afterwards, out of consideration for his limp, had been made supervisor of the woodpile, gardener, and a sort of nondescript servitor of his master's luxurious needs. Nay, in larger and deeper characters must his history be writ, he having been, in days gone by, one of those ministers of the gospel whom conscientious Kentucky masters often urged to the exercise of spiritual functions in behalf of their benighted people."]

JAMES LANE ALLEN

About two years after the close of the war, therefore, the colonel and Peter were to be found in the city, ready to turn over a new leaf in the volumes of their lives, which already had an old-fashioned binding, a somewhat musty odor, and but few written leaves remaining.

After a long, dry summer you may have seen two gnarled old apple trees, that stood with interlocked arms on the western slope of some quiet hillside, make a melancholy show of blooming out again in the autumn of the year and dallying with the idle buds that mock their sapless branches. Much the same was the belated, fruitless efflorescence of the colonel and Peter.

The colonel had no business habits, no political ambition, no wish to grow richer. He was too old for society, and without near family ties. For some time he wandered through the streets like one lost,— sick with yearning for the fields and woods, for his cattle, for familiar faces. He haunted Cheapside and the courthouse square, where the farmers always assembled when they came to town; and if his eye lighted on one, he would buttonhole him on the street corner and lead him into a grocery and sit down for a quiet chat. Sometimes he would meet an aimless, melancholy wanderer like himself, and the two would go off and discuss over and over again their departed days; and several times he came unexpectedly upon some of his old servants who had fallen into bitter want, and who more than repaid him for the help he gave by contrasting the hardships of a life of freedom with the ease of their shackled years.

In the course of time, he could but observe that human life in the town was reshaping itself slowly and painfully, but with resolute energy. The colossal structure of slavery had fallen, scattering its ruins far and wide over the state; but out of the very débris was being taken the material to lay the deeper foundations of the new social edifice. Men and women as old as he were beginning life over and trying to fit themselves for it by changing the whole attitude and habit of their minds, — by taking on a new heart and spirit. But when a great building falls, there is always some rubbish, and the colonel and others like him were part of this. Henceforth they possessed only an antiquarian sort of interest, like the stamped bricks of Nebuchadnezzar.

Nevertheless he made a show of doing something, and in a year or two opened on Cheapside a store for the sale of hardware and agricultural implements. He knew more about the latter than anything else; and, furthermore, he secretly felt that a business of this kind would enable him to establish in town a kind of headquarters for the farmers. His account books were to be kept on a system of twelve months' credit; and he mentally resolved that if one of his customers could n't pay then, he should have another year's time.

Business began slowly. The farmers dropped in and found a good lounging place. On county-court days, which were great market days for the sale of sheep, horses, mules, and cattle in front of the colonel's door, they swarmed in from the hot sun and sat around on the counter and the plows and machines till the entrance was blocked to other customers. When a customer did come in, the colonel, who was probably talking with some old acquaintance, would tell him just to look around and pick out what he wanted and the price would be all right. If one of those acquaintances asked for a pound of nails, the colonel would scoop up some ten pounds and say, "I reckon that's about a pound, Tom." He had never seen a pound of nails in his life; and if one had been weighed on his scales, he would have said the scales were wrong. He had no great idea of commercial dispatch. One morning a lady came in for some carpet tacks, an article that he had overlooked. But he at once sent off an order for enough to have tacked a carpet pretty well all over Kentucky; and when they came, two weeks later, he told Peter to take her up a double handful with his compliments. He had laid in, however, an ample and especially fine assortment of pocket-knives, for that instrument had always been to him one of gracious and very winning qualities. Then when a friend dropped in he would say, "General, don't you need a new pocket-knife?" and, taking out one, would open all the blades and commend the metal and the handle. The "general" would inquire the price, and the colonel, having shut the blades, would hand it to him, saying in a careless, fond way, "I reckon I won't charge you anything for that." His mind could not come down to the low level of such ignoble barter, and he gave away the whole case of knives.

These were the pleasanter aspects of his business life, which did not lack as well its tedium and crosses. Thus there were many dark stormy days when no one he cared to see came in; and he then became rather a pathetic figure, wandering absently around amidst the symbols of his past activity, and stroking the plows, like dumb companions. Or he would stand at the door and look across at the old courthouse, where he had seen many a slave sold and had listened to the great Kentucky orators. Once, too, while he was deep in conversation, a brisk young farmer drove up to the door in a sulky and called in pretty sharply that he wanted him to go out and set up a machine. The colonel's mind just then was busy with certain scenes of great power in his own past life, and had swelled to the old heroic proportions; wherefore, burning over the indignity, he seized an ax handle and started out in a manner that led the young man to drive quickly away.

But what hurt him most was the talk of the newer farming and the abuse of the old which he was forced to hear; and he generally refused to handle the improved implements and mechanical devices by which labor and waste were to be saved.

Altogether he grew tired of "the thing," and sold out at the end of the year with a loss of over a thousand dollars, though he insisted he had done a good business.

As he was then seen much on the streets again and several times heard to make remarks in regard to the sidewalks, gutters, and crossings, when they happened to be in bad condition, the *Daily Press* one morning published a card stating that if Colonel Romulus Fields would consent to make the race for mayor he would receive the support of many Democrats, adding a tribute to his virtues and his influential past. It touched the colonel, and he walked down town with a rather commanding figure. But it pained him to see how many of his acquaintances returned his salutations very coldly; and just as he was passing the Northern Bank he met the young opposition candidate,—a little red-haired fellow, walking between two ladies, with a rosebud in his buttonhole,—who refused to speak at all, but made the ladies laugh by some remark he uttered as the colonel passed. The card had been inserted humorously, but he took it seriously; and when his friends found this out, they rallied round him. The day of election drew near. They told him he would have to buy votes. He said he would n't buy a vote to be mayor of the New Jerusalem. They told him he must "mix" and "treat." He refused. Foreseeing he had no chance, they besought him to withdraw. He said he would not. They told him he would n't poll twenty votes. He replied that *one* would satisfy him, provided it was neither begged nor bought. When his defeat was announced he accepted it as another evidence that he had no part in the newer day, and regretted it only because there was thus lost to him another chance of redeeming his idleness.

A sense of this weighed heavily on him at times; but it is not likely that he realized how pitifully he was undergoing a moral shrinkage in consequence of mere disuse. Actually, extinction had set in with him long prior to dissolution, and he was dead years before his heart ceased beating. The very basic virtues on which had rested his once spacious and stately character were now but the moldy corner stones of a crumbling ruin.

It was a subtle evidence of deterioration in manliness that he had taken to dress. When he had lived in the country, he had never dressed up unless he came to town. When he had moved to town, he thought he must remain dressed up all the time; and this fact first fixed his attention on a matter which afterwards began to be loved for its own sake. Usually he wore a Derby hat, a black diagonal coat, gray trousers, and a white necktie. But the article of attire in which he took chief pleasure was hose; and the better to show the gay colors of these, he wore low-cut shoes of the finest calfskin, turned up at the toes. Thus his feet kept pace with the present, however far his head may have lagged in the past; and it may be that this stream of fresh fashions, flowing perennially over his lower extremities like water about the roots of a tree, kept him from drying up altogether. Peter always polished his shoes with too much blacking, perhaps thinking that the more the blacking the greater the proof of love. He wore his clothes about a season and a half — having several suits — and then passed them on to Peter, who, foreseeing the joy of such an inheritance, bought no new ones. In the act of transferring them the colonel made no comment until he came to the hose, from which he seemed unable to part without a final tribute of esteem, as: " These are fine, Peter "; or, " Peter, these are nearly as good as new." Thus Peter too was dragged through the whims of fashion. To have seen the colonel walking about his grounds and garden followed by Peter, just a year and a half behind in dress and a yard and a half behind in space, one might well have taken the rear figure for the colonel's double, slightly the worse for wear, somewhat shrunken, and cast into a heavy shadow. . . .

Peter, meantime, had been finding out that his occupation too was gone.

Soon after moving to town, he had tendered his pastoral services to one of the fashionable churches of the city, — not because it was fashionable, but because it was made up of his brethren. In reply he was invited to preach a trial sermon, which he did with gracious unction. It was a strange scene, as one calm Sunday morning he stood on the edge of the pulpit, dressed in a suit of the colonel's old clothes, with one hand in his trousers pocket, and his lame leg set a little forward at an angle familiar to those who know the statues of Henry Clay.

How self-possessed he seemed, yet with what a rush of memories did he pass his eyes slowly over that vast assemblage of his emancipated people! With what feelings must he have contrasted those silk hats, and walking canes, and broadcloths;

those gloves and satins, laces and feathers, jewelry and fans —
that whole many-colored panorama of life — with the weary,
sad, and sullen audiences that had often heard him of old under
the forest trees or by the banks of some turbulent stream!

In a voice husky, but heard beyond the flirtation of the uttermost pew, he took his text: "Consider the lilies of the field,
how they grow; they toil not, neither do they spin." From
this he tried to preach a new sermon, suited to the newer day.
But several times the thoughts of the past were too much for
him, and he broke down with emotion. The next day a grave
committee waited on him and reported that the sense of the
congregation was to call a colored gentleman from Louisville.
Private objections to Peter were that he had a broken leg, wore
Colonel Fields's second-hand clothes, which were too big for
him, preached in the old-fashioned way, and lacked self-control
and repose of manner.

Peter accepted his rebuff as sweetly as Socrates might have
done. Humming the burden of an old hymn, he took his
righteous coat from a nail in the wall and folded it away in a
little brass-nailed deerskin trunk, laying over it the spelling book
and the Pilgrim's Progress, which he had ceased to read. Thence-
forth his relations to his people were never intimate, and even
from the other servants of the colonel's household he stood apart.
In paying them, the colonel would sometimes say, "Peter, I
reckon I'd better begin to pay you a salary; that's the style
now." But Peter would turn off, saying he did n't "have no
use fur no salary."

Thus both of them dropped more and more out of life, but
as they did so, only drew more and more closely to each other.
The colonel had bought a home on the edge of the town, with
some ten acres of beautiful ground surrounding. A high osage-
orange hedge shut it in, and forest trees, chiefly maples and elms,
gave to the lawn and house abundant shade. Wild-grape vines,

the Virginia creeper, and the climbing oak swung their long festoons from summit to summit, while honeysuckles, clematis, and the Mexican vine clambered over arbors and trellises, or along the chipped stone of the low, old-fashioned house. Just outside the door of the colonel's bedroom slept an ancient sundial.

The place seemed always in half-shadow, with hedgerows of box, clumps of dark holly, darker firs half a century old, and aged, crapelike cedars.

It was in the seclusion of this retreat, which looked almost like a wild bit of country set down on the edge of the town, that the colonel and Peter spent more of their time as they fell farther in the rear of onward events. There were no such flower gardens in the city, and pretty much the whole town went thither for its flowers, preferring them to those that were to be had for a price at the nurseries. There was perhaps a suggestion of pathetic humor in the fact that it should have called on the colonel and Peter, themselves so nearly defunct, to give the flowers for so many funerals ; but, it is certain, almost weekly the two old gentlemen received this chastening admonition of their all-but-spent mortality. The colonel cultivated the rarest fruits also, and had under glass varieties that were not friendly to the climate ; so that by means of the fruits and flowers there was established a pleasant social bond with many who otherwise would never have sought them out. But others came for better reasons. To a few deep-seeing eyes the colonel and Peter were momentous figures, disappearing types of a once vast social system, ruined landmarks on a fading historic landscape, and their devoted friendship was the last steady burning-down of that pure flame of love which can never again shine out in the future of the two races. Hence a softened charm invested the drowsy quietude of that shadowy paradise in which the old master without a slave and the old slave without a master still kept up a brave pantomime of their obsolete relations. No one ever saw in their intercourse aught but the finest courtesy, the most delicate consideration. The very tones of their voices in addressing each other were as good as sermons on gentleness, their antiquated playfulness as melodious as the babble of distant water. To be near them was to be exorcised of evil passions. The sun of their day had indeed long since set; but, like twin clouds lifted high and motionless into some far quarter of the gray twilight skies, they were still radiant with the glow of the invisible orb.

Henceforth the colonel's appearances in public were few and regular. He went to church on Sundays, where he sat on the edge of the choir in the center of the building, and sang an ancient bass of his own improvisation to the older hymns, and glanced furtively around to see whether anyone noticed that he could not sing the new ones. At the Sunday-school picnics the committee of arrangements allowed him to carve the mutton, and after dinner to swing the smallest children gently beneath the trees. He was seen on Commencement Day at Morrison Chapel, where he always gave his bouquet to the valedictorian, whose address he preferred to any of the others. In the autumn he might sometimes be noticed sitting high up in the amphitheater at the fair and looking over into the ring where the judges were grouped around the music-stand. Once he had been a judge himself, with a blue ribbon in his buttonhole, while the band played "Sweet Alice, Ben Bolt," and "Gentle Annie." The ring seemed full of young men now, and no one thought of offering him the privileges of the grounds. In his day the great feature of the exhibition had been cattle; now everything was turning into a horse show. He was always glad to get home again to Peter, his true yokefellow. For just as two old oxen — one white and one black — that have long toiled under the same yoke will, when turned out to graze at last in the widest pasture, come and put themselves horn to horn and flank to flank, so the colonel and Peter were never so happy as when ruminating side by side. . . .

It was in the twilight of a late autumn day in the same year that nature gave the colonel the first direct intimation to prepare for the last summons. They had been passing along the garden walks, where a few pale flowers were trying to flourish up to the very winter's edge, and where the dry leaves had gathered unswept and rustled beneath their feet. All at once the colonel turned to Peter, who was a yard and a half behind, as usual, and said: " Give me your arm, Peter "; and thus the two, for the first time in all their lifetime walking abreast, passed slowly on.

" Peter," said the colonel, gravely, a minute or two later, " we are like two dried-up stalks of fodder. I wonder the Lord lets us live any longer."

" I reck'n He 's managin' to use us *some* way, or we would n' be heah," said Peter.

" Well, all I have to say is, that if He 's using me, He can't be in much of a hurry for his work," replied the colonel.

" He uses snails, en I *know* we ain' ez slow ez *dem*," argued Peter, composedly.

" I don't know. I think a snail must have made more progress since the war than I have."

The idea of his uselessness seemed to weigh on him, for a little later he remarked, with a sort of mortified smile : " Do you think, Peter, that we would pass for what they call representative men of the New South ? "

" We done *had* ou' day, Marse Rom," replied Peter. " We got to pass fur what we *wuz*. Mebbe de Lohd 's got mo' use fur us yit 'n people has," he added, after a pause.

From this time on the colonel's strength gradually failed him ; but it was not until the following spring that the end came. A night or two before his death his mind wandered backward, after the familiar manner of the dying, and his delirious dreams showed the shifting, faded pictures that renewed themselves for the last time on his wasting memory. It must have been that he was once more amidst the scenes of his active farm life, for his broken snatches of talk ran thus:

"Come, boys, get your cradles! Look where the sun is! You are late getting to work this morning. That is the finest field of wheat in the county. Be careful about the bundles! Make them the same size and tie them tight. That swath is too wide, and you don't hold your cradle right, Tom.

"Sell Peter! Sell Peter Cotton! No, sir! You might buy *me* some day and work *me* in your cotton field; but as long as he's mine, you can't buy Peter, and you can't buy any of my negroes.

"Boys! boys! If you don't work faster, you won't finish this field to-day. You'd better go in the shade and rest now. The sun's very hot. Don't drink too much ice water. There's a jug of whisky in the fence corner. Give them a good dram around, and tell them to work slow till the sun gets lower."

Once during the night a sweet smile played over his features as he repeated a few words that were part of an old rustic song and dance. Arranged, not as they now came broken and incoherent from his lips, but as he once had sung them, they were as follows:

> "O Sister Phœbe! How merry were we
> When we sat under the juniper-tree,
>     The juniper-tree, heigho!
> Put this hat on your head! Keep your head warm;
> Take a sweet kiss! It will do you no harm,
>     Do you no harm, I know!"

After this he sank into a quieter sleep, but soon stirred with a look of intense pain.

"Helen! Helen!" he murmured. "Will you break your promise? Have you changed in your feeling towards me? I have brought you the pinks. Won't you take the pinks, Helen?"

Then he sighed as he added, "It wasn't her fault. If she had only known—"

Who was the Helen of that far-away time? Was this the colonel's love-story? How much remained untold?

But during all the night, whithersoever his mind wandered, at intervals it returned to the burden of a single strain,—the harvesting. Towards daybreak he took it up again for the last time:

"O boys, boys, *boys*! If you don't work faster you won't finish the field to-day. Look how low the sun is!—I am going to the house. They can't finish the field to-day. Let them do what they can, but don't let them work late. I want Peter to go to the house with me. Tell him to come on."

In the faint gray of the morning Peter, who had been watching by the bedside all night, stole out of the room, and going into the garden pulled a handful of pinks—a thing he had never done before—and, reëntering the colonel's bedroom, put them in a vase near his sleeping face. Soon afterwards the colonel opened his eyes and looked around him. At the foot of the bed stood Peter, and on one side sat the physician and a friend. The night lamp burned low, and through the folds of the curtains came the white light of early day.

"Put out the lamp and open the curtains," he said feebly. "It's day." When they had drawn the curtains aside, his eyes fell on the pinks, sweet and fresh with the dew on them. He stretched out his hand and touched them caressingly, and his eyes sought Peter's with a look of grateful tenderness.

"I want to be alone with Peter for a while," he said, turning his face towards the others.

When they were left alone, it was some minutes before they could speak. Peter, not knowing what he did, had gone to the window and hid himself behind the curtains, drawing them tightly around his form as though to shroud himself from the coming sorrow.

At length the colonel said, " Come here ! "

Peter, almost staggering forward, fell at the foot of the bed, and, clasping the colonel's feet with one arm, pressed his cheek against them.

" Come closer ! "

Peter crept on his knees and buried his head on the colonel's thigh.

" Come up here, — *closer* "; and putting one arm around Peter's neck he laid the other hand softly on his head, and looked long and tenderly into his eyes.

" Peter," he said with ineffable gentleness, " if I had served my Master as faithfully as you have served yours, I should not feel ashamed to stand in his presence."

" If my Marseter is ez mussiful to me ez you have been, he will save my soul in heaven."

" I have fixed things so that you will be comfortable after I am gone. When your time comes, I should like you to be laid close to me. We can take the long sleep together. Are you willing ? "

" That 's whar I want to be laid."

The colonel stretched out his hand to the vase, and, taking the bunch of pinks, said very calmly : " Leave these in my hand when I am dead ; I 'll carry them with me." A moment more, and he added : " If I should n't wake up any more, good-by, Peter ! "

" Good-by, Marse Rom ! "

And they shook hands. After this the colonel lay back on the pillows. His soft, silvery hair contrasted strongly with his childlike, unspoiled, open face. To the day of his death, as is apt to be true of those who have lived pure lives but never married, he had a boyish strain in him, a softness of nature, showing itself even now in the gentle expression of his mouth. His brown eyes had in them the same boyish look when, just as he was falling asleep, he scarcely opened them to say, "Pray, Peter."

Peter, on his knees, and looking across the colonel's face towards the open door, through which the rays of the rising sun streamed in upon his hoary head, prayed while the colonel fell asleep, adding a few words for himself now left alone.

Several hours later memory led the colonel back again through the dim gateway of the past, and out of that gateway his spirit finally took flight into the future.

Peter lingered a year. The place went to the colonel's sister, but he was allowed to remain in his quarters. With much thinking of the past, his mind fell into a lightness and a weakness. Sometimes he would be heard crooning the burden of old hymns, or sometimes seen sitting beside the old brass-nailed trunk, fumbling with the spelling-book and the Pilgrim's Progress. Often too he walked out to the cemetery on the edge of the town, and each time could hardly find the colonel's grave amidst the multitude of the dead. One gusty day in spring, the Scotch sexton, busy with the blades of blue grass springing from the animated mold, saw his familiar figure standing motionless beside the colonel's resting place. He had taken off his hat — one of the colonel's last bequests — and laid it on the colonel's headstone. On his body he wore a strange coat of faded blue, patched and weather-stained and so moth-eaten that parts of the curious tails had dropped entirely away. In one hand he held an open Bible, and on a much-soiled page he was pointing with his finger to the following words: "I would not have you ignorant, brethren, concerning them which are asleep."

It would seem that, impelled by love and faith, and guided by his wandering reason, he had come forth to preach his last sermon on the immortality of the soul over the dust of his dead master.

The sexton led him home, and soon afterwards a friend, who had loved them both, laid him beside the colonel.

It was perhaps fitting that his winding sheet should be the vestment in which, years agone, he had preached to his fellow slaves in bondage; for if it so be that the dead of this planet shall come forth from their graves clad in the trappings of mortality, then Peter should arise on the Resurrection Day wearing his old jeans coat.

## WILLIAM SIDNEY PORTER (" O. HENRY ")

[William Sidney Porter, better known by his pen name " O. Henry," was born in 1862 at Greensboro, North Carolina. His disposition early led him into a roving life, and he successively lived on a cattle ranch in Texas, did newspaper work in Houston and Austin, spent a while in South America, moved to New Orleans, and in 1902 settled in New York, where he was living at the time of his death, in 1910. He achieved widespread popularity as a writer of short stories, which in the collected edition of his works fill some nine or ten volumes.]

### TWO RENEGADES [1]

In the Gate City of the South the Confederate Veterans were reuniting; and I stood to see them march, beneath the tangled flags of the great conflict, to the hall of their oratory and commemoration.

While the irregular and halting line was passing I made onslaught upon it and dragged forth from the ranks my friend

[1] Reprinted from " Roads of Destiny " by permission of the holder of the copyright, Doubleday, Page & Company.

Barnard O'Keefe, who had no right to be there. For he was a Northerner born and bred; and what should he be doing hallooing for the Stars and Bars among those gray and moribund veterans? And why should he be trudging, with his shining, martial, humorous, broad face, among those warriors of a previous and alien generation?

I say I dragged him forth, and held him till the last hickory leg and waving goatee had stumbled past. And then I hustled him out of the crowd into a cool interior; for the Gate City was stirring that day, and the hand organs wisely eliminated "Marching through Georgia" from their repertories.

"Now, what deviltry are you up to?" I asked of O'Keefe when there were a table and things in glasses between us.

O'Keefe wiped his heated face and instigated a commotion among the floating ice in his glass before he chose to answer.

"I am assisting at the wake," said he, "of the only nation on earth that ever did me a good turn. As one gentleman to another, I am ratifying and celebrating the foreign policy of the late Jefferson Davis, as fine a statesman as ever settled the financial question of a country. Equal ratio — that was his platform — a barrel of money for a barrel of flour — a pair of $20 bills for a pair of boots — a hatful of currency for a new hat — say, ain't that simple compared with W. J. B.'s little old oxidized plank?"

"What talk is this?" I asked. "Your financial digression is merely a subterfuge. Why are you marching in the ranks of the Confederate Veterans?"

"Because, my lad," answered O'Keefe, "the Confederate government in its might and power interposed to protect and defend Barnard O'Keefe against immediate and dangerous assassination at the hands of a bloodthirsty foreign country, after the United States of America had overruled his appeal for protection and had instructed Private Secretary Cortelyou to reduce his estimate of the Republican majority for 1905 by one vote."

"Come, Barney," said I, "the Confederate States of America has been out of existence for nearly forty years. You do not look older yourself. When was it that the deceased government exerted its foreign policy in your behalf?"

"Four months ago," said O'Keefe, promptly. "The infamous foreign power I alluded to is still staggering from the official blow dealt it by Mr. Davis's contraband aggregation of states. That's why you see me cakewalking with the ex-rebs to the illegitimate tune about simmon seeds and cotton. I vote for the Great Father in Washington, but I am not going back on Mars' Jeff. You say the Confederacy has been dead forty years? Well, if it hadn't been for it, I'd have been breathing to-day with soul so dead I couldn't have whispered a single 'cuss-word' about my native land. The O'Keefes are not over-burdened with ingratitude."

I must have looked bewildered. "The war was over," I said vacantly, "in —"

O'Keefe laughed loudly, scattering my thoughts.

"Ask old Doc Millikin if the war is over!" he shouted, hugely diverted. "Oh, no! Doc hasn't surrendered yet. And the Confederate States! Well, I just told you they bucked officially and solidly and nationally against a foreign government four months ago and kept me from being shot. Old Jeff's country stepped in and brought me off under its wing while Roosevelt was having a gunboat repainted and waiting for the National Campaign Committee to look up whether I had ever scratched the ticket."

"Isn't there a story in this, Barney?" I asked.

"No," said O'Keefe; "but I'll give you the facts. You know how I went down to Panama when this irritation about a canal began. I thought I'd get in on the ground floor. I did, and had to sleep on it, and drink water with little zoos in it; so, of course I got the Chagres fever. That was in a little town called San Juan on the coast.

"After I got the fever hard enough to kill a Port-au-Prince nigger, I had a relapse in the shape of Doc Millikin.

"There was a doctor to attend a sick man! If Doc Millikin had your case, he made the terrors of death seem like an invitation to a donkey party. He had the bedside manners of a Piute medicine man and the soothing presence of a dray loaded with bridge girders. When he laid his hand on your fevered brow you felt like Cap. John Smith just before Pocahontas went his bail.

"Well, this old medical outrage floated down to my shack when I sent for him. He was built like a shad, and his eyebrows was black, and his white whiskers trickled down from his chin like milk coming out of a sprinkling pot. He had a nigger boy along carrying an old tomato can full of calomel, and a saw.

"Doc felt my pulse, and then he began to mess up some calomel with an agricultural implement that belonged to the trowel class. . . .

"By this time Doc Millikin had thrown up a line of fortifications on square pieces of paper; and he says to me: 'Yank, take one of these powders every two hours. They won't kill you. I'll be around again about sundown to see if you're alive.'

"Old Doc's powders knocked the Chagres. I stayed in San Juan, and got to knowing him better. He was from Mississippi, and the red-hottest Southerner that ever smelled mint. He made Stonewall Jackson and R. E. Lee look like Abolitionists. He had a family somewhere down near Yazoo City; but he stayed away from the States on account of an uncontrollable liking he had for the absence of a Yankee government. Him and me got as thick personally as the emperor of Russia and the dove of peace, but sectionally we didn't amalgamate.

" 'T was a beautiful system of medical practice introduced by old Doc into that isthmus of land. He 'd take that bracket saw and the mild chloride and his hypodermic, and treat anything from yellow fever to a personal friend.

" Besides his other liabilities Doc could play a flute for a minute or two. He was guilty of two tunes — ' Dixie ' and another one that was mighty close to ' Suwanee River ' — you might say it was one of its tributaries. He used to come down and sit with me while I was getting well, and aggrieve his flute and say unreconstructed things about the North. You 'd have thought the smoke from the first gun at Fort Sumter was still floating around in the air.

[O'Keefe tells how, participating in a Colombian revolution on the insurgent side, he was captured by the government troops and after a trial was sentenced to be shot in two weeks. His appeal to the American consul for protection proving ineffectual, he requests the consul to have Doc Millikin come to see him.]

" Doc comes and looks through the bars at me, surrounded by dirty soldiers, with even my shoes and canteen confiscated, and he looks mightily pleased.

" ' Hello, Yank,' says he, ' getting a little taste of Johnson's Island, now, ain't ye ? '

" ' Doc,' says I, ' I 've just had an interview with the U. S. consul. I gather from his remarks that I might just as well have been caught selling suspenders in Kishineff under the name of Rosenstein as to be in my present condition. It seems that the only maritime aid I am to receive from the United States is some navy plug to chew. Doc,' says I, ' can't you suspend hostilities on the slavery question long enough to do something for me ? '

" ' It ain't been my habit,' Doc Millikin answers, ' to do any painless dentistry when I find a Yank cutting an eyetooth. So the Stars and Stripes ain't landing any marines to shell the huts of the Colombian cannibals, hey? Oh, say, can you see by the dawn's early light the star-spangled banner has fluked in the fight? What's the matter with the War Department, hey? It's a great thing to be a citizen of a gold-standard nation, ain't it?'

"'Rub it in, Doc, all you want,' says I. 'I guess we're weak on foreign policy.'

"'For a Yank,' says Doc, putting on his specs and talking more mild, 'you ain't so bad. If you had come from below the line I reckon I would have liked you right smart. Now since your country has gone back on you, you have to come to the old doctor whose cotton you burned and whose mules you stole and whose niggers you freed to help you. Ain't that so, Yank?'

"'It is' says I, heartily, 'and let's have a diagnosis of the case right away, for in two weeks' time all you can do is to hold an autopsy and I don't want to be amputated if I can help it.'

"'Now,' says Doc, businesslike, 'it's easy enough for you to get out of this scrape. Money'll do it. You've got to pay a long string of 'em from General Pomposo down to this anthropoid ape guarding your door. About ten dollars will do the trick. Have you got the money?'

"'Me?' says I. 'I've got one Chile dollar, two *real* pieces, and a *medio*.'

"'Then if you've any last words, utter 'em,' says that old reb. 'The roster of your financial budget sounds quite much to me like the noise of a requiem.'

"'Change the treatment,' says I. 'I admit that I'm short. Call a consultation or use radium or smuggle me in some saws or something.'

"'Yank,' says Doc Millikin, 'I've a good notion to help you. There's only one government in the world that can get you out of this difficulty; and that's the Confederate States of America, the grandest nation that ever existed.'

" Just as you said to me I says to Doc: ' Why, the Confederacy ain't a nation. It 's been absolved forty years ago.'

"' That 's a campaign lie,' says Doc. ' She 's running along as solid as the Roman Empire. She 's the only hope you 've got. Now, you, being a Yank, have got to go through with some preliminary obsequies before you can get official aid. You 've got to take the oath of allegiance to the Confederate government. Then I 'll guarantee she does all she can for you. What do you say, Yank? — it 's your last chance.'

"' If you 're fooling with me, Doc,' I answers, ' you 're no better than the United States. But as you say it 's the last chance, hurry up and swear me. I always did like corn whisky and possum anyhow. I believe I'm half Southerner by nature. I'm willing to try the Ku-Klux in place of the khaki. Get brisk.'

" Doc Millikin thinks awhile, and then he offers me this oath of allegiance to take without any kind of chaser:

"' I, Barnard O'Keefe, Yank, being of sound body but a Republican mind, do hereby swear to transfer my fealty, respect, and allegiance to the Confederate States of America, and the government thereof in consideration of said government, through its official acts and powers, obtaining my freedom and release from confinement and sentence of death brought about by the exuberance of my Irish proclivities and my general pizenness as a Yank.'

" I repeated these words after Doc, but they seemed to me a kind of hocus-pocus; and I don't believe any life-insurance company in the country would have issued me a policy on the strength of 'em.

" Doc went away, saying he would communicate with his government immediately.

" Say — you can imagine how I felt — me to be shot in two weeks and my only hope for help being in a government that 's been dead so long that it is n't even remembered except on

Decoration Day and when Joe Wheeler signs the voucher for his pay check. But it was all there was in sight; and somehow I thought Doc Millikin had something up his old alpaca sleeve that was n't all foolishness.

"Around to the jail comes old Doc again in about a week. I was fleabitten, a mite sarcastic, and fundamentally hungry.

"'Any Confederate ironclads in the offing?' I asks. 'Do you notice any sounds resembling the approach of Jeb Stewart's cavalry overland or Stonewall Jackson sneaking up in the rear? If you do, I wish you 'd say so.'

"'It 's too soon yet for help to come,' says Doc.

"'The sooner the better,' says I. 'I don't care if it gets in fully fifteen minutes before I am shot; and if you happen to lay eyes on Beauregard or Albert Sidney Johnston or any of the relief corps, wigwag 'em to hike along.'

"'There 's been no answer received yet,' says Doc.

"'Don't forget,' says I, 'that there 's only four days more. I don't know how you propose to work this thing, Doc,' I says to him; 'but it seems to me I 'd sleep better if you had got a government that was alive and on the map — like Afghanistan or Great Britain, or old man Kruger's kingdom, to take this matter up. I don't mean any disrespect to your Confederate States, but I can't help feeling that my chances of being pulled out of this scrape was decidedly weakened when General Lee surrendered.'

"'It 's your only chance,' says Doc; 'don't quarrel with it. What did your own country do for you?'

"It was only two days before the morning I was to be shot, when Doc Millikin came around again.

"'All right, Yank,' says he. 'Help 's come. The Confederate States of America is going to apply for your release. The representatives of the government arrived on a fruit steamer last night.'

"'Bully!' says I — 'bully for you, Doc! I suppose it's marines with a Gatling. I am going to love your country all I can for this.'

"'Negotiations,' says old Doc, 'will be opened between the two governments at once. You will know later on to-day if they are successful.'

"About four in the afternoon a soldier in red trousers brings a paper round to the jail, and they unlocks the door and I walks out. The guard at the door bows and I bows, and I steps into the grass and wades around to Doc Millikin's shack.

"Doc was sitting in his hammock, playing 'Dixie,' soft and low and out of tune, on his flute. I interrupted him at 'Look away! look away!' and shook his hand for five minutes.

"'I never thought,' says Doc, taking a chew fretfully, 'that I'd ever try to save any blame Yank's life. But, Mr. O'Keefe, I don't see but what you are entitled to be considered part human, anyhow. I never thought Yanks had any of the rudiments of decorum and laudability about them. I reckon I might have been too aggregative in my tabulation. But it ain't me you want to thank — it's the Confederate States of America.'

"'And I'm much obliged to 'em,' says I. 'It's a poor man that would not be patriotic with a country that's saved his life. I'll drink to the Stars and Bars whenever there's a flagstaff and a glass convenient. But where,' says I, 'are the rescuing troops? If there was a gun fired or a shell burst, I didn't hear it.'

"Doc Millikin raises up and points out the window with his flute at the banana steamer loading with fruit.

"'Yank,' says he, 'there's a steamer that's going to sail in the morning. If I was you, I'd sail on it. The Confederate government's done all it can for you. There wasn't a gun fired. The negotiations was carried on secretly between the two nations by the purser of that steamer. I got him to do it because I did n't want to appear in it. Twelve thousand dollars was paid to the officials in bribes to let you go.'

"'Man!' says I, sitting down hard, 'twelve thousand — how will I ever — who could have — where did the money come from?'

"'Yazoo City,' says Doc Millikin. 'I've got a little saved up there. Two barrels full of it. It looks good to these Colombians. 'T was Confederate money, every dollar of it. Now do you see why you 'd better leave before they try to pass some of it on an expert?'

"'I do,' says I.

"'Now let 's hear you give the password,' says Doc Millikin.

"'Hurrah for Jeff Davis!' says I.

"'Correct,' says Doc. 'And let me tell you something: The next tune I learn on my flute is going to be "Yankee Doodle." I reckon there 's some Yanks that are not so pizen. Or, if you was me, would you try "The Red, White, and Blue"?'"

# ESSAYISTS AND DESCRIPTIVE WRITERS

## SUSAN DABNEY SMEDES

[Mrs. Susan Dabney Smedes was born at Raymond, Mississippi, in 1840, and was the daughter of Thomas S. Dabney, a planter whose life forms the basis of her description of life on a Southern plantation, entitled "Memorials of a Southern Planter." She was married in 1860 to Lyell Smedes, but was in a few months left a widow. Her life has been largely devoted to philanthropic work. Her home at present is Sewanee, Tennessee.]

## A SOUTHERN PLANTER'S IDEALS OF HONOR[1]

And now a great blow fell on Thomas Dabney. Shortly before the war he had been asked by a trusted friend to put his name as security on some papers for a good many thousand dollars. At the time he was assured that his name would only be wanted to tide over a crisis of two weeks, and that he would never hear of the papers again. It was a trap set, and his unsuspicious nature saw no danger, and he put his name to the papers. Loving this man, and confiding in his honor as in a son's, he thought no more of the transaction.

It was now the autumn of 1866. One night he walked upstairs to the room where his children were sitting, with a paper in his hand. "My children," he said, "I am a ruined man. The sheriff is downstairs. He has served this writ on me. It is for a security debt. I do not even know how many more such papers have my name to them." His face was white as

1 Reprinted from "Memorials of a Southern Planter," by permission of the holder of the copyright, James Pott & Company.

he said these words. He was sixty-eight years of age, with a large and helpless family on his hands, and the country in such a condition that young men scarcely knew how to make a livelihood.

The sheriff came with more writs. Thomas roused himself to meet them all. He determined to pay every dollar.

But to do this he must have time. The sale of everything that he owned would not pay all these claims. He put the business in the hands of his lawyer, Mr. John Shelton, of Raymond, who was also his intimate friend. Mr. Shelton contested the claims, and this delayed things till Thomas could decide on some way of paying the debts.

A gentleman to whom he owed personally several thousand dollars courteously forbore to send in his claim. Thomas was determined that he should not on this account fail to get his money, and wrote urging him to bring a friendly suit, that, if the worst came, he should at least get his proportion. Thus urged, the friendly suit was brought, the man deprecating the proceeding, as looking like pressing a gentleman.

And now the judgments, as he knew they would, went against him one by one. On the 27th of November, 1866, the Burleigh plantation was put up at auction and sold, but the privilege of buying it in a certain time reserved to Thomas. At this time incendiary fires were common. There was not much law in the land. We heard of the ginhouses and cotton-houses that were burned in all directions. One day as Thomas came back from a business journey the smoldering ruins of his ginhouse met his eye. The building was itself valuable and necessary. All the cotton that he owned was consumed in it. He had not a dollar. He had to borrow the money to buy a postage stamp, not only during this year but during many years to come. It was a time of deepest gloom. Thomas had been wounded to the bottom of his affectionate heart by the perfidy of the man who had brought this on his house. In the midst of the grinding poverty that now fell in full force on him, he heard of the reckless extravagance of this man on the money that should have been used to meet these debts.

Many honorable men in the South were taking the benefit of the bankrupt law. Thomas's relations and friends urged him to take the law. It was madness, they said, for a man of his age, in the condition the country was then in, to talk of settling the immense debts that were against him. He refused with scorn to listen to such proposals. But his heart was well-nigh broken.

He called his children around him, as he lay in bed, not eating and scarcely sleeping.

"My children," he said, "I shall have nothing to leave you but a fair name. But you may depend that I shall leave you that. I shall, if I live, pay every dollar that I owe. If I die, I leave these debts to you to discharge. Do not let my name be dishonored. Some men would kill themselves for this. I shall not do that. But I shall die."

The grief of betrayed trust was the bitterest drop in his cup of suffering. But he soon roused himself from this depression and set about arranging to raise the money needed to buy in the plantation. It could only be done by giving up all the money brought in by the cotton crop for many years. This meant rigid self-denial for himself and his children. He could not bear the thought of seeing his daughters deprived of comforts. He was ready to stand unflinchingly any fate that might be in store for him. But his tenderest feelings were stirred for them. His chivalrous nature had always revolted from the sight of a woman doing hard work. He determined to spare his daughters all such labor as he could perform. General Sherman had said that he would like to bring every Southern woman to the washtub. "He shall never bring my daughters to the washtub," Thomas Dabney said. "I will do the washing myself." And he did it for two years. He was in his seventieth year when he began to do it.

This may give some idea of the labors, the privations, the hardships, of those terrible years. The most intimate friends of Thomas, nay, his own children, who were not in the daily life at Burleigh, have never known the unprecedented self-denial, carried to the extent of acutest bodily sufferings, which he practiced during this time. A curtain must be drawn over this part of the life of my lion-hearted father!

When he grew white and thin, and his frightened daughters prepared a special dish for him, he refused to eat the delicacy. It would choke him, he said, to eat better food than they had, and he yielded only to their earnest solicitations. He would have died rather than ask for it. When the living was so coarse and so ill-prepared that he could scarcely eat it, he never failed, on rising from the table, to say earnestly and reverently, as he stood by his chair, "Thank the Lord for this much."

During a period of eighteen months no light in summer, and none but a fire in winter, except in some case of necessity, was seen in the house. He was fourteen years in paying these debts that fell on him in his sixty-ninth year. He lived but three years after the last dollar was paid.

## BASIL LANNEAU GILDERSLEEVE

[Basil Lanneau Gildersleeve was born in Charleston, South Carolina, in 1831. After graduating from Princeton he studied in several German universities and then returned to the United States to engage in teaching. For several years he was professor of Latin and Greek in the University of Virginia, and since 1876 he has been professor of Greek in Johns Hopkins University. While he is well known as the author of textbooks and monographs in his chosen field of scholarship, he has also shown himself in such volumes as " Essays and Studies " and " Hellas and Hesperia " to be gifted as an English stylist.]

## THE CREED OF THE OLD SOUTH [1]

A few months ago, as I was leaving Baltimore for a summer sojourn on the coast of Maine, two old soldiers of the war between the states took their seats immediately behind me in the car and began a lively conversation about the various battles in which they had faced each other more than a quarter of a century ago, when a trip to New England would have been no holiday jaunt for one of their fellow travelers. The veterans went into the minute detail that always puts me to shame, when I think how poor an account I should give if pressed to describe the military movements that I have happened to witness; and I may as well acknowledge at the outset that I have as little aptitude for the soldier's trade as I have for the romancer's. Single incidents I remember as if they were of yesterday. Single pictures have burned themselves into my brain. But I have no vocation to tell how fields were lost and won, and my experience of military life was too brief and fitful to be of any value to the historian of the war. For my own life that experience has been of the utmost significance, and despite the heavy price I have had to pay for my outings, despite the daily reminder of five long months of intense suffering, I have no regrets. An able-bodied young man, with a long vacation at his disposal, could not have done otherwise, and the right to teach Southern youth for nine months was earned by sharing the fortunes of their fathers and brothers at the front for three. Self-respect is everything; and it is

[1] Reprinted from " The Creed of the Old South," by permission of the holder of the copyright, the Johns Hopkins Press.

something to have belonged in deed and in truth to an heroic generation, to have shared in a measure its perils and privations. But that heroic generation is apt to be a bore to a generation whose heroism is of a different type, and I doubt whether the young people in our car took much interest in the very audible conversation of the two veterans. Twenty-five years hence, when the survivors will be curiosities, as were Revolutionary pensioners in my childhood, there may be a renewal of interest. As it is, few of the present generation pore over " The Battles and Leaders of the Civil War," and a grizzled old Confederate has been heard to declare that he intended to bequeath his copy of that valuable work to someone outside of the family, so provoked was he at the supineness of his children. And yet, for the truth's sake, all these battles must be fought over and over again, until the account is cleared and until justice is done to the valor and skill of both sides.

The two old soldiers were talking amicably enough, as all old soldiers do, but they " yarned," as all old soldiers do, and though they talked from Baltimore to Philadelphia, and from Philadelphia to New York, their conversation was lost on me, for my thoughts went back into my own past, and two pictures came up to me from the time of the war.

In the midsummer of 1863 I was serving as a private in the First Virginia Cavalry. Gettysburg was in the past and there was not much fighting to be done, but the cavalry was not wholly idle. Raids had to be intercepted, and the enemy was not to be allowed to vaunt himself too much; so that I gained some experience of the hardships of that arm of the service and found out by practical participation what is meant by a cavalry charge. To a looker-on nothing can be finer. To the one who charges, or is supposed to charge, — for the horse seemed to me mainly responsible, — the details are somewhat cumbrous. Now in one of these charges some of us captured a number of the opposing force, among them a young lieutenant. Why this particular capture should have impressed me so, I cannot tell, but memory is a tricky thing. A large red fox scared up from his lair by the fight at Castleman's Ferry stood for a moment looking at me, and I shall never forget the stare of that red fox. At one of our fights near Kernstown a spent bullet struck a horse on the side of his nose, which happened to be white, and left a perfect imprint of itself; and the jerk of the horse's head and the outline of the bullet are present to me still. The explosion of a particular caisson, the shriek of a special shell, will ring in one's ears for life. A captured lieutenant was no novelty, and yet this captured lieutenant caught my eye and held it. A handsomer young fellow, a more noble-looking, I never beheld among Federals or Confederates, as he stood there, bareheaded, among his captors, erect and silent. His eyes were full of fire, his lips showed a slight quiver of scorn, and his hair seemed to tighten its curls in defiance. Doubtless I had seen as fine specimens of young manhood before, but if so, I had seen without looking, and this man was evidently what we called a gentleman.

Southern men were proud of being gentlemen, although they have been told in every conceivable tone that it was a foolish pride — foolish in itself, foolish in that it did not have the heraldic backing that was claimed for it; the utmost concession being that a number of "deboshed" younger sons of decayed gentry had been shipped to Virginia in the early settlement of that colony. But the very pride played its part in making us what we were proud of being, and whether descendants of the aforesaid "deboshed," of simple English yeoman, of plain Scotch-Irish Presbyterians (a doughty stock), or of Huguenots of various ranks of life, we all held to the same standard, and showed, as was thought, undue exclusiveness on this subject. But this prisoner was the embodiment of the best type of Northern youth, with a spirit as high, as resolute, as could be found in the ranks of Southern gentlemen; and though in theory all enlightened Southerners recognized the high qualities of some of our opponents, this one noble figure in "flesh and blood" was better calculated to inspire respect for "those people," as we had learned to call our adversaries, than many pages of "gray theory."

A little more than a year afterwards, in Early's Valley campaign, — a rude school of warfare, — I was serving as a volunteer aid on General Gordon's staff. The day before the disaster of Fisher's Hill I was ordered, together with another staff officer, to accompany the general on a ride to the front. The general had a well-known weakness for inspecting the outposts — a weakness that made a position in his suite somewhat precarious. The officer with whom I was riding had not been with us long, and when he joined the staff he had just recovered from wounds and imprisonment. A man of winning appearance, sweet temper, and attractive manners, he soon made friends of the military family, and I never learned to love a man so much in so brief an acquaintance, though hearts knit quickly in the stress of war. He was highly educated, and foreign residence and travel had widened his vision without affecting the simple faith and thorough consecration of the Christian. Here let me say that the bearing of the Confederates is not to be understood without taking into account the deep religious feeling of the army and its great leaders. It is a historical element, like any other, and is not to be passed over in summing up the forces of the conflict. "A soldier without religion," says a Prussian officer, who knew our army as well as the German, "is an instrument without value," and it is not unlikely that the knowledge of the part that faith played in sustaining the Southern people may have lent emphasis to the expression of his conviction.

We rode together towards the front, and as we rode our talk fell on Goethe and on Faust, and of all passages the soldiers' song came up to my lips — the song of soldiers of fortune, not the chant of men whose business it was to defend their country. Two lines, however, were significant:

> Kühn ist das Mühen,
> Herrlich der Lohn.

We reached the front. An occasional "zip" gave warning that the sharpshooters were not asleep, and the quick eye of the general saw that our line needed rectification, and how. Brief orders were given to the officer in command. My comrade was left to aid in carrying them out. The rest of us withdrew. Scarcely had we ridden a hundred yards towards camp when a shout was heard, and, turning round, we saw one of the men running after us. "The captain had been killed." The peace of heaven was on his face as I gazed on the noble features that afternoon. The bullet had passed through his official papers and found his heart. He had received his discharge, and the glorious reward had been won.

This is the other picture that the talk of the two old soldiers called up — dead Confederate against living Federal; and these two pictures stand out before me again, as I am trying to make others understand and to understand myself what it was to be a Southern man twenty-five years ago; what it was to accept with the whole heart the creed of the Old South. The image of the living Federal bids me refrain from harsh words in the presence of those who were my captors. The dead Confederate bids me uncover the sacred memories that the dust of life's Appian Way hides from the tenderest and truest of those whose business it is to live and work. For my dead comrade of the Valley campaign is one of many — some of them my friends, some of them my pupils as well. The eighteenth of July, 1861, laid low one of my Princeton College roommates; on the twenty-first, the day of the great battle, the other fell — both bearers of historic names, both upholding the cause of their state with as unclouded a conscience as any saint in the martyrology ever wore; and from that day to the end, great battle and outpost skirmish brought me, week by week, a personal loss in men of the same type. . . .

The war began, the war went on. Passion was roused to fever heat. Both sides " saw red," that physiological condition which to a Frenchman excuses everything. The proverbial good humor of the American people did not, it is true, desert the country, and the Southern men who were in the field, as they were much happier than those who stayed at home, if I may judge by my own experience, were often merry enough by the camp fire and exchanged rough jests with the enemy's pickets. But the invaded people were very much in earnest, however lightly some of their adversaries treated the matter, and as the pressure of the war grew tighter, the more somber did life become. A friend of mine, describing the crowd that besieged the Gare de Lyon in Paris, when the circle of fire was drawing round the city and foreigners were hastening to escape, told me that the press was so great that he could touch in every direction those who had been crushed to death as they stood and had not had room to fall. Not wholly unlike this was the pressure brought to bear on the Confederacy. It was only necessary to put out your hand and you touched a corpse; and that not an alien corpse, but the corpse of a brother or a friend. Every Southern man becomes grave when he thinks of that terrible stretch of time, partly, it is true, because life was nobler, but chiefly because of the memories of sorrow and suffering. A professional Southern humorist once undertook to write in dialect a " Comic History of the War," but his heart failed him, as his public would have failed him, and the serial lived only for a number or two.

The war began, the war went on. War is a rough game. It is an omelet that cannot be made without breaking eggs, not only eggs *in esse*, but also eggs *in posse*. So far as I have read about war, ours was no worse than other wars. While it lasted, the conduct of the combatants on either side was represented in the blackest colors by the other. Even the ordinary and legitimate doing to death was considered criminal if the deed was done by a ruthless rebel or ruffianly invader. Noncombatants were especially eloquent. In describing the end of a brother who had been killed while trying to get a shot at a Yankee, a Southern girl raved about the "murdered patriot" and the "dastardly wretch" who had anticipated him. But I do not criticize, for I remember an English account of the battle of New Orleans, in which General Pakenham was represented as having been picked off by a "sneaking Yankee rifle." Those who were engaged in the actual conflict took more reasonable views, and the annals of the war are full of stories of battlefield and hospital in which a common humanity asserted itself. But brotherhood there was none. No alienation could have been more complete. Into the fissure made by the disruption poured all the bad blood that had been breeding from Colonial times, from Revolutionary times, from "bleeding Kansas" and the engine-house at Harper's Ferry; and a great gulf was fixed, as it seemed forever, between North and South. The hostility was a very satisfactory one — for military purposes.

The war began, the war went on — this politicians' conspiracy, this slaveholders' rebellion, as it was variously called by those who sought its source, now in the disappointed ambition of the Southern leaders, now in the desperate determination of a slaveholding oligarchy to perpetuate their power and to secure forever their proprietorship in their "human chattels." On this theory the mass of the Southern people were but puppets in the hands of political wirepullers or blind followers of hectoring "patricians." To those who know the Southern people nothing can be more absurd — to those who know their personal independence, to those who know the deep interest which they have always taken in politics, the keen intelligence with which they have always followed the questions of the day. The courthouse green was the political university of the Southern masses, and the hustings the professorial chair, from which the great political and economical questions of the day were presented, to say the least, as fully and intelligently as in the newspapers to which so much enlightenment is attributed. There was no such system of rotten boroughs, no such domination of a landed aristocracy, throughout the South as has been imagined, and venality, which is the disgrace of current politics, was practically unknown. The men who represented the Southern people in Washington came from the people, and not from a ring. Northern writers who have ascribed the firm control in Congress of the national government which the South held so long to the superior character, ability, and experience of its representatives do not seem to be aware that the choice of such representatives and their prolonged tenure show that in politics, at least, the education of the Southerner had not been neglected. The rank and file then were not swayed simply by blind passion or duped by the representatives of political gamesters. Nor did the lump need the leavening of the large percentage of men of the upper classes who served as privates, some of them from the beginning to the end of the war. The rank and file were, to begin with, in full accord with the great principles of the war, and were sustained by the abiding conviction of the justice of the cause. Of course there were in the Southern army, as in every army, many who went with the multitude in the first enthusiastic rush, or who were brought into the ranks by the needful process of conscription ; but it is not a little remarkable that few of the poorest and the most ignorant could be induced to forswear the

cause and to purchase release from the sufferings of imprisonment by the simple process of taking the oath. Those who
have seen the light of battle on the faces of these humble
sons of the South or witnessed their steadfastness in camp,
on the march, in the hospital, have not been ashamed of their
brotherhood.

There is such a thing as fighting for a principle, an idea;
but principle and idea must be incarnate, and the principle of
state rights was incarnate in the historical life of the Southern
people. Of the thirteen original states, Virginia, North Carolina,
South Carolina, and Georgia were openly and officially upon
the side of the South. Maryland as a state was bound hand
and foot. We counted her as ours, for the Potomac and Chesapeake Bay united as well as divided. Everyone was something more than a certain aggregate of square miles wherein
dwelt an uncertain number of uncertain inhabitants, something
more than a territory transformed into a state by the magic of
political legerdemain — a creature of the central government,
and duly loyal to its creator.

In claiming this individuality, nothing more is claimed for
Virginia and for South Carolina than would be conceded to
Massachusetts and Connecticut; and we believed then that
Massachusetts and Connecticut would not have behaved otherwise than we did, if the parts had been reversed. The
brandished sword would have shown what manner of *placida
quies* would have ensued, if demands had been made on Massachusetts at all commensurate with the federal demands on
Virginia. These older Southern states were proud of their history, and they showed their pride by girding at their neighbors.
South Carolina had her fling at Georgia, her fling at North
Carolina; and the wish that the little State had been scuttled
at an early day was a plagiarism from classical literature that
might have emanated from the South as well as from the North.

Virginia assumed a superiority that was resented by her Southern sisters as well as by her Northern partners. The Old North State derided the pretensions of the commonwealths that flanked her on either side, and Georgia was not slow to give South Carolina as good as she sent. All this seemed to be harmless banter, but the rivalry was old enough and strong enough to encourage the hopes of the Union leaders that the Confederacy would split along state lines. The cohesive power of the Revolutionary War was not sufficiently strong to make the states sink their contributions to the common cause in the common glory. Washington was the one national hero, and yet the Washington Light Infantry of Charleston was named, not after the illustrious George, but after his kinsman, William. The story of Lexington and Concord and Bunker Hill did not thrill the South Carolinian of an earlier day, and those great achievements were actually criticized. Who were Putnam and Stark that South Carolinians should worship them, when they had a Marion and a Sumter of their own? Vermont went wild, the other day, over Bennington as she did not over the centenary of the surrender at Yorktown. Take away this local patriotism and you take out all the color that is left in American life. That the local patriotism may not only consist with a wider patriotism, but may serve as a most important element in a wider patriotism, is true. Witness the strong local life in the old provinces of France. No student of history, no painter of manners can neglect it. In " Gerfaut," a novel written before the Franco-Prussian War, Charles de Bernard represents an Alsatian shepherd as saying, " I am not French; I am Alsatian." " *Trait de patriotisme de clocher assez commun dans la belle province du Rhin*," adds the author, little dreaming of the national significance of that " patriotisme de clocher." The Breton's love of his home is familiar to everyone who has read his " Renan," and Blanche Willis Howard, in " Guenn," makes her priest exclaim: " Monsieur, I would fight with France against any other nation, but I would fight with Brittany against France. I love France. I am a Frenchman. But first of all I am a Breton." The Provençal speaks of France as if she were a foreign country, and fights for her as if she were his alone. What is true of France is true in a measure of England. Devonshire men are notoriously Devonshire men first and last. If this is true of what have become integral parts of a kingdom or republic by centuries of incorporation, what is to be said of the states that had never renounced their sovereignty, that had only suspended it in part ?

The example of state pride set by the older states was not lost on the younger Southern states, and the Alabamian and the Mississippian lived in the same faith as did the stock from which they sprang; and the community of views, of interest, of social order, soon made a larger unit and prepared the way for a true nationality, and with the nationality a great conflict. The heterogeneousness of the elements that made up the Confederacy did not prove the great source of weakness that was expected. The Border states looked on the world with different eyes from the Gulf states. The Virginia farmer and the Creole planter of Louisiana were of different strains; and yet there was a solidarity that has never failed to surprise the few Northerners who penetrated the South for study and pleasure. There was an extraordinary ramification of family and social ties throughout the Southern states, and a few minutes' conversation sufficed to place any member of the social organism from Virginia to Texas. Great schools, like the University of Virginia, within the Southern border did much to foster the community of feeling, and while there were not a few Southerners at Harvard and Yale, and while Princeton was almost a Southern college, an education in the North did not seem to nationalize the Southerner. On the contrary, as in the universities of the

Middle Ages, groups were formed in accordance with nativity; and sectional lines, though effaced at certain points, were strengthened at others. There may have been a certain broadening of view; there was no weakening of home ties. West Point made fewer converts to this side and to that than did the Northern wives of Southern husbands, the Southern wives of Northern husbands.

All this is doubtless controvertible, and what has been written may serve only to amuse or to disgust those who are better versed in the facts of our history and keener analysts of its laws. All I vouch for is the feeling; the only point that I have tried to make is the simple fact that, right or wrong, we were fully persuaded in our own minds, and that there was no lurking suspicion of any moral weakness in our cause. Nothing could be holier than the cause, nothing more imperative than the duty of upholding it. There were those in the South who, when they saw the issue of the war, gave up their faith in God, but not their faith in the cause.

## WILLIAM PETERFIELD TRENT

[William Peterfield Trent was born at Richmond, Virginia, in 1862. After graduating from the University of Virginia and pursuing postgraduate studies at Johns Hopkins University, he became professor of English in the University of the South, Sewanee, Tennessee. This position he held from 1888 to 1900, when he accepted a professorship in English literature in Columbia University, New York City, which he now holds. His many books on historical and literary subjects (especially notable being "Life of William Gilmore Simms," "Authority of Criticism," and "A History of American Literature") have made him known of the foremost critics of literature in the United States. While at the University of the South he was the first editor of the *Sewanee Review* — a magazine important to literary and historical research in the South.]

## THE DIVERSITY AMONG SOUTHERNERS[1]

A " Solid South " would seem to presuppose a homogeneous
Southern people coextensive with the geographical, or rather
political, area thus designated ; but to draw this inference would
be to make a mistake almost equal to that made by the European who thinks Chicago a three or four hours' ride from
New York, and confounds our Eastern and Western populations.
If political opinions and prejudices be not taken into account,
the typical Charlestonian will be found to differ as much from
the average inhabitant of Nashville as the typical New Yorker
does from his rival of Chicago. The Virginian and the Georgian
have points of contact, to be sure, but they differ radically in
many important respects — just as radically as a citizen of
New Jersey does from a citizen of Wisconsin. They may, perhaps, differ more radically, on account of the fact that state
lines are more strictly drawn in the South than in any other
portion of the Union. It is, of course, measurably true to affirm
that the Southern people are descendants in the main of that
portion of the English people " who had been least modernized,
who still retained a large element of the feudal notion." The
usual assumption that the civilization of the North is Puritan,
while that of the South is Cavalier, rests on a substantial though
small basis of fact. It is further true that the institution of
slavery gave a more or less uniform patriarchal tone to society
in every Southern state. But when all the points of resemblance are numbered and estimated, it will still be found that
the tidewater South differs from the Southwest as much as
New England does from the Northwest, that each state of a
subsection differs from its neighbors, and that there are important lines of cleavage within some of the states themselves.

[1] Reprinted from the article " Dominant Tendencies of the South," *Atlantic
Monthly*, Vol. LXXIX, page 42.

Such a general proposition, however, is of little value unless it is accompanied by particular illustrations.

The two leading types of Southern population are plainly the Virginian and the South Carolinian of the tidewater. For this fact there are both historical and physiographical reasons. Virginia was the first and South Carolina the second Southern colony to be settled by well-to-do Englishmen who desired to found permanent homes. The introduction of slavery and its application to staple crops speedily gave an aristocratic tone to society in both provinces; but between them, in North Carolina, and to the south of them, in Georgia, there were fewer wealthy settlers and no staple crops to speak of, so that from the first, society in these provinces was more or less democratic in spite of slavery. Before, however, the gentry of the coast could expand and occupy the country lying between the Blue Ridge and the Alleghenies, and beyond the latter range of mountains, a very different sort of people had moved in and taken possession. Hardy Scotch-Irish Presbyterians, thrifty German Lutherans, sober and industrious Quakers, had occupied the "up country," and in North Carolina had spread toward the coast. Among these people, owing to their habits and the nature of their soil, slavery could take no strong hold; hence they remained democratic and distinct from their tidewater neighbors, as indeed they are to this day. So it came to pass that when, after the Revolution, tidewater Virginians, in consequence of debt and the impoverishment of the land, determined to emigrate, they passed over the two mountain ranges and settled in Kentucky, or went as far to the southwest as Alabama, later on, while the hardy mountain people, hungry for land and eager for adventure, moved along the valleys and over convenient passes and founded settlements, the more important of which were destined to coalesce into the distinctively democratic commonwealth of Tennessee. Meanwhile, the invention of the cotton gin made it worth the South Carolinian's while to bide at home, and opened up to immigration and settlement the states bordering on the Gulf. As in the case of all new countries, the inflowing population was extremely mixed, but the man who had most slaves could clear his land and start his cotton soonest; and so throughout the lower tier of southwestern states aristocracy triumphed, on the whole, over democracy, being somewhat aided by the presence of French and Spanish populations at Mobile and New Orleans. But in the midst of all this movement and confusion the tidewater Virginians and South Carolinians stood for political and social ideals before which the rest of the South and the Southwest bowed until the advent of Jackson and his frontier Democrats to power. The Virginian fell before the storm, but the South Carolinian bent and rose again. Slavery, not Tennessee democracy, represented the aspirations of the Southern people during the three momentous decades before the Civil War, and slavery's banner Calhoun and his South Carolinians were obviously best fitted to bear. So it has come about that the early prestige of Virginia and the later prestige of South Carolina have invested the "low country" inhabitants of those states — for it is "low country" ideals that have prevailed — with an importance in the eyes of their fellow Southerners and of the rest of the world that is only just beginning to be shaken by the progress of commonwealths that have learned better how to utilize their material resources. But what now can one say of these two types of Southerners?

In the first place, they are nearer to the type of Englishmen that originally settled in the two colonies than might be expected, when the lapse of time is considered. They are distinctly less American in their habits of thought and action than are Georgians or Tennesseeans, New Yorkers, or Iowans. In the cities one naturally finds all sorts and conditions of people, but in the country and in the bosom of indigenous families one finds oneself continually confronted with some survival or recrudescence of English trait or custom. There is a certain colonialism in the attitude assumed by many of these good folks toward all things modern and American that strikes one as odd in people who gave Washington and the Pinckneys to the cause of independence. There is a persistence in customs, a loyalty to beliefs and traditions, a *naïveté* of self-satisfaction that cannot be called conceit, a clannishness, an attachment to the soil, that are radically English and thoroughly picturesque, but are certainly not American.

These and similar traits the tidewater inhabitants of the two states have in common. And yet they differ to such a degree that even the superficial observer has no difficulty in distinguishing them without having recourse to such external peculiarities as dialect or physical appearance. The Virginian is more democratic than the South Carolinian; he has more bonhomie; he is not nearly so punctilious, or stern, or fiery. A true South Carolinian gentleman would never have sat in the White House with slippers worn down at the heels, as Jefferson did. Many Virginian gentlemen would not have done it, either, but they would have comprehended how it was possible to do it. In some way or other, the Virginian developed from a seventeenth-century into an eighteenth-century English squire. He became more or less an easy-going optimist, fond of good company and good living, never so vulgar as Squire Western, but likely to fall into careless, slipshod habits unless upheld, as was often the case, by the refined women about him. With the South Carolinian it seems to have been different. What with the infusion of sober Huguenot blood, what with the masterful qualities necessitated by his isolated position among great masses of black barbarians, he took himself and life more seriously than the Virginian did, and he does so to this day. He has the earnestness and much of the courtly charm of the best type of seventeenth-century Englishman. If the Virginian gentleman is a Squire Allworthy, the South Carolinian is, if it can be conceived, a Colonel Hutchinson fighting on the Royalist side. One even finds that a Virginian boy of the better classes has more bonhomie and less dignity than a South Carolinian of similar age and breeding. The Virginian loves his state and is proud of her history, but on alien soil, amid a pleasant company, he can forget her. The South Carolinian is rarely so unbending, and is, unintentionally no doubt, supercilious toward all other peoples and states. He is not merely glad to hail from his native state, he is not merely anxious to return thither to die, he is miserable whenever and as long as he is not living there. Nay, he actually wishes to be rooted to a particular parish or town. The *genius loci* is the god he worships, and he stands for everything that is not cosmopolitan. Hence he is *par excellence* the Southern conservative, so thoroughgoing in his provincialism that it ceases to appear narrow and small, and reaches the infinite if not the sublime. On this side, as indeed in general intensity of nature, he goes far beyond the Virginian. The latter is conservative and slow to move, yet after all he is a disciple of Jefferson, and he cannot help remembering that his kinsfolk peopled Kentucky and that there are men of Virginian stock thriving in all parts of the country. But even on him the waves of progress have had to dash and dash in order to produce any effect, and he stands to-day, with the South Carolinian, like a promontory jutting out into a rising sea. His promontory is, however, a little greener than that of his neighbor.

Such, in the main, is the material on which the *Zeitgeist* has had to work in the two Southern states that were in the lead before the Civil War practically leveled everything. Very different, as we have seen, is the material in the state lying between the Old Dominion and the commonwealth that had a philosopher for godfather. The North Carolinian is, and has always been, the typical Southern democrat. If he has not progressed rapidly, it is not because he has been unwilling to give up his traditions, though he has them, but because he has always been more or less hampered by physical difficulties, and more or less cast in the shade by his greater neighbors. He has ever been unpretending, but his virtues have been many and solid. He has had his history miswritten, but instead of uttering bitter complaints has set to work to rewrite it. He has labored indefatigably, although with small success as yet, to obtain a good system of public instruction, seeing that large portions of his state would without this remain unexploited for generations. He is still backward in many respects, and still has to bide taunts about not having produced many great men, about smelling of turpentine, and about allowing the practice of "dipping" to continue within his borders. But like the patient, thoroughgoing democrat he is, he takes it all good-naturedly, and has determined not to be last in the race of progress that he is running with his neighbors, though he does at times stop to listen, open-mouthed, to a quack proclaiming the virtues of some political nostrum.

The South Carolinian has always arrogated to himself the name "Carolinian," and he has never been on very familiar terms with his northern neighbor. His feeling for his southern neighbor, the Georgian, is also one of mere tolerance, for the latter has long been called the Southern Yankee, and fairly deserves the appellation. He has much of the shrewdness and push that mark the typical "Down-Easter," and he has a considerable share of that worthy's moral earnestness. In addition he has a good deal of the Virginian's geniality and love of comfort, of the North Carolinian's unpretending democracy, and of the South Carolinian's tendency to exhibitions of fiery temper.

But over and above everything else he has an honest and hearty and not unfounded pride in Georgia, and a sort of masonic affiliation with every person, animal, institution, custom — in short, *thing* — that can be called Georgian. He may not always stand for culture, but he does always stand for patriotism, state and national. He loves success, strength, straightforwardness, and the solid virtues generally, — neither is he averse to the showy ones, — but above all he loves virtue in action. Though possessed of a strong, clear intellect, he is more particularly a man of five senses, of which he makes as good use as he can. He may not always taste the sweetness or see the light of the highest civilization, but he has a good healthy appetite for life. In fine, the Georgian is the Southerner of all others who comes nearest to being a normal American. There are, to be sure, varieties of Georgians, and different phases of civilization are represented in different sections of the state, but the features of character that make for uniformity are more numerous and important than those that make for divergence. The various elements that compose the population — original settlers, incomers from Virginia and the two Carolinas — seem to have been fused, save perhaps on the coast about Savannah, rather than to have preserved their individuality, and the result is the typical Georgian, energetic, shrewd, thrifty, brave, religious, patriotic, tending in the extremes of society to become narrow and hard, or self-assertive and pushing.

The Floridian on the one hand, and the Alabamian on the other, may be fairly described as modified Georgians. Florida, being a comparatively new state, settled under great difficulties and by various stocks, has not until recent years played any great part in Southern history, and even now represents little that is suggestive of an indigenous civilization. This is not true of Alabama, save of the mineral region in the northern part of the state; but the Alabamian, while a distinct personality, has never impressed himself upon the South as his neighbors on the Atlantic coast have done. He seems to hold partly by the Georgian and partly by the Virginian (with whom he is often connected by ties of blood), and has many of the best qualities of both. He is either a "limbered-up" Virginian or a mellowed Georgian. He is also a much less strenuous type of man than his neighbor to the west of him, although in their dates of settlement and in their physiographical features the two states do not present striking points of difference. As for the Mississippian, he too possesses well-defined but mixed characteristics. He seems to hold by the South Carolinian on the one hand, and by the Tennesseean on the other, which is another way of saying that he is a Southwesterner whose natural democratic proclivities have been somewhat modified by institutions and customs of an aristocratic cast. On his large plantation, amid his hundreds of slaves, it was a matter of course that he should develop some of the South Carolinian's masterful traits, while his position as a frontiersman and pioneer necessarily gave him a basis of character not dissimilar to that of the hardy settler on the Watauga or the Cumberland. To understand the Mississippian, then, or indeed any Southwesterner as far as the Rio Grande, we must know something about the Tennesseean.

This stalwart citizen of a state which has already played an important part in our history, and which from its position and resources ought to play a still more important part in the future, naturally holds by the North Carolinian in many of his characteristics. He can generally point to Scotch-Irish ancestors from whom he has inherited the love of independence and the sturdy democratic virtues that characterize the people of the mountain sections of the states on his eastern border, but he owes to these ancestors something that differentiates him from his kinspeople east of the Alleghenies. The latter have been somewhat abashed, somewhat kept in check, by their contact with the civilization of the tidewater, but he wears upon his forehead, whether he dwell on hill or plain, that "freedom of the mountaineer" of which Wordsworth sang. His fathers, whether they owned slaves or not, never ceased to be democrats, and so he is a democrat through and through, of a less unpretending type than the North Carolinian. Through the valor and the exertions of those fathers he has a wide and fair domain in which to choose his dwelling place, but whether he has his abode among the mineral treasures of his mountains, or in the bluegrass plains, or amid the low-lying fields that whiten with the cotton boll, he is always and everywhere the open-handed, self-reliant, easily excited son of equality and freedom that Wellington's regulars went down before in the fatal trenches of New Orleans. In fact, the Tennesseean is not, strictly speaking, a Southerner at all. The basis of his character is Western, and though his sympathies were divided in the Civil War, and though he helps to make up the "Solid South," he has really as little affiliation with the Southerners of the Atlantic coast as Andrew Jackson had with John C. Calhoun. He has not, indeed, the murderous intentions of his great hero and idol, but when he counts himself as being *of* the Southern people he ought to change his preposition and say that he is *with* them.

The other Southwestern states naturally have more distinctively Southern features than Tennessee, but we need hardly go into particulars. Arkansas and Texas are as yet too new to have stood for much in the history of Southern culture, and save in certain localities they are still in the transition stage common to pioneer states. When their various strains of population have been fused and their immense territory has been really settled, the emerging civilization will be almost inevitably Western in tone. It will not be Western in exactly the same way that the civilization of Wisconsin and Illinois is Western, but then the civilization of the latter states differs from that of

Nebraska, or Colorado, or the Dakotas. Yet it will most assuredly not be Southern in any true sense of the term, for in this country the meridians of longitude have on the whole prevailed over the parallels of latitude.

In Louisiana a Southern civilization has been developed in the lower part of the state, and will probably always dominate it. The Louisianian of this section is quite different from his Western compatriots of the towns on the Texas and Arkansas borders, and he possibly comes nearer to the foreigner's idea of what a Southerner is than any other of the types that have been described. Perhaps this is because most foreigners get their ideas of the South from "Uncle Tom's Cabin." Be this as it may, the typical Louisianian seems to understand the *dolce far niente* better than the Virginian; he keeps social life going with less trouble than the South Carolinian; he would never think of bustling and working like a Georgian; he would die of the blues if he had to exchange the picturesque contrasts of his chief city and the lower half of his state with the gray-colored uniformity of the life that the North Carolinian has led for generations. But if the Louisianian has enjoyed life, he has not had the wisdom to develop all portions of his interesting commonwealth, and he has never taken a commanding position among his Southern brethren. With him, however, our modest efforts at portraiture must cease.

# POETS

## PAUL HAMILTON HAYNE

[Paul Hamilton Hayne was born in Charleston, South Carolina, in 1830. His family belonged to the wealthy and aristocratic circle of that city. After graduating from Charleston College, Hayne studied law, but his love of literature proved too strong for the practice of his profession. In 1857 he became editor of *Russell's Magazine*, which he made a decided success. Before the war Hayne had published three volumes of poetry, made up chiefly of pieces which he had contributed to various periodicals. At the outbreak of hostilities he became an aide on Governor Pickens's staff, but after a brief service he was forced to resign on account of ill health. Finding himself impoverished at the close of the war, he moved to the pine barrens of Georgia and about eighteen miles from Augusta built a very plain cottage, which he called "Copse Hill." Here he struggled bravely with poverty as best he could, through his contributions of poetry and other kinds of writing to the magazines. Gradually his genius gained recognition throughout the country at large and he came to have the title

PAUL HAMILTON HAYNE

of "the Laureate of the South." In 1882 a complete edition of his poems was published in Boston. Shortly after the publication of this volume, Hayne's health began to give way, and he died in 1886.]

## A DREAM OF THE SOUTH WINDS [1]

O fresh, how fresh and fair
Through the crystal gulfs of air,
The fairy South Wind floateth on her subtle wings of balm!
And the green earth lapped in bliss,
To the magic of her kiss
Seems yearning upward fondly through the golden-crested calm!

From the distant Tropic strand,
Where the billows, bright and bland,
Go creeping, curling round the palms with sweet, faint undertune,
From its fields of purpling flowers
Still wet with fragrant showers,
The happy South Wind lingering sweeps the royal blooms of June.

All heavenly fancies rise
On the perfume of her sighs,
Which steep the inmost spirit in a languor rare and fine,
And a peace more pure than sleep's
Unto dim, half-conscious deeps,
Transports me, lulled and dreaming, on its twilight tides divine.

Those dreams! ah me! the splendor,
So mystical and tender,
Wherewith like soft heat-lightnings they gird their meaning round,
And those waters, calling, calling,
With a nameless charm enthralling,
Like the ghost of music melting on a rainbow spray of sound!

1 The selections from Hayne are reprinted by permission of the holder of the copyright, Lothrop, Lee & Shepard Co.

Touch, touch me not, nor wake me,
Lest grosser thoughts o'ertake me,
From earth receding faintly with her dreary din and jars, —
What viewless arms caress me?
What whispered voices bless me,
With welcomes dropping dewlike from the weird and wondrous
stars?

Alas! dim, dim, and dimmer
Grows the preternatural glimmer
Of that trance the South Wind brought me on her subtle wings of
balm,
For behold! its spirit flieth,
And its fairy murmur dieth,
And the silence closing round me is a dull and soulless calm!

## ASPECTS OF THE PINES

Tall, somber, grim, against the morning sky
They rise, scarce touched by melancholy airs,
Which stir the fadeless foliage dreamfully,
As if from realms of mystical despairs.

Tall, somber, grim, they stand with dusky gleams
Brightening to gold within the woodland's core,
Beneath the gracious noontide's tranquil beams —
But the weird winds of morning sigh no more.

A stillness, strange, divine, ineffable,
Broods round and o'er them in the wind's surcease,
And on each tinted copse and shimmering dell
Rests the mute rapture of deep-hearted peace.

Last, sunset comes — the solemn joy and might
    Borne from the West when cloudless day declines —
Low, flutelike breezes sweep the waves of light,
    And lifting dark green tresses of the pines,

Till every lock is luminous — gently float,
    Fraught with hale odors up the heavens afar
To faint when twilight on her virginal throat
    Wears for a gem the tremulous vesper star.

## MACDONALD'S RAID — 1780

I remember it well; 't was a morn dull and gray,
And the legion lay idle and listless that day,
A thin drizzle of rain piercing chill to the soul,
And with not a spare bumper to brighten the bowl,
When Macdonald arose, and unsheathing his blade,
Cried, " Who 'll back me, brave comrades ?   I'm hot for a raid.
Let the carbines be loaded, the war harness ring,
Then swift death to the Redcoats, and down with the King ! "

We leaped up at his summons, all eager and bright,
To our finger tips thrilling to join him in fight;
Yet he chose from our numbers *four* men and no more.
" Stalwart brothers," quoth he, " you 'll be strong as fourscore,
If you follow me fast wheresoever I lead,
With keen sword and true pistol, stanch heart and bold steed.
Let the weapons be loaded, the bridle bits ring,
Then swift death to the Redcoats, and down with the King ! "

In a trice we were mounted; Macdonald's tall form
Seated firm in the saddle, his face like a storm
When the clouds on Ben Lomond hang heavy and stark,
And the red veins of lightning pulse hot through the dark;

His left hand on his sword belt, his right lifted free,
With a prick from the spurred heel, a touch from the knee,
His lithe Arab was off like an eagle on wing —
" Ha ! death, death to the Redcoats, and down with the King ! "

'T was three leagues to the town, where, in insolent pride
Of their disciplined numbers, their works strong and wide,
The big Britons, oblivious of warfare and arms,
A soft *dolce* were wrapped in, not dreaming of harms,
When fierce yells, as if borne on some fiend-ridden rout,
With strange cheer after cheer, are heard echoing without,
Over which, like the blast of ten trumpeters, ring,
" Death, death to the Redcoats, and down with the King ! "

Such a tumult we raised with steel, hoof-stroke, and shout,
That the foemen made straight for their inmost redoubt,
And therein, with pale lips and cowed spirits, quoth they,
" Lord, the whole rebel army assaults us to-day.
Are the works, think you, strong ? God of heaven, what a din !
'T is the front wall besieged — have the rebels rushed in ?
It must be ; for, hark ! hark to that jubilant ring
Of ' Death to the Redcoats, and down with the King ! ' "

Meanwhile, through the town like whirlwind we sped,
And ere long be assured that our broadswords were red ;
And the ground here and there by an ominous stain
Showed how the stark soldier beside it was slain :
A fat sergeant-major, who yawed like a goose,
With his waddling bowlegs, and his trappings all loose,
By one back-handed blow the Macdonald cuts down,
To the shoulder-blade, cleaving him sheer through the crown,
And the last words that greet his dim consciousness ring
With " Death, death to the Redcoats, and down with the King ! "

Having cleared all the streets, not an enemy left
Whose heart was unpierced, or whose headpiece uncleft,
What should we do next, but — as careless and calm
As if we were scenting a summer morn's balm
'Mid a land of pure peace — just serenely drop down
On a few constant friends who still stopped in the town.
*What* a welcome they gave us! One dear little thing,
As I kissed her sweet lips, did I dream of the King? —

Of the King or his minions? No; war and its scars
Seemed as distant just then as the fierce front of Mars
From a love-girdled earth; but, alack! on our bliss,
On the close clasp of arms and kiss showering on kiss,
Broke the rude bruit of battle, the rush thick and fast
Of the Britons made 'ware of our rash *ruse* at last;
So we haste to our coursers, yet flying, we fling
The old watchwords abroad, "Down with Redcoats and King!"

As we scampered pell-mell o'er the hard-beaten track
We had traversed that morn, we glanced momently back,
And beheld their long earthworks all compassed in flame;
With a vile plunge and hiss the huge musket balls came,
And the soil was plowed up, and the space 'twixt the trees
Seemed to hum with the war song of Brobdingnag bees;
Yet above them, beyond them, victoriously ring
The shouts, "Death to the Redcoats, and down with the King!"

Ah! *that* was a feat, lads, to boast of! What men
Like you weaklings to-day had durst cope with *us* then?
Though I say it who should not, I am ready to vow
I'd o'ermatch a half score of your fops even now —

The poor puny prigs, mincing up, mincing down,
Through the whole wasted day the thronged streets of the town:
Why, their dainty white necks 't were but pastime to wring —
Ay! *my* muscles are firm still; *I* fought 'gainst the King!

Dare you doubt it? well, give me the weightiest of all
The sheathed sabers that hang there, uplooped on the wall;
Hurl the scabbard aside; yield the blade to my clasp;
Do you see, with one hand how I poise it and grasp
The rough iron-bound hilt? With this long hissing sweep
I have smitten full many a foeman with sleep —
That forlorn, final sleep! God! what memories cling
To those gallant old times when we fought 'gainst the King.


### THE PINE'S MYSTERY

Listen! the somber foliage of the Pine
    A swart Gitana of the woodland trees,
In answering what we may but half divine
    To those soft whispers of the twilight breeze!

Passion and mystery murmur through the leaves,
    Passion and mystery, touched by deathless pain,
Whose monotone of long, low anguish grieves
    For something lost that shall not live again!


### THE WILL AND THE WING

To have the will to soar, but not the wings,
    Eyes fixed forever on a starry height,
Whence stately shapes of grand imaginings
    Flash down the splendors of imperial light;

And yet to lack the charm that makes them ours,
    The obedient vassals of that conquering spell,
Whose omnipresent and ethereal powers
    Encircle Heaven, nor fear to enter Hell;

COPSE HILL

Paul Hamilton Hayne's unpretentious home after the war, situated
about eighteen miles from Augusta, Georgia

This is the doom of Tantalus — the thirst
    For beauty's balmy fount to quench the fires
Of the wild passion that our souls have nurst
    In hopeless promptings — unfulfilled desires.

Yet would I rather in the outward state
    Of Song's immortal temple lay me down,
A beggar basking by that radiant gate,
    Than bend beneath the haughtiest empire's crown!

For sometimes, through the bars, my ravished eyes
   Have caught brief glimpses of a life divine,
And seen afar, mysterious rapture rise
   Beyond the veil that guards the inmost shrine.


## THE AXE AND PINE

All day, on bole and limb the axes ring,
And every stroke upon my startled brain
Falls with the power of sympathetic pain;
I shrink to view each glorious forest king
Descend to earth, a wan, discrownéd thing.
Ah, Heaven! beside these foliaged giants slain,
How small the human dwarfs, whose lust for gain
Hath edged their brutal steel to smite and sting!
Hark! to those long-drawn murmurings, strange and drear!
The wail of Dryads in their last distress;
O'er ruined haunts and ravished loveliness
Still tower those brawny arms; tones coarsely loud
Rise still beyond the greenery's waning cloud,
While falls the insatiate steel, sharp, cold, and sheer!


## MIDSUMMER IN THE SOUTH

I love Queen August's stately sway,
And all her fragrant south winds say,
With vague, mysterious meanings fraught,
Of unimaginable thought;
Those winds, 'mid change of gloom and gleam,
Seem wandering thro' a golden dream —
The rare midsummer dream that lies
In humid depths of nature's eyes,
Weighing her languid forehead down

Beneath a fair but fiery crown:
Its witchery broods o'er earth and skies,
Fills with divine amenities
The bland, blue spaces of the air,
And smiles with looks of drowsy cheer
'Mid hollows of the brown-hued hills;
And oft, in tongues of tinkling rills,
A softer, homelier utterance finds
Than that which haunts the lingering winds!

I love midsummer's azure deep,
Whereon the huge white clouds, asleep,
Scarce move through lengths of tranced hours;
Some, raised in forms of giant towers —
Dumb Babels, with ethereal stairs
Scaling the vast height — unawares
What mocking spirit, ether-born,
Hath built those transient spires in scorn,
And reared towards the topmost sky
Their unsubstantial fantasy!
Some stretched in tenuous arcs of light
Athwart the airy infinite,
Far glittering up yon fervid dome,
And lapped by cloudland's misty foam,
Whose wreaths of fine sun-smitten spray
Melt in a burning haze away;
Some throned in heaven's serenest smiles,
Pure-hued, and calm as fairy isles,
Girt by the tides of soundless seas —
The heavens' benign Hesperides.

I love midsummer uplands, free
To the bold raids of breeze and bee,
Where, nested warm in yellowing grass,

I hear the swift-winged partridge pass,
With whir and boom of gusty flight,
Across the broad heath's treeless height:
Or, just where, elbow-poised, I lift
Above the wild flower's careless drift
My half-closed eyes, I see and hear
The blithe field sparrow twittering clear
Quick ditties to his tiny love;
While, from afar, the timid dove,
With faint, voluptuous murmur, wakes
The silence of the pastoral brakes.

I love midsummer sunsets, rolled
Down the rich west in waves of gold,
With blazing crests of billowy fire.
But when those crimson floods retire,
In noiseless ebb, slow-surging, grand,
By pensive twilight's flickering strand,
In gentler mood I love to mark
The slow gradations of the dark;
Till, lo! from Orient's mists withdrawn,
Hail! to the moon's resplendent dawn;
On dusky vale and haunted plain
Her effluence falls like balmy rain;
Gaunt gulfs of shadow own her might;
She bathes the rescued world in light,
So that, albeit my summer's day
Erewhile did breathe its life away,
Methinks, whate'er its hours had won
Of beauty, born from shade and sun,
Hath not perchance so wholly died,
But o'er the moonlight's silvery tide
Comes back, sublimed and purified!

## IRWIN RUSSELL

[Irwin Russell was born in Port Gibson, Mississippi, in 1853. After graduating from the St. Louis University in 1869 he chose

IRWIN RUSSELL

the profession of law, but the young lawyer never had a case in court because his interests were turning steadily to literature. His first contribution to *Scribner's Monthly* appeared in 1876. During the yellow-fever epidemic of 1878 he lost his father, and, thrown on his own resources, he started to New York, intending to make a livelihood through writing. Soon after arriving there he was stricken with a dangerous fever. When he recovered he shipped on a vessel for New Orleans and worked his passage by coal heaving. In New Orleans he spent several months of poverty and distress, attempting to earn a living by writing for newspapers. His life of promise was ended in 1879 under pitiable circumstances. Nine years later his poems were collected into a small volume.]

### NEBUCHADNEZZAR [1]

You, Nebuchadnezzah, whoa, sah !
Whar is you tryin' to go, sah ?
I'd hab you fur to know, sah,
    I's a-holdin' ob de lines.

[1] The selections from Russell are reprinted through the kind permission of the holder of the copyright, the Century Company.

You better stop dat prancin';
You 's pow'ful fond ob dancin',
But I 'll bet my yeah 's advancin'
    Dat I 'll cure you ob yo' shines.


Look heah, mule! Better min' out;
Fus' t'ing you know you 'll fin' out
How quick I 'll wear dis line out
    On yo' ugly, stubbo'n back.
You need n't try to steal up
An' lif' dat precious heel up;
You 's got to plow dis fiel' up;
    You has, sah, fur a fac'.


Dar, *dat's* de way to do it!
He 's comin' right down to it;
Jes watch him plowin' troo it!
    Dis nigger ain't no fool.
Some folks dey would 'a' beat him;
Now, dat would only heat him —
I know jes how to treat him:
    You mus' *reason* wid a mule.


He minds me like a nigger.
If he wuz only bigger
He 'd fotch a mighty figger,
    He would, I *tell* you! Yes, sah!
*See* how he keeps a-clickin'!
He 's as gentle as a chickin,
An' nebber thinks o'kickin' —
    *Whoa dar! Nebuchadnezzah!*


\* \* \* \* \* \*

Is dis heah me, or not me?
Or is de debbil got me?
Wuz dat a cannon shot me?
   Hab I laid heah more 'n a week?
Dat mule do kick amazin'!
De beast wuz sp'iled in raisin' —
But now I 'spect he 's grazin'
   On de oder side de creek.


## SELLING A DOG

H'yar, Pot-liquor! What you at? You heah me callin' you?
H'yar, sah! Come an' tell dis little gemmen howdy-do!
Dar, sah, *ain't* dat puppy, jes as fat as he kin roll?
Maybe you won't b'liebe it, but he 's only six mon's ol'!


'Coon dog? Lord! young marster, he 's jes at 'em all de while;
*I* b'liebe dat he kin smell a 'coon fur half a mile.
I don' like to sell him, fur he 's wuf his weight in gol';
If *you* did n't want him, sah, he nebber *should* be sol'.


If you takes him off wid you, I 'll feel like I wuz lost.
He 's de bes' young fightin' dog I ebber come acrost.
Jes look at dem eyes, young marster; what a sabbage face! —
He won't let no stranger nigger come about de place.


You know Henry Wilson's Bob, dat whipped your fader's Dan?
Pot-liquor jes chucked dat dog so bad he could n't stan'!
Well, sah, if you wants him, now I 'll tell you what I 'll do, —
You kin hab him fur a dollar, seein 's how it 's *you*.

Now, Marster Will, you *knows* it — he 's wuf mo 'n dat, a heap ;
R'al'y, I 's a-doin' wrong to let him go so cheap.
Don't you tell nobody, now, what wuz de price you paid —
My ol' 'oman 's gwine to gib me fits, sah, I 's afraid !

T'anks you, sah ! Good-mornin', sah ! You tell yo' ma, fur me,
I has got de fines' turkeys dat she ebber see ;
Dey is jes as good as any pusson ebber eat.
If she wants a *gobbler*, let her sen' to Uncle Pete.

Dar ! I 's done got rid ob dat ar wretched dog at las' !
Drownin' time wuz comin' fur him mighty precious fas' !
Sol' him fur a dollar — Well ! An' goodness knows de pup
Is n't wuf de powder it 'd take to blow him up !

### DAT PETER

I 'se been a-watchin' people an' deir doings all my life,
An' sometimes I obsarves to Sophonisby — dat 's my wife —
Dat nuffin' seldom happens what I does n't 'spect to see :
                    But Peter,
                    Dat Peter !
                        He gits away wid me.

You see he 's been to Oakland, an' his larnin' is profound ;
I heered him sayin' yes'day dat the yearth kep' turnin' round !
Dat 'pears to me ridiculous — but I nebber wuz to school —
                    And Peter,
                    Dat Peter !
                        He 'lows dat I 'se a fool.

Well, mebbe so; I mout be, but I does n't think it 's true;
I aint so wise as Peter, but I knows a ting or two:
Ef I kain't run as fast as some, I manages to crawl —
                But Peter,
                Dat Peter!
                    He thinks he knows it all.


He wears a suit ob store-clo'es, an' a fine fibe dollar hat!
Who eber heard de like afore ob sich gwine on as dat?
He iles his har, he do; an' goes a-sparkin' eb'ry night;
                Why Peter,
                Dat Peter!
                    I guess he thinks he 's white.


I really think ef Peter would rent a leetle patch ob land,
An' settle down to crappin', dat he 'd hold a better hand;
De debbil's gwine to set him back afore his game is done;
                But Peter,
                Dat Peter!
                    He say he 's twenty-one.


Well, let de nigger slide — I could say suffin' ef I mout,
But I has oder matters to be projeckin' about.
I 'se jubious how he 'll come out — hab to wait a while an' see.
                But Peter,
                Dat Peter!
                    He 's most too much for me.

## SIDNEY LANIER

[Sidney Lanier was born in Macon, Georgia, in 1842. His ancestors had been for generations musicians. At fourteen he entered the sophomore class of Oglethorpe College at Midway, Georgia, and graduated in 1860. He was at once appointed a tutor in the col-

**SIDNEY LANIER**

lege, but the war broke out shortly and he joined the Confederate army. He saw service in Virginia, and toward the close of the war was put in charge of a blockade-running vessel. His vessel was captured in 1864, and he was confined for five months in Point Lookout prison. The exposure and hardships of this experience germinated the seeds of consumption, against which he had to fight the rest of his life and to which he finally succumbed. After the war Lanier lived in Georgia and Alabama, earning a living as teacher, hotel clerk, and lawyer. But finding that his health grew no better and feeling that he was wasting his genius in uncongenial pursuits, he decided to devote himself to literature and music. In 1873 he went to Baltimore and found employment as first flutist in the Peabody Symphony Orchestra. In Baltimore he found musicians, literary people, and libraries, and his genius would undoubtedly have blossomed rapidly had it not been for ill health. Recurring attacks of his malady compelled him to seek health in visits to the mountains of North Carolina and the mild climate of Florida. In 1879 he was appointed lecturer on English literature at Johns Hopkins University, a position which assured an income and which was entirely congenial. His health, however, was rapidly failing, and finally the sufferer was obliged to quit work and go to the mountains of North Carolina. There in the little village of Lynn his brave fight closed in the early autumn of 1881.]

## THE TOURNAMENT

### JOUST FIRST

Bright shone the lists, blue bent the skies,
　　And the knights still hurried amain
To the tournament under the ladies' eyes,
　　Where the jousters were Heart and Brain.

Flourished the trumpets : entered Heart,
　　A youth in crimson and gold.
Flourished again : Brain stood apart,
　　Steel-armored, dark and cold.

Heart's palfrey caracoled gayly round,
　　Heart tra-li-ra'd merrily ;
But Brain sat still, with never a sound,
　　So cynical-calm was he.

Heart's helmet-crest bore favors three
　　From his lady's hand caught ;
While Brain wore a plumeless casque ; not he
　　Or favor gave or sought.

The herald blew ; Heart shot a glance
　　To find his lady's eye,
But Brain gazed straight ahead his lance
　　To aim more faithfully.

They charged, they struck ; both fell, both bled.
　　Brain rose again, ungloved,
Heart, dying, smiled and faintly said,
　　" My love to my beloved."

### JOUST SECOND

A-many sweet eyes wept and wept,
  A-many bosoms heaved again;
A-many dainty dead hopes slept
  With yonder Heart-knight prone o'er the plain.


Yet stars will burn through any mists,
  And the ladies' eyes, through rains of fate,
Still beamed upon the bloody lists
  And lit the joust of Love and Hate.


O strange! or ere a trumpet blew,
  Or ere a challenge-word was given,
A knight leapt down i' the lists; none knew
  Whether he sprang from earth or heaven.


His cheek was soft as a lily-bud,
  His gray eyes calmed his youth's alarm;
Nor helm nor hauberk nor even a hood
  Had he to shield his life from harm.


No falchion from his baldric swung,
  He wore a white rose in its place.
No dagger at his girdle hung,
  But only an olive branch, for grace.


And, "Come, thou poor mistaken knight,"
  Cried Love, unarmed, yet dauntless there,
"Come on, God pity thee! — I fight
  Sans sword, sans shield; yet, Hate, beware!"

Spurred furious Hate; he foamed at mouth,
   His breath was hot upon the air,
His breath scorched souls, as a dry drought
   Withers green trees and burns them bare.


Straight drives he at his enemy,
   His hairy hands grip lance in rest,
His lance it gleams full bitterly,
   God! — gleams, true-point, on Love's bare breast!


Love's gray eyes glow with a heaven-heat,
   Love lifts his hand in a saintly prayer;
Look! Hate hath fallen at his feet!
   Look! Hate hath vanished in the air!


Then all the throng looked kind on all;
   Eyes yearned, lips kissed, dumb souls were freed;
Two magic maids' hands lifted a pall
   And the dead knight, Heart, sprang on his steed.


Then Love cried, " Break me his lance, each knight!
   Ye shall fight for blood-athirst Fame no more."
And the knights all doffed their mailèd might
   And dealt out dole on dole to the poor.


Then dove-lights sanctified the plain,
   And hawk and sparrow shared a nest.
And the great sea opened and swallowed Pain,
   And out of this water-grave floated Rest!

## SONG OF THE CHATTAHOOCHEE[1]

Out of the hills of Habersham,
    Down the valleys of Hall,
The hurrying rain,[a] to reach the plain,
    Has run[b] the rapid and leapt[c] the fall,
Split at the rock and together again,
Accepted his[d] bed, or narrow or wide,
And fled[e] from folly on every side,
    With a lover's pain to attain the plain,
      Far from the hills of Habersham,
      . Far from the valleys of Hall.


All down the hills of Habersham,
    All through the valleys of Hall,
The rushes cried, *Abide, abide*;
    The willful water weeds held me thrall,
The laurel, slow-laving, turned my tide,[f]
The ferns and the fondling grass said *stay*,
The dewberry dipped for to win[g] delay,
    And the little reeds sighed, *Abide, abide*,
      *Here in the hills of Habersham*,
      *Here in the valleys of Hall*.

---

[1] First published in *Scott's Magazine*, from which it is here taken. Lanier's later revisions are given in footnotes, and the study of these will show the development of the poet's artistic sense.

   *a*. Changed to " I hurry amain."
   *b*. Changed to " I run."
   *c*. Changed to " leap."
   *d*. Changed to " accept my."
   *e*. Changed to " flee."
   *f*. Changed to " The laving laurel turned my tide."
   *g*. Changed to " work."

High over the hills of Habersham,
        Veiling the valleys of Hall,
    The hickory told me manifold
        Fair tales of shade, the poplar tall
    Wrought me her shadowy self to hold,
The chestnut, the oak, the walnut, the pine,
Overleaning, with flickering meaning and sign,
        Said, *Pass not so cold these manifold*
            *Deep shades of the hills of Habersham,*
            *These glades in the valleys of Hall.*


    And oft in the hills of Habersham,
        And oft in the valleys of Hall,
    The white quartz shone, and the smooth brookstone
        Barred[h] me of passage with friendly brawl,
    And many a metal lay sad, alone,[i]
And the diamond, the garnet, the amethyst,
And the crystal that prisons a purple mist,
        Showed lights like my own from each cordial stone
            In the clefts of the hills of Habersham,
            In the beds of the valleys of Hall.


    But oh, not the hills of Habersham,
        And oh, not the valleys of Hall,
    Shall hinder the rain from attaining the plain,[j]
        For downward the voices of duty call —
    Downward to toil and be mixed with the main.

---

*h.* Changed to "did bar."

*i.* This and the three following lines changed to

> And many a luminous jewel lone —
> Crystals clear or a-cloud with mist,
> Ruby, garnet, and amethyst —
>     Made lures with the lightnings of streaming stone.

*j.* Changed to " Avail! I am fain for to water the plain."

The dry fields burn and the mills are to turn,
And a thousand meadows*k* mortally yearn,
   And the final*l* main from beyond the plain
      Calls o'er the hills of Habersham,
      And calls through the valleys of Hall.


## THE CRYSTAL [1]

At midnight, death's and truth's unlocking time,
When far within the spirit's hearing rolls
The great soft rumble of the course of things —
A bulk of silence in a mask of sound —
When darkness clears our vision that by day
Is sun-blind, and the soul 's a ravening owl
For truth, and flitteth here and there about
Low-lying woody tracts of time and oft
Is minded for to sit upon a bough,
Dry-dead and sharp, of some long-stricken tree
And muse in that gaunt place, — 't was then my heart,
Deep in the meditative dark, cried out:

Ye companies of governor-spirits grave,
Bards, and old bringers-down of flaming news
From steep-walled heavens, holy malcontents,
Sweet seers, and stellar visionaries, all
That brood about the skies of poesy,
Full bright ye shine, insuperable stars;
Yet, if a man look hard upon you, none
With total luster blazeth, no, not one

*k.* Changed to "myriad of flowers."
*l.* Changed to "lordly."
[1] This poem appeared in the *Independent*, July 15, 1880, from which it is taken.
The passage in which Lanier reviews the world's great names, — Shakespeare,
Homer, Socrates, Buddha, Dante, Milton, Æschylus, Lucretius, etc., — only to
find some flaw in each, is here omitted.

But hath some heinous freckle of the flesh
Upon his shining cheek, not one but winks
His ray, opaqued with intermittent mist
Of defect; yea, you masters all must ask
Some sweet forgiveness, which we leap to give,
We lovers of you, heavenly-glad to meet
Your largess so with love, and interplight
Your geniuses with our mortalities. . . .

But Thee, but Thee, O sovereign Seer of time,
But Thee, O poet's Poet, Wisdom's Tongue,
But Thee, O man's best Man, O love's best Love,
O perfect life in perfect labor writ,
O all men's Comrade, Servant, King, or Priest, —
What *if* or *yet*, what mole, what flaw, what lapse,
What least defect or shadow of defect,
What rumor, tattled by an enemy,
Of inference loose, what lack of grace
Even in torture's grasp, or sleep's, or death's, —
Oh, what amiss may I forgive in Thee,
Jesus, good Paragon, thou Crystal Christ?

## SUNRISE [1]

In my sleep I was fain of their fellowship, fain
Of the live-oak, the marsh, and the main.
The little green leaves would not let me alone in my sleep;
Up breathed from the marshes, a message of range and of sweep,
Interwoven with waftures of wild sea-liberties, drifting,
Came through the lapped leaves sifting, sifting,
Came to the gates of sleep.

[1] First published in the *Independent*, December 14, 1882, from which it is
here taken.

Then my thoughts, in the dark of the dungeon-keep
Of the Castle of Captives hid in the City of Sleep,
Upstarted, by twos and by threes assembling:
The gates of sleep fell a-trembling
Like as the lips of a lady that forth falter *yes*,
   Shaken with happiness:
   The gates of sleep stood wide.


I have waked, I have come, my beloved! I might not abide:
I have come ere the dawn, O beloved, my live-oaks, to hide
   In your gospeling glooms, — to be
As a lover in heaven, the marsh my marsh and the sea my sea.


Tell me, sweet burly-barked, man-bodied Tree
That mine arms in the dark are embracing, dost know
From what fount are these tears at thy feet which flow?
They rise not from reason, but deeper inconsequent deeps.
   Reason's not one that weeps.
   What logic of greeting lies
Betwixt dear over-beautiful trees and the rain of the eyes?


O cunning green leaves, little masters! like as ye gloss
All the dull-tissued dark with your luminous darks that emboss
The vague blackness of night into pattern and plan,
   So,
(But would I could know, but would I could know,)
With your question embroid'ring the dark of the question of
  man, —
So, with your silences purfling this silence of man
While his cry to the dead for some knowledge is under the ban,
   Under the ban, —
  So, ye have wrought me

Designs on the night of our knowledge, — yea, ye have taught me,
So,
That haply we know somewhat more than we know.


   Ye lispers, whisperers, singers in storms,
   Ye consciences murmuring faiths under forms,
   Ye ministers meet for each passion that grieves,
   Friendly, sisterly, sweetheart leaves,
Oh, rain me down from your darks that contain me
Wisdoms ye winnow from winds that pain me, —
Sift down tremors of sweet-within-sweet
That advise me of more than they bring, — repeat
Me the woods-smell that swiftly but now brought breath
From the heaven-side bank of the river of death, —
Teach me the terms of silence, — preach me
The passion of patience, — sift me, — impeach me, —
And there, oh there
As ye hang with your myriad palms upturned in the air,
Pray me a myriad prayer.


My gossip, the owl, — is it thou
That out of the leaves of the low-hanging bough,
As I pass to the beach, art stirred?
Dumb woods, have ye uttered a bird?


Reverend Marsh, low-couched along the sea,
Old chemist, rapt in alchemy,
Distilling silence, — lo,
That which our father-age had died to know —
The menstruum that dissolves all matter — thou
Hast found it: for this silence, filling now
The globèd clarity of receiving space,
This solves us all: man, matter, doubt, disgrace,

Death, love, sin, sanity,
Must in yon silence' clear solution lie.
Too clear! That crystal nothing who 'll peruse?
The blackest night could bring us brighter news.
Yet precious qualities of silence haunt
Round these vast margins, ministrant.
Oh, if thy soul 's at latter gasp for space,
With trying to breathe no bigger than thy race
Just to be fellowed, when that thou hast found
No man with room, or grace enough of bound
To entertain that New thou tell'st, thou art, —
'T is here, 't is here, thou canst unhand thy heart
And breathe it free, and breathe it free,
By rangy marsh, in lone sea-liberty.
The tide 's at full: the marsh with flooded streams
Glimmers, a limpid labyrinth of dreams.
Each winding creek in grave entrancement lies
A rhapsody of morning-stars. The skies
Shine scant with one forked galaxy, —
The marsh brags ten: looped on his breast they lie.

Oh, what if a sound should be made!
Oh, what if a bound should be laid
To this bow-and-string tension of beauty and silence a-spring, —
To the bend of beauty the bow, or the hold of silence the string!
I fear me, I fear me yon dome of diaphanous gleam
Will break as a bubble o'erblown in a dream, —
Yon dome of too-tenuous tissues of space and of night,
Overweighted with stars, overfreighted with light,
Oversated with beauty and silence, will seem
       But a bubble that broke in a dream,
If a bound of degree to this grace be laid,
       Or a sound or a motion made.

But no: it is made: list! somewhere, — mystery, where?
   In the leaves? in the air?
In my heart? is a motion made:
'T is a motion of dawn, like a flicker of shade on shade.
In the leaves 't is palpable: low multitudinous stirring
Upwinds through the woods; the little ones, softly conferring,
Have settled my lord's to be looked for; so; they are still;
But the air and my heart and the earth are a-thrill, —
And look where the wild duck sails round the bend of the river, —
   And look where a passionate shiver
   Expectant is bending the blades
Of the marsh-grass in serial shimmers and shades, —
And invisible wings, fast fleeting, fast fleeting,
   Are beating
The dark overhead as my heart beats, — and steady and free
Is the ebb-tide flowing from marsh to sea —
   (Run home, little streams,
   With your lapfuls of stars and dreams), —
And a sailor unseen is hoisting a-peak,
For list, down the inshore curve of the creek
   How merrily flutters the sail, —
And lo, in the East! Will the East unveil?
The East is unveiled, the East hath confessed
A flush: 't is dead; 't is alive; 't is dead, ere the West
Was aware of it: nay, 't is abiding, 't is withdrawn:
Have a care, sweet Heaven! 'T is Dawn.

Now a dream of a flame through that dream of a flush is up-
  rolled:
To the zenith ascending, a dome of undazzling gold
Is builded, in shape as a beehive, from out of the sea:
The hive is of gold undazzling, but oh, the Bee,
The star-fed Bee, the build-fire Bee,

Of dazzling gold is the great Sun-Bee
That shall flash from the hive-hole over the sea.
Yet now the dewdrop, now the morning gray,
Shall live their little lucid sober day
Ere with the sun their souls exhale away.
Now in each pettiest personal sphere of dew
The summ'd morn shines complete as in the blue
Big dewdrop of all heaven: with these lit shrines
O'er-silvered to the farthest sea-confines,
The sacramental marsh one pious plain
Of worship lies. Peace to the ante-reign
Of Mary Morning, blissful mother mild,
Minded of nought but peace, and of a child.

Not slower than Majesty moves, for a mean and a measure
Of motion, — not faster than dateless Olympian leisure
Might pace with unblown ample garments from pleasure to
    pleasure, —
The wave-serrate sea-rim sinks unjarring, unreeling,
Forever revealing, revealing, revealing,
Edgewise, bladewise, halfwise, wholewise, — 't is done!
            Good-morrow, lord Sun!
With several voice, with ascription one,
The woods and the marsh and the sea and my soul
Unto thee, whence the glittering stream of all morrows doth roll,
Cry good and past-good and most heavenly morrow, lord Sun.

O Artisan born in the purple, — Workman Heat, —
Parter of passionate atoms that travail to meet
And be mixed in the death-cold oneness, — innermost Guest
At the marriage of elements, — fellow of publicans, — blest
King in the blouse of flame, that loiterest o'er
The idle skies, yet laborest fast evermore, —

Thou in the fine forge-thunder, thou, in the beat
Of the heart of a man, thou Motive, — Laborer Heat:
Yea, Artist, thou, of whose art yon sea 's all news,
With his inshore greens and manifold mid-sea blues,
Pearl-glint, shell-tint, ancientest perfectest hues,
Ever shaming the maidens, — lily and rose
Confess thee, and each mild flame that glows
In the clarified virginal bosoms of stones that shine,
        It is thine, it is thine:

Thou chemist of storms, whether driving the winds a-swirl
Or a-flicker the subtiler essences polar that whirl
In the magnet earth, — yea, thou with a storm for a heart,
Rent with debate, many-spotted with question, part
From part oft sundered, yet ever a globèd light,
Yet ever the artist, ever more large and bright
Than the eye of a man may avail of: — manifold One,
I must pass from thy face, I must pass from the face of the Sun:

Old Want is awake and agog, every wrinkle a-frown;
The worker must pass to his work in the terrible town:
But I fear not, nay, and I fear not the thing to be done;
I am strong with the strength of my lord the Sun:
How dark, how dark soever the race that must needs be run,
        I am lit with the Sun.

Oh, never the mast-high run of the seas
  Of traffic shall hide thee,
Never the hell-colored smoke of the factories
      Hide thee,
Never the reek of the time's fen-politics
      Hide thee,

And ever my heart through the night shall with knowledge
    abide thee,
And ever by day shall my spirit, as one that hath tried thee,
Labor, at leisure, in art, — till yonder beside thee
        My soul shall float, friend Sun,
        The day being done.

## JOHN BANISTER TABB

[John Banister Tabb, more commonly called Father Tabb, was
born in Virginia in 1845. During the Civil War he served on a
blockade runner, and, being captured, he was imprisoned in Point
Lookout prison, where he became the friend of Sidney Lanier. In
1872 he began to teach and to write verses, and in 1884 he privately
published his first volume of poems. In the meantime he had been
ordained a priest in the Roman Catholic Church, and had become
professor of English in St. Charles College, Maryland. There he
died in 1909. He has published, at various times, some seven or
eight volumes of verse.]

### MY STAR [1]

Since the dewdrop holds the star
    The long night through,
Perchance the satellite afar
    Reflects the dew.

And while thine image in my heart
    Doth steadfast shine ;
There, haply, in thy heaven apart
    Thou keepest mine.

[1] The selections from Tabb are here reprinted through the kind permission
of the holder of the copyright, Small, Maynard & Company.

## KILLDEE

Killdee! Killdee! far o'er the lea
   At twilight comes the cry.
Killdee! a marsh-mate answereth
   Across the shallow sky.

Killdee! Killdee! thrills over me
   A rhapsody of light,
As star to star gives utterance
   Between the day and night.

Killdee! Killdee! O Memory,
   The twin birds, Joy and Pain,
Like shadows parted by the sun,
   At twilight meet again!

## CLOVER

Little masters, hat in hand
Let me in your presence stand,
Till your silence solve for me
This your threefold mystery.

Tell me — for I long to know —
How, in darkness there below,
Was your fairy fabric spun,
Spread and fashioned, three in one.

Did your gossips gold and blue,
Sky and Sunshine, choose for you,
Ere your triple forms were seen,
Suited liveries of green?

Can ye, — if ye dwelt indeed
Captives of a prison seed, —
Like the Genie, once again
Get you back into the grain?

Little masters, may I stand
In your presence, hat in hand,
Waiting till you solve for me
This your threefold mystery?

## FAME

Their noonday never knows
    What names immortal are:
'T is night alone that shows
    How star surpasseth star.

## JOHN HENRY BONER

[John Henry Boner was born in Salem, North Carolina, in 1845, of
Moravian lineage. He was at first connected as printer and as editor
with newspapers in North Carolina. In 1871 he secured government
employment in Washington. Subsequently he engaged in literary
work in New York. On account of impaired health he was forced
to give up his work in New York and to return to Washington,
where for a while he acted as proofreader in the Government Print-
ing Office. He died in Washington in 1903.]

### MOONRISE IN THE PINES [1]

The sultry day is ending,
    The clouds are fading away,
Orange with purple is blending,
    And purple is turning to gray;

[1] The selections from Boner are here reprinted through the permission of
the holder of the copyright, Mrs. Boner.

The gray grows darker and denser
    Till it and the earth are one;
A star swings out like a censer,
    And the brief warm night is begun.


The brown moth floats and poises
    Like a leaf in the windless air;
Aroused by insect noises
    The gray toad leaves his lair;
Sounding the dusk depth quickly
    The bull bats fall and rise,
And out of the grasses thickly
    Swarm glistering fireflies.


Now darkness heavy, oppressive,
    And silent completes the gloom.
The breathless night is excessive
    With fragrance of perfume,
For the land is enmeshed and ablaze
    With vines that blossom and trail,
Embanking the traveled ways
    And festooning the fences of rail.


Afar in the southern sky
    Heat-lightning flares and glows,
Vividly tinting the clouds that lie
    At rest with a shimmer of rose —
Tremulous, flitting, uncertain,
    As a mystical light might shine
From under an ebon curtain
    Before a terrible shrine.

And the slumberous night grows late.
 The midnight hush is deep.
Under the pines I wait
 For the moon ; and the pine trees weep
Great drops of dew, that fall
 Like footsteps here and there,
And they sadly whisper and call
 To each other high in the air.

They rustle and whisper like ghosts,
 They sigh like souls in pain,
Like the movement of stealthy hosts
 They surge, and are silent again.
The midnight hush is deep,
 But the pines — the spirits distrest —
They move in somnambulant sleep —
 They whisper and are not at rest.

Lo ! a light in the East opalescent
 Softly suffuses the sky
Where flocculent clouds are quiescent,
 Where like froth of the ocean they lie —
Like foam on the beach they crimple
 Where the wave has spent its swirl,
Like the curve of a shell they dimple
 Into iridescent pearl.

And the light grows brighter and higher
 Till far through the trees I see
The rim of a globe of fire
 That rolls through the darkness to me,

And the aisles of the forest gleam
    With a splendor unearthly, that shines
Like the light of a lurid dream
    Through the colonnaded pines.


## THE LIGHT'OOD FIRE

When wintry days are dark and drear
    And all the forest ways grow still,
When gray snow-laden clouds appear
    Along the bleak horizon hill,
When cattle all are snugly penned
    And sheep go huddling close together,
When steady streams of smoke ascend
    From farmhouse chimneys — in such weather
        Give me old Carolina's own,
        A great log house, a great hearthstone,
        A cheering pipe of cob or brier
        And a red, leaping light'ood fire.


When dreary day draws to a close
    And all the silent land is dark,
When Boreas down the chimney blows
    And sparks fly from the crackling bark,
When limbs are bent with snow or sleet
    And owls hoot from the hollow tree,
With hounds asleep about your feet,
    Then is the time for reverie.
        Give me old Carolina's own,
        A hospitable wide hearthstone,
        A cheering pipe of cob or brier
        And a red, rousing light'ood fire.

## POE'S COTTAGE AT FORDHAM

Heré lived the soul enchanted
  By melody of song;
Here dwelt the spirit haunted
  By a demoniac throng;
Here sang the lips elated;
Here grief and death were sated;
Here loved and here unmated
  Was he, so frail, so strong.

POE'S COTTAGE AT FORDHAM

Here wintry winds and cheerless
  The dying firelight blew,
While he whose song was peerless
  Dreamed the drear midnight through,

And from dull embers chilling
Crept shadows darkly filling
The silent place, and thrilling
   His fancy as they grew.


Here, with brow bared to heaven,
   In starry night he stood,
With the lost star of seven
   Feeling sad brotherhood.
Here in the sobbing showers
Of dark autumnal hours
He heard suspected powers
   Shriek through the stormy wood.


From visions of Apollo
   And of Astarte's bliss,
He gazed into the hollow
   And hopeless vale of Dis ;
And though earth were surrounded
By heaven, it still was mounded
With graves.  His soul had sounded
   The dolorous abyss.


Proud, mad, but not defiant,
   He touched at heaven and hell.
Fate found a rare soul pliant
   And rung her changes well.
Alternately his lyre,
Stranded with strings of fire,
Led earth's most happy choir
   Or flashed with Israfel.

No singer of old story
　　Luting accustomed lays,
No harper for new glory,
　　No mendicant for praise,
He struck high chords and splendid,
Wherein were fiercely blended
Tones that unfinished ended
　　With his unfinished days.

Here through this lowly portal,
　　Made sacred by his name,
Unheralded immortal
　　The mortal went and came.
And fate that then denied him,
And envy that decried him,
And malice that belied him,
　　Have cenotaphed his fame.

## WILL HENRY THOMPSON

[Will Henry Thompson was born in 1848 at Calhoun, Georgia.
Like his brother, Maurice Thompson, who has been more widely
known through his poems and his novels, Will Henry Thompson
served in the Confederate army, and later engaged in the practice of
law in Indiana. In 1889 he moved to Seattle, Washington, where he
has achieved prominence as an attorney. He is noted as an orator,
and he has written a small amount of poetry of high quality.]

### THE HIGH TIDE AT GETTYSBURG

A cloud possessed the hollow field,
The gathering battle's smoky shield.
Athwart the gloom the lightning flashed,
And through the cloud some horsemen dashed,
And from the heights the thunder pealed.

Then at the brief command of Lee
Moved out that matchless infantry,
With Pickett leading grandly down,
To rush against the roaring crown
Of those dread heights of destiny.

Far heard above the angry guns
A cry across the tumult runs, —
The voice that rang through Shiloh's woods
And Chickamauga's solitudes,
The fierce South cheering on her sons!

Ah, how the withering tempest blew
Against the front of Pettigrew!
A Khamsin wind that scorched and singed
Like that infernal flame that fringed
The British squares at Waterloo!

A thousand fell where Kemper led;
A thousand died where Garnett bled:
In blinding flame and strangling smoke
The remnant through the batteries broke
And crossed the works with Armistead.

" Once more in Glory's van with me! "
Virginia cried to Tennessee;
" We two together, come what may,
Shall stand upon these works to-day! "
(The reddest day in history.)

Brave Tennessee!  In reckless way
Virginia heard her comrade say:
" Close round this rent and riddled rag! "
What time she set her battle flag
Amid the guns of Doubleday.

But who shall break the guards that wait
Before the awful face of Fate?
The tattered standards of the South
Were shriveled at the cannon's mouth,
And all her hopes were desolate.

In vain the Tennesseean set
His breast against the bayonet!
In vain Virginia charged and raged,
A tigress in her wrath uncaged,
Till all the hill was red and wet!

Above the bayonets, mixed and crossed,
Men saw a gray, gigantic ghost
Receding through the battle cloud,
And heard across the tempest loud
The death cry of a nation lost!

The brave went down! Without disgrace
They leaped to Ruin's red embrace.
They only heard Fame's thunders wake,
And saw the dazzling sunburst break
In smiles on Glory's bloody face!

They fell, who lifted up a hand
And bade the sun in heaven to stand!
They smote and fell, who set the bars
Against the progress of the stars,
And stayed the march of Motherland!

They stood, who saw the future come
On through the fight's delirium!
They smote and stood, who held the hope
Of nations on that slippery slope
Amid the cheers of Christendom.

God lives! He forged the iron will
That clutched and held that trembling hill.
God lives and reigns! He built and lent
The heights for Freedom's battlement
Where floats her flag in triumph still!

Fold up the banners! Smelt the guns!
Love rules. Her gentler purpose runs.
A mighty mother turns in tears
The pages of her battle years,
Lamenting all her fallen sons!

## SAMUEL MINTURN PECK

[Samuel Minturn Peck was born in Tuscaloosa, Alabama, in 1854. After graduating from the University of Alabama he studied medicine in New York. He began writing about his twenty-fifth year, and has collected his poems into several volumes published at various intervals. He has also written stories collected under the title "Alabama Sketches."]

### A SOUTHERN GIRL [1]

Her dimpled cheeks are pale;
She's a lily of the vale, ·
    Not a rose.
In a muslin or a lawn
She is fairer than the dawn
    To her beaux.

Her boots are slim and neat,—
She is vain about her feet
    It is said.

[1] The selections from Samuel Minturn Peck are here reprinted through the permission of the holder of the copyright, Frederick A. Stokes Company.

She amputates her *r*'s,
But her eyes are like the stars
    Overhead.


On a balcony at night
With a fleecy cloud of white
    Round her hair —
Her grace, ah, who could paint?
She would fascinate a saint,
    I declare.


'Tis a matter of regret,
She's a bit of a coquette,
    Whom I sing:
On her cruel path she goes
With a half a dozen beaux
    To her string.


But let all that pass by,
As her maiden moments fly
    Dew empearled;
When she marries, on my life,
She will make the dearest wife
    In the world.


## THE GRAPEVINE SWING

When I was a boy on the old plantation,
  Down by the deep bayou,
The fairest spot of all creation,
  Under the arching blue;

When the wind came over the cotton and corn,
   To the long slim loop I'd spring
With brown feet bare, and a hat brim torn,
   And swing in the grapevine swing.

Swinging in the grapevine swing,
Laughing where the wild birds sing,
     I dream and sigh
     For the days gone by
Swinging in the grapevine swing.

Out — o'er the water lilies bonnie and bright,
   Back — to the moss-grown trees;
I shouted and laughed with a heart as light
   As a wild rose tossed by the breeze.
The mocking bird joined in my reckless glee,
   I longed for no angel's wing,
I was just as near heaven as I wanted to be
   Swinging in the grapevine swing.

Swinging in the grapevine swing,
Laughing where the wild birds sing, —
     Oh, to be a boy
     With a heart full of joy,
Swinging in the grapevine swing!

I'm weary at noon, I'm weary at night,
   I'm fretted and sore of heart,
And care is sowing my locks with white
   As I wend through the fevered mart.
I'm tired of the world with its pride and pomp,
   And fame seems a worthless thing.
I'd barter it all for one day's romp,
   And a swing in the grapevine swing.

Swinging in the grapevine swing,
Laughing where the wild birds sing,
    I would I were away
    From the world to-day,
Swinging in the grapevine swing.

## AUNT JEMIMA'S QUILT

A miracle of gleaming dyes
   Blue, scarlet, buff and green ;
O ne'er before by mortal eyes
   Such gorgeous hues were seen !
So grandly was its plan designed,
   So cunningly 't was built,
The whole proclaimed a master mind —
   My Aunt Jemima's quilt.

Each friendly household far and wide
   Contributed its share ;
It chronicled the countryside
   In colors quaint and rare.
From belles and brides came rich brocade
   Enwrought with threads of gilt ;
E'en buxom widows lent their aid
   To Aunt Jemima's quilt.

No tapestry from days of yore,
   No web from Orient loom,
But paled in beauteous tints before
   This strange expanse of bloom.
Here glittering stars and comet shone
   O'er flowers that never wilt ;
Here fluttered birds from worlds unknown
   On Aunt Jemima's quilt.

O, merry was the quilting bee,
    When this great quilt was done;
The rafters rang with maiden glee,
    And hearts were lost and won.
Ne'er did a throng of braver men
    In war clash hilt to hilt,
Than sought the smiles of beauty then
    Round Aunt Jemima's quilt.

This work of art my aunt esteemed
    The glory of the age;
No poet's eyes have ever beamed
    More proudly o'er his page.
Were other quilt to this compared,
    Her nose would upward tilt;
Such impudence was seldom dared
    O'er Aunt Jemima's quilt.

Her dear old hands have gone to dust,
    That once were lithe and light;
Her needles keen are thick with rust,
    That flashed so nimbly bright.
And here it lies by her behest,
    Stained with the tears we spilt,
Safe folded in this cedar chest —
    My Aunt Jemima's quilt.

## WILLIAM HAMILTON HAYNE

[William Hamilton Hayne, the son of Paul Hamilton Hayne, was born in Charleston, South Carolina, in 1856. He was educated mainly at his father's home, "Copse Hill," near Augusta, Georgia. Like his father he has devoted himself wholly to literature, beginning to publish verses in newspapers and magazines in 1879. His collected poems were published in 1892 under the title "Sylvan Lyrics and Other Verses." Mr. Hayne lives at Augusta, Georgia.]

WILLIAM HAMILTON HAYNE

### A MEADOW SONG[1]

O come to the meadow, with me,
For the lark is hovering high,
To bathe in the light of the sun
And the south winds wandering by !

[1] The selections from William Hamilton Hayne are here reprinted through the permission of the author.

A thrush by the rivulet's rim
   Grows gay from the breath of the grass,
And sings to his sweetheart, the brook,
   That mirrors his love like a glass!

O come to the meadow with me —
   Bird-music is gleeful and good
With Nature's full chorus of winds
   From the wonderful heart of the wood!
Forget-me-nots gleam in the grass,
   For the morning is mirthful with love —
From robins that roam in the glen
   To the palpitant wings of the dove.

O come to the meadow with me,
   To the rivulet's emerald edge,
And hear the low lilt of the stream
   Where the dewdrops encircle the sedge;
The young leaves look up to the sky,
   And the redbirds come hither to roam —
They love the brook's lyrical flow
   And its delicate fretwork of foam!

O come to the meadow with me
   While the music of morning is heard,
And the rapture of fetterless song
   Is sent from the heart of a bird!
Come hither and wander with me,
   For Nature is breathing of love
From violets veiled in the grass
   To the tremulous wings of the dove!

## WHEN DOGWOOD BRIGHTENS THE GROVES
## OF SPRING

When dogwood brightens the groves of spring
 And the gold of jasmine gleams,
When mating birds in the forest sing,
 Ah! that is the time for dreams,
For thoughts of love that are always new —
 Though as old as the ancient world —
Forever fresh as the Maytime dew
 In the breast of the rose impearled.


When timid green on the thorn tree grows —
 Like love at the verge of hate —
And air from the apple orchard flows
 Through the springtide's open gate,
When drowsy winds o'er the lilies pass,
 And the wings of the thrush are shy;
When violets bloom in the new-born grass,
 With the tints of a tropic sky;


When jonquils borrow the sun's warm ray,
 And the woodbine lures the bee;
When the heart that was once a waif and stray
 Returns like a ship from sea —
Ah! that is the time that no man grieves
 Who woos with the wooing dove,
For the hearts of men and the hearts of leaves
 Are throbbing with hope and love!

## ROBERT BURNS WILSON

[Robert Burns Wilson was born in Washington County, Pennsylvania, in 1850. Early in life he became a resident of Frankfort, Kentucky. In addition to writing poetry he has studied painting and exhibited his pictures with great success. During the later years of his life his home was chiefly in New York, where he died in 1916.]

### TO A CROW

Bold, amiable, ebon outlaw, grave and wise!
For many a good green year hast thou withstood —
By dangerous, planted field and haunted wood —
All the devices of thine enemies,
Gleaning thy grudgéd breath with watchful eyes
And self-relying soul.  Come ill or good,
Blithe days thou see'st, thou feather Robin Hood!
Thou mak'st a jest of farm-land boundaries.
Take all thou may'st, and never count it crime
To rob the greatest robber of the earth,
Weak-visioned, dull, self-lauding man, whose worth
Is in his own esteem.  Bide thou thy time;
Thou know'st far more of Nature's lore than he,
And her wide lap shall still provide for thee.

### BALLAD OF THE FADED FIELD

Broad bars of sunset-slanted gold
    Are laid along the field, and here
The silence sings, as if some old
    Refrain, that once rang long and clear
Came softly, stealing to the ear
    Without the aid of sound.  The rill
Is voiceless, and the grass is sere,
    But beauty's soul abideth still.

Trancelike the mellow air doth hold
 The sorrow of the passing year;
The heart of Nature groweth cold,
 The time of falling snow is near;
On phantom feet, which none may hear,
 Creeps — with the shadow of the hill —
The semblance of departed cheer,
 But beauty's soul abideth still.


The dead, gray-clustered weeds enfold
 The well-known summer path, and drear
The dusking hills, like billows rolled
 Against the distant sky, appear.
From lonely haunts, where Night and Fear
 Keep ghostly tryst, when mists are chill,
The dark pine lifts a jaggéd spear,
 But beauty's soul abideth still.


### Envoy

Dear love, the days that once were dear
 May come no more: life may fulfill
Her fleeting dreams with many a tear,
 But beauty's soul abideth still.


## FRANK LEBBY STANTON

[Frank Lebby Stanton was born in Charleston, South Carolina, in 1857. He has served various newspapers, but seems finally to have associated himself with the Atlanta *Constitution*. To this paper he has for several years past contributed a column daily of verses and short sketches. In this way his poems have become familiar to newspaper readers and are widely popular.]

## A PLANTATION DITTY

De gray owl sing fum de chimbly top:
 "Who — who — is — you-oo?"
En I say: "Good Lawd, hit's des po' me,
En I ain't quite ready fer de Jasper Sea;
I'm po' en sinful, en you 'lowed I'd be;
 Oh, wait, good Lawd, 'twell ter-morror."

De gray owl sing fum de cypress tree:
 "Who — who — is — you-oo?"
En I say: "Good Lawd, if you look you'll see
 Hit ain't nobody but des po' me,
En I like ter stay 'twell my time is free;
 Oh, wait, good Lawd, 'twell ter-morror."

## THE GRAVEYARD RABBIT

In the white moonlight, where the willow waves,
He halfway gallops among the graves —
A tiny ghost in the gloom and gleam,
Content to dwell where dead men dream.

 But wary still!
 For they plot him ill;
For the graveyard rabbit hath a charm
(May God defend us!) to shield from harm.

Over the shimmering slab he goes —
Every grave in the dark he knows;
But his nest is hidden from human eye
Where headstones broken on old graves lie.

Wary still!
  For they plot him ill;
For the graveyard rabbit, though sceptics scoff,
Charmeth the witch and the wizard off!

The black man creeps, when the night is dim,
Fearful, still, on the track of him;
Or fleetly follows the way he runs,
For he heals the hurts of conjured ones.

Wary still!
  For they plot him ill;
The soul's bewitched that would find release, —
To the graveyard rabbit go for peace!

He holds their secret — he brings a boon
Where winds moan wild in the dark of the moon;
And gold shall glitter and love smile sweet
To whoever shall sever his furry feet!

Wary still!
  For they plot him ill;
For the graveyard rabbit hath a charm
(May God defend us!) to shield from harm.


## ANSWERING TO ROLL CALL

This one fought with Jackson, and faced the fight with Lee;
That one followed Sherman as he galloped to the sea;
But they are marchin' on together just as friendly as can be,
And they'll answer to the roll call in the mornin'.

They'll rally to the fight
  In the stormy day and night,
  In bonds that no cruel fate shall sever;

While the stormwinds waft on high
Their ringing battle-cry:
"Our country, — our country forever!"

The brave old flag above them is rippling down its red, —
Each crimson stripe the emblem of the blood by heroes shed;
It shall wave for them victorious or droop above them, — dead,
For they 'll answer to the roll call in the mornin'.

They 'll rally to the fight
In the stormy day and night,
In bonds that no cruel fate shall sever;
While the stormwinds waft on high
Their ringing battle-cry:
"Our country, — our country forever!"

## MADISON JULIUS CAWEIN

[Madison Julius Cawein was born in Louisville, Kentucky, in 1865. After graduating from the high school of that city, he engaged in business, but found time for the writing of poetry and the study of literature. His first volume of verse, "Blooms of the Berry," published in 1887, made but little impression until, in 1888, Mr. W. D. Howells praised it in the "Editor's Study" of *Harper's Magazine*. This drew attention to Cawein's work, and gradually his circle of admirers was enlarged. In all, Cawein published some twenty columns of poems, the best of which he collected toward the close of his life in a volume entitled "Selected Poems." He died in Louisville in 1914.]

MADISON JULIUS CAWEIN

## THE WHIPPOORWILL

Above long woodland ways that led
To dells the stealthy twilights tread,
The west was hot geranium-red;
   And still, and still,
Along old lanes, the locusts sow
With clustered curls the Maytimes know,
Out of the crimson afterglow,
We heard the homeward cattle low,
And then the far-off, far-off woe
   Of " whippoorwill ! " of " whippoorwill ! "

Beneath the idle beechen boughs
We heard the cowbells of the cows
Come slowly jangling toward the house,
   And still, and still,
Beyond the light that would not die
Out of the scarlet-haunted sky,
Beyond the evening star's white eye
Of glittering chalcedony,
Drained out of dusk the plaintive cry
   Of " whippoorwill ! " of " whippoorwill ! "

What is there in the moon, that swims
A naked bosom o'er the limbs,
That all the wood with magic dims?
   While still, while still,
Among the trees whose shadows grope
Mid ferns and flowers the dewdrops ope, —
Lost in faint deeps of heliotrope
Above the clover-scented slope, —
Retreats, despairing past all hope,
   The whippoorwill, the whippoorwill.

## EVENING ON THE FARM

From out the hills where twilight stands,
Above the shadowy pasture-lands,
    With strained and strident cry,
Beneath pale skies that sunset bands,
        The bull bats fly.


A cloud hangs over, strange of shape,
And, colored like the half-ripe grape,
    Seems some uneven stain
On heaven's azure, thin as crape,
        And blue as rain.


Byways, that sunset's sardonyx
O'erflares, and gates the farm-boy clicks,
    Through which the cattle came,
The mullein's stalks seem giant wicks
        Of downy flame.


From woods no glimmer enters in,
Above the streams that, wandering, win
    From out the violet hills,
Those haunters of the dusk begin,
        The whippoorwills.


Adown the dark the firefly marks
Its flight in golden-emerald sparks;
    And, loosened from its chain,
The shaggy watchdog bounds and barks,
        And barks again.

Each breeze brings scents of hill-heaped hay;
And now an owlet, far away,
    Cries twice or thrice, " T-o-o-w-h-o-o-";
And cool dim moths of mottled gray
       Flit through the dew.

The silence sounds its frog-bassoon,
Where, on the woodland creek's lagoon,
    Pale as a ghostly girl
Lost 'mid the trees, looks down the moon,
       With face of pearl.

Within the shed where logs, late hewed,
Smell forest-sweet, and chips of wood
    Make blurs of white and brown,
The brood-hen huddles her warm brood
       Of teetering down.

The clattering guineas in the tree
Din for a time; and quietly
    The henhouse, near the fence,
Sleeps, save for some brief rivalry
       Of cocks and hens.

A cowbell tinkles by the rails,
Where, streaming white in foaming pails,
    Milk makes an uddery sound;
While overhead the black bat trails
       Around and round.

The night is still. The slow cows chew
A drowsy cud. The bird that flew
    And sang is in its nest.
It is the time of falling dew,
       Of dreams and rest.

The brown bees sleep; and round the walk,
The garden path, from stalk to stalk
    The bungling beetle booms,
Where two soft shadows stand and talk
      Among the blooms.

The stars are thick; the light is dead
That dyed the west; and Drowsyhead,
    Tuning his cricket-pipe,
Nods, and some apple, round and red,
      Drops overripe.

Now down the road, that shambles by,
A window, shining like an eye
    Through climbing rose and gourd,
Shows where Toil sups and these things lie —
      His heart and hoard.

## JOHN CHARLES McNEILL

[John Charles McNeill was born in Scotland County, North Carolina, in 1874. After graduating from Wake Forest College, he practiced law in Lumberton, North Carolina, for some time. Later he accepted a position on the staff of the Charlotte, North Carolina, *Observer*, and devoted his entire time to writing until his death, in 1907. Though he published only two small collections of verse, yet these were sufficient to show that he was remarkably gifted as a poet.]

### AWAY DOWN HOME [1]

'T will not be long before they hear
    The bull bat on the hill,
And in the valley through the dusk
    The pastoral whippoorwill.

[1] The selections from McNeill are published here through the permission of the holder of copyright, The Stone-Barringer Publishing Co.

A few more friendly suns will call
   The bluets through the loam
And star the lanes with buttercups
   Away down home.

JOHN CHARLES McNEILL

"Knee-deep!" from reedy places
   Will sing the river frogs.
The terrapins will sun themselves
   On all the jutting logs.
The angler's cautious oar will leave
   A trail of drifting foam
Along the shady current
   Away down home.

The mocking bird will feel again
   The glory of his wings,
And wanton through the balmy air
   And sunshine while he sings,

With a new cadence in his call,
   The glint-wing'd crow will roam
From field to newly furrowed field
   Away down home.

When dogwood blossoms mingle
   With the maples' modest red,
And sweet arbutus wakes at last
   From out her winter's bed,
'T would not seem strange at all to meet
   A dryad or a gnome,
Or Pan or Psyche in the woods
   Away down home.

Then come with me, thou weary heart!
   Forget thy brooding ills,
Since God has come to walk among
   His valleys and his hills.
The mart will never miss thee,
   Nor the scholar's dusty tome,
And the Mother waits to bless thee,
   Away down home.

## AN IDYL

Upon a gnarly, knotty limb
   That fought the current's crest,
Where shocks of reeds peeped o'er the brim,
   Wild wasps had glued their nest.

And in a sprawling cypress' grot,
   Sheltered and safe from flood,
Dirt-daubers each had chosen a spot
   To shape his house of mud.

In a warm crevice of the bark
   A basking scorpion clung,
With bright blue tail and red-rimmed eyes,
   And yellow, twinkling tongue.

A lunging trout flashed in the sun,
   To do some petty slaughter,
And set the spiders all a-run
   On little stilts of water.

Toward noon upon the swamp there stole
   A deep, cathedral hush,
Save where, from sun-splotched bough and bole,
   Sweet thrush replied to thrush.

An angler came to cast his fly
   Beneath a baffling tree.
I smiled, when I had caught his eye,
   And he smiled back at me.

When stretched beside a shady elm
   I watched the dozy heat,
Nature was moving in her realm,
   For I could hear her feet.

## BAREFOOTED

The girls all like to see the bluets in the lane
   And the saucy Johnny Jump-ups in the meadow,
But we boys, we want to see the dogwood blooms again
   Throwin' a sort of summer-lookin' shadow;
For the very first mild mornin' when the woods are white
   (And we need n't even ask a soul about it)
We leave our shoes right where we pulled them off at night,
   And, barefooted once again, we run and shout it:

You may take the country over —
When the bluebird turns a rover,
And the wind is soft and hazy,
And you feel a little lazy,
And the hunters quit the possums —
It's the time for dogwood blossoms.

We feel so light we wish there were more fences here;
We'd like to jump and jump them, all together!
No seeds for us, no guns, or even 'simmon beer,
No nothin' but the blossoms and fair weather!
The meadow is a little sticky right at first,
But a few short days 'll wipe away that trouble.
To feel so good and gay, I wouldn't mind the worst
That could be done by any field o' stubble.
O, all the trees are seemin' sappy!
O, all the folks are smilin' happy!
And there's joy in every little bit of room;
But the happiest of them all
At the Shanghai rooster's call
Are we barefoots when the dogwoods burst abloom!

## SUNDOWN

Hills, wrapped in gray, standing alone in the west;
Clouds, dimly lighted, gathering slowly;
The star of peace at watch above the crest —
Oh, holy, holy, holy!

We know, O Lord, so little what is best;
Wingless, we move so lowly;
But in thy calm all-knowledge let us rest —
Oh, holy, holy, holy!

## WALTER MALONE

[Walter Malone was born in De Soto County, Mississippi, in 1866. After graduating from the University of Mississippi, he began the practice of law, in which he was very successful. In 1905 he was appointed judge. His home was in Memphis, Tennessee, with the exception of the years from 1897 to 1900, during which he was engaged in literary pursuits in New York City. He published several volumes of poetry, most of the earlier volumes being published in 1904 in a collective edition entitled " Poems." He died in Memphis in 1915.]

### OCTOBER IN TENNESSEE

Far, far away, beyond the hazy height,
　　The turquois skies are hung in dreamy sleep;
Below, the fields of cotton, fleecy-white,
　　Are spreading like a mighty flock of sheep.

Now, like Aladdin of the days of old,
　　October robes the weeds in purple gowns;
He sprinkles all the sterile fields with gold,
　　And all the rustic trees wear royal crowns.

The straggling fences all are interlaced
　　With pink and azure morning-glory blooms,
The starry asters glorify the waste,
　　While grasses stand on guard with pikes and plumes.

Yet still amid the splendor of decay
　　The chill winds call for blossoms that are dead,
The cricket chirps for sunshine passed away,
　　And lovely summer songsters that have fled.

And lonesome in a haunt of withered vines,
　　Amid the flutter of her withered leaves,
Pale Summer for her perished kingdom pines,
　　And all the glories of her golden sheaves.

In vain October wooes her to remain
   Within the palace of his scarlet bowers,
Entreats her to forget her heartbreak pain,
   And weep no more about her faded flowers.

At last November, like a conqueror, comes
   To storm the golden city of his foe ;
We hear his rude winds, like the roll of drums,
   Bringing their desolation and their woe.

The sunset, like a vast vermilion flood,
   Splashes its giant glowing waves on high,
The forest flames with foliage red as blood,
   A conflagration sweeping to the sky.

Then all the treasures of that brilliant state
   Are gathered in a mighty funeral pyre ;
October, like a king resigned to fate,
   Dies in his forests, with their sunset fire.

## SURVIVALS OF OLD BRITISH BALLADS

### BARBARA ALLEN

There was a young man who lived in our town,
   His given name was William ;
He was taken sick, and very sick,
   And death was in his dwelling.

It was the merry month of May,
   When the green buds were swelling,
Sweet William on his deathbed lay
   For the love of Barbara Allen.

He sent his servant down in town;
  He went into her dwelling:
"My master's sick, and sent for you,
  If your name be Barbara Allen."

And slowly, slowly did she rise,
  And slowly she went to him,
And all she said when she got there,
  "Young man, I think you are dying."

"Oh, yes, I'm sick, I'm very sick,
  And death is with me, darling,
I'll die, I'll die, I'll surely die,
  If I don't get Barbara Allen."

"Oh, yes, you are sick, and very sick,
  And death is in your dwelling;
You'll die, you'll die, you'll surely die,
  For you will never get Barbara Allen.

"Remember on last Wednesday night
  When we were at a wedding,
You passed your wine to the girls all around
  And slighted Barbara Allen."

He turned his pale face to the wall,
  He turned his back upon her:
"Adieu, adieu to the friends all around,
  And adieu to Barbara Allen."

She had not got ten miles from town,
  When she heard a swamp bird singing;
And every time the swamp bird sung
  Was woe to Barbara Allen.

She had not got three miles from town,
　　When she heard a death bell ringing,
And in her ear it seemed to say,
　　" Hard-hearted Barbara Allen."

She looked to the east, and she looked to the west,
　　And she saw his corpse a-coming ;
" I could have saved that young man's life
　　By giving him Barbara Allen ! "

" O mother, O mother, go make my bed,
　　Make it of tears and sorrow ;
Sweet William died for me to-day,
　　And I will die for him to-morrow.

" O father, O father, go dig my grave,
　　Dig it deep and narrow ;
Sweet William died for true love's sake,
　　And I shall die of sorrow."

Sweet William died on Saturday night,
　　And Barbara died on Sunday ;
Her mother died for the love of both
　　And was buried alone on Monday.

Sweet William was buried in the new churchyard,
　　And Barbara beside him :
And out of his grave sprang a lily-white rose,
　　And out of hers a briar.

## LORD THOMAS AND FAIR ELEANOR

Lord Thomas, he was a bold forester,
　　And a chaser of the king's deer,
Fair Eleanor, she was a brave woman,
　　Lord Thomas, he loved her dear !

"Now, riddle my riddle, dear Mother," he cried,
  "And riddle it all into one:
For whether to marry the Fair Eleanor,
  Or to bring you the Brown Girl home?"

"The Brown Girl, she hath both houses and lands,
  Fair Eleanor, she hath none:
Therefore I charge you, upon my blessing,
  To bring me the Brown Girl home!"

He clothed himself in gallant attire,
  His merrymen all in green,
And every borough that he rode through,
  They took him to be some king.

And when he reached Fair Eleanor's bower,
  He knocked thereat, therein,
And who so ready as Fair Eleanor
  To let Lord Thomas in?

"What news? What news, Lord Thomas?" she cried,
  "What news dost thou bring unto me?"
"I come to bid thee to my wedding,
  And that is sad news for thee!"

"Now Heaven forbid, Lord Thomas," she cried,
  "That any such thing should be done!
I thought to have been, myself, thy bride,
  And thou to have been the bridegroom!"

"Now, riddle my riddle, dear Mother," she cried,
  "And riddle it all into one:
For whether to go to Lord Thomas's wedding,
  Or whether I tarry at home?"

"There be many that be thy friend, Daughter,
　But a thousand be thy foe:
Therefore I charge thee, upon my blessing,
　To Lord Thomas's wedding don't go!"

"There be many that be my friend, Mother,
　Though a thousand be my foe:
So, betide my life, betide my death,
　To Lord Thomas's wedding I'll go!"

She decked herself in gallant attire,
　Her tiremen all in green,
And every borough that she rode through,
　They took her to be some queen.

And when she reached Lord Thomas's door,
　She knocked thereat, therein,
And who so ready as Lord Thomas
　To let Fair Eleanor in?

"Be this your bride, Lord Thomas?" she cried,
　"Methinks she looks wondrous brown!
Thou mightest have had as fair a woman
　As ever the sun shone on!"

"Despise her not, Fair Ellen!" he cried.
　"Despise her not unto me!
For better I love thy little finger
　Than all of her whole body!"

The Brown Girl, she had a little penknife,
　Which was both long and sharp,
And between the broad ribs and the short,
　She pierced Fair Eleanor's heart!

"O art thou blind, Lord Thomas?" she cried,
  "Or canst thou not plainly see
My own heart's blood run trickling down,
  Run trickling down to my knee?"

Lord Thomas, he had a sword at his side,
  And as he walked up the hall,
He cut the bride's head from her shoulders,
  And flung it against the wall!

He placed the hilt against the ground,
  The point against his heart!
So never three lovers together did meet,
  And sooner again did part!

They buried Fair Ellen beneath an oak tree,
  Lord Thomas beneath the church spire,
And out of her bosom there grew a red rose,
  And out of her lover's a briar!

They grew and grew, till they reached the church top,
  They grew till they reached the church spire,
And there they entwined, in a true lover's knot,
  For true lovers all to admire!

## THE HANGMAN'S TREE

"Hangman, hangman, howd yo hand,
  O howd it wide and far!
For theer I see my father cooming
  Riding through the air.

"Father, father, ha yo brought me goold?
  Ha yo paid my fee?
Or ha yo coom to see me hung
  Beneath the hangman's tree?"

" I ha naw brought yo goold,
 I ha naw paid yo fee,
But I ha coom to see yo hung
 Beneath the hangman's tree."

" Hangman, hangman, howd yo hand,
 O howd it wide and far !
For theer I see my mother cooming
 Riding through the air.

" Mother, mother, ha yo brought me goold ?
 Ha yo paid my fee ?
Or ha yo coom to see me hung
 Beneath the hangman's tree ? "

" I ha naw brought yo goold,
 I ha naw paid yo fee,
But I ha coom to see yo hung
 Beneath the hangman's tree."

" Hangman, hangman, howd yo hand,
 O howd it wide and far !
For theer I see my sister cooming
 Riding through the air.

" Sister, sister, ha yo brought me goold ?
 Ha yo paid my fee ?
Or ha yo coom to see me hung
 Beneath the hangman's tree ? "

" I ha naw brought yo goold,
 I ha naw paid yo fee,
But I ha coom to see yo hung
 Beneath the hangman's tree."

" Hangman, hangman, howd yo hand,
   O howd it wide and far !
For theer I see my sweetheart cooming
   Riding through the air.

" Sweetheart, sweetheart, ha yo brought me goold ?
   Ha yo paid my fee ?
Or ha yo coom to see me hung
   Beneath the hangman's tree ?"

" Oh, I ha brought yo goold,
   And I ha paid yo fee,
And I ha coom to take yo froom
   Beneath the hangman's tree."

### THE WIFE OF USHER'S WELL

There was a lady fair and gay,
   And children she had three :
She sent them away to some northern land,
   For to learn their grameree.

They had n't been gone but a very short time,
   About three months to a day,
When sickness came unto that land
   And swept those babies away.

There is a King in the heavens above
   That wears a golden crown :
She prayed that He would send her babies home
   To-night or in the morning soon.

It was about one Christmas time,
   When the night was long and cool,
She dreamed of her three little lonely babes
   Come running in their mother's room.

The table was fixed and the cloth was spread,
    And on it put bread and wine :
" Come sit you down, my three little babes,
    And eat and drink of mine."


" We will neither eat your bread, dear mother,
    Nor we 'll neither drink your wine ;
For to our Saviour we must return
    To-night or in the morning soon."


The bed was fixed in the back room ;
    On it was some clean white sheet,
And on the top was a golden cloth,
    To make those little babies sleep.


" Wake up ! wake up ! " says the oldest one,
    " Wake up ! its almost day.
And to our Saviour we must return
    To-night or in the morning soon.


" Green grass grows at our head, dear mother,
    Green moss grows at our feet ;
The tears that you shed for us three babes,
    Won't wet our winding sheet."


## GEORGE COLLINS

George Collins rode home one cold winter night,
    George Collins rode home so fine,
George Collins rode home one cold winter night,
    He taken sick and died.

A fair young lady in her father's house
  A-sewing her silk so fine
And when she heard that George was dead
  She threw it down and cried.


"O daughter, don't weep! O daughter, don't mourn!
  There are more boys than one."
"O mother dear! he has my heart,
  And now he's dead and gone.


"The happiest hours I ever spent
  Were when I was by his side;
The saddest news I ever heard
  Was when George Collins died."


She followed him up, she followed him down;
  She followed him to his grave,
And there she fell on her bended knees;
  She wept; she mourned; she prayed.


"Unscrew the coffin; lay back the lid;
  Roll down the linen so fine;
And let me kiss his cold pale lips,
  For I know he will never kiss mine."

# NOTES

## INTRODUCTION

### LITERATURE IN THE COLONIAL SOUTH

Although the limits placed upon this volume preclude selections from the colonial writers of the South, yet some account of their work is a necessary introduction to the later literature. From the earliest days of the Virginia colony there was considerable activity in writing. The first book written in Virginia, though published away, was Captain John Smith's "A True Relation of Virginia," written in 1608. A later book, written during his stay in Virginia, was entitled "A Map of Virginia." Both of these books were descriptive of the country and the Indians, and as the writer was a keen observer and a graphic narrator, his accounts are interesting. In 1610 William Strachey, secretary of the Virginia colony, wrote at Jamestown and sent to London for publication his "A True Repertory of the Wrack and Redemption of Sir Thomas Gates, Knight, upon and from the Islands of the Burmudas." This was an account of the disaster by a member of the expedition that accompanied Sir Thomas Gates, and is memorable for a vivid description of a storm at sea. It is commonly thought that this book may have been a source of suggestion to Shakespeare for the opening incident of his play "The Tempest," there being interesting parallels between the two accounts. The earliest poetry written in Virginia was a translation of ten books of Ovid's "Metamorphoses," made by George Sandys during his stay in the colony as its treasurer. But these writers may hardly be claimed as American writers. As a matter of fact, they were Englishmen, who eventually went back to their English home, writing for Englishmen in order to describe what they had seen and felt in the new country.

It seems, therefore, on the whole more fitting to place the beginning of literature in the South at the time when native-born writers began to write for their countrymen and to take for their subject matter local history, politics, and conditions. One of the first evidences of a growth of national consciousness was the popular uprising of 1676 known as Bacon's Rebellion. This gave to the people a national hero and a realization of independence of England, not only geographically, but politically. From this event the colonists began to talk of Virginia as their mother state. The literature that was produced in the hundred years following Bacon's Rebellion bears strong traces of this new spirit. While much of it continued to be of a descriptive and historical character, yet a good deal of it was of a political kind inspired by local or intercolonial disputes. Virginia produced more of this literature than any other colony, but in the course of time other colonies, such as Maryland, North Carolina, South Carolina, and Georgia, made their contributions.

In the anonymous Burwell Papers an account is given of the first great thrill in colonial life — Bacon's Rebellion. In Colonel William Byrd one discovers the most sprightly and interesting writer in the colonies before Franklin. In Robert Beverley one perceives the country gentleman interested not only in his plantation but interested also in its past history and its present economic and social conditions. These are but a few of the more readable of those who illustrate the awakened interest in local life. As might be expected these writers imitated in their style and literary methods the writers of England. In the eighteenth century the periodical essays of Addison and Steele had set the fashion for a type of light and delicately neat prose, and it is possible that Southern writers would have gone on to a literature of manners and customs that would have approached the observant, personal, and quaintly humorous manner of *The Tatler*, *The Spectator*, and other essays of the same kind. But the great political questions connected with the Revolution eventually absorbed the intellectual life of the Southern colonists. The stress of these events did not produce much that could, in the narrower sense of the term, be called literature, but in the writings of the time there is such a vivid reflection of what the people were thinking and feeling that the words of orators and political writers have the imaginative lift of literature. Men like Richard Henry Lee and Patrick Henry, among the orators, and Thomas Jefferson, James Madison, and George Washington, among the political writers, were some of those who produced contributions that it is difficult to avoid calling literature.

# PART I. THE OLD SOUTH IN LITERATURE

Following the Revolution came the great material development of the country, and in connection with this a great intellectual and literary development in the Northern states. But in the South the social and economic conditions continued to be those of a rural aristocracy based on slavery. While such a life was full of graciousness and hospitality and all the high social virtues that come of a feudal aristocracy, it nevertheless tended towards conservatism and individualism. These qualities operated strongly in the interval between the Revolution and the Civil War to make the country gentleman of the South desire to have things remain as they were politically and economically. They also made him see intensely the claims of his own state and section to the exclusion of others, such a feeling culminating in the doctrine of state rights. Another marked condition in Southern life in this period was a stunting poverty of popular education. The children of rich families had private tutors and were able to attend college, but the great mass of the common people were without the most rudimentary education.

Such conditions tended to retard intellectual and literary development. When the North was producing the Knickerbocker school, represented by Irving, Bryant, and Cooper, and the New England group of writers among whom were Hawthorne and Emerson, the South was, comparatively speaking, producing a meager amount of literature. But the chief cause of lack of literary development in the old South was that the South expended its intellectual life in oratory at the county courthouse or the state capitol or the halls of Congress. Such notable names and interesting personalities as Pinckney, Walsh, Houston, Preston, Randolph, Clay, Calhoun, Benton, and Hayne belong to the group of antebellum orators and statesmen.

The orators of the old South have not been excelled in our national history. They were clever debaters on the science and art of statecraft. They diligently studied public questions, they had read the classic orators, and they constructed their speeches on the best models of that ancient art. In these old Southern statesmen the finest tradition of the school of Burke and Pitt and Fox still lived. Thus the energy of the most gifted men was spent on political discussion; the old-time Southerner was a politician by instinct and training, and his ambition was political. To him the spoken word was more than the written word. Consequently he sought preferment at the bar, on the bench, in the forum, and not in the world of letters.[1]

[1] Metcalf, " American Literature," page 257.

## ESSAYISTS AND DESCRIPTIVE WRITERS

It is strange that the South, with its fondness for the literature of the eighteenth century, did not produce more essayists, especially after the manner of Addison and Steele's *The Tatler* and *The Spectator*. As it is, William Wirt is almost the only writer of this form. Others, however, have left, incidentally to other purposes, as the selections below from Crockett, Audubon, and Elliott show, vivid descriptions of certain phases of Southern life.

### WILLIAM WIRT

This and the following selection have been taken from Wirt's "Letters of the British Spy." This book of essays pretended to be copies of letters written by a young Englishman of rank, during a tour of the United States, to a member of the English Parliament. The letters presented, in the leisurely eighteenth-century fashion of Addison, geographical descriptions, delineations of public men, moral and political discussions, and literary views. The value of the book to the present generation lies chiefly in the fact that it shows how the eighteenth century ruled in the mind of a Southerner at the beginning of the nineteenth century.

### THE BRITISH SPY'S OPINION OF *THE SPECTATOR* (PAGE 1)

*The Spectator :* the series of periodical essays written by Addison and Steele. — **Bacon:** Francis Bacon, the English philosopher and statesman of the Elizabethan age. — **Boyle:** Robert Boyle, a noted English scientific and philosophical writer of the seventeenth century.
QUESTIONS. 1. What literary ideals does the writer approve? 2. Were these ideals passing away in England and in other sections of the United States while surviving in the South?

### AN OLD VIRGINIA PREACHER (PAGE 4)

The preacher is said to have been Rev. James Waddell, a noted Presbyterian preacher of Virginia who in his latter years was blind.
**Orange:** a county in Virginia.
QUESTIONS. 1. Describe the preacher and his preaching. 2. Has the South been noted for the production of preachers of exceptional power?

## DAVID CROCKETT

This selection is from "The Life of David Crockett by Himself" — an autobiography written in order to correct false impressions about the writer. After Crockett's election to Congress his eccentricities of dress and manner made him a notable figure in Washington, and a publisher seized the occasion to issue, in 1834, an anonymous book entitled "Sketches and Eccentricities of Colonel David Crockett," without the latter's approval. To correct the impressions of this book, Crockett, now nearing fifty, set to work to write the story of his life and produced a book which, in spite of literary deficiencies, is one of the most racy and amusing books of its kind. His achievement is all the more remarkable because he did not learn to write until, when nearly thirty, an appointment as justice of the peace compelled him to do so in a degree sufficient to keep his records and to draw legal papers. Bear hunts, Indian fights, and other thrilling adventures make up the contents of the book, and in spite of inelegancies of expression it gives a good picture of pioneer life.

### THE BEAR HUNT (PAGE 8)

harricane: canebrake. — cracks: caused by earthquakes.

QUESTION. What methods, according to this selection, were employed in hunting bears?

### JOHN JAMES AUDUBON

This selection is from the journal in which Audubon recorded not merely details relating to his scientific interests, but many adventures and sketches of the country and its inhabitants in the sections visited by him.

### EARLY SETTLERS ALONG THE MISSISSIPPI (PAGE 14)

The scene of this sketch is the swamps of Louisiana, which in Audubon's time were very sparsely settled.

QUESTIONS. 1. What causes induced the squatters to leave their homes? 2. How did they travel? 3. What obstacles did they overcome in their new homes? 4. What qualities caused them to prosper? 5. Has the South retained or lost such qualities among its white working classes?

## WILLIAM ELLIOTT

Elliott's "Carolina Sports by Land and Water," from which this selection is taken, belongs to the type of literature of which Izaak Walton's "The Complete Angler" is the undisputed head. Elliott's book is in two parts: the first gives interesting narratives of the author's adventures in connection with fishing; the second is devoted to experiences in hunting wildcats, deer, and other game. The setting for it was the coastal section of South Carolina southeast of Charleston.

### A Deer Hunt (Page 19)

**malice prepense:** premeditated malice.

QUESTIONS. 1. What details regarding the hunting of deer does this selection give? 2. How is vividness secured in the account?

**Other Essayists and Descriptive Writers.** Worthy of mention but impossible of representation in this volume are the following writers : *South Carolina* . Hugh Swinton Legare (1797–1843), Henry J. Nott (1797–1837), Caroline Howard Gilman (1794–1888), Louisa Susannah McCord (1810–1879); *Alabama:* Octavia Walton LeVert (1810–1877).

## ROMANCERS AND STORY WRITERS

The writing of romantic fiction in the old South was centered mainly in the fifteen years between 1835 and 1850. This was the period of expansion for the South in two directions. In the region of ideas many great questions were coming to the front for settlement, and in the field of material conquest the settlement of the rich Southwest was going on. Under the stimulus of these conditions men began to realize the wealth of material in Southern history and traditions, and began to work it into fiction.

The spirit in which this work was done was imitative of what was being done in fiction in England and in the New England States. In England, under the influence of the romantic movement, the novel had developed into the romance of historical imagination represented by Scott's Waverley series. In New England, fiction began toward the end of the eighteenth century and followed the tendencies of fiction in England, until its early development culminated in the romances of Cooper, who practically created the American frontier story and the American historical novel. The success of Cooper's work stimulated writers in the South to follow in his footsteps, and rapidly romances of the same general type, with Southern incidents as their basis, came into existence. The foremost antebellum writers of fiction in the South were Poe, Simms, Kennedy, and Cooke. Of these the last three are to be grouped together as representing the interest in writing historical romances. Poe stands apart from these in the methods and ideals followed in his tales.

## EDGAR ALLAN POE

It has been so long popular to think of Poe as "a world artist, unrelated to his local origin, unindebted to it," that it may seem almost absurd to look for any representation of Southern life in Poe's stories. Nevertheless, so distinguished a critic as Professor Woodberry holds that Poe is as much a product of the South as Whittier was of New England. As he puts it, "His breeding and education were Southern; his manners, habits of thought, and moods of feeling were Southern; his sentimentalism, his conception of womanhood and its qualities, of manhood and its behavior, his weaknesses of character, have the stamp of his origin; his temperament, even his sensibilities, his gloom and dream, his response to color and music, were of his race and place."

## THE FALL OF THE HOUSE OF USHER (PAGE 28)

This story, first published in 1839, is generally accepted as, from the point of view of craftsmanship, Poe's finest tale.

*ennuyé:* wearied, bored. — **Von Weber:** A German composer of the late eighteenth and early nineteenth centuries. — **Fuseli:** a Swiss artist who lived from 1742 to 1825, and who painted a series of imaginative pictures illustrating Shakespeare and Milton. — "**The Haunted Palace**": the allegorical significance is plainly hinted at. The word *Porphyrogene* in line 22 of the poem on page 38 is formed from two Greek words, meaning "purple" and "begotten"; hence born in the purple, royal.

**Watson,** etc.: these are the names of obscure scientists, more prominent in Poe's day than in the present. — **Satyrs and Ægipans:** in classical mythology the satyrs were creatures with the body of a man and the feet, hair, and horns of a goat; *ægipans* is an epithet of Pan, the satyr-like rural god. — **Gothic:** the black-letter type of the Middle Ages. — *Vigiliæ Mortuorum,* etc.: "Vigils for the Dead according to the

Choir of the Church of Mayence." — **"Mad Trist" of Sir Launcelot Canning :** no book with this title is known, and the title was undoubtedly coined by Poe and the quotations invented by him to fit the context.

QUESTIONS. 1. What effect does Poe evidently seek to produce in this story? 2. Show whether the parts are skillfully related to one another and to the whole. 3. In what respects is the story characteristic of the South? 4. Can the description of Usher be taken as self-portraiture on Poe's part?

## JOHN PENDLETON KENNEDY

These selections are taken from "Swallow Barn, or a Sojourn in the Old Dominion," published in 1832. The author's design was to present sketches descriptive of country life in Virginia, in a series of letters supposed to be written by Mark Littleton to a friend in New York, giving his impressions of a Virginia home which he is visiting. So desultory is the book in its manner that it can hardly be called a novel. Its best description is in the words of the preface, "a series of detached sketches linked together by the hooks and eyes of a traveler's notes ... and may be described as variously and interchangeably partaking of the complexion of a book of travel, a diary, a collection of letters, a drama, and a history." Nevertheless, the author has succeeded in presenting a full picture of life in the old homesteads on the James River.

### SELECTIONS FROM "SWALLOW BARN"

#### SWALLOW BARN, AN OLD VIRGINIA ESTATE (PAGE 50)

*chevaux-de-frise :* a contrivance consisting of pieces of timber with spikes of iron used to defend a passage.

#### THE MISTRESS OF SWALLOW BARN (PAGE 57)

**tertian :** an intermittent fever which returns every three days.

#### TRACES OF THE FEUDAL SYSTEM (PAGE 59)

**rod of Aaron:** the wonder-working rod used by Moses and Aaron. See Bible, Book of Exodus. — **Mr. Chub :** a parson who has charge of the school on the Meriwether estate. — **Mr. Burke :** the celebrated English orator and statesman of the eighteenth century. — **Rip :** the thirteen-year-old son of the Meriwethers.

## The Quarter (Page 64)

*chapeau de bras :* a type of military helmet.

Questions. 1. What is said of the house, Swallow Barn? 2. What of the surrounding buildings? 3. How extensive was the estate? 4. What were the products of the plantation? 5. Describe the appearance and character of the owner, Frank Meriwether; of Mrs. Meriwether. 6. Does the account of the negro quarters show that the slaves were happy and contented? 7. In what ways did the life on these old estates evidence traces of the feudal system? 8. Discuss whether such a condition was a help or a hindrance to the development of the South.

## Selections from " Horseshoe Robinson "

Very different from the leisurely " Swallow Barn" is Kennedy's stirring romance of the Revolution, "Horseshoe Robinson." In the introduction Kennedy has told the circumstances under which he formed the acquaintance of the principal character and came into possession of the leading incidents of the novel. On a visit to the western section of South Carolina in 1819, he spent the night at a house where he met Horseshoe Robinson, then an old man, who had been summoned to give relief to a boy who had dislocated his shoulder in a fall from a horse. "Horseshoe," says Kennedy, "yielded himself to my leading and I got out of him a rich stock of adventure, of which his life was full. It was long after midnight before our party broke up; and when I got to my bed it was to dream of Horseshoe and his adventures. I made a record of what he told me, whilst the memory of it was still fresh, and often afterwards reverted to it, when accident or intentional research brought into my view events connected with the times and scenes to which this story had reference."

Kennedy also adds that after the publication of the novel in 1835 he commissioned a friend to send the old man — who had by that time moved to Alabama — a copy of the book. "The report brought me was that the old man listened very attentively to the reading of it, and took a great interest in it.

"'What do you say to all of this?' was the question addressed to him after the reading was finished. His reply is a voucher which I desire to preserve: 'It is all true and right — in its right place — excepting about them women, which I disremember. That mought be true, too; but my memory is treacherous — I disremember.'"

### Horseshoe Robinson (Page 68)

**Gates:** General Horatio Gates of the American army, who had forced the British under Burgoyne to surrender after the battle of Saratoga in 1777. In 1780 he was put in command of the Southern forces of the Revolutionary army. Owing to his poor generalship his forces were defeated near Camden, South Carolina, on August 16, 1780, by Lord Cornwallis, and a few months later Gates was superseded by General Greene. Gates thereupon retired to his home in Virginia.

### Horseshoe captures Five Prisoners (Page 77)

**cock-a-whoop:** boastful.

### The Battle of King's Mountain (Page 90)

**King's Mountain:** a ridge rising a few hundred feet above the surrounding country just within the limits of South Carolina and about thirty miles southwest of Charlotte, North Carolina. Here was fought on October 7, 1780, a battle between the English and Tory force of one thousand one hundred and twenty-five under Lieutenant-Colonel Ferguson and about one thousand Georgia, North Carolina, South Carolina, Tennessee, and Kentucky backwoodsmen under William Campbell, James Williams, Benjamin Cleveland, Isaac Shelby, and John Sevier. The engagement lasted about an hour, resulting in so decisive a defeat for the English that Cornwallis was compelled to postpone for a time his invasion of North Carolina. — **Froissart:** a French chronicler of the fourteenth century.

QUESTIONS. 1. In a review of this book Poe praised the character of Horseshoe Robinson by writing, "In short, he is the man of all others we would like to have riding by our side in any very hazardous adventure." What traits of character does Horseshoe exhibit that would justify this opinion? 2. Are the other characters vividly enough drawn to enable you to analyze their characteristics? 3. What levels of Southern society are represented in the story? 4. Give some of the details regarding the life of each of these levels. 5. What impressions of the devotion of the people to the cause of liberty are given?

## WILLIAM GILMORE SIMMS

Of Simms's numerous novels "The Yemassee," from which the selection below is taken, is perhaps his nearest approach to artistic success. While lacking many essential points of greatness, it is a bold, spirited romance, full of invention and narrative power. If considerations of space had permitted, some selections from his great Revolutionary romance, "The Partisan," would have been included in this volume. This book is scarcely less interesting and successful than "The Yemassee" and portrays the same period of history as Kennedy's "Horseshoe Robinson." The two stories are, however, by no means duplicates; Simms's story has as its background the swamps of South Carolina in which Marion, the "Swamp Fox," and his followers found refuge.

## SELECTIONS FROM "THE YEMASSEE"

### THE ATTACK ON THE BLOCK HOUSE (PAGE 105)

The blockhouse was a familiar means of defense from Indians in the early days of settlement in America. It was a structure built of stout logs, in which were loopholes through which rifles might be fired. This particular blockhouse is described in an earlier chapter of "The Yemassee" as consisting of two stories, the lower story being a single apartment, but the upper story, reached by a ladder, was divided into two rooms, one of which, more securely built than the other, was for the protection of the women and children.

*amour propre:* vanity. — **Ariel:** the sprite in Shakespeare's "The Tempest" who performs the bidding of Prospero.

QUESTIONS. 1. What preparations for defense did the inmates of the blockhouse make? 2. What methods of attack were used by the Indians? 3. What traits of character did Granger's wife display? 4. Was the life of pioneer days conducive to giving women such qualities of character as she shows?

## JOHN ESTEN[1] COOKE

The selections here given are from "The Virginia Comedians." This book, published in 1854, is generally considered the best of the dozen or so romances written by Cooke with scenes laid in colonial and Revolutionary times and in the Civil War. Cooke's aspirations in this story were, in his own words, "to paint the Virginia phase of American society, to do for the Old Dominion what Cooper has done for the Indians, Simms for the Revolutionary down in South Carolina, Irving for the Dutch Knickerbockers, and Hawthorne for the weird

[1] Pronounced *Easten.*

Puritan life of New England." The scene is laid around Williamsburg, the colonial capital of Virginia, in the years immediately preceding the Revolution. In Cooke's mind this was a striking period of social transition. "It was the period of the culmination of the old régime," says Cooke in the preface to the 1883 edition. "A splendid society had burst into flower, and was enjoying itself in the sunshine and under the blue skies of the most beautiful of lands. On the surface the era is tranquil, but beneath is the volcano. Passion smolders under the laughter; the homespun coat jostles the embroidered costume; men are demanding social equality, as they will soon demand a republic; and the splendid old régime is about to vanish in the storm of Revolution." The novel is, therefore, a picture of the "golden days," and in this way it is perhaps best to take the book. The reader who looks for story interest will find himself disappointed. There is plenty of action, — ardent love-making, duels, and the like, — and there is bright talk, but the plot is not well sustained throughout. Its weakness is evidenced by the fact that the book is now published as two separate books, "Beatrice Hallam" and its sequel, "Captain Ralph," either of which can be read without the other.

## Selections from "The Virginia Comedians"

### Mr. Champ Effingham of Effingham Hall (Page 124)

**Kidderminster:** an English manufacturing town noted for its carpet industry. — **tout ensemble:** whole. — **point de Venise:** Venetian point lace. — **Mr. Joseph Addison's serial:** the *Spectator* essays.

### Governor Fauquier's Ball (Page 128)

**House of Burgesses:** the legislative body of colonial Virginia. — **Governor Fauquier:** a colonial governor of Virginia, whose term extended from 1758 to 1768. — **the Raleigh:** the noted tavern at Williamsburg. — **Benedick:** one of the characters in Shakespeare's "Much Ado About Nothing." — **the Twopenny-Act:** see *the action brought by the Reverend Mr. Maury*, etc., page 132. In the early days of Virginia the salaries of the clergy were paid in tobacco, the clergy receiving the advantage of a rise in price and suffering from a low price. In 1758 the legislature of Virginia enacted a law to the effect that these salaries should be paid in paper currency at a less amount than the price of tobacco in that year. This provoked a protest, one of the test suits being filed by the Reverend James Maury. — *vox argentea* of Cicero : the silver voice of Cicero, the Roman orator.

**Mr. Patrick Henry :** the orator and statesman born in Hanover County, Virginia, in 1736. `In 1763 he came into prominence by his brilliant plea for the defense in the suit brought by the Reverend James Maury. His later career as an orator of Revolutionary times is too well known to be repeated. — **Anacreon :** a Greek lyric poet who lived in the fifth century B.C.

**Mr. Wythe, Colonel Bland,** etc.: prominent characters in the history of colonial Virginia. — **tictac :** a kind of backgammon. — **spadille :** a game of cards. — **Corydons and Chloes :** names common in pastoral poetry for shepherds and shepherdesses. Here they are used as equivalent to beaux and belles. — *petit maître :* coxcomb. — **Myrtilla :** see note above. — **Cordelia :** a character in Shakespeare's "King Lear." — **Circe :** a character in classical mythology who by her powers of enchantment transformed human beings into animals, such as wolves, lions, etc.

As the early Southern novels were so largely of the historical type, it is interesting to note the episodes of Southern history that formed their backgrounds. A list arranged in the order of the historical situations contained in them will not only serve to suggest the more important of these novels but will outline an interesting course of reading.

The list would begin with William Caruthers' "Cavaliers of Virginia" and St. George Tucker Jr.'s "Hansford," both of which record that dramatic episode of colonial history known as Bacon's Rebellion. Next would come William Caruthers' "Knights of the Horseshoe," based on the romantic expedition made by Governor Spotswood of Virginia to the summit of the Blue Ridge, whence he and his companions looked over for the first time into the Shenandoah valley. These would be followed by John Pendleton Kennedy's "Rob of the Bowl," giving an account of the struggle between Episcopalianism and Roman Catholicism in Maryland under the second Lord Baltimore. Then would come William Gilmore Simms's "Yemassee," with its background of the uprising of the Yemassee Indians in 1715. In John Esten Cooke's "The Virginia Comedians" and its sequel "Henry St. John, Gentleman" we are carried on to the splendid flowering of Virginia life just before the Revolution. With William Gilmore Simms again in his several novels — "The Partisan," "Katherine Walton," "Mellichampe," "The Scout," "Eutaw," "The Forayers," and "Woodcraft" — we have various phases of the Revolution. To this same period belongs John Pendleton Kennedy's "Horseshoe Robinson." The great exodus into the Mississippi valley and the Southwest, which was the great thrill in Southern life in the early nineteenth century, found expression in the series of Border Romances by William Gilmore Simms, which well reflect pioneer existence in the various new states — "Guy Rivers" for Georgia, "Richard Hurdis" for Alabama, "Border Beagles" for

Mississippi, "Beauchampe" for Kentucky. Next would come that remarkable novel prophetic of the startling events to come in the Civil War period, Nathaniel Beverly Tucker's "The Partisan Leader." Caroline Lee Hentz's "The Planter's Northern Bride," a reply to Mrs. Stowe's "Uncle Tom's Cabin," would bring the chain of events down almost to the opening of the Civil War. John Esten Cooke's "Surrey of Eagle's Nest," "Mohun," and "Hilt to Hilt" would be found accounts by an eyewitness of the notable campaigns of the Civil War in Virginia.

**Other Romancers and Story Writers.** Not represented in this book are the following writers: *Virginia:* John Beauchamp Jones (1810–1866); *North Carolina:* Calvin H. Wiley (1819–1887); *Georgia:* Francis Robert Goulding (1810–1881); *Kentucky:* Catherine Anne Warfield (1816–1877); *Louisiana:* Sarah Anne Dorsey (1829–1879).

## HUMORISTS

Between 1835 and 1855 there sprang up in the South a group of humorists whose work is of interest on several accounts. In the first place, it was a distinctive contribution to American literature. The people of the antebellum South were a happy people who cared more for laughter than for tears. It was characteristic of the Southerner, and still is, even in the present day, that in whatever assemblage he might be there was the matching of jokes and anecdotes. In the second place, this humorous writing was an attempt to produce literature for its own sake. As has been shown, much of the earlier writing was writing done for a purpose, such as orations, political essays, journals, biographies, and the like. Almost the first effort in the South to produce literature for its own sake was in the field of humorous writing. A third reason why this humorous writing should command attention lies in the fact that it was popular with the Southern people before the war. Whatever opinion may be held about its intrinsic literary worth, there is no gainsaying the fact that it was the joy and delight of the Southern people, and in it they thought they found a faithful delineation of certain phases of their life. A final reason for giving attention to the work of these writers is that they are the forerunners of the realistic writers of the new South who have so successfully depicted in short stories and novels the scenes and characters of various sections of the South.

The salient features of this Southern humorous literature were the natural outgrowth of the conditions amidst which it was produced. It was a humor of locality. Those who produced it perceived that in the South there were strongly marked types. This was true of the Southern gentleman, with his marked accent and mannerisms, and it was still more true of the middle and lower classes and their peculiarities. It was the humor of dialect. In that day bad spelling in rough imitation of dialect was considered as a necessary adjunct to humor. It was, moreover, humor of situation. It delighted in boisterous and rather crude situations of discomfiture. Even people of refinement would find diversion in the roughest pranks and would laugh unrestrainedly over a predicament that was both painful and unfortunate. It had two other characteristics which relate not to its materials but to its sources. In the first place, it originated through the newspaper sketch and has all the freshness of that type of literature; and, in the second place, it is, like all other Southern literature of this period, the work of the amateur.

## AUGUSTUS BALDWIN LONGSTREET

From the first Georgia was a much more democratic state than Virginia or South Carolina. Its population was a sturdy race which separation from the more aristocratic sections had rendered peculiarly individual. The country dances, the gander pullings, the militia drills, the debating societies, the fox hunts, the shooting matches, the horse races, and the like which formed so large a part of the everyday life of the rural sections of Georgia are vividly portrayed by Longstreet in "Georgia Scenes," from which are taken the two following selections.

### THE HORSE SWAP (PAGE 151)

In this sketch Longstreet has given a very lively picture of a characteristic feature of country life in the South.

*cracklins :* a well-cooked, crisp rind of pork. — *tout ensemble :* whole appearance. — **tacky :** ugly horse. — **make a pass at me :** make me an offer. — **banter :** proposal. — **boot :** money given to make an exchange equal. — **brought him to a hack :** caused him to hesitate. — **rues and after claps :** bitternesses and regrets.

QUESTIONS. 1. Describe the methods of the horse swap. 2. What impressions of the character of the rural population of Georgia does the sketch give?

### THE TURN OUT (PAGE 161)

*fescues, abisselfas,* and *anpersants :* the author explains these terms as follows : "*The fescue* was a sharpened wire or other instrument used by the preceptor to point out the letters to the children. *Abisselfa* is a

contraction of the words 'a by itself, a.' It was usual, when either of
the vowels constituted a syllable of a word, to pronounce it, and denote
its independent character by the words just mentioned, thus: 'a by itself *a*, c-o-r-n, corn, *acorn*.' The character which stands for the word
'and' (&) was probably pronounced by the same accompaniment but
in terms borrowed from the Latin language, thus: '& per se' (by itself)
&. Hence *anpersants*."

**Mrs. Trollope:** an English writer who, after visiting the United
States, wrote a very grossly exaggerated and unfavorable account of the
American people. — **school-butter:** the author's note on this expression is as follows: "I have never been able to satisfy myself clearly as
to the literal meaning of these terms. They were considered an unpardonable insult to a country school, and always justified an attack by the
whole fraternity upon the person who used them in their hearing."

QUESTIONS. 1. What characteristics of the schoolmaster are brought
out? of the boys? 2. Comment on the democratic relation of schoolmaster and pupils shown by this incident.


## WILLIAM TAPPAN THOMPSON

The selection here given is from "Major Jones's Courtship," which
consists of a series of letters describing the courtship of Mary Stallings
by Major Joseph Jones, who is a typical countryman and small planter
of the middle class in Georgia — a vigorous and uneducated product of
plantation life. Although both Mary and the Major are tenderly inclined
towards each other and the old folks are willing to the match, yet it is
only after various amusing situations that their love attains a happy culmination. The book is natural and faithful in its picture of country life
in more primitive times, and is full of lively and wholesome humor.


### MAJOR JONES'S COURTSHIP (PAGE 170)

**Miss Carline and Miss Kesiah:** older sisters of the Major's sweetheart, Mary Stallings, whose widowed mother owns the plantation adjoining the Major's. — **old Miss Stallins:** Mary Stallings's mother.
The designation "Mrs." is often pronounced *Miss* among country people in the South. — **jice:** joist. — **ager:** ague, chill. — **Cato:** a common
name for negroes.

QUESTIONS. 1. Give in your own words an account of the incident.
2. Comment on the character of the humor.

## JAMES GLOVER BALDWIN

Baldwin's "Flush Times in Alabama and Mississippi," from which this selection is taken, is a volume of humorous sketches drawn from the writer's experiences in the "Shinplaster Era" — a time when in the recently opened Southwest business flourished upon the fictitious basis of universal credit and indefinite extension. Of these "flush times" Baldwin was himself a part, and he gives a very vivid interpretation of it.

### OVID BOLUS, ESQ. (PAGE 176)

This extract from the sketch with the same title presents very meagerly a piece of humor held by some to equal Mark Twain at his best.

**Prince Hal . . . Falstaff:** characters in Shakespeare's "King Henry IV."—**belles-lettres:** polite or elegant literature.—*nati consumere fruges:* born to consume the fruits of the earth. — **D'Orsay:** a leader of society in Paris and London in the early nineteenth century. — *manage:* horsemanship. — **Murat:** a celebrated cavalry leader in Napoleon's army.

## HOW THE FLUSH TIMES SERVED THE VIRGINIANS (PAGE 180)

This extract forms a portion of the sketch entitled "How the Times served the Virginians. Virginians in a New Country. The Rise, Decline, and Fall of the Rag Empire" — as brilliant a piece of social characterization as can be found anywhere.

**verdant Moses:** the reference is to an episode in Goldsmith's "The Vicar of Wakefield," chap. xii. — **resolutions of '98:** a set of resolutions drafted by Madison which were passed by the Virginia legislature as a protest against the extension of the powers of the federal government at the expense of the states, as a result of the liberal interpretation the Federalists were placing upon the Constitution, and in particular by the enactment of the Alien and Sedition Acts. — **Martha:** one of the characters in Scott's "The Fortunes of Nigel." She was the daughter of old Trapbois, a miser and usurer. — **saws of Poor Richard:** maxims of prudence and thrift contained in Benjamin Franklin's "Poor Richard's Almanac." — **Webster:** Daniel Webster, the American orator. — **University:** the University of Virginia. — **Greene:** a county in Alabama.

QUESTIONS. 1. What characteristics of the Virginians are set forth? 2. By what means did they attempt to repair their lost fortunes in the Flush Times?

**Other Humorists.** Among the writers of humorous sketches are several others of somewhat less importance than those represented in this book. The list would include the following. *Alabama:* Johnson Jones Hooper (1815–1863); *Tennessee:* George Washington Harris (1814–1869); *Georgia:* John Basil Lamar (1812–1862), Charles Henry Smith (" Bill Arp ") (1826–1903); *Louisiana and Arkansas:* Thomas Bangs Thorp (1815–1878).

# POETS

What was found to be true of Southern prose in antebellum times — that it was literature of effort rather than accomplishment — is likewise true of the poetry of this period. The quantity was surprisingly large. The statement has been made that a list of approximately two hundred and fifty writers of verse could be made out, from 1805 to 1860, and that there was not a year in which numbers of volumes of poetry were published. Yet in all this company there were few who can be called writers of genuine power. It is strange that the South, the home of a great people, had no great poet before the war. Poe was, to be sure, great in many respects, but he was not great enough in interest in real life to be called an interpreter of Southern life in his poetry.

Poetry in the South before the war was largely written by amateurs. It was looked upon, as Paul Hamilton Hayne has declared, as " the choice recreation of gentlemen, as something fair and good, to be courted in a dainty amateur fashion." In consequence, there is not the great thought and deep passion of masterpieces, but a general air of amateurishness. There is also upon it, as in all Southern literature of this time except the humor, the mark of imitation and, so, of artificiality. It never seemed simple, natural, unforced. Furthermore, the Southern poet was unfortunate in his models. Instead of going to the serious, elevated poems of Wordsworth or to the greater poetry of Byron, he took as his models the light, graceful work of the Cavalier lyrists, — Suckling, Herrick, and Carew, — or the sentimentalism of Tom Moore, or the rhetoric of Byron, or perhaps the faultless but insipid early poems of Tennyson. As to the theme, it was generally love, fortunate or the reverse, although the whole gamut of the Muse's lyre was run in kind and in subject matter. The Southern poets, moreover, had less individuality of expression than almost any other group of poets in the world. The poetry might all have been written by one man. Even Poe, except for his dominant mood of morbidness, simply carried to perfection what every other poet of the South was trying to do. Southern poetry has, as conspicuous qualities, beauty, melody, and exquisite rhythm. In the poets of the lower South, especially, the local coloring is noteworthy, and the interpretation of nature's moods and outward aspects is done with delicate artistic sensibility. Here and there, however, out of the general mass of those who attempted poetry some few did best what others did indifferently, and these are they whom both criticism and common consent have agreed to call the representative poets. But even these have won their place, not by the bulk of their work, but rather by some single poem. This fact, however, is no disparagement of their work. It is a worthy achievement to have produced even a single poem which men will cherish.

## ST. GEORGE TUCKER

### Resignation (Page 188)

Questions. 1. Trace the thought of the poem through its successive stages. 2. Assign reasons for this poem being widely popular.

## FRANCIS SCOTT KEY

### The Star-Spangled Banner (Page 190)

When the British bombarded Baltimore in 1814, Key, who had gone under flag of truce to the British fleet in order to secure the release of a friend, a prisoner in the hands of the British, was compelled to remain on board one of the British vessels all night, and was therefore a witness of the bombardment. When he saw the American flag still floating over Fort McHenry the next morning, he wrote his famous poem, jotting down portions of it on the back of a letter. The version given here follows the original manuscript except in some instances of punctuation.

Questions. 1. What reference does the poem have to the specific occasion? 2. To what feelings does it give expression? 3. Does the poem live by reason of its merit or its patriotic appeal?

## RICHARD HENRY WILDE

### My Life is like the Summer Rose (Page 192)

This poem is expressive of the gentle melancholy that a perfectly happy, comfortable Southern youth of the earlier part of the nineteenth century was fond of assuming simply because such a Byronic affectation was fashionable.

**Tampa's desert strand:** Florida.

QUESTIONS. 1. Which of the three images used to suggest the transitoriness of life is the best and why? 2. What is the central thought of the poem? 3. Is the poem distinctively Southern in its scenery?

### To the Mocking-Bird (Page 193)

**Yorick:** a jester at the Danish court whose skull, just dug up, leads Hamlet to moralizing (cf. "Hamlet," V, i). — **Abbot of Misrule:** in olden days the leader of the revels at Christmas, who, in mockery of the Church's absolution of sins, absolved his followers of all their wisdom. — **Jacques:** one of Shakespeare's characters who morbidly delights in dwelling on the moral discrepancies of the world. Shakespeare's spelling of the name is *Jaques.*

QUESTION. What aspects of the mocking bird's song are dwelt upon?

## EDWARD COATE PINKNEY

### Song (Page 194)

QUESTIONS. 1. What does the first stanza tell of the poet's experience? 2. What does the second add to this?

### A Serenade (Page 194)

This poem was written in honor of Miss Georgiana McCausland, whom the poet afterwards married.

QUESTION. What is the thought of the poem?

### A Health (Page 195)

This poem was written in honor of Mrs. Rebecca Somerville of Baltimore. Professor Lounsbury gives this poem high praise in saying, " It would be difficult to find anywhere in English literature a more exquisite tribute to womanhood."

QUESTIONS. 1. What qualities of woman are spoken of? 2. What has been the typical attitude of the Southern man toward the other sex?

## MIRABEAU BUONAPARTE LAMAR

### THE DAUGHTER OF MENDOZA (PAGE 197)

It is said that this poem was inspired by a beautiful woman whom Lamar had met in Central America.

**Mendoza:** a river of the Argentine Republic.

QUESTIONS. 1. What details of the woman's beauty are given? 2. What has been the effect of this meeting upon the poet? 3. These stanzas have been spoken of as "lilting and sparkling." Illustrate.

## ALBERT PIKE

### TO THE MOCKING BIRD (PAGE 198)

**Æolian strain:** music like that produced by the wind harp.

QUESTIONS. 1. What idea regarding the mocking bird does each stanza contain? 2. Read Keats's "Ode to the Nightingale" and give an opinion as to how far Pike may have been indebted to Keats's poem.

## PHILIP PENDLETON COOKE

### FLORENCE VANE (PAGE 200)

This widely known song of Cooke is said to be purely a romance of the writer's imagination.

**Thy heart was as a river,** etc.: Cooke explained the meaning of these obscure lines as follows: "Florence did not want the capacity to love, but directed her love to no object. Her passions went flowing like a lost river." His next sentence in this explanation is an interesting example of the influence Byron exerted over these early Southern lyrists. "Byron has a kindred idea expressed by the same figure. Perhaps his verses were in my mind when I wrote my own:

"She was the ocean to the river of his thoughts,
Which terminated all. — 'The Dream'"

QUESTIONS. 1. What situation is given in the poem? 2. Does it seem artificial in its sentiment? 3. What is responsible for its charm?

### LIFE IN THE AUTUMN WOODS (PAGE 202)

**car**: according to mythology the sun was a chariot driven through the heavens by the god Apollo. — **Shakespeare's melancholy courtier**: Jaques in " As You Like It." — **Ardennes**: some have thought that the forest of Arden, where is laid the scene of " As You Like it," must have been taken from the forest of Ardennes in French Flanders. — **Amiens**: in " As You Like It," a lord attending on the banished duke. — **little recked**: see " As You Like It," II, i, in which Jaques in an excess of sentimentality weeps over the killing of a deer.

QUESTIONS. 1. What descriptions of the delights of hunting does the poem give? 2. How does the poet show himself to be appreciative of nature?

### THEODORE O'HARA

### THE BIVOUAC OF THE DEAD (PAGE 205)

This poem commemorates the Kentuckians who fell in the Mexican War at the battle of Buena Vista. It was read by the author when the remains of these soldiers were brought to Frankfort, Kentucky, in 1847 for burial.

**Came down the serried foe**: the Mexicans under Santa Anna. — **Long had the doubtful conflict raged**: the battle raged for ten hours with varying success. — **stout old chieftain**: General Zachary Taylor. **Angostura's plain**: the plateau on which the battle was fought, so called from the mountain pass of Angostura leading to it from the south. — **Dark and Bloody Ground**: this is the meaning of the Indian word " Kentucky." — **Spartan mother's**: Kentucky is here likened to the Spartan mothers who wished to have their sons return with their shields or upon them.

QUESTIONS. 1. What pictures of the battle and details concerning it are given? 2. What tribute is paid to the fallen soldiers? 3. What qualities are to be expected in a martial poem? 4. Does this poem exhibit these?

### ALEXANDER BEAUFORT MEEK

### A SONG (PAGE 209)

QUESTIONS. 1. Who is the speaker? 2. What comparisons does the speaker use to indicate feeling? 3. Which of these is the most poetic, and why?

## LAND OF THE SOUTH (PAGE 210)

This is a selection from a longer poem, entitled "The Day of Freedom."

**Helvyn:** Switzerland. — **Tempe:** a valley in Thessaly famous for its attractiveness.

QUESTIONS. 1. What aspects of the South are presented? 2. What is the basis of the poet's devotion to the South? 3. To what extent will he go to show his devotion?

## THE MOCKING BIRD (PAGE 211)

**Mime:** mimic. — **Petrarch:** an Italian poet of the fourteenth century noted as a writer of sonnets. — **Laura:** the woman Petrarch loved and addressed in his sonnets. — **Anacreon:** a Greek lyric poet. — **Troubadour:** one of a school of poets which flourished in the southern part of France in the Middle Ages.

QUESTIONS. 1. To whom is the poet speaking? 2. What literary reminiscences are used in the description of the mocking bird? 3. Which of these is the most pleasing, and why? 4. Compare this tribute to the mocking bird with other poems on the same subject found in this volume.

## HENRY ROOTES JACKSON

### THE RED OLD HILLS OF GEORGIA (PAGE 213)

QUESTIONS. 1. What aspects of Georgia scenery are referred to? 2. What characteristics of Southerners are mentioned? 3. Is it typical of the Southern people that they are home lovers? 4. Does this poem well express such a feeling?

### MY WIFE AND CHILD (PAGE 215)

By a curious confusion this poem came to be attributed to General T. J. ("Stonewall") Jackson and is supposed to have been written by him during the Civil War. It was, however, written in 1846 by Henry Rootes Jackson while in the Mexican campaign.

QUESTIONS. 1. Note the picture of the camp in the first stanza. 2. What glimpses of home life are given in the subsequent stanzas? 3. What prayer does the poet make for his wife and child?

### JAMES MATTHEWS LEGARÉ [1]

## To a Lily (Page 217)

**Venus:** reference is to the legend that Venus rose first from the foam of the sea.

QUESTIONS. 1. What comparisons does the poet make between the lily and his beloved? 2. Does the poem seem sincere in its sentiment?

## Haw Blossoms (Page 217)

QUESTIONS. 1. What scene is described in the first five stanzas? 2. What meditations on this scene are given in the next seven stanzas? 3. What lesson is brought out in the last two stanzas?

### WILLIAM GILMORE SIMMS

## Oh, the Sweet South (Page 220)

QUESTIONS. 1. What is the thought of the first stanza? 2. What characteristics of the South are mentioned in the second stanza?

## The Swamp Fox (Page 222)

This poem is found in Simms's historical romance "The Partisan." The Swamp Fox was a common designation for General Francis Marion, a Revolutionary leader in South Carolina, whose shrewdness in attack and escape won this nickname.

**Tarleton:** a distinguished leader of the British forces in the South during the Revolutionary War. — **Santee:** Marion's principal field of operations lay between the Santee and the Peedee rivers. — **The Colonel:** at this time Marion held the rank of colonel. Subsequently he was advanced to the rank of general. — **cooter:** a Southern colloquialism for a fresh-water tortoise or turtle.

QUESTIONS. 1. What details of the life of Marion and his men are mentioned? 2. Compare this poem with Bryant's "Song of Marion's Men."

[1] Pronounced *Legaree.*

## EDGAR ALLAN POE
### To Helen (Page 225)

This poem is a tribute of devotion to his boyhood friend, Mrs. Stannard. This lady's name was Jane, but Poe has given her in the poem the name of " Helen " as more fitting his tribute to her as a classic embodiment of beauty.

**beauty :** the beauty of Helen of Troy. — **Nicéan barks :** it is impossible to say exactly what this allusion means. It is altogether likely that Poe has here simply used some word of his own formed with a vague suggestion of antiquity. — **wanderer :** Odysseus, or Ulysses. — **hyacinth :** lovely as Hyacinthus, favorite of Apollo. — **Naiad :** a nymph who presided over lakes, brooks, and fountains. The term is therefore suggestive of exquisite grace. — **Psyche :** the Greek word for " soul " and also the name of a beautiful maiden whom Cupid loved and wedded.

QUESTIONS. 1. Is this poem notable for its thought or for its grace of delicacy? 2. Lines 9 and 10 are two of Poe's best-known and most frequently quoted lines. Explain the fitness of the words " glory " and " grandeur."

### Israfel (Page 227)

**"Whose heart-strings are a lute " :** Israfel, the angel of music, was supposed to have the sweetest voice of all God's creatures. — **hymns :** the reference is to " the music of the spheres " which the stars were supposed to make in their courses. **levin :** lightning. — **Pleiads :** Poe here refers to the legend of a lost Pleiad by his use of the past tense, " Which were seven." — **Where Love 's a grown-up God :** Poe seems to think of the god of love, usually represented as a boy, as grown to full manhood in heaven, for love becomes perfect there.

QUESTIONS. 1. What is the vision of power that the poet has, and what dismays him? 2. Compare the closing thought with that of Shelley's " To a Skylark."

### The Raven (Page 228)

Poe has fully set forth his methods and his purpose in this poem in the essay entitled " Philosophy of Composition."

**lost Lenore :** Poe is said to have told Mrs. A. B. Shelton, formerly Miss Royster (his first sweetheart, whose father brought the love

affair to speedy termination), that she was the Lenore of " The Raven."
— **Raven**: frequently in literature a bird of ill omen. — **Pallas**: Min-
erva, goddess of wisdom. — **Plutonian**: characteristic of Pluto, god of
the underworld, where utter darkness reigned.

" **Wretch** ": the lover addresses himself. — **nepenthe**: a drink
thought by the ancients to banish sorrow; later it came to mean anything that quieted physical or mental anguish, as, for instance, opium.
— **balm in Gilead**: a Biblical phrase signifying remedy or consolation
for sorrow. — **Aidenn**: a form for Eden coined by Poe for the rime. —
**the lamplight o'er him streaming**: in answer to criticism of this line
Poe explained, " My conception was that of the bracket candelabrum
affixed against the wall, high up above the door and bust."

QUESTIONS. 1. Reconstruct the dramatic situation. 2. According to
Poe the interpretation of the poem was to be found by taking the fact
that the Raven stood for " Mournful and Never-ending remembrance "
in connection with lines 101, 107, and 108. With this clue explain the
significance of the poem.

## ULALUME (PAGE 233)

This poem was published in December, 1847. As Poe's wife had died
under distressing circumstances in the preceding January, the poem
evidently is an expression of the poet's mood under his bereavement.

**Auber**: coined by Poe. — **Weir**: coined by Poe for the sake of
rime. — **Psyche**: the Greek word for soul. — **scoriac rivers**: rivers of
lava. — **Yaanek**: another of Poe's specially coined words. — **boreal pole**:
probably the Antarctic regions. — **senescent**: growing old. — **Astarte**:
the moon goddess of the Phœnicians. — **crescent**: suggestive of hope.

**Dian**: the moon goddess of the Romans, who was chaste and cold
to the advances of lovers. — **where the worm never dies**: an expression
from the Bible implying the gnawing of the unending grief. — **stars of
the Lion**: the constellation Leo. — **Lethean**: with the power of the
river Lethe in Hades, which, according to classical mythology, induced
forgetfulness. — **sibyllic**: mysterious. The Sibyls in classical mythology were priestesses of Apollo who were inspired to utter mysterious
prophecies. — **legended**: with an inscription.

QUESTION. This poem has been commonly regarded as a mere experiment in verbal melody with very little meaning. Bearing in mind
what was said above as to the circumstances of the composition of the
poem, endeavor to interpret the poem as an expression of the poet's
feeling at that time.

## ANNABEL LEE (PAGE 237)

This poem was published in the New York *Tribune* two days after Poe's death, and is one of his last poems. According to general acceptance Annabel Lee stands for the poet's wife, who had died about three years before.

**highborn kinsmen:** the angels who took Poe's wife from him.

QUESTIONS. 1. This poem has more definiteness of incident than Poe's poems usually show. What are the details of the incident? Should the sentiment be called morbid? 2. What qualities make this one of the most popular of Poe's poems?

## ELDORADO (PAGE 238)

This poem is another one of the last of Poe's poems.

**Eldorado:** a fabled city or country abounding in gold and precious stones. Figuratively the word is used to denote any place of great wealth. Poe evidently uses the word in the sense of the poet's kingdom.

QUESTIONS. 1. Explain the meaning of the poem. 2. Can it be said to apply to Poe's life?

**Other Poets.** To the various states named belong the following poets who have not been represented in this book but who have attained some reputation in and beyond their respective states. *Maryland:* Charles Henry Wharton (1748–     ), John Shaw (1778–1809), Severn Teackle Wallis (1816–1894), George Henry Miles (1824–1871); *Virginia:* William Munford (1775–1825), William Maxwell (1784–1857), Richard Dabney (1787–1825), Henry Throop Stanton (1834–1899); *South Carolina:* Caroline Howard Gilman (1794–1888), Mary E. Lee (1813–1849), Catherine Gendron Poyas (1813–1882); *North Carolina:* Mary Bayard Clarke (1827–1886), Theophilus Hunter Hill (1836–1901), Edwin Wiley Fuller (1847–1875); *Kentucky:* George Denison Prentice (1802–1870), Amelia Welby (1819–1852); *West Virginia:* Daniel Bedinger Lucas (1836–     ); *Alabama:* Augustus J. Requier (1825–1887). *Mississippi:* Rosa Vertner Jeffrey (1826–1894); *Georgia:* Thomas Holley Chivers (1807–1858).

# PART II. POETRY OF THE CIVIL WAR

## JAMES RYDER RANDALL

## MY MARYLAND (PAGE 240)

This poem was written while the author was teaching in Louisiana. In April, 1861, he read in one of the New Orleans newspapers an account of how the Massachusetts troops had been fired upon in their passage through his native city, Baltimore. Unable to sleep in his excitement over the occurrence, he rose at midnight and hastily composed this poem.

**Carroll:** Charles Carroll of Carrollton, one of the signers of the Declaration of Independence. — **Howard:** John Eager Howard, a distinguished Revolutionary soldier. — **Ringgold:** Samuel Ringgold, who was killed in the Mexican War at the battle of Palo Alto. — **Watson:** William Henry Watson, a colonel in the Mexican War who was killed at Monterey. — **Lowe:** Enoch Lewis Lowe, a soldier in the Mexican War and later governor of Maryland. — **May:** Charles Augustus May, a distinguished leader at the battle of Monterey. — *Sic semper:* the full form of the Latin motto is *Sic semper tyrannis*, "Thus always to tyrants." — **Vandal:** a term for the Northerners.

QUESTIONS. 1. What lines of the poem show the immediate motive for its writing? 2. What is the basis of the poet's appeal to Maryland to join the Southern cause? 3. Is it an appeal simply to feeling or is it an appeal to reason?

## JOHN PELHAM (PAGE 243)

The hero celebrated in this poem was a young Alabamian who, although barely twenty-two, had signally distinguished himself in the Confederate army. His death in the cavalry fight at Kelly's Ford, March 17, 1863, caused profound grief throughout the army.

**Marcellus:** the nephew and son-in-law of the Emperor Augustus, and his intended successor, who met an untimely death.

QUESTIONS. 1. What references are made to Pelham's career? 2. What tribute is paid to him?

## ALBERT PIKE

### DIXIE (PAGE 244)

This poem is perhaps the best of many written in the South to the stirring tune "Dixie." It of course bears no relation to the insignificant words that the tune originally had.

QUESTION. By what means does the poet make his appeal?

## HARRY McCARTHY

### THE BONNIE BLUE FLAG (PAGE 246)

Like "Dixie" this famous song originated in the theater and first became popular in New Orleans in 1861.

## JOHN ESTEN COOKE

### The Band in the Pines (Page 247)

For note in regard to Pelham see page 498.

QUESTIONS. 1. What does the poet mean by the "band in the pine wood"? 2. What is the central thought of the poem?

## JOHN REUBEN THOMPSON

### Ashby (Page 249)

**dragoon**: Turner Ashby was a dashing brigadier general of cavalry. He was killed in a skirmish near Harrisonburg, Virginia, in 1862. — **Paynim**: pagan. — **Templestowe**: the place where occurred the tournament described in the forty-third chapter of "Ivanhoe."

### Music in Camp (Page 250)

The incident which was the basis of this poem occurred during the winter of 1862–1863, when the Northern and Southern armies were encamped on opposite sides of the Rappahannock River in Virginia.

QUESTIONS. 1. What are the details of the incident? 2. What is its significance?

### The Burial of Latane (Page 253)

Captain Latane was killed in the Pamunkey expedition of General J. E. B. Stuart. His brother managed to carry the body to the near-by plantation of Mrs. Brockenbrough. The Federal soldiers, however, refused to allow a clergyman to come to conduct the funeral. Accordingly, accompanied by a few other ladies, a little girl with her apron filled with flowers, and a few faithful slaves who stood near, Mrs. Brockenbrough herself read the burial service and committed the gallant soldier's body to the earth.

*Victrix et vidua :* victorious and bereft.

## WILLIAM GORDON McCABE

### Dreaming in the Trenches (Page 255)

This poem was written in 1864, while the author was in the trenches before Petersburg.

**Montrose:** James Graham, Marquis of Montrose, of the seventeenth century, a supporter of Charles I. — **the old** *Romance*: Malory's "Morte d'Arthur." — *Tristram:* a knight of King Arthur's Round Table who was the lover of Iseult, wife of his uncle, King Mark of Cornwall.

QUESTIONS. 1. What is the poet's dream? 2. What determination does he express in the last stanza?

## CHRISTMAS NIGHT OF '62 (PAGE 256)

QUESTIONS. 1. What details of the soldier's bivouac are suggested? 2. What are the poet's thoughts on this Christmas night?

## JOHN PEGRAM (PAGE 258)

General Pegram was a distinguished Confederate cavalry leader who was killed at the head of his division near Hatcher's Run, Virginia, in February, 1865, aged thirty-three.

QUESTION. What tribute is paid to Pegram as a man and as a soldier?

## JOHN WILLIAMSON PALMER

### STONEWALL JACKSON'S WAY (PAGE 259)

This poem was written at Oakland, Maryland, September 17, 1862, while the battle of Antietam was in progress. It is probably the most graphic and condensed pen portrait of Jackson ever made.

"**Blue-light Elder**": Presbyterian elder. — **Banks:** a general in the Federal army. — **Massa:** a nickname among the soldiers for General Jackson. — **pray:** it was General Jackson's custom never to begin a battle without a prayer, and after a victory to give public thanks to God. — *In forma pauperis:* as a poor man. — **Hill:** A. P. Hill, a prominent Confederate general. — **Pope:** John Pope, a general in the Federal army. — **Stuart:** General J. E. B. Stuart, a Confederate cavalry commander.

QUESTIONS. 1. What characteristics of General Jackson are presented? 2. Is the touch of humor in this poem an advantage or not?

## HENRY LYNDEN FLASH

### Stonewall Jackson (Page 261)

In connection with the battle of Chancellorsville on May 2, 1863, General Jackson with a small escort advanced in front of his lines, between eight and nine o'clock in the evening, to reconnoiter. As he was returning his party was mistaken for Federal soldiers and was fired upon by the Confederates. Jackson was so severely wounded in the left arm and the right hand that on the following day his left arm was amputated. He seemed in a fair way to recover, but pneumonia set in, from which he died, May 10, 1863.

QUESTION. What is the underlying thought of the poem?

## THADDEUS OLIVER

### All Quiet along the Potomac To-night (Page 262)

The authorship of this poem has been generally ascribed to Ethel Lynn Beers, a New England writer. But recent evidence for a different view seems conclusive. Professor C. Alphonso Smith presents the evidence for Thaddeus Oliver's authorship as follows:

This poem was first published unsigned on October 21, 1861, "in a Northern newspaper." In *Harper's Weekly*, of November 30th, 1861, it reappeared with Mrs. Beers' initials attached. Mr. Oliver, however, wrote the poem in August, 1861, and read it to several friends in camp with him in Virginia. In a letter dated "Camp 2d Ga. Regt. near Centreville, Va., October 3rd, 1861," Mr. John D. Ashton, of Georgia, writing to his wife says: "Upon my arrival at home, should I be so fortunate as to obtain the hoped-for furlough, I will read you the touching and beautiful poem mentioned in my letter of last week, 'All Quiet along the Potomac To-night,' written by my girlishly modest friend, Thaddeus Oliver, of the Buena Vista Guards."

For further evidence see *Southern Historical Society Papers*, Vol. VIII, pages 255-260.

QUESTIONS. 1. Show that the poem gives a vivid picture of a grim reality. 2. In what way does the incident make a human appeal?

## MARIE RAVENEL DE LA COSTE

### Somebody's Darling (Page 264)

This poem was one of the best-loved Confederate poems and for many years was to be found in every scrapbook and heard on every school stage.

## CAROLINE AUGUSTA BALL

### The Jacket of Gray (Page 266)

Like "Somebody's Darling" this poem was widely popular, because it expressed the feelings and experience of many a home.

## MARGARET JUNKIN PRESTON

### Gone Forward (Page 268)

This poem is based upon the last words of General Lee.
**Red-Cross knights:** the insignia of the Christian knights of the Middle Ages was often a red cross.

QUESTION. What significance does the poet attribute to Lee's last words?

### The Shade of the Trees (Page 269)

This poem is founded upon the last words of General T. J. ("Stonewall") Jackson.

QUESTION. What significance does the poet ascribe to the last words of Jackson?

## ANONYMOUS

### The Soldier Boy (Page 270)

All that is known regarding the authorship of this poem is embodied in the initials "H. M. L." prefixed to it and the date, "Lynchburg, May 18, 1861."
**Damascus:** sword blades made in Damascus have been noted for their temper. — **falchion:** sword.

QUESTION. What ideals of soldierly honor does this poem present?

### "The Brigade must not Know, Sir" (Page 271)

This poem was written in 1863, presumably shortly after the death of General "Stonewall" Jackson.

QUESTIONS. 1. Note the contrasts and the climax in the dialogue of the first three stanzas. 2. What account of the burial and what tribute to Jackson are made in the last three stanzas?

## The Confederate Flag (Page 272)

This poem first appeared in the *Metropolitan Record*. Nothing further is known in regard to its author or its date.

QUESTIONS. 1. In what spirit is the outcome of the war accepted? 2. What may the South continue to take pride in?

## Lines on a Confederate Note (Page 273)

So much uncertainty exists regarding the author of this unique poem that it seems best not to attempt to ascribe it to an author. In the Smithsonian Institution, Washington, D.C., there is a Confederate note with a version of this poem inscribed upon the back of it and signed by Miss M. J. Turner of North Carolina. There is no proof, however, that this is the original copy. The poem is frequently ascribed to Major A. S. Jonas of Mississippi, who was a member of the staff of General Stephen D. Lee, and the following account is usually given of its composition. After being paroled Major Jonas went to Richmond to secure transportation home. At the Powhatan Hotel his company met a Miss Anna Rush, a young girl from the North. She showed them a batch of Confederate notes printed upon one side which she was taking home as souvenirs. Handing one to each officer, she requested them to write something on the back. The officers complied and this poem is said to have been Major Jonas's contribution.

## ABRAM JOSEPH RYAN

### The Conquered Banner (Page 275)

This poem was written a short time after the surrender of General Lee, but was not published until 1868, when it appeared in Father Ryan's paper, *The Banner of the South*.

QUESTIONS. 1. What features of this poem would make it touch the Southern heart? 2. Judged purely as poetry, should it be ranked high? 3. While the poet is intensely Southern in his feeling, is he evidencing unrelenting bitterness? 4. Is the poem despairing in regard to the future of the South? 5. Compare this poem with "The Confederate Flag."

## The Sword of Robert Lee (Page 277)

This poem appeared in *The Banner of the South* in 1868, a few weeks after " The Conquered Banner."

QUESTIONS.  1. What qualities of Lee as a man and a leader does Ryan suggest?  2. Are there others that he might have brought forward?

## HENRY TIMROD

### Carolina (Page 279)

This stirring lyric was written in the exciting days of 1861, when the states were debating the question of secession.

**Eutaw's battle-bed:** the battle of Eutaw Springs during the Revolutionary War, in which the Americans under General Greene defeated the British. — **Rutledge:** John Rutledge, the president and commander in chief of South Carolina during the Revolution.

**Laurens:** John Laurens, a young patriot and soldier who was killed in the skirmish at the close of the Revolution. — **Marion:** the famous partisan leader of the Revolution. — **Huns:** Northern troops. — **From Sachem's Head to Sumter's wall:** from mountains to sea, Sachem's Head (more usually Cæsar's Head) being a mountain in northeastern South Carolina, and Sumter being the fort in Charleston harbor. — **armorial trees:** palmetto trees on the coat-of-arms of South Carolina.

QUESTION. By what appeals does the poet seek to stir the patriotism of the citizens of his state?

## A Cry to Arms (Page 282)

**byre:** cow house. — **cot:** cottage; here equivalent to home.

QUESTIONS.  1. Upon whom does the poet call, and what is each asked to leave?  2. What is demanded of them?

## Charleston (Page 284)

This poem was evidently written late in 1861, or early in 1862, when Fort Sumter and Fort Moultrie were both in the hands of the Confederates and the Union warships were blockading the coast.

**second summer:** Indian summer. — **Sumter:** Fort Sumter in Charleston harbor. — **Calpe:** a Greek name for Gibraltar. — **Moultrie:** Fort

Moultrie in Charleston harbor. — **Saxon lands:** Charleston was the port through which the Confederacy obtained supplies from England on ships that ran the Federal blockade.

QUESTIONS. 1. What picture of the city is given? 2. What is said of her future?

## SPRING (PAGE 286)

**germs:** seeds. — **South:** the south wind. — **Dryad:** a tree nymph.

QUESTIONS. 1. What aspect of spring is presented in the first part of the poem? 2. What references to stirring events of Timrod's time does the last part of the poem contain?

## THE COTTON BOLL (PAGE 288)

**Small sphere:** the boll or seed capsule of the cotton. — **cirque:** a circular valley. — **Uriel:** one of the seven archangels. — **touched our very swamps:** the reference is to William Gilmore Simms, a fellow Charlestonian and friend of Timrod, who had written poems and romances in which the swamps were the backgrounds. — **Poet of "The Woodlands":** William Gilmore Simms, whose country place in Barnwell County, South Carolina, was called "Woodlands."

**flute's ... trumpet's ... west wind's:** intended to symbolize different types of Simms's literary work. — **Cornwall:** the southernmost county of England, bounded on three sides by water. It is noted for its mines of copper and tin, which extend in some places far under the sea. — **bruit:** report. — **Goth:** the Northern soldiers. — **The Port which ruled the Western seas:** New York. At that time it was considered by many Southerners, especially South Carolinians, as an unjust competitor for trade with Charleston.

QUESTIONS. 1. What incident starts the poet's train of thought? 2. What poetic description of the South as the land of cotton is given in lines 29–55? 3. What details of Southern scenery are given in lines 56–92? 4. The work of what other Southern writer is referred to in lines 93–101? 5. What are Timrod's thoughts in lines 102–120 about the usefulness of the South's cotton to the world? 6. What contrast between this peaceful mission of the South and the present state of warfare in the South does the poet see in lines 122–145? 7. What hopes for the success of the Southern cause does the poet express in the remainder of the poem? 8. What qualities tend to make this a notable poem? 9. Is it too discursive?

## THE LILY CONFIDANTE (PAGE 293)

QUESTIONS. 1. Whom does the lover select as the confidante of his secret? 2. What question does he ask the lily? 3. What answer does the lily make?

## MAGNOLIA CEMETERY ODE (PAGE 295)

This lyric was sung on the occasion of decorating the graves of the Confederate dead in Magnolia Cemetery, Charleston, South Carolina, in 1867. It has been greatly admired, one of the most notable expressions of admiration being that of Whittier when he said that it was "in its simple grandeur, the noblest poem ever written by a Southern poet." More recently Professor Trent has said of it, "One need not fear for this once to compare a South Carolina poem with the best lyric of the kind in the literature of the world."

**no marble column:** a monument was later erected, consisting of a bronze color bearer on a granite pedestal.

QUESTIONS. 1. What is the wish of the poet for the fallen heroes? 2. In what way does the poem show Southern gallantry? 3. With what picture does the poem close?

## FRANCIS ORRAY TICKNOR

### LITTLE GIFFEN (PAGE 297)

This poem relates an almost literally true story. The boy was Isaac Newton Giffen, the son of an East Tennessee blacksmith. After being severely wounded, probably in the battle of Chickamauga, he was nursed back to life by Dr. and Mrs. Ticknor at their home, "Torch Hill." It is believed that he was afterwards killed in the battles around Atlanta.

**Johnston:** General Joseph Johnston, a Confederate commander. The battles of Dallas and Kenesaw Mountain are perhaps referred to. — **Golden Ring:** the Round Table, King Arthur's group of knights.

QUESTIONS. 1. Note the conciseness of detail with which the incident is told. 2. What does the poem show regarding the loyalty of the poorer classes in the South to the cause of the Confederacy?

### The Virginians of the Valley (Page 298)

This poem was written early in the war, just after Virginia had become the scene of conflict.

"**Golden Horse-shoe**" **Knights** : the followers of Governor Spotswood of Virginia who made with him the famous expedition to the top of the Blue Ridge Mountains were each given a golden horseshoe in token of the achievement, thus establishing a sort of Virginia knighthood.

QUESTIONS. 1. What references to Virginia's past in the first two stanzas? 2. What tribute to her in the last stanza?

### Unknown (Page 299)

The poet's dedication of this poem is "To the Women of the South decorating graves of Unknown Soldiers.".

QUESTIONS. 1. What scene is described? 2. Why the expression "doubly dead," line 8?

### Page Brook (Page 300)

The title is the name of an old Southern homestead that had been desolated by the war.

QUESTION. What contrasts are made between the home as it now is and as it formerly was?

### Loyal (Page 301)

This poem was written to commemorate the courage of General Pat Cleburne. At the battle of Franklin, Tennessee, in November, 1864, which General John B. Gordon has called "the bloodiest battle of modern times," he was, against his judgment, ordered to take some well-manned breastworks. He replied to the order, "General, I will take the works or fall in the effort." He was killed in the attempt. — **The Douglas** : Lord Douglas, the friend of Robert Bruce, who, when the latter's wish to go on a crusade was frustrated by death, fulfilled Bruce's request to take his heart to Jerusalem. — **Who sheltered** : such Southerners as Cleburne and his men.

QUESTION. The poem consists of eight stanzas of introduction with a final stanza of application. What is the thought of each of these parts?

## PART III. THE NEW SOUTH IN LITERATURE

After the Civil War had swept away the old civilization of the South, and the Southern states had passed through the trying period of reconstruction in adjusting themselves to the new racial, educational, industrial, and political problems, there came to the South great industrial prosperity. In the wake of this prosperity has come a new outburst of literary energy, surpassing the older literature in freshness and variety, and the South has come to take a more important place in the literature of the nation. This new literature has achieved more in prose than in poetry.

### HUMORISTS

The writing of humorous sketches of social life which we have seen formed a conspicuous part of the literature of the old South was continued until the movement became merged with the writing of short stories portraying with "local color" the life of various sections.

### RICHARD MALCOLM JOHNSTON

This selection is from "The Dukesborough Tales." The subtitle, "Old Times in Middle Georgia," suggests the scope of the book. It was essentially reminiscences of the "grim and rude but hearty old times in Georgia." Dukesborough was simply Powelton, Hancock County Georgia, near which the author had been born, and the characters were representative of the democratic Georgia "cracker" class.

### THE GOOSEPOND SCHOOLMASTER (PAGE 303)

The selection here given is descriptive of a type of schoolmaster that was not infrequently found in the country school of the South. These schools were commonly known as "old field schools."

### GEORGE WILLIAM BAGBY

#### JUD BROWNIN'S ACCOUNT OF RUBINSTEIN'S PLAYING (PAGE 308)

The speaker is supposed to be an ignorant countryman.

**Rubinstein:** a noted Russian pianist who made a concert tour in the United States.

## NOVELISTS AND STORY WRITERS

About 1875 there began to appear in Northern magazines sketches and short stories by Southern writers which betokened the beginning of a new development in Southern fiction. With the passing of the old generation of fiction writers, the historical romance imitating Scott or Cooper and the crudely humorous character sketch disappeared. Their places were taken by the work of the new group of writers, who dealt in a realistic way with the various phases of Southern life. The difference between the old and the new fashion in fiction was expressed in the remark of John Esten Cooke, shortly before his death, about the new school: "They see, as I do, that fiction should faithfully reflect life, and they obey the law, while I was born too soon, and am now too old to learn my trade anew."

The new group of writers opened their eyes to the abundant material in the South calling for interpreters. One of their number has said: "Never in the history of the country has there been a generation of writers who came into such an inheritance of material." This was true; for the antebellum writers, with the exception of the humorists, had their sight obscured by the supposed uniformity of Southern life to such an extent that they failed to appreciate the wealth of picturesque material at hand. But the vanishing of the old feudal system with its attendant spirit of caste revealed more clearly than before the variety of type in Southern life, and writers began to realize the value of this material. Thus the creole of Louisiana, the mountaineer of the Appalachians, the "cracker" of Georgia, the inhabitants of the blue-grass region of Kentucky, the negro — all these and others found their observant interpreters.

This group of writers of fiction have been distinguished from their predecessors by regard for careful, artistic workmanship. In their work is to be found little of the carelessness that mars the work of the older school even in its best representatives, as, for instance, Simms and Longstreet. In ideals of craftsmanship the newer writers have been followers of Poe, the result being carefulness of structure and regard for distinction of style. Their success in the short story with local color has been marked enough to command the respect of the country at large. But when these writers have turned from fiction of this shorter compass to that of the scope of the novel they have frequently shown a weakness in structure that has marred somewhat their achievement in this form.

Though Southern fiction since the war has been provincial it has not been sectional. Without exception the writers have echoed the words of Joel Chandler Harris: "What does it matter whether I am a Northerner or a Southerner if I am true to truth, and true to the larger truth, my own self? My idea is that truth is more important than sectionalism, and that literature that can be labeled Northern, Southern, Western, or Eastern, is not worth labeling at all"; and, as he put it at another time, "Whenever we have a Southern literature, it will be American and cosmopolitan as well. Only let it be the work of genius, and it will take all sections by storm." Essentially the same spirit is to be found in the claim of Thomas Nelson Page that in his writings he never wittingly wrote a line which he did not hope might bring about a better understanding between the North and the South, and finally lead to a more perfect Union. Thus Southern writers have endeavored to further that most important task of the present generation — the promotion of a real national spirit.

## GEORGE WASHINGTON CABLE

### THE DANCE IN PLACE CONGO (PAGE 314)

QUESTIONS. 1. What details are given about Congo Square? 2. What musical instruments are used in connection with the dance? 3. Describe the "bamboula."

## JOEL CHANDLER HARRIS

In the several volumes of Uncle Remus stories — "Uncle Remus, his Songs and his Sayings," "Nights with Uncle Remus," to mention only the two earliest and most important of these collections — Joel Chandler Harris has done his most distinctive work as a writer in preserving the folklore of the negro in his American environment. As he himself stated, he was simply the compiler and editor of the stories that he had picked up in his contact with negroes. But he is absolutely the creator of the setting of the stories, — Uncle Remus, the group of negroes associated with him, the little boy to whom the stories are told, and the rest, — which gives one of the best-sustained studies American literature has of the old plantation negro. Inasmuch as character is something more appreciated by readers generally than folklore, it may be surmised that the primary interest in the Uncle Remus books is more frequently than not this delineation of the gentle old darky.

## BRER RABBIT GROSSLY DECEIVES BRER FOX (PAGE 324)

This tale was first published in the *Atlanta Constitution*, December 21, 1879, in the department entitled "Uncle Remus's Folk Lore." It is here reprinted from that source.

**Tar-baby:** see "The Wonderful Tar-baby Story" in "Uncle Remus, his Songs and his Sayings." — **pusly:** parsley.

## THE CUNNING FOX IS AGAIN VICTIMIZED (PAGE 328)

This story appeared in the *Atlanta Constitution*, December 25, 1879, from which it is here taken.

**ingun:** onion. — **patter-rollers:** patrols, that is, officers commissioned to look out for negroes who had slipped away without permission from their plantations.

QUESTIONS. 1. How does the introduction of Uncle Remus, the little boy, etc. add to the interest of the stories? 2. The author has suggested that the stories of the rabbit and the fox may be to some extent allegorical. Attempt an interpretation of this character. 3. What significance is to be attached to the fact that the rabbit is generally victorious? 4. Is the rabbit intended to typify the negro race?

## MARY NOAILLES MURFREE ("CHARLES EGBERT CRADDOCK")

### THE "HARNT" THAT WALKS CHILHOWEE (PAGE 332)

This selection is from one of the stories in the writer's first volume, "In the Tennessee Mountains."

**cor'ner:** coroner. — **laurel:** rhododendron, which in the vernacular of the mountains is called laurel.

QUESTIONS. 1. What is the story of Reuben Crabb? 2. What does Clarsie do for him? 3. What characteristics of the mountaineers are exhibited in this story?

## THOMAS NELSON PAGE

### MARSE CHAN (SUMMARY) (PAGE 342)

The author has given the following account of how the story came to be written:

Just then a friend showed me a letter which had been written by a young girl to her sweetheart in a Georgia regiment, telling him that she had discovered that she loved him after all, and that if he would get a furlough and come home she would marry him. . . . Then, as if she feared such a temptation might be too strong for him, she added a postscript in these words: "Don't come without a furlough; for if you don't come honorable, I won't marry you." This letter had been taken from the pocket of a private dead on the battlefield of one of the battles around Richmond, and, as the date was only a week or two before the battle occurred, its pathos struck me very much. I remember I said, "The poor fellow got his furlough through a bullet." The idea remained with me, and I went to my office one morning and began to write "Marse Chan," which was finished in about a week.

## JAMES LANE ALLEN

### TWO GENTLEMEN OF KENTUCKY (PAGE 348)

**Cheapside:** the scene of the story is Lexington, Kentucky. Cheapside is one of the business streets of that city, so named from the famous Cheapside of London.

QUESTIONS. 1. What characteristics are ascribed to Colonel Romulus Fields? 2. What to Peter? 3. Do such traits of character among whites and blacks in the South give encouragement to believe that the two races can find a common basis whereon they can live in friendship?

## WILLIAM SIDNEY PORTER ("O. HENRY")

The roving life of Porter gave him a wide range of acquaintance with human types in different sections of the country and in different levels of society. As Professor Stuart P. Sherman has said, "He has made a great harvest of the sounds and sights and smells of New York City in chop house, 'lobster-palace,' flat, tenement, park, police court, Broadway, Coney Island. He knows, too, the roads and railways branching into the South, and stretching across the West; the various features and characters of towns and cities from Chicago down the Mississippi Valley to New Orleans and out to 'Frisco; the ranchers and miners and the picturesque riff-raff of adventurers floating through Arizona, Texas, Mexico, and South America, and the returned wanderer from the Philippines." Such a statement should not, however, be understood to mean that his stories are mere studies in localism. Against such a view Porter always protested, as in the following remark, "They say I know New York well. Just change Twenty-Third Street in one of my New York stories to Main Street, rub out the Flatiron Building, and insert Town Hall, and the story will fit any up-State town just as well. So long as a story is true to human nature all you need to do to fit any town is to change the local color. You can make all the characters of the 'Arabian Nights' parade up and down Broadway." The result is that Porter has exhibited in mass a great range of human nature, and if he has not created characters distinctive because of passions which raise them above the crowd, he has depicted wide areas and aspects of society hitherto untouched by the short story. It is this aspect of his work that justifies Professor C. Alphonso Smith's statement, "O. Henry has socialized the short story."

## Two Renegades (Page 363)

This story is typical of a number of Porter's stories in having its scene laid in South America. It is also characteristic in its portrayal of the picaresque type of character and in its original diction. It has not been deemed necessary by the present editor to explain its slang and its allusions to matters contemporary at the time when Porter wrote the story.

QUESTIONS. 1. What were the characteristics of Doc Millikin? 2. In what way does the story show the obliterating of sectional animosities? 3. Point out characteristic features of the writer's style.

**Other Novelists and Story-Writers.** Some of the more important writers of fiction in the South since the Civil War are named in the list that follows. *Maryland :* Francis Hopkinson Smith (1838–1915), Lucy Meacham Thruston (1862–    ) ; *Virginia :* Mary Virginia Terhune ("Marion Harland") (1831–    ), Mrs. Burton Harrison (1846–    ), Molly Elliot Seawell (1860–    ), Amélie Rives (1863–    ), Mary Johnston (1870–    ), Ellen Glasgow (1874–    ), James Branch Cabell (1879–    ), Henry Sydnor Harrison (1880–    ) ; *North Carolina :* Frances Christian Tiernan ("Christian Reid") (1846–    ), Thomas Dixon (1864–    ) ; *Georgia :* Harry Stillwell Edwards (1854–    ), Will N. Harben (1858–    ) ; *Kentucky :* John Fox, Jr. (1863–    ), Alice Hegan Rice (1870–    ) ; *Tennessee :* Sarah Barnwell Elliott (18  –    ), Frances Hodgson Burnett (1849–    ), Will Allen Dromgoole (18  –    ), John Trotwood Moore (1858–    ), Virginia Frazer Boyle (1863–    ) ; *Mississippi :* Katherine Sherwood Bonner McDowell ("Sherwood Bonner") (1849–1883), Harris Dickson (1868–    ) ; *Alabama :* Augusta Evans Wilson (1835–1909) ; *Louisiana :* Albion Tourgée (1838–1905), Grace King (1852–    ), Kate Chopin (1851–1904), Ruth McEnery Stuart (1856–    ), Mary Evelyn Moore Davis (1852–1909).

## ESSAYISTS AND DESCRIPTIVE WRITERS

The literary development of the new South has not produced notable writers of essays, if the term be taken in the narrower sense. But this is no disparagement to Southern writers. The essay characterized by a personal, confidential attitude of the writers toward their subjects and their readers and by an informal, familiar style — what is commonly called the familiar essay — is a rare form that few in English or American literature seem able to do well. If the term be extended in scope to include the short article discussing in a systematic way some topic of literary, historical, or social interest, the large number of such articles by Southern writers in the various magazines and reviews give the South a respectable showing in this phase of literary activity. The saving of space has required that the representatives in this field selected for this volume be confined to a very small number.

### SUSAN DABNEY SMEDES

This selection is from Mrs. Smedes's "Memorials of a Southern Planter," a book which may be regarded as a series of essays. In this book she endeavored to give a faithful picture of her father, Thomas S. Dabney. He was born in Virginia in 1798, but in early manhood he moved to Mississippi and bought in Hinds County an extensive plantation which he called "Burleigh." At the close of the war he found himself impoverished.

### A SOUTHERN PLANTER'S IDEALS OF HONOR (PAGE 373)

QUESTION. In what ideals does Thomas Dabney seem typical of the Southern planter of the old South?

### BASIL LANNEAU GILDERSLEEVE
### THE CREED OF THE OLD SOUTH (PAGE 377)

Of the article from which the selection here given is taken, Mr. William Archer, an English critic, has written in his "America To-day" as follows: "I met a scholar-soldier in the South who had given expression to the sentiment of his race and generation in an essay — one might almost say an elegy — so chivalrous in spirit and so fine in literary form that it moved me well-nigh to tears. Reading it at a public library, I found myself so visibly affected by it that my neighbor at the desk glanced at me in surprise, and I had to pull myself sharply together."

**Kühn ist,** etc.: bold is the venture, splendid the pay. — **Gare de Lyon:** the terminal station in Paris of the railway from Paris to Lyons. — *in esse:* in being. — *in posse:* in possibility. — *placida quies:* calm repose.

QUESTIONS. 1. What two incidents represent the writer's memory of the war? 2. What does he consider the real issue causing the war? 3. What was the attitude of the Southern people on that issue?

## WILLIAM PETERFIELD TRENT

### THE DIVERSITY AMONG SOUTHERNERS (PAGE 389)

This selection is an extract from an article entitled "Dominant Forces in Southern Life," which originally appeared in the *Atlantic Monthly* for January, 1907.

**Squire Western:** a pleasure-loving country gentleman, a creation of Fielding in "Tom Jones." — **Squire Allworthy:** another character in Fielding's "Tom Jones." — **Colonel Hutchinson:** John Hutchinson, a Puritan soldier who, in the Great Rebellion, fought against the Royalists. — *Zeitgeist:* spirit of the age. — **had a philosopher for godfather:** the allusion is to the fact that John Locke, the eminent English philosopher, drew up a scheme for the management of the colony of North Carolina. — "**dipping**": a colloquial expression for taking snuff.

QUESTIONS. 1. What are the characteristic differences between the Southern states as here set forth? 2. Test the validity of the writer's statements by your own experience. Would you modify them in any way?

## POETS

Despite the fact that in the literature of the new South prose has increased its lead on poetry, yet in this period poetry makes an impressive showing. By the year 1875 — the beginning of the South's new development — most of the antebellum writers either were dead or had come to a standstill in their work, the most notable exception being Paul Hamilton Hayne. Although well past middle life at the close of the war, he maintained such a steady and persistent stream of work up to the time of his death in 1886 that it seems proper to consider him among the poets of the new South. Further justification for so doing is found in the fact that he voiced some of the new tendencies in Southern life. One of the most marked of these tendencies was the spirit of nationalism. The later poets have given expression to the growing belief in the South that the results of the war must be accepted by all in good faith and that all should rejoice that the nation has survived undivided. Hayne was one of the first to give expression to such a thought in his poetry.

In addition to the spirit of nationalism just spoken of, the poetry of the new South shows two other tendencies. The first of these is realism. The sentimentalism, the melancholy, and the indifference to Southern landscape and character shown in the older poetry has given place to an eagerness to use Southern local color. The second tendency is an increased effort in the direction of conscientious and skillful workmanship. While, perhaps, the poets of the South, in common with the poets of other sections of the country, have interested themselves in execution rather than in conception, yet the results of their efforts give grounds for the optimistic words of Professor Edwin Mims, " In such poetry — notable alike for its artistry and its poetic feeling — one sees the promise of the future of Southern poetry. When the present age of criticism has passed, when the South has become adjusted to its new life, and when again the great poets shall be heard in England and America, we may confidently expect the coming of a great creative era." [1]

## PAUL HAMILTON HAYNE

### A Dream of the South Winds (Page 400)

Questions. 1. What aspects of the south winds does the poet touch upon? 2. Note how the awakening from the dream is managed at the close.

### Aspects of the Pines (Page 401)

Questions. 1. What aspects of the appearance of the pines are suggested in this poem? 2. What effect of the pines on the spirit of man is suggested?

[1] " The South in the Building of the Nation," Vol. VII, page 54.

## MACDONALD'S RAID — 1780 (PAGE 402)

Macdonald was one of General Marion's men, who led four companions into the fortified post of Georgetown, South Carolina, held by three hundred of the British soldiers and brought out his men unharmed.

**Ben Lomond :** a mountain of central Scotland. — **Arab :** Arabian horse. — *dolce :* idleness. — **Brobdingnag :** the land of giants visited by Gulliver.

QUESTIONS. 1. Who relates the incident? 2. What details of it are given?

## THE PINE'S MYSTERY (PAGE 405)

Hayne had a peculiar fondness for the pine. He made it the subject not only of the two poems herein given, but of several other poems, all of them in his happiest vein.

**Gitana :** a gypsy dancer.

. QUESTION. Has the poet given a good description of the pine's mournful tone?

## THE WILL AND THE WING (PAGE 405)

**Tantalus :** in Grecian mythology a Phrygian king who was punished in the lower world by being placed in the midst of a lake whose waters reached to his chin but receded whenever he sought to allay his thirst, while over his head hung branches laden with fruit which likewise receded whenever he stretched out his hand to grasp them.

QUESTION. What conception of his art does the poet give?

## THE AXE AND PINE (PAGE 407)

**Dryads :** in classical mythology, spirits who inhabited trees.

QUESTIONS. 1. What is the poet lamenting? 2. Explain the last four lines.

## MIDSUMMER IN THE SOUTH (PAGE 407)

**Hesperides :** in mythology the sisters who guarded the golden apples of the sunset.

QUESTIONS. 1. What aspects of midsummer are brought out? 2. Which of these is treated with the greatest poetic ability?

### IRWIN RUSSELL

Irwin Russell's greatest distinction lies in his being the first to point out the literary possibilities of the negro. The negro had appeared incidentally in Southern literature, but Russell was the first to make him not only the leading but the sole character. Thomas Nelson Page has admitted that Russell was his teacher in this field, and Joel Chandler Harris gives Russell the same distinction, saying, " Russell described the old-time darky that was even in his time beginning to disappear."

## NEBUCHADNEZZAR (PAGE 410)

**yeah 's advancin' :** advances of supplies which the negro had secured from some merchant against the value of his crops.

QUESTIONS. 1. Relate the incident. 2. Is the habit of philosophizing with the animals a negro may be working with characteristic of the race ? 3. Is the humorous acceptance of discomfiture also one of their characteristics ?

## - SELLING A DOG (PAGE 412)

QUESTIONS. 1. Who is speaking ? 2. To whom ? 3. What characteristics of the negro as a trader are shown.?

## DAT PETER (PAGE 413)

QUESTION. What characteristics of the younger generation of negroes is brought out in this poem ?

### SIDNEY LANIER

## THE TOURNAMENT (PAGE 416)

This was one of the earliest poems of Lanier. The first part was written in 1862, amid the horrors of war, while the poet was in camp near Wilmington, North Carolina. The second part was written three years later at his home in Macon, Georgia, whither he had returned after the war. The poem was first published in " The Round Table," in 1867.

QUESTIONS. 1. Interpret the meaning of the first joust. 2. Does the last stanza of this part of the poem seem to give the poet's attitude toward the war in which he was engaged ? If so, what does it seem to be ?

3. Interpret the meaning of the second joust. 4. What application does this part of the poem have to conditions after the war? 5. Note the poet's emphasis on the need of the world of love as a vital element.

## Song of the Chattahoochee (Page 419)

This poem was first published in *Scott's Magazine*, Atlanta, Georgia, from which it is here taken.

The Chattahoochee is a river in Georgia that rises in the mountains of that state, passes in its upper course through the counties of Hall and Habersham, and flows through the lowlands into the Gulf of Mexico.

Questions. 1. What reason does the river assign for resisting all temptations to stay in its onward course? 2. Apply this to life. 3. Is the rippling and animated movement of the poem appropriate to the song of a mountain stream?

## The Crystal (Page 421)

Questions. 1. Under what conditions did the poet begin his musings? 2. What conclusion did he reach in regard to great mankind? 3. In what way is Christ different from these so far as stainlessness of character is concerned?

## Sunrise (Page 422)

This is Lanier's last completed poem. It was first published in *The Independent*, December 14, 1882, from which it is here taken. In the words of Mrs. Lanier, it was written "while the sun of life seemed fairly at the setting, and the hand which first penciled its lines had not strength to carry nourishment to the lips." The poet is supposed to be standing where he can look out over the salt marshes of Glynn County, Georgia.

**gospeling glooms**: glooms that teach high truths. — **purfling**: embroidering. — **menstruum**: a solvent. — **Olympian leisure**: the leisure of the deities of Olympus. Explain the force of "dateless" in this connection. — **born in the purple**: of imperial rank, purple being the official color of the Roman emperors. — **innermost Guest At the marriage of elements**: an allusion to the chemical action of the sun in the world of matter. — **fellow of publicans**: one who associates with everybody. The publicans, or tax collectors, of the Roman Empire were a despised class among the Jews and other Roman dependents.

QUESTIONS. 1. How have the marshes called to the poet in his slumbers? How is his awakening described? 2. In what spirit does he go out to the live-oaks and the marshes? 3. By what terms does he address the trees and the leaves? What question does the poet ask? 4. What is the poet's petition? 5. What bird emerges from the trees? 6. What is the thought of the stanza addressed to the "reverend marsh"? 7. Give the details of the full tide. 8. Explain the line "The bow-and-string tension of beauty and silence." 9. How is the motion of the dawn described? 10. In what terms does Lanier describe the first flush of the eastern sky? 11. Trace his description of the slow rising of the sun above the horizon. 12. Give the substance of the apostrophe to heat. 13. What is the thought about the worker and his toil? 14. In what spirit does the poet return to the haunts of men after this contact with nature?

## JOHN BANISTER TABB

Father Tabb's poems are all short, a favorite form being the quatrain. Critics have aptly called them cameos — the most delicate art in the smallest compass. Poetry of this sort demands the most refined technique, and that of Father Tabb is almost perfect.

### MY STAR (PAGE 429)

QUESTIONS. 1. What is the thought of the first stanza? 2. What application is made of it in the second stanza?

### KILLDEE (PAGE 430)

**Killdee:** the killdee, or killdeer, is a bird of the plover family that is named from its cry "Kill-dee, Kill-dee."

QUESTIONS. 1. What description is found in the first two stanzas? 2. What reflection does the poet put in the last stanzas?

## JOHN HENRY BONER

Edmund Clarence Stedman wrote of Boner as "that gentlest of minstrels who caught his music from the whispering pines."

### MOONRISE IN THE PINES (PAGE 431)

**bull bats:** a colloquial name for the nighthawk. — **Heat-lightning:** more or less extensive and vivid flashes of lightning without thunder, seen at the close of a warm day.

QUESTIONS. 1. What details of the evening scene are presented in lines 1–32? 2. What aspects of the pines are presented in lines 33–48? 3. What elements has the poet emphasized in his description of the moonrise, lines 49–64?

## THE LIGHT'OOD FIRE (PAGE 434)

**light'ood :** a dialectal term applied to very dry pitchy and pine wood used for making a fire quickly. — **Boreas :** the north wind.

## POE'S COTTAGE AT FORDHAM (PAGE 435)

**here unmated :** the reference is to the death of Poe's wife. — **Apollo :** the Greek god of wisdom and prophecy. — **Astarte :** the Phœnician goddess of love. — **Dis :** the lower regions. — **stranded :** stringed — a bold use of the term. — **Israfel :** see Poe's poem with the title, page 227, and the notes thereon. — **cenotaphed :** erected a monument, or cenotaph, to his fame.

QUESTION. What thoughts arise in the poet's mind at the recollection of Poe's cottage?

## WILL HENRY THOMPSON

## THE HIGH TIDE AT GETTYSBURG (PAGE 437)

It seems to be one of the laws of literature that the best poetry is not produced under the immediate stimulus of the event, but, as Wordsworth expressed it, originates "from emotion recollected in tranquillity." At any rate, this particular poem, written in 1888, has been regarded by many as the most notable achievement in the verse inspired by that great struggle.

The battle of Gettysburg was a development of General Lee's pushing forward into Pennsylvania in 1863. At Gettysburg he met the Federal forces under General Meade, and after three days of fierce fighting (July 1, 2, 3) he was forced to retreat southward. This battle has been regarded as the turning-point in the Civil War, the fortunes of the Confederacy steadily waning thereafter.

**Pickett :** General George E. Pickett, who led the final charge of the Confederates in the battle. — **Shiloh's woods :** an important battle of the war, fought near Shiloh Church near Pittsburg Landing, Tennessee, April 6 and 7, 1862. — **Chickamauga's solitudes :** one of the most hotly contested battles of the war, fought September 19 and 20, 1863, near

Chickamauga Creek, about twelve miles east of Chattanooga, Tennessee. — **Pettigrew:** General J. J. Pettigrew, a Confederate officer who was killed during the retreat from Gettysburg. — **A Khamsin wind:** a hot, dry wind of the African deserts. — **Kemper:** General J. L. Kemper of the Confederate forces. — **Garnett:** General R. B. Garnett, who was killed while leading Pickett's charge. — **Armistead:** General L. A. Armistead, who was killed in Pickett's charge. — **Doubleday:** General Abner Doubleday of the Federal army.

QUESTIONS: 1. What details of the battle are given? 2. Show that a spirit of broadest patriotism breathes through the poem.

### SAMUEL MINTURN PECK

#### A SOUTHERN GIRL (PAGE 440)

QUESTION. What characteristics of the Southern girl are brought out?

#### THE GRAPEVINE SWING (PAGE 441)

**bayou:** a sluggish stream which forms an inlet into a river or other body of water.

QUESTIONS. .1. Under what circumstances does the poet long for a return to the joys of the grapevine swing? 2. What details of Southern scenery are depicted?

#### AUNT JEMIMA'S QUILT (PAGE 443)

QUESTION. What details of an old-fashioned quilting party can be gathered from this poem?

### WILLIAM HAMILTON HAYNE

#### A MEADOW SONG (PAGE 445)

QUESTION. What constitutes the appeal to come to the meadow?

#### WHEN DOGWOOD BRIGHTENS THE GROVES OF SPRING (PAGE 447)

QUESTIONS. 1. What aspects of spring are described? 2. What corresponding feelings are ascribed to men?

### ROBERT BURNS WILSON

#### To a Crow (Page 448)

**Robin Hood :** an outlaw hero of English legend.
QUESTIONS. 1. What characteristics of the crow are mentioned?
2. What contrast does the poet draw between the bird and man?

#### Ballad of the Faded Field (Page 448)

QUESTIONS. 1. Note details presented to picture the field. 2. What is the thought the poet wishes to emphasize?

### FRANK LEBBY STANTON

#### Answering to Roll Call (Page 451)

QUESTION. How is this poem expressive of the spirit of nationalism?

### MADISON JULIUS CAWEIN

#### Evening on the Farm (Page 454)

**bull bats :** nighthawks. — **teetering :** seesawing.
QUESTIONS. 1. Carefully point out all the details of the picture presented. 2. Does it seem lifelike?

### JOHN CHARLES McNEILL

#### Away Down Home (Page 456)

QUESTIONS. 1. What details of the coming of spring are given? 2. With what thought does the poem close?

#### An Idyl (Page 457)

QUESTIONS. 1. What details of the poem are given? 2. Explain the last two lines.

#### Barefooted (Page 459)

QUESTION. What boyish feelings has the poet tried to describe?

## WALTER MALONE

### OCTOBER IN TENNESSEE (PAGE 461)

**Aladdin:** a character in the "Arabian Nights" who becomes possessed of a magic lamp and ring, by rubbing which genii appear to do his bidding.

**Other Poets.** A list of some of the more important poets of the later period in Southern literature not represented in this book is given below. *Maryland:* Virginia Woodward Cloud (186 – ), Lizette Woodworth Reese (1856– ); *Virginia:* James Barron Hope (1827–1887), Armistead Churchill Gordon (1855– ), James Lindsay Gordon (1860–1904); *North Carolina:* Henry Jerome Stockard (1858–1914), Benjamin Sledd (1864– ); *South Carolina:* George Herbert Sass (1845–1908), Yates Snowden (1858– ), Carlyle McKinley (1847–1904); *Georgia:* Robert Loveman (1864– ); *Florida:* Will Wallace Harney (1831– ); *West Virginia:* Danske Dandridge (1858– ), Waitman Barbe (1864– ); *Kentucky:* John Patterson (1861– ), Lucien V. Rule (1871– ), Cale Young Rice (1872– ); *Tennessee:* Will T. Hale (1857– ), John Trotwood Moore (1858– ), Will Allen Dromgoole (18 – ), Virginia Frazer Boyle (1863– ); *Mississippi:* Lafayette Rupert Hamlin (1861–1902); Stark Young (1881– ); *Alabama:* Clifford Lanier (1844–1908), Howard Weeden (1847–1905), Martha Young ( – ); *Louisiana:* Mary Ashley Townsend (1832–1901), Eliza Jane Poitevant Nicholson ("Pearl Rivers") (1849–1896); *Texas:* William Lawrence Chittenden (1862– ), Clarence Ousley (1863– ).

## SURVIVALS OF OLD BRITISH BALLADS

An account of Southern literature would be incomplete without some reference to the ballads and songs of popular composition, sometimes called folk-songs, in which the South is very rich. Though these songs have endured from the earliest periods of Southern civilization, yet they have only recently begun to be collected into print. Such poetry has important historical value because it renders a picture of the life, the tastes, and the feelings of those elements of the population of the South which are largely untouched by books and education. With the wider diffusion of education in recent years among the masses of the people, this folk-poetry has begun to pass rapidly away, and it therefore behooves the Southern people to find and preserve this valuable material before it is too late to do so. The folklore and ballad societies existing in almost every state as centers for carrying on this work of collection should have the interest and active support of everyone.

The distinctive features of these ballads and songs arise largely from the circumstances of their origin. They were originally extemporized in the presence of an audience; on subsequent occasions reproduced partly from memory, partly under the inspiration of new listeners and new conditions; then transmitted from singer to singer, and reshaped by each. Thus there was evolved a composite product defying ascription to a single author which, though crude and homely as poetry, was admirably fitted for immediate effect upon hearers who were neither subtle nor critical.

One of the most widely discussed phases of this folk-poetry has been the survivals of old British ballads. Many of these old ballads were brought by the early settlers to the American colonies and have continued alive by oral transmission in their transplanted home, even after they had ceased to exist in this way in England. Of the three hundred and five English and Scotch ballads known to scholars, forty-two have been found existing down to recent times in the Southern states. Many of them are remarkably close to original versions collected in England and Scotland; others have so degenerated as to be hardly recognizable. According to information available in 1916, the five most commonly found survivals of old British ballads in the South are the following: "Bonnie Barbara Allen," "Lady Isabel and the Elf Knight," "Lord Thomas and Fair Annet," "Lord Lovel," and "The Maid Freed from the Gallows." The version of "Barbara Allen" (Child, 84 [1]) here reproduced was found among the country whites of Mississippi in 1909 by Professor E. C. Perrow. That of "Lord Thomas and Fair Eleanor" (Child, 73) was reported from South Carolina in 1914. Those of "The Hangman's Tree" (Child, 95) and of "The Wife of Usher's Well" (Child, 79) were discovered by Miss Backus in the mountains of North Carolina. The version of "George Collins" (Child, 85) comes also from the mountains of North Carolina.

**Other Traditional Songs.** Of much interest are the traditional songs native to the South which have developed where under suitable conditions the ballad-making impulse has asserted itself and created a song around an unfortunate love affair, the capture of an outlaw, a battle of the Civil War, or other suitable material. Of much interest also are the negro songs. In the life of this race music plays a large part, especially in religious exercises and in collective labor. Many of the negro's songs are taken from the whites, but more are of his own devising and show all the characteristic features of popular composition.

[1] This and the following references are to the authoritative collection — Professor F. J. Child's "English and Scottish Popular Ballads."

# SELECTED BIBLIOGRAPHY OF
# SOUTHERN LITERATURE

This list aims at giving the more important books useful in the further study of Southern literature. References to histories of American literature and to collections of selections from American writers have been omitted, though nearly all the standard works in these fields treat to some extent Southern writers. Neither have editions and biographies of individual authors been included except for some very special reason. Fuller bibliographies may be found in Moses' "The Literature of the South" and in Alderman and Kent's "Library of Southern Literature."

## HISTORICAL AND SOCIAL

BROWN, W. G. The Lower South in American History.

CHANDLER, J. A. C., and others. The South in the Building of the Nation, 12 vols.

CURRY, J. L. M. The Southern States — their Relation to the Constitution and to the Union.

DODD, W. E. Statesmen of the Old South.

HART, A. B. The Southern South.

MURPHY, E. G. The Present South.

MURPHY, E. G. The Basis for Ascendency.

PAGE, T. N. The Old South.

PAGE, T. N. Social Life in Virginia.

PAGE, T. N. The Old Dominion: her Making and her Manners.

PAGE, W. H. The Rebuilding of Old Commonwealths.

RHODES, J. F. History of the United States (1850–1877), 8 vols.

TRENT, W. P. Southern Statesmen of the Old Régime.

WILSON, W. History of the American People.

WILSON, W. Division and Reunion (1829–1889).

## LITERARY

### Selections from Southern Writers

ABERNATHY, J. W.  The Southern Poets (selected poems of Lanier, Timrod, and Hayne).

ALDERMAN, E. A. (General Editor), and KENT, C. W. (Literary Editor).  Library of Southern Literature, 16 vols. (The fullest and most important collection of the work of Southern writers. The selections are well chosen, but the critical sketches are by many different persons and are of varying degrees of value.)

BREVARD, CAROLINE M.  Literature of the South.

BROCK, SALLIE A.  The Southern Amaranth.

CLARKE, JENNIE T.  Songs of the South: Choice Selections from Southern Poets.

DAVIDSON, J. W.  The Living Writers of the South. (A valuable book for writers living at the date of its publication, 1869; contains many uncollected poems.)

FAGAN, W. L.  Southern War Songs.

FORREST, MARY.  Women of the South Distinguished in Literature (1861).

HOLLIDAY, C.  Three Centuries of Southern Poetry (1607–1907).

HUBNER, C.  Representative Southern Poets.

HUBNER, C.  War poets of the South and Confederate Campfire Songs.

KENT, C. W.  Southern Poems.

MANLY, LOUISE.  Southern Literature from 1579 to 1895.

MASON, EMILY V.  The Southern Poems of the War.

MIMS, EDWIN (Editor).  The South in the Building of the Nation, Vol. VIII. (Contains a history of Southern fiction, with illustrative extracts.)

MIMS, E., and PAYNE, B. R.  Southern Prose and Poetry.

MOORE, F.  Songs and Ballads of the Southern People, 1861–1865.

ORGAIN, KATE.  Southern Authors in Poetry and Prose.

PAINTER, F. V.  Poets of the South.

PAINTER, F. V.  Poets of Virginia.

SIMMS, W. G.  War Poetry of the South.

STOCKARD, J. E.  A Study in Southern Poetry.

TARDY, MARY. Living Female Writers of the South (contains selections from those living in 1872).

TRENT, W. P. Southern Writers.

WATTERSON, H. W. Oddities in Southern Life and Character (valuable for its selections from the humorists).

WAUCHOPE, G. A. The Writers of South Carolina.

WEBER, W. L. Selections from Southern Poets.

WHARTON, H. M. War Songs and Poems of the Southern Confederacy.

——, War Lyrics and Songs of the South. (This book, edited by a group of Southern women and published in England in 1866, is one of the best as well as one of the earliest collections of its kind.)

## BIOGRAPHY AND CRITICISM

BASKERVILL, W. M. Southern Writers, 2 vols. (Valuable for biographical and critical studies of writers since 1870. Volume I is altogether by the late Professor Baskervill; Volume II contains contributions by his friends and former pupils who desired to complete his projected work.)

HENNEMAN, J. B. (Editor). The South in the Building of the Nation, Vol. VIII. (Contains valuable articles on the literary and intellectual life of the South.)

HOLLIDAY, C. A. History of Southern Literature.

LINK, S. A. Pioneers of Southern Literature, 2 vols.

MIMS, E., Life of Lanier.

PICKETT, MRS. J. C. Literary Hearthstones of Dixie.

RAYMOND, IDA. Southland Writers, 2 vols.

RUTHERFORD, MILDRED L. The South in History and Literature.

SHEPHERD, H. E. Authors of Maryland.

TRENT, W. P. Life of William Gilmore Simms.

Several of the books listed on the preceding page under the heading "Selections from Southern Writers" are useful for biographies and criticisms. In this connection Trent's "Southern Writers" and Alderman and Kent's "Library of Southern Literature" are to be especially mentioned. Much important biographical and critical matter will be found in magazines, particularly the *Sewanee Review* and the *South Atlantic Quarterly*.